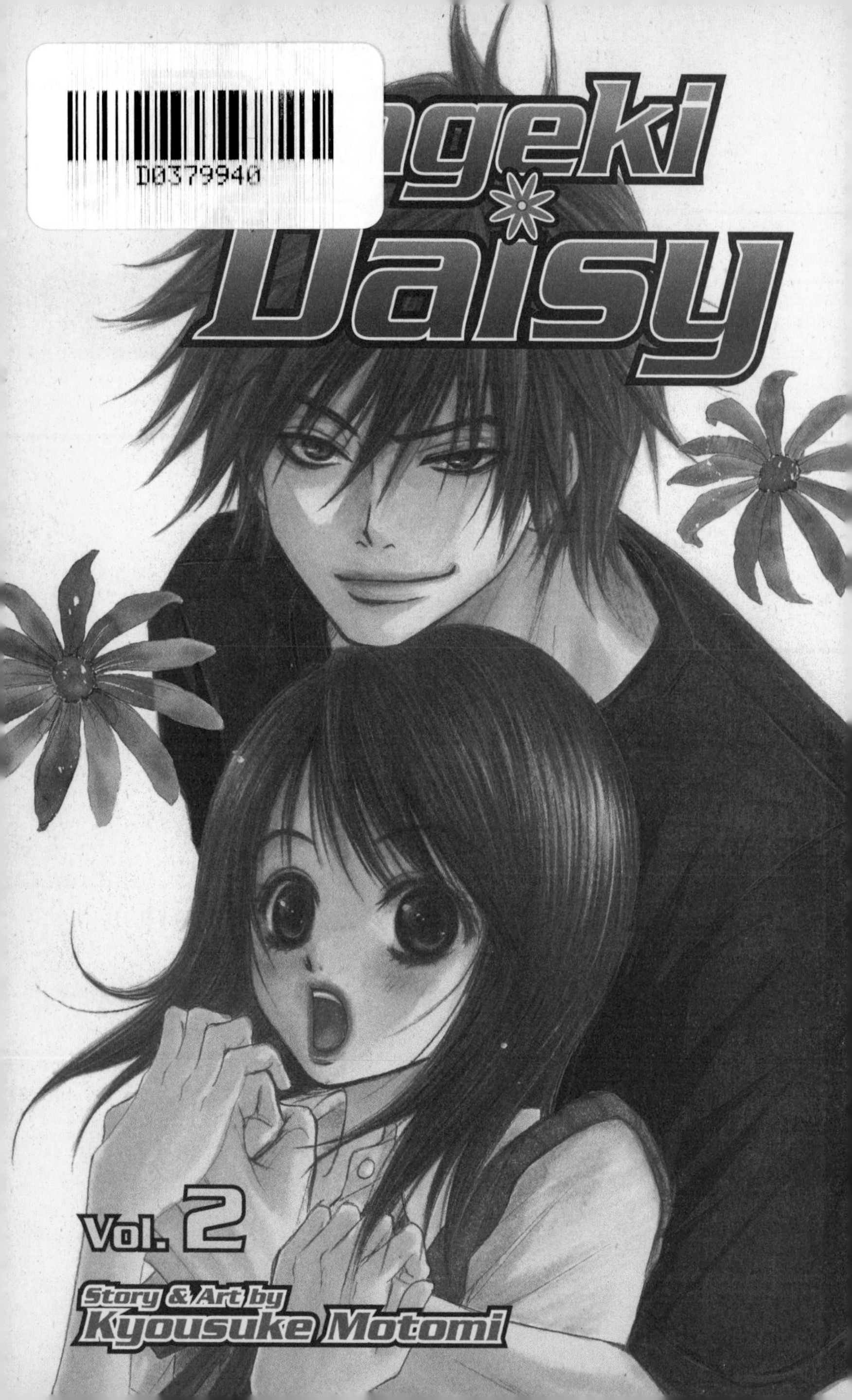
ngeki Daisy
Vol. 2
Story & Art by
Kyousuke Motomi

Dengeki Daisy

Volume 2 CONTENTS

DAISY

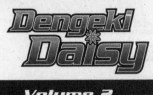

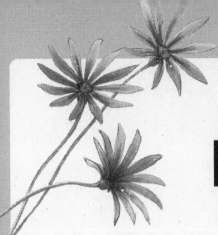

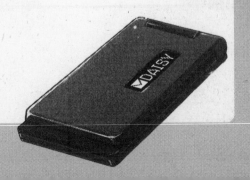

CHAPTER 5: I'LL BE CLOSE TO YOU WHEN THE TIME COMES.

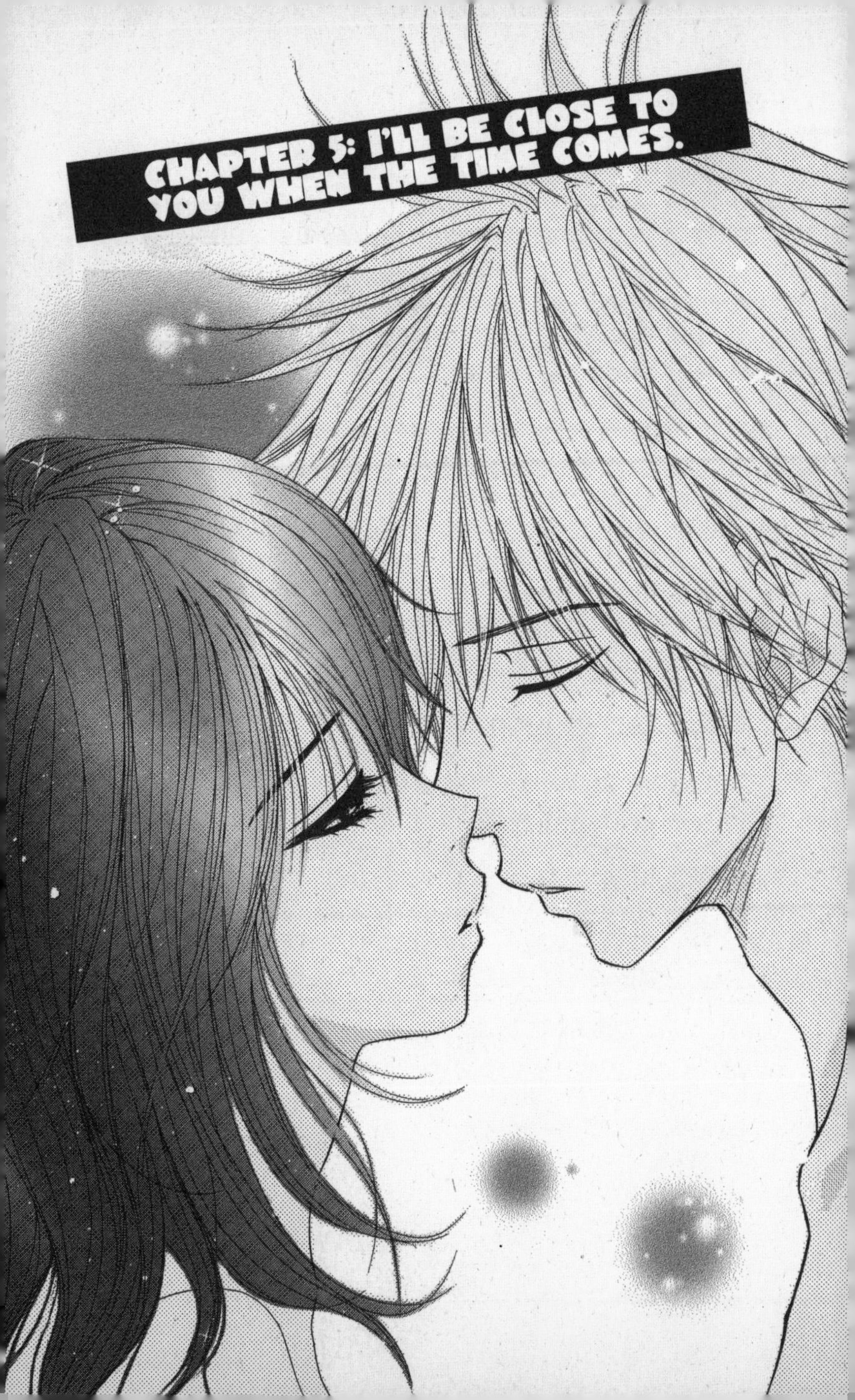

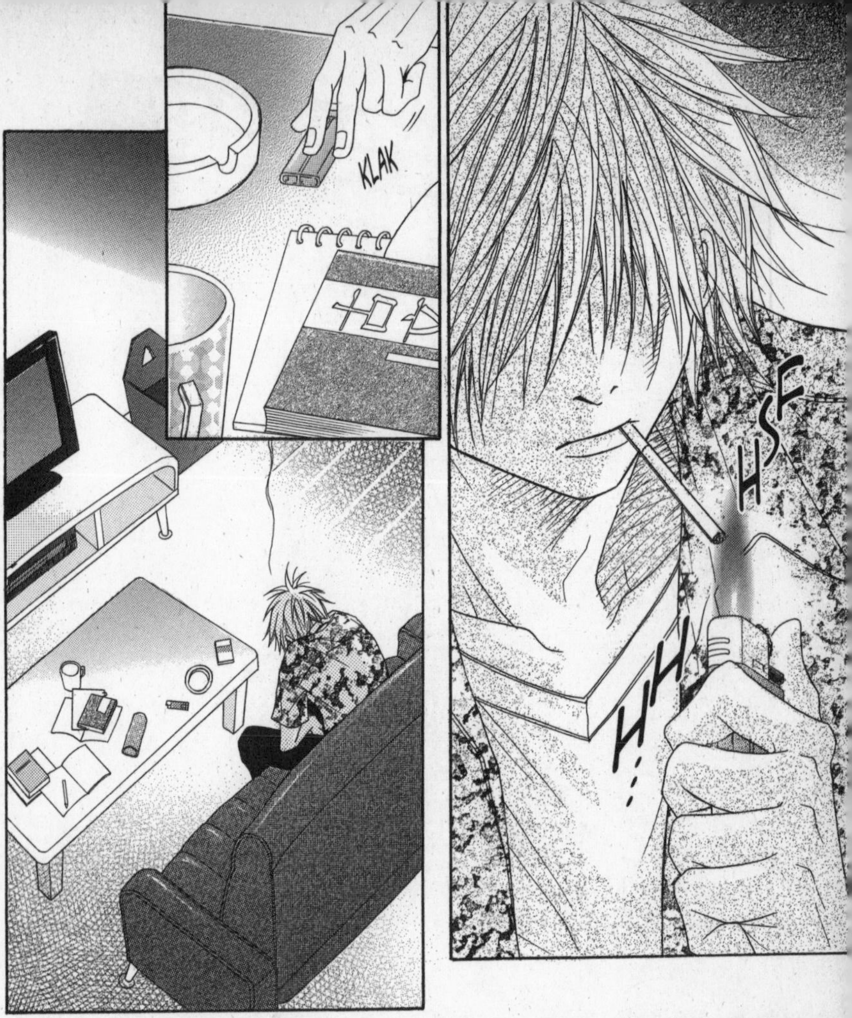
HSF
HH...
KLAK

HELLO, EVERYONE!! I'M KYOUSUKE MOTOMI. ***DENGEKI DAISY.*** THIS IS A VERY, VERY HAPPY VOLUME 2 (FOR ME). I'D BE EVEN HAPPIER IF YOU ENJOY IT. SO THANK YOU IN ADVANCE!!

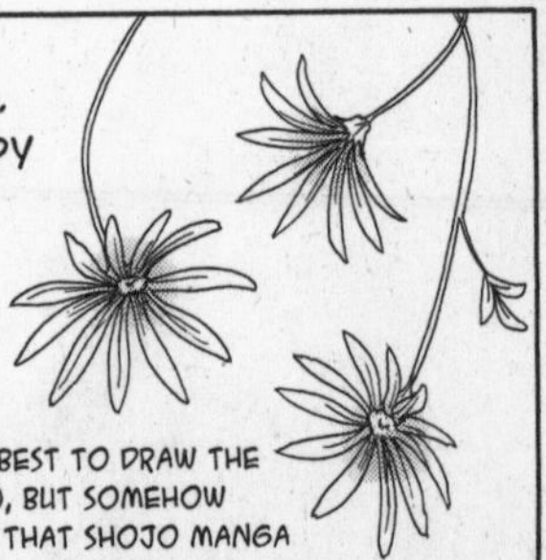

I REALLY DID MY BEST TO DRAW THE FLOWERS (DAISIES), BUT SOMEHOW THEY'RE LACKING THAT SHOJO MANGA FEEL. HOW ODD...

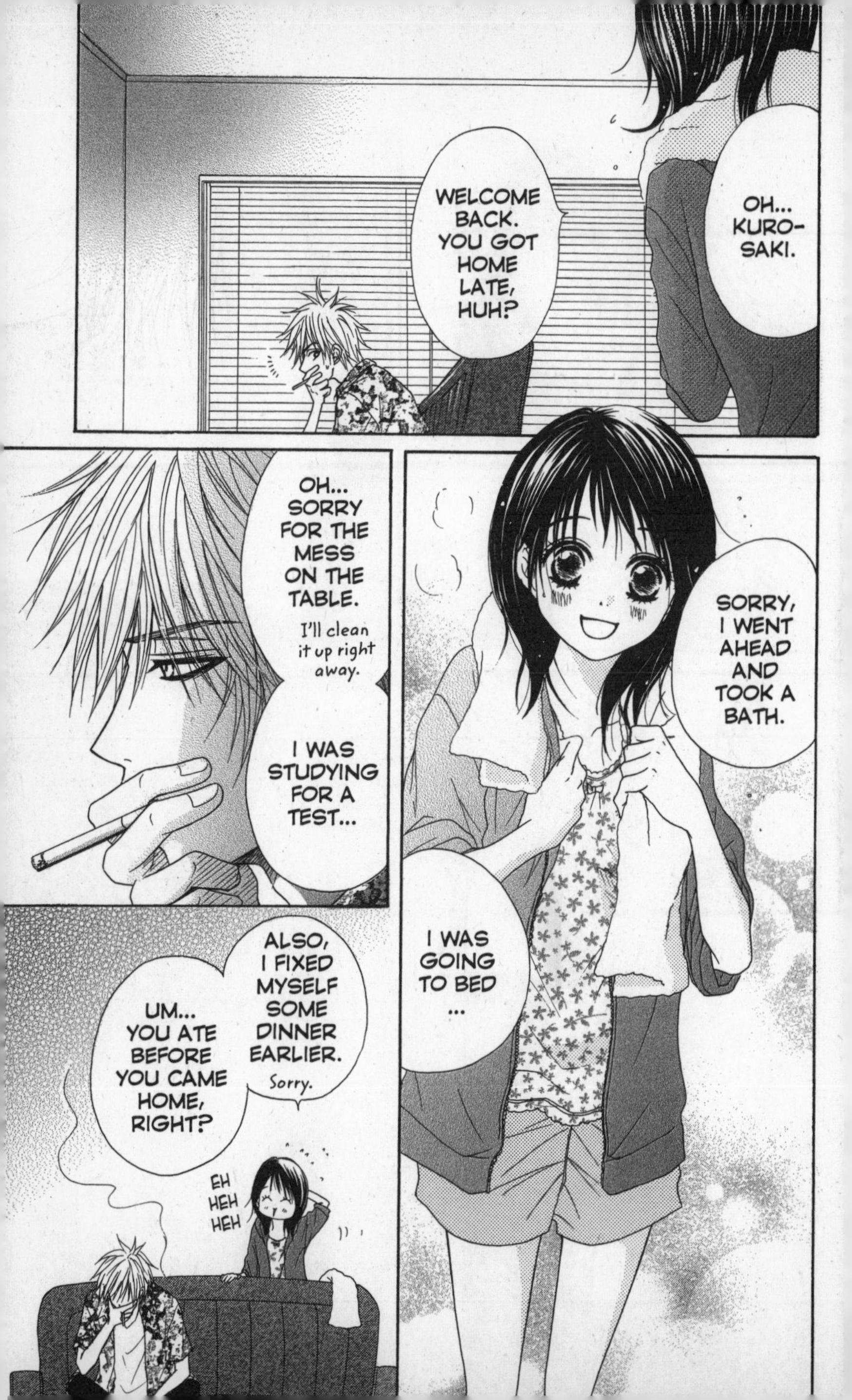
OH... KURO-SAKI.
WELCOME BACK. YOU GOT HOME LATE, HUH?
SORRY, I WENT AHEAD AND TOOK A BATH.
I WAS GOING TO BED ...
OH... SORRY FOR THE MESS ON THE TABLE.
I'll clean it up right away.
I WAS STUDYING FOR A TEST...
ALSO, I FIXED MYSELF SOME DINNER EARLIER.
Sorry.
UM... YOU ATE BEFORE YOU CAME HOME, RIGHT?
EH HEH HEH

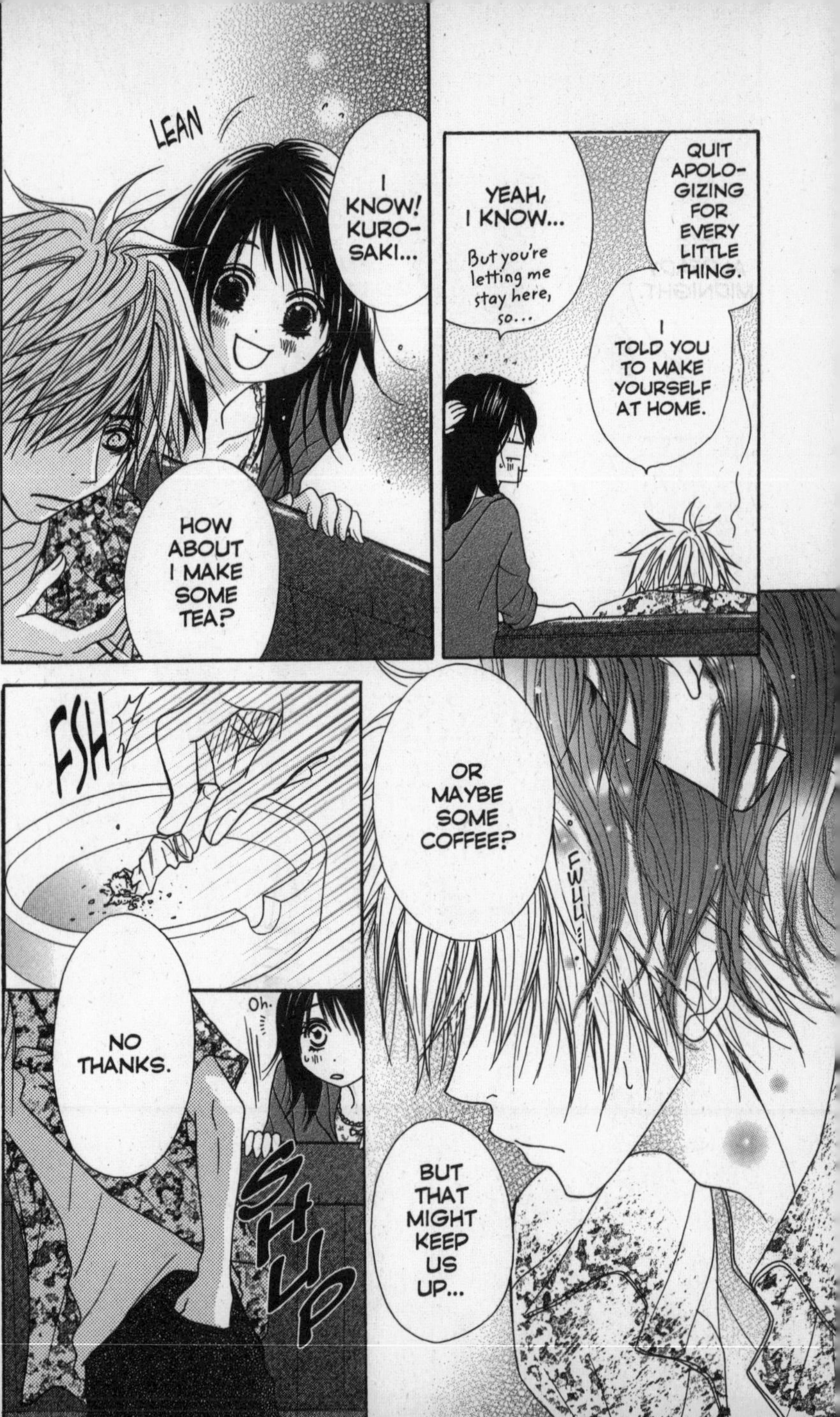
QUIT APOLOGIZING FOR EVERY LITTLE THING.
YEAH, I KNOW...
But you're letting me stay here, so...
I TOLD YOU TO MAKE YOURSELF AT HOME.
LEAN
I KNOW! KUROSAKI...
HOW ABOUT I MAKE SOME TEA?
OR MAYBE SOME COFFEE?
FWUU
BUT THAT MIGHT KEEP US UP...
FSH
NO THANKS.
Oh.
SHUP

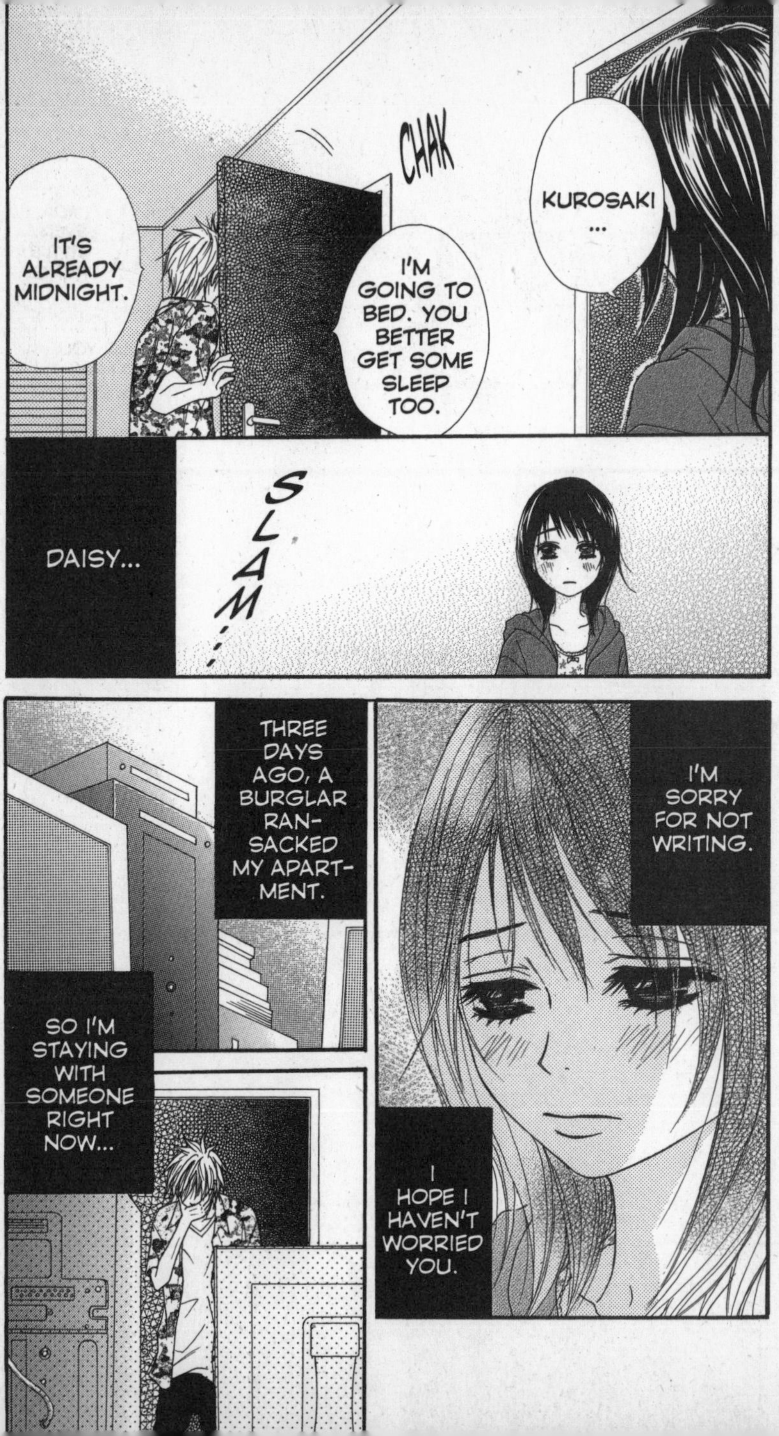
KUROSAKI ...
CHAK
I'M GOING TO BED. YOU BETTER GET SOME SLEEP TOO.
IT'S ALREADY MIDNIGHT.
SLAM...
DAISY...
I'M SORRY FOR NOT WRITING.
I HOPE I HAVEN'T WORRIED YOU.
THREE DAYS AGO, A BURGLAR RAN-SACKED MY APART-MENT.
SO I'M STAYING WITH SOMEONE RIGHT NOW...

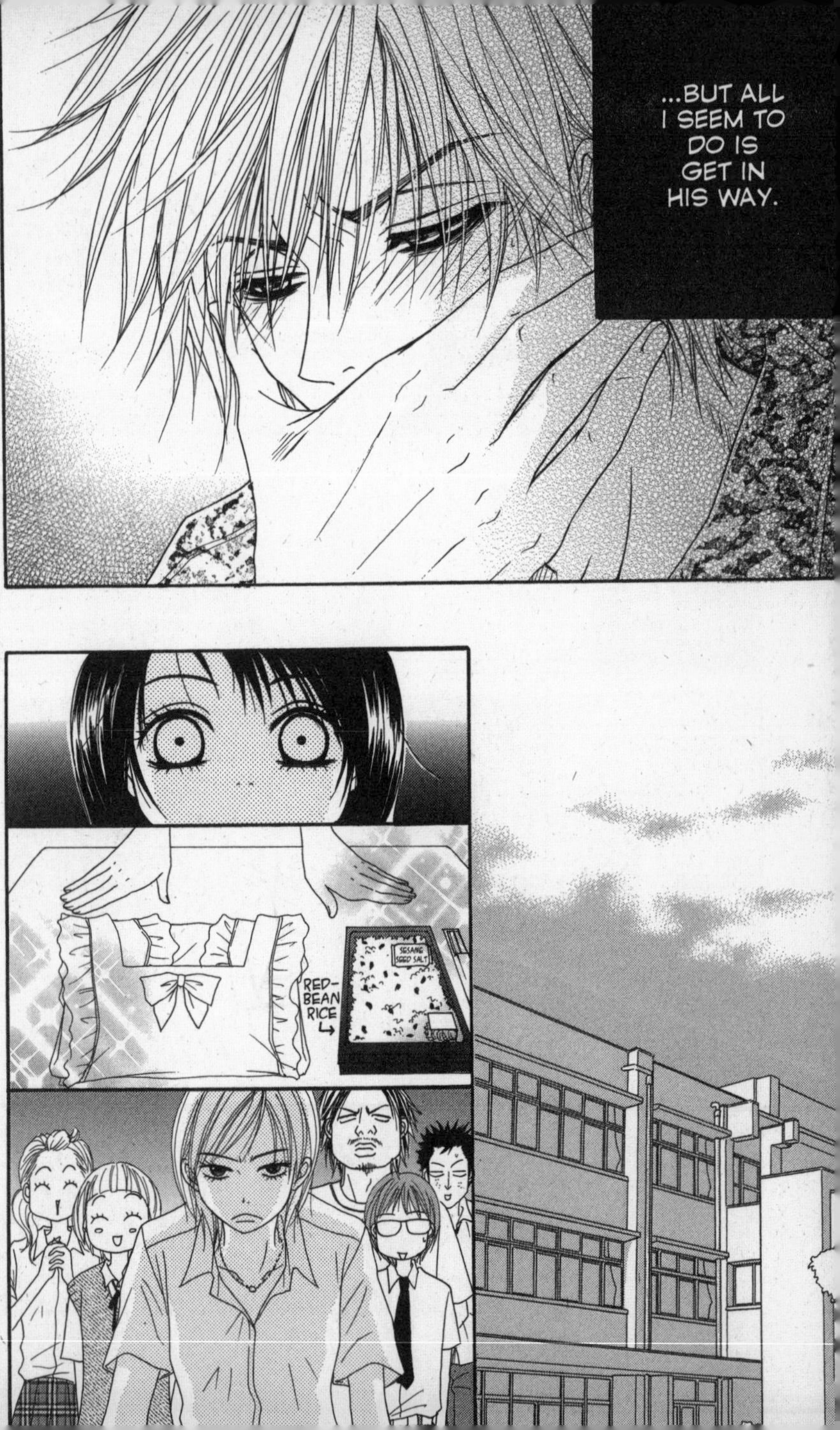
...BUT ALL I SEEM TO DO IS GET IN HIS WAY.
SESAME SEED SALT
RED-BEAN RICE

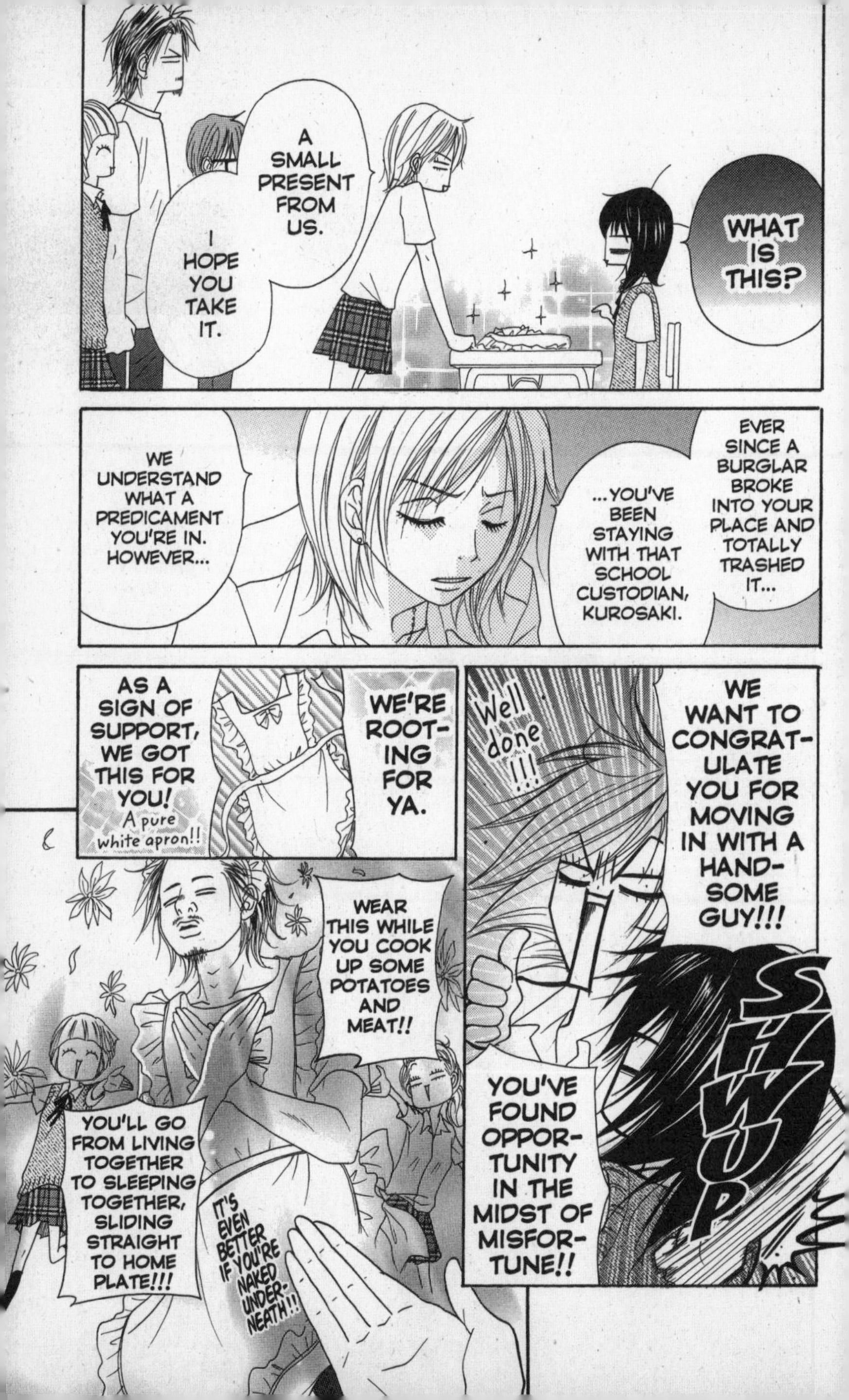
WHAT IS THIS?
A SMALL PRESENT FROM US.
I HOPE YOU TAKE IT.
EVER SINCE A BURGLAR BROKE INTO YOUR PLACE AND TOTALLY TRASHED IT...
...YOU'VE BEEN STAYING WITH THAT SCHOOL CUSTODIAN, KUROSAKI.
WE UNDERSTAND WHAT A PREDICAMENT YOU'RE IN. HOWEVER...
WE WANT TO CONGRATULATE YOU FOR MOVING IN WITH A HANDSOME GUY!!!
Well done!!!
YOU'VE FOUND OPPORTUNITY IN THE MIDST OF MISFORTUNE!!
SHWUP
WE'RE ROOTING FOR YA.
AS A SIGN OF SUPPORT, WE GOT THIS FOR YOU!
A pure white apron!!
WEAR THIS WHILE YOU COOK UP SOME POTATOES AND MEAT!!
YOU'LL GO FROM LIVING TOGETHER TO SLEEPING TOGETHER, SLIDING STRAIGHT TO HOME PLATE!!!
IT'S EVEN BETTER IF YOU'RE NAKED UNDERNEATH!!

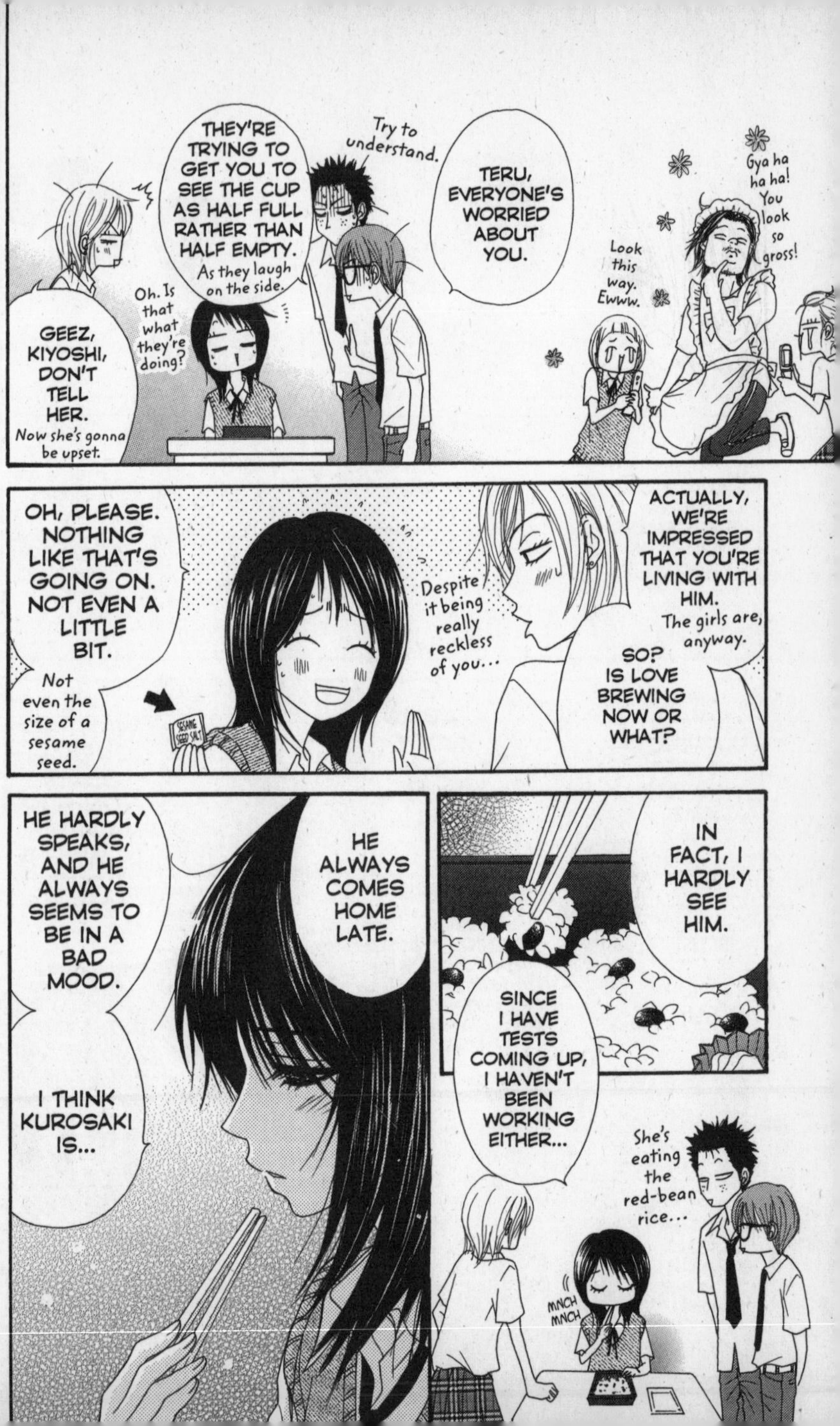

Gya ha ha! You look so gross!
Look this way. Ewww.
TERU, EVERYONE'S WORRIED ABOUT YOU.
Try to understand.
THEY'RE TRYING TO GET YOU TO SEE THE CUP AS HALF FULL RATHER THAN HALF EMPTY.
As they laugh on the side.
Oh. Is that what they're doing?
GEEZ, KIYOSHI, DON'T TELL HER.
Now she's gonna be upset.
ACTUALLY, WE'RE IMPRESSED THAT YOU'RE LIVING WITH HIM.
The girls are, anyway.
SO? IS LOVE BREWING NOW OR WHAT?
Despite it being really reckless of you...
OH, PLEASE. NOTHING LIKE THAT'S GOING ON. NOT EVEN A LITTLE BIT.
SESAME SEED SALT
Not even the size of a sesame seed.
IN FACT, I HARDLY SEE HIM.
SINCE I HAVE TESTS COMING UP, I HAVEN'T BEEN WORKING EITHER...
She's eating the red-bean rice...
MNCH MNCH
HE ALWAYS COMES HOME LATE.
HE HARDLY SPEAKS, AND HE ALWAYS SEEMS TO BE IN A BAD MOOD.
I THINK KUROSAKI IS...

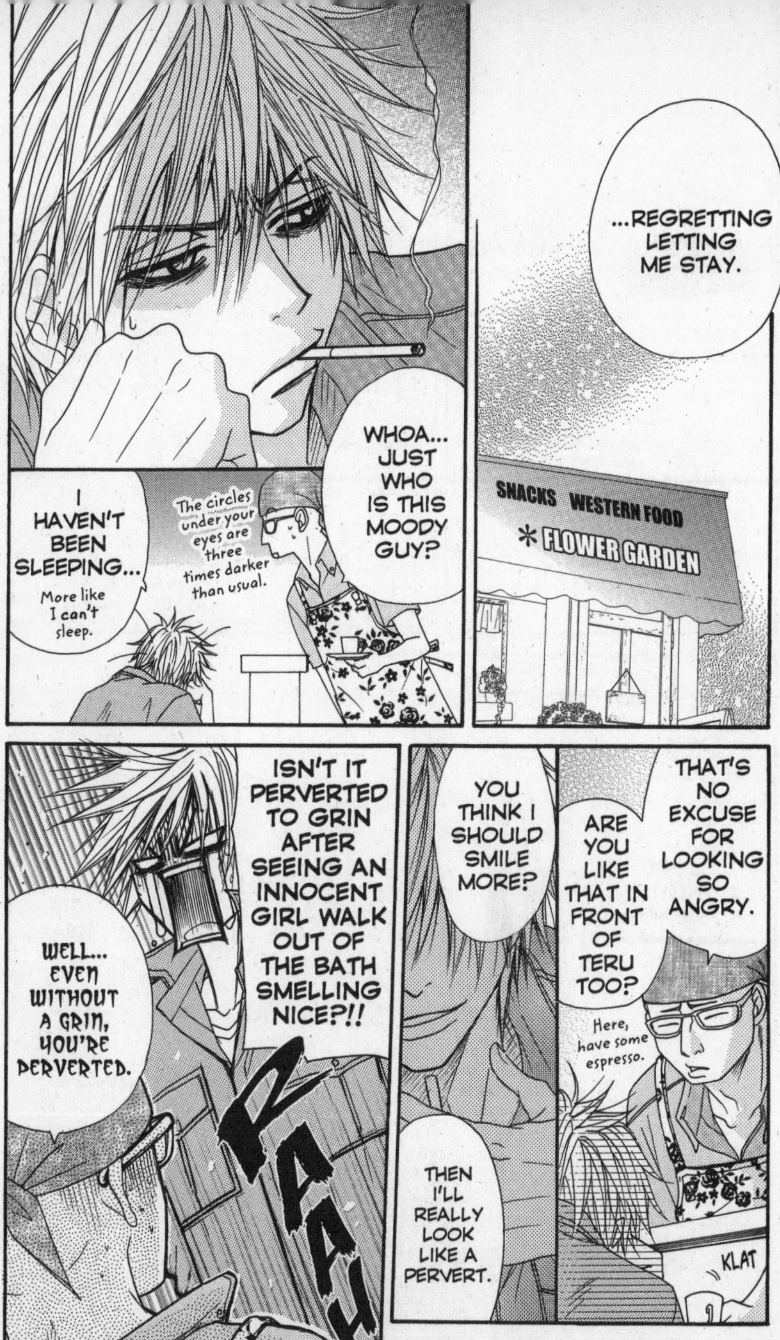
...REGRETTING LETTING ME STAY.
SNACKS WESTERN FOOD
* FLOWER GARDEN
WHOA... JUST WHO IS THIS MOODY GUY?
The circles under your eyes are three times darker than usual.
I HAVEN'T BEEN SLEEPING...
More like I can't sleep.
THAT'S NO EXCUSE FOR LOOKING SO ANGRY.
ARE YOU LIKE THAT IN FRONT OF TERU TOO?
Here, have some espresso.
KLAT
YOU THINK I SHOULD SMILE MORE?
THEN I'LL REALLY LOOK LIKE A PERVERT.
ISN'T IT PERVERTED TO GRIN AFTER SEEING AN INNOCENT GIRL WALK OUT OF THE BATH SMELLING NICE?!!
WELL... EVEN WITHOUT A GRIN, YOU'RE PERVERTED.
RAAH

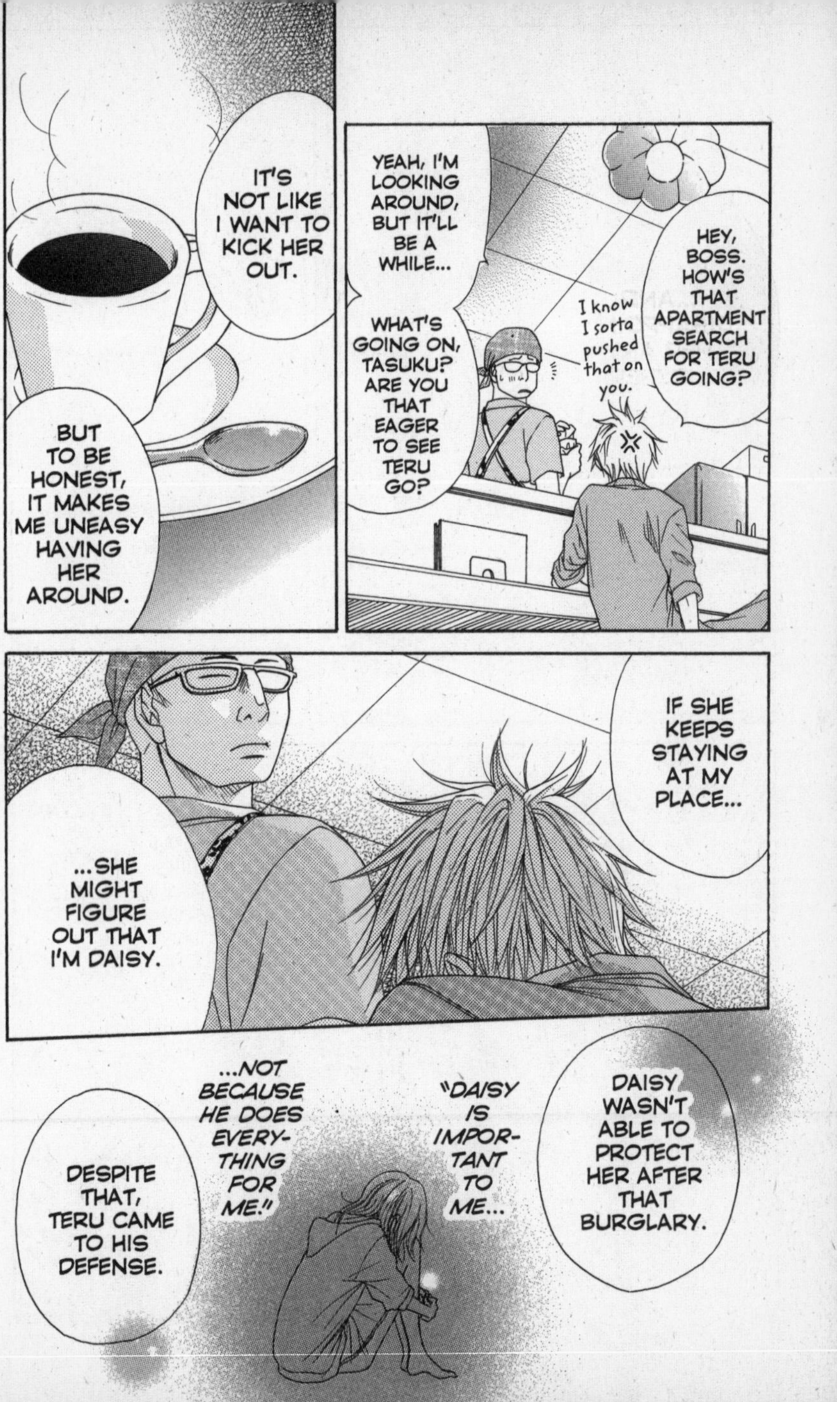
HEY, BOSS. HOW'S THAT APARTMENT SEARCH FOR TERU GOING?
I know I sorta pushed that on you.
YEAH, I'M LOOKING AROUND, BUT IT'LL BE A WHILE...
WHAT'S GOING ON, TASUKU? ARE YOU THAT EAGER TO SEE TERU GO?
IT'S NOT LIKE I WANT TO KICK HER OUT.
BUT TO BE HONEST, IT MAKES ME UNEASY HAVING HER AROUND.
IF SHE KEEPS STAYING AT MY PLACE...
...SHE MIGHT FIGURE OUT THAT I'M DAISY.
DAISY WASN'T ABLE TO PROTECT HER AFTER THAT BURGLARY.
"DAISY IS IMPORTANT TO ME...
...NOT BECAUSE HE DOES EVERY-THING FOR ME."
DESPITE THAT, TERU CAME TO HIS DEFENSE.

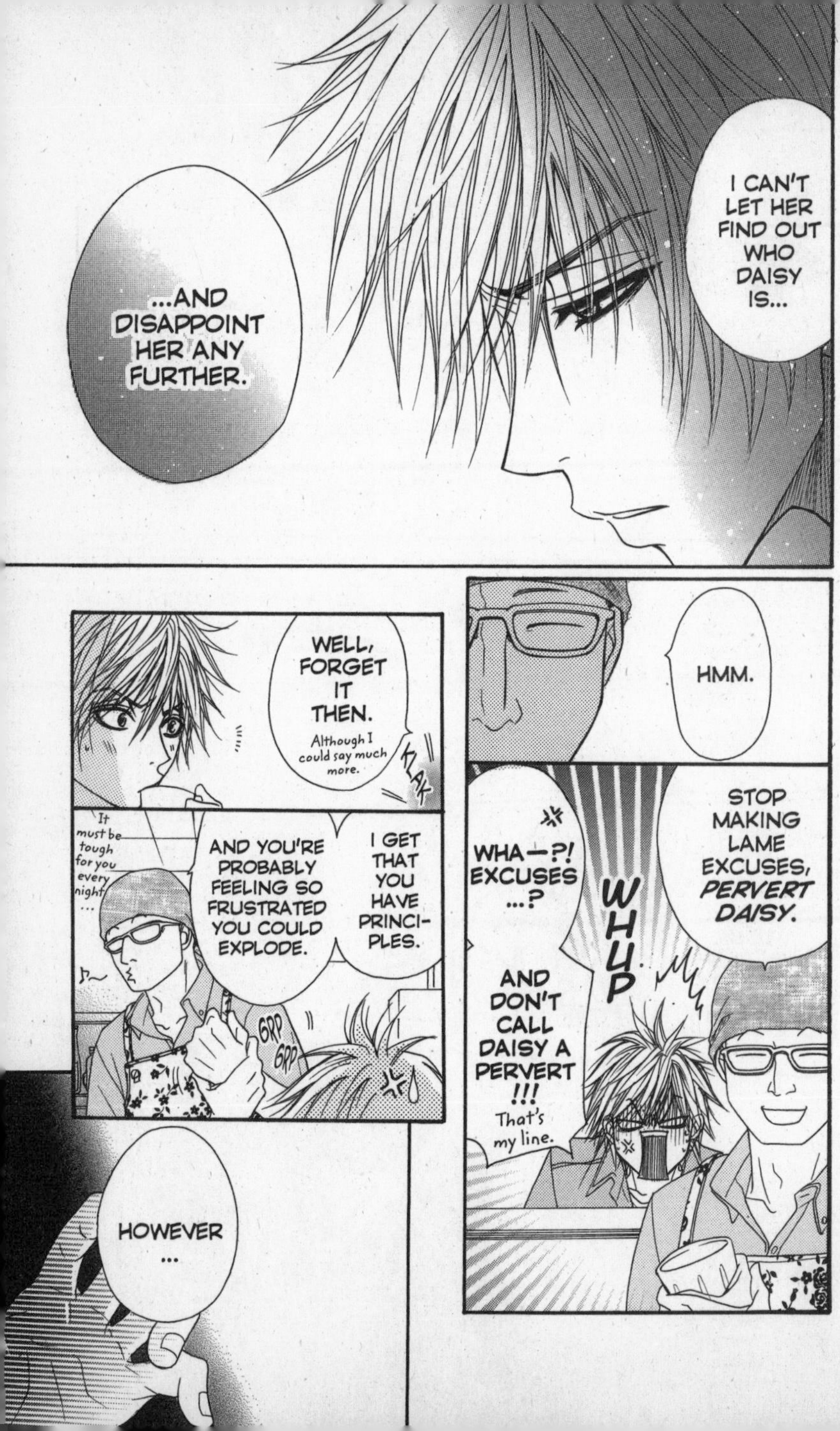

I CAN'T LET HER FIND OUT WHO DAISY IS...
...AND DISAPPOINT HER ANY FURTHER.
HMM.
WELL, FORGET IT THEN.
Although I could say much more.
KLAK
I GET THAT YOU HAVE PRINCIPLES.
AND YOU'RE PROBABLY FEELING SO FRUSTRATED YOU COULD EXPLODE.
It must be tough for you every night...
GRP GRP
STOP MAKING LAME EXCUSES, *PERVERT DAISY.*
WHUP
WHA—?! EXCUSES ...?
AND DON'T CALL DAISY A PERVERT!!!
That's my line.
HOWEVER ...

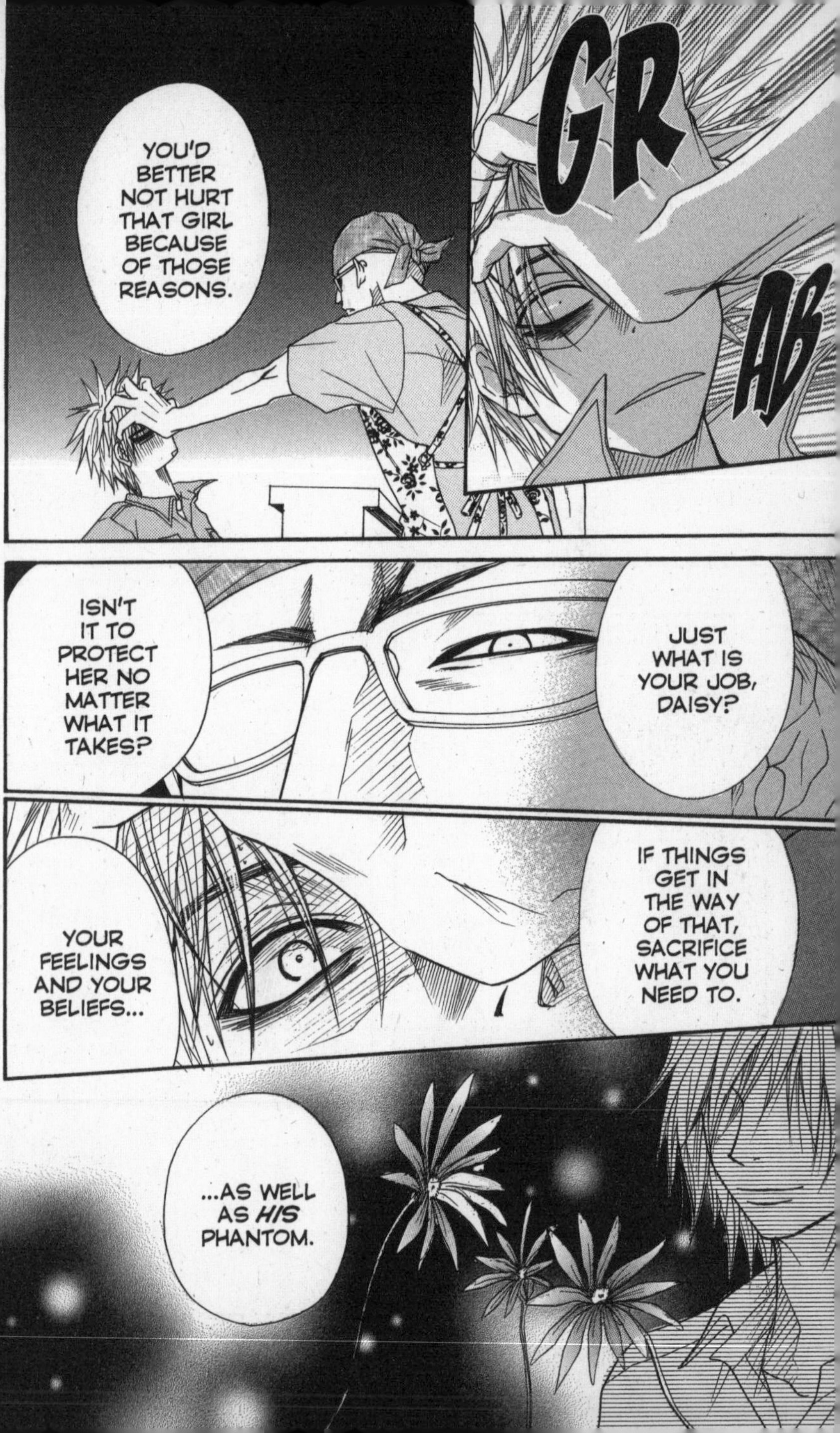
GR
AB
YOU'D BETTER NOT HURT THAT GIRL BECAUSE OF THOSE REASONS.
JUST WHAT IS YOUR JOB, DAISY?
ISN'T IT TO PROTECT HER NO MATTER WHAT IT TAKES?
IF THINGS GET IN THE WAY OF THAT, SACRIFICE WHAT YOU NEED TO.
YOUR FEELINGS AND YOUR BELIEFS...
...AS WELL AS *HIS* PHANTOM.

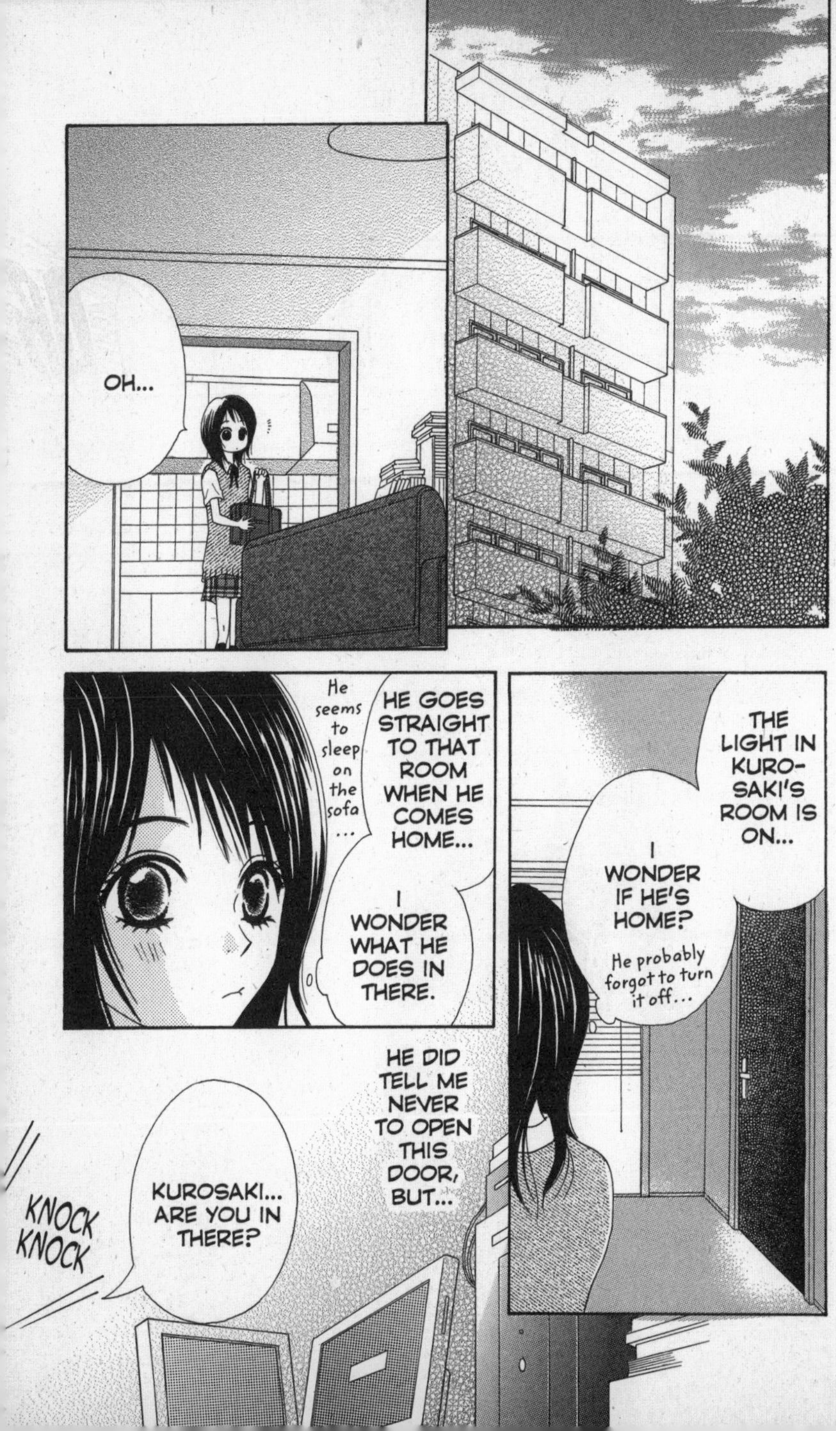
OH...
THE LIGHT IN KUROSAKI'S ROOM IS ON...
I WONDER IF HE'S HOME?
He probably forgot to turn it off...
HE GOES STRAIGHT TO THAT ROOM WHEN HE COMES HOME...
He seems to sleep on the sofa...
I WONDER WHAT HE DOES IN THERE.
HE DID TELL ME NEVER TO OPEN THIS DOOR, BUT...
KUROSAKI... ARE YOU IN THERE?
KNOCK KNOCK

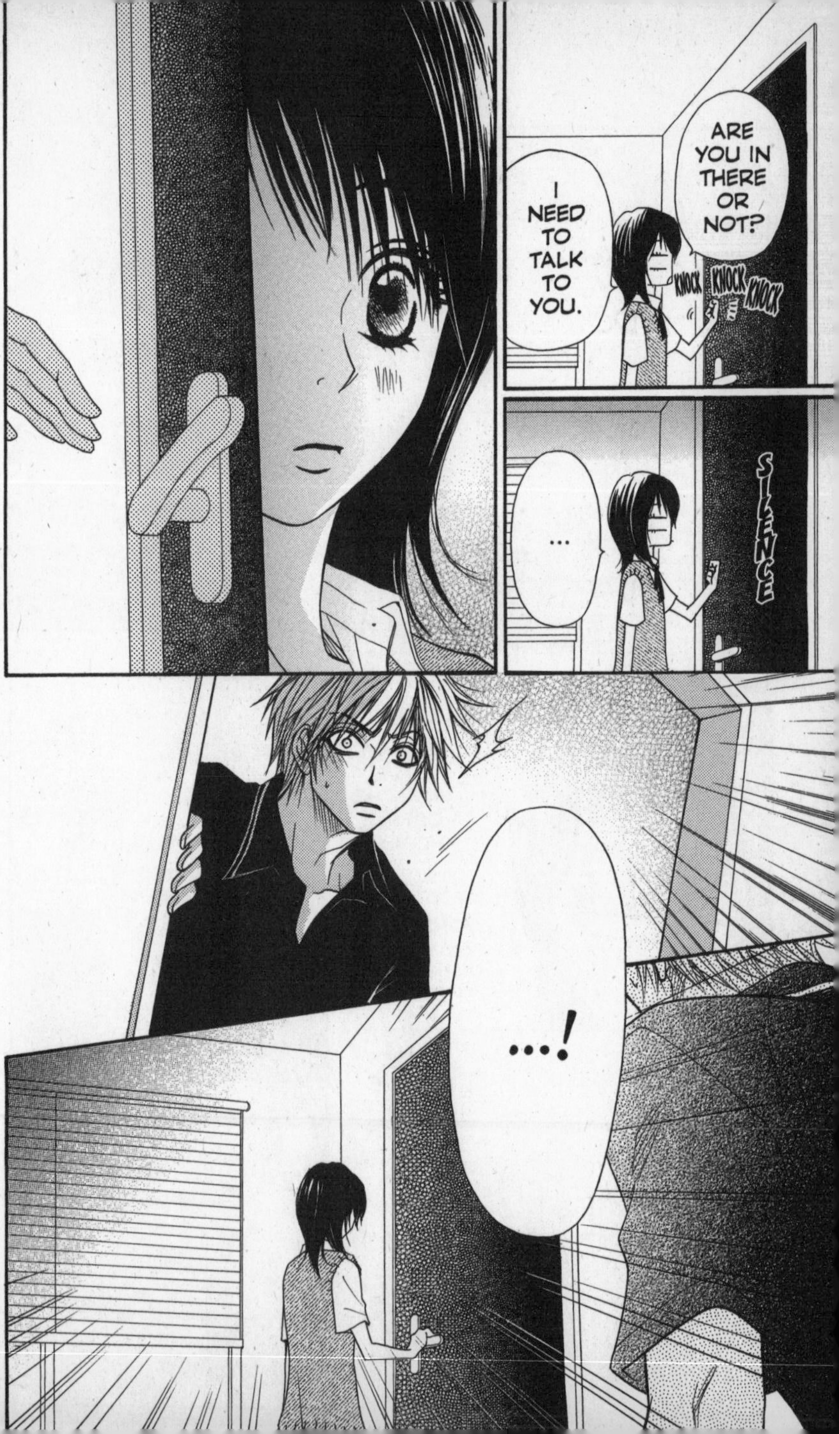
ARE YOU IN THERE OR NOT?
KNOCK KNOCK KNOCK
I NEED TO TALK TO YOU.
SILENCE
...
...!

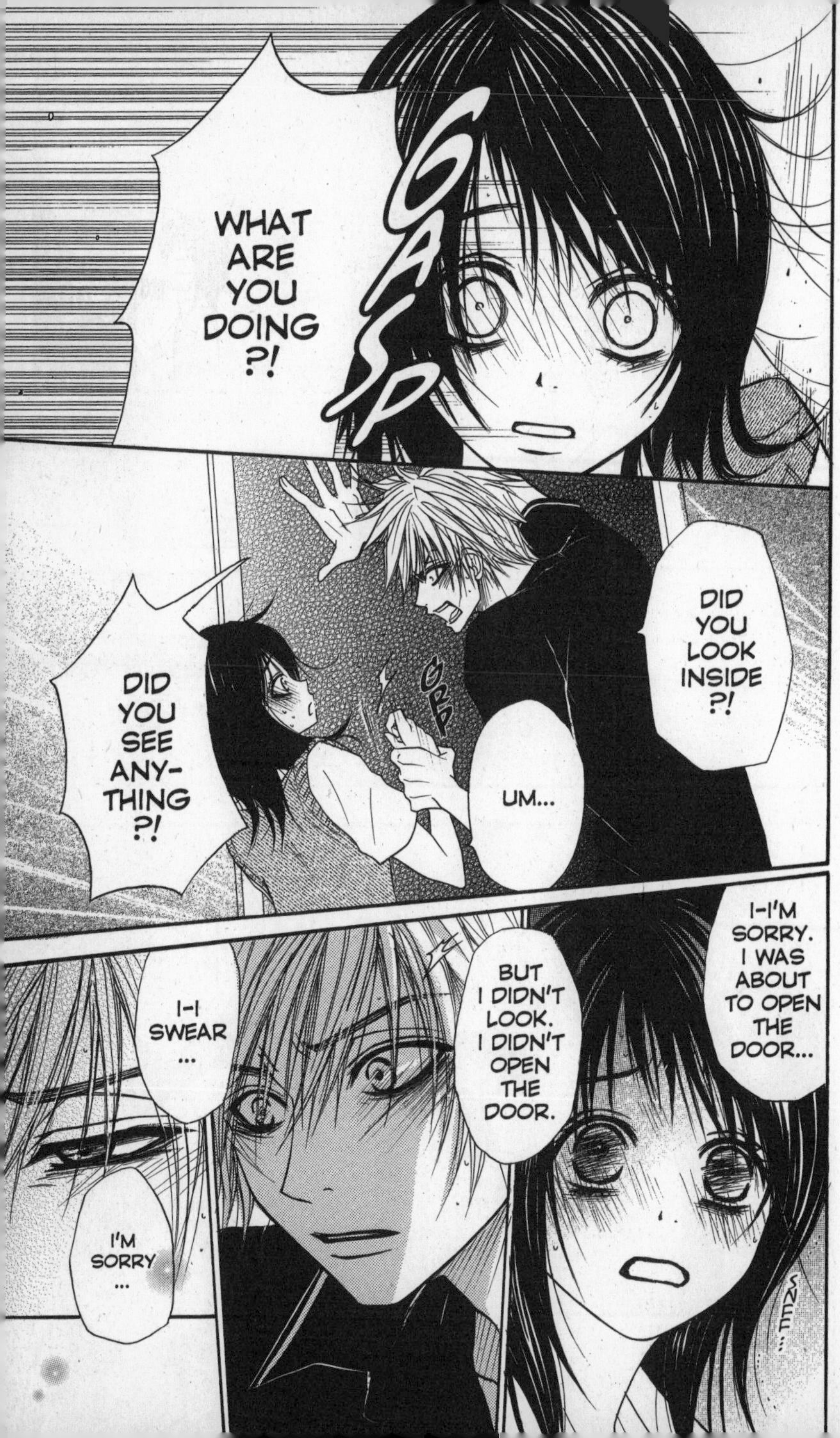
GASP
WHAT ARE YOU DOING?!
DID YOU LOOK INSIDE?!
UM...
DID YOU SEE ANYTHING?!
I-I'M SORRY. I WAS ABOUT TO OPEN THE DOOR...
BUT I DIDN'T LOOK. I DIDN'T OPEN THE DOOR.
I-I SWEAR...
SNFF...
I'M SORRY...

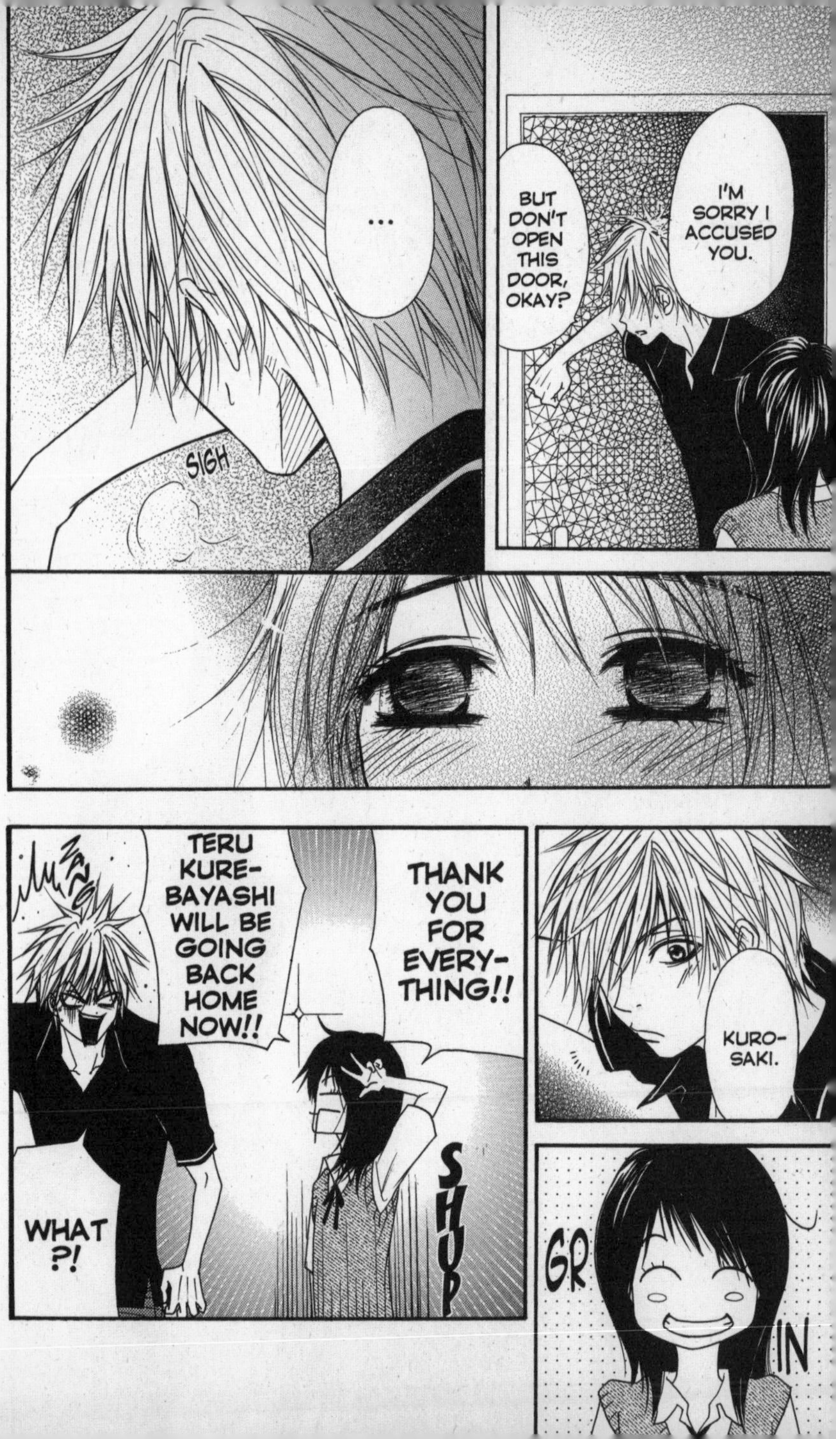
I'M SORRY I ACCUSED YOU.
BUT DON'T OPEN THIS DOOR, OKAY?
...
SIGH
KURO-SAKI.
GRIN
THANK YOU FOR EVERY-THING!!
TERU KURE-BAYASHI WILL BE GOING BACK HOME NOW!!
SHUP
WHAT?!

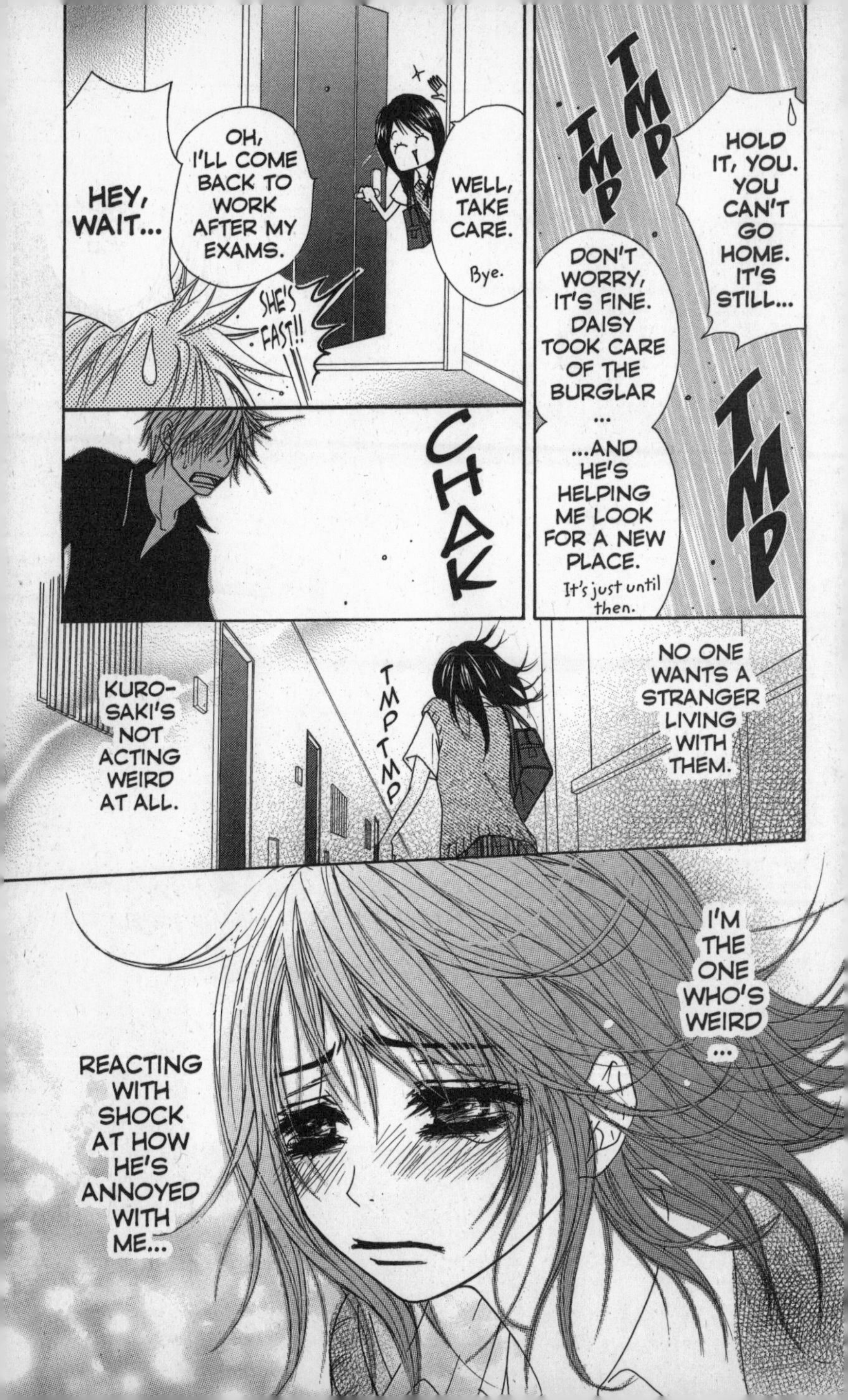
HOLD IT, YOU. YOU CAN'T GO HOME. IT'S STILL...
TMP TMP
DON'T WORRY, IT'S FINE. DAISY TOOK CARE OF THE BURGLAR ...
...AND HE'S HELPING ME LOOK FOR A NEW PLACE.
It's just until then.
TMP
WELL, TAKE CARE.
Bye.
OH, I'LL COME BACK TO WORK AFTER MY EXAMS.
HEY, WAIT...
SHE'S FAST!!
CHAK
NO ONE WANTS A STRANGER LIVING WITH THEM.
TMP TMP
KURO-SAKI'S NOT ACTING WEIRD AT ALL.
I'M THE ONE WHO'S WEIRD ...
REACTING WITH SHOCK AT HOW HE'S ANNOYED WITH ME...

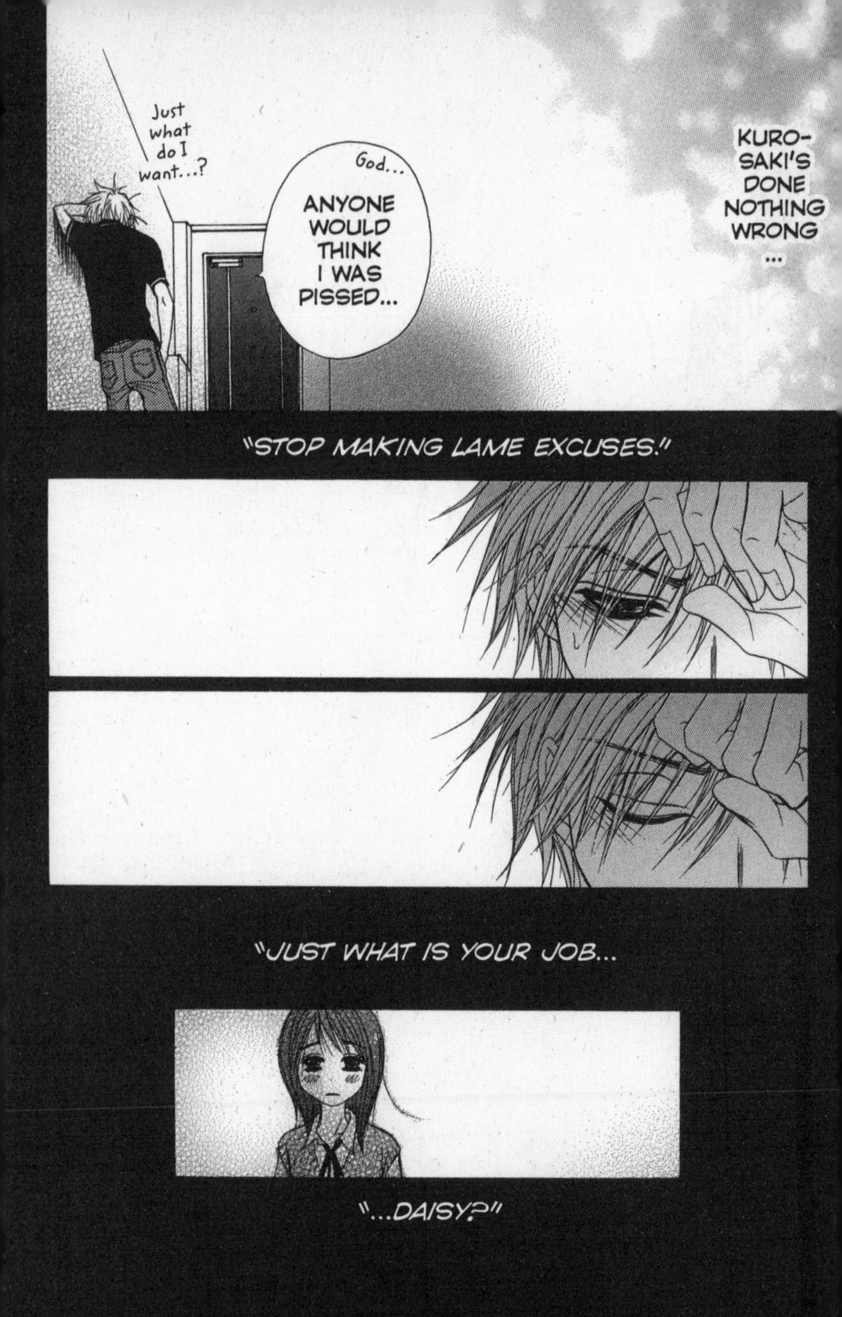
KURO-SAKI'S DONE NOTHING WRONG...
God... ANYONE WOULD THINK I WAS PISSED...
Just what do I want...?
"STOP MAKING LAME EXCUSES."
"JUST WHAT IS YOUR JOB...
"...DAISY?"

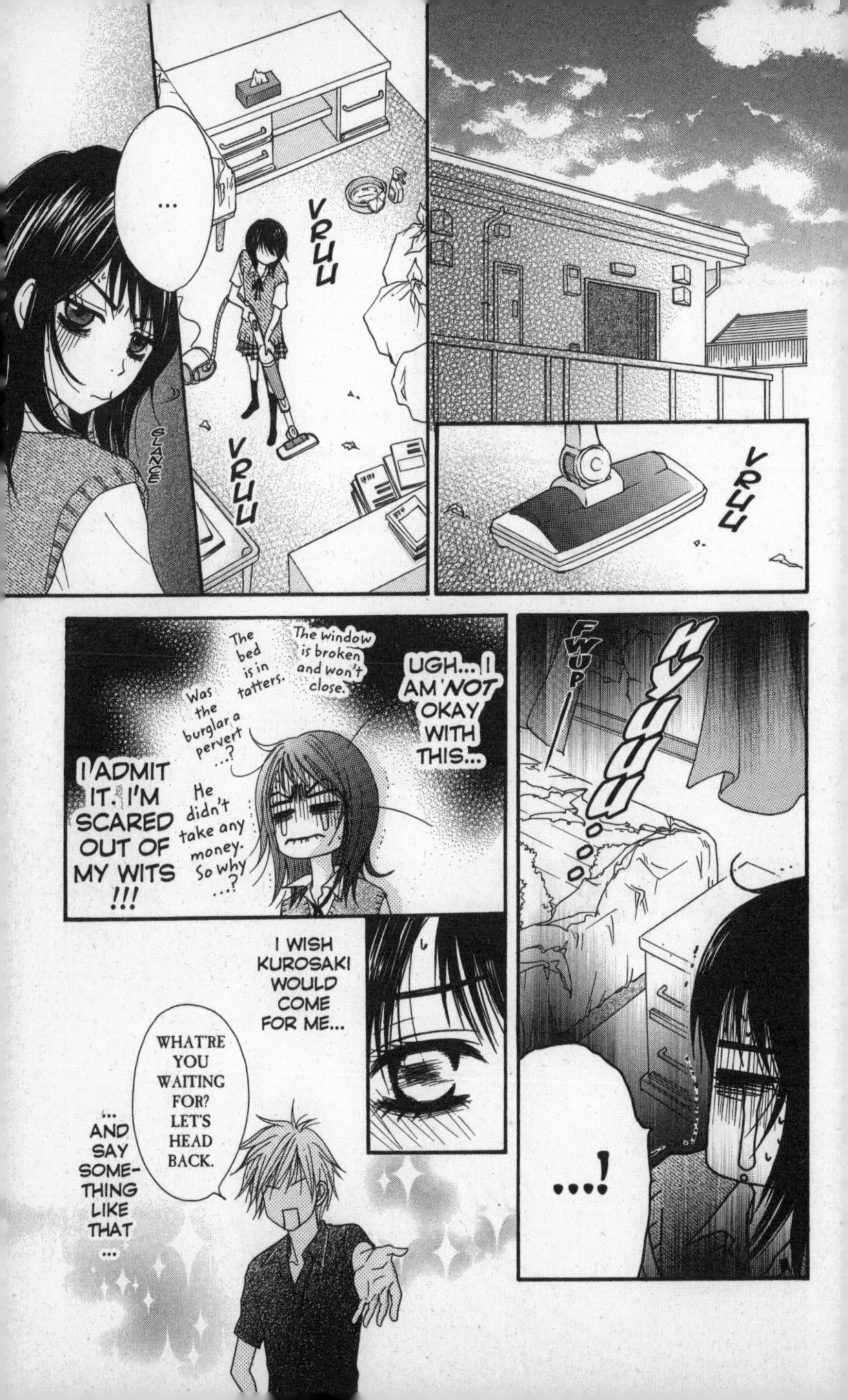
VRUU
...
VRUU
VRUU
GLANCE
FWUP
HYUUUUU
ooo
...
...!
UGH... I AM NOT OKAY WITH THIS...
The window is broken and won't close.
The bed is in tatters.
Was the burglar a pervert...?
He didn't take any money. So why...?
I ADMIT IT. I'M SCARED OUT OF MY WITS!!!
I WISH KUROSAKI WOULD COME FOR ME...
WHAT'RE YOU WAITING FOR? LET'S HEAD BACK.
...AND SAY SOMETHING LIKE THAT...

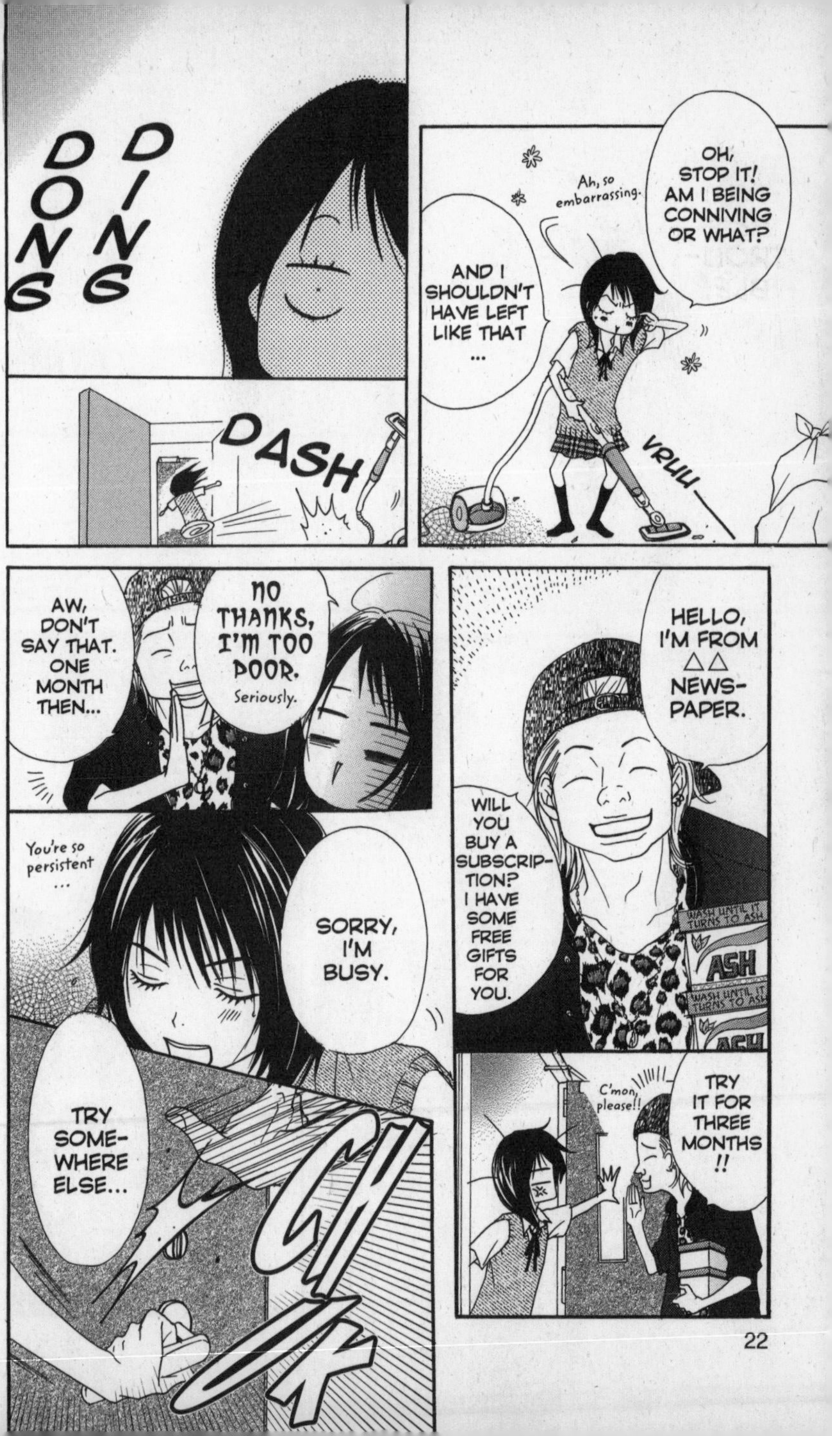
OH, STOP IT! AM I BEING CONNIVING OR WHAT?
Ah, so embarrassing.
AND I SHOULDN'T HAVE LEFT LIKE THAT ...
VRUU—
DING DONG
DASH
HELLO, I'M FROM △△ NEWSPAPER.
WILL YOU BUY A SUBSCRIPTION? I HAVE SOME FREE GIFTS FOR YOU.
WASH UNTIL IT TURNS TO ASH
ASH
NO THANKS, I'M TOO POOR.
Seriously.
AW, DON'T SAY THAT. ONE MONTH THEN...
TRY IT FOR THREE MONTHS!!
C'mon, please!!
SORRY, I'M BUSY.
You're so persistent ...
TRY SOMEWHERE ELSE...
CHIK

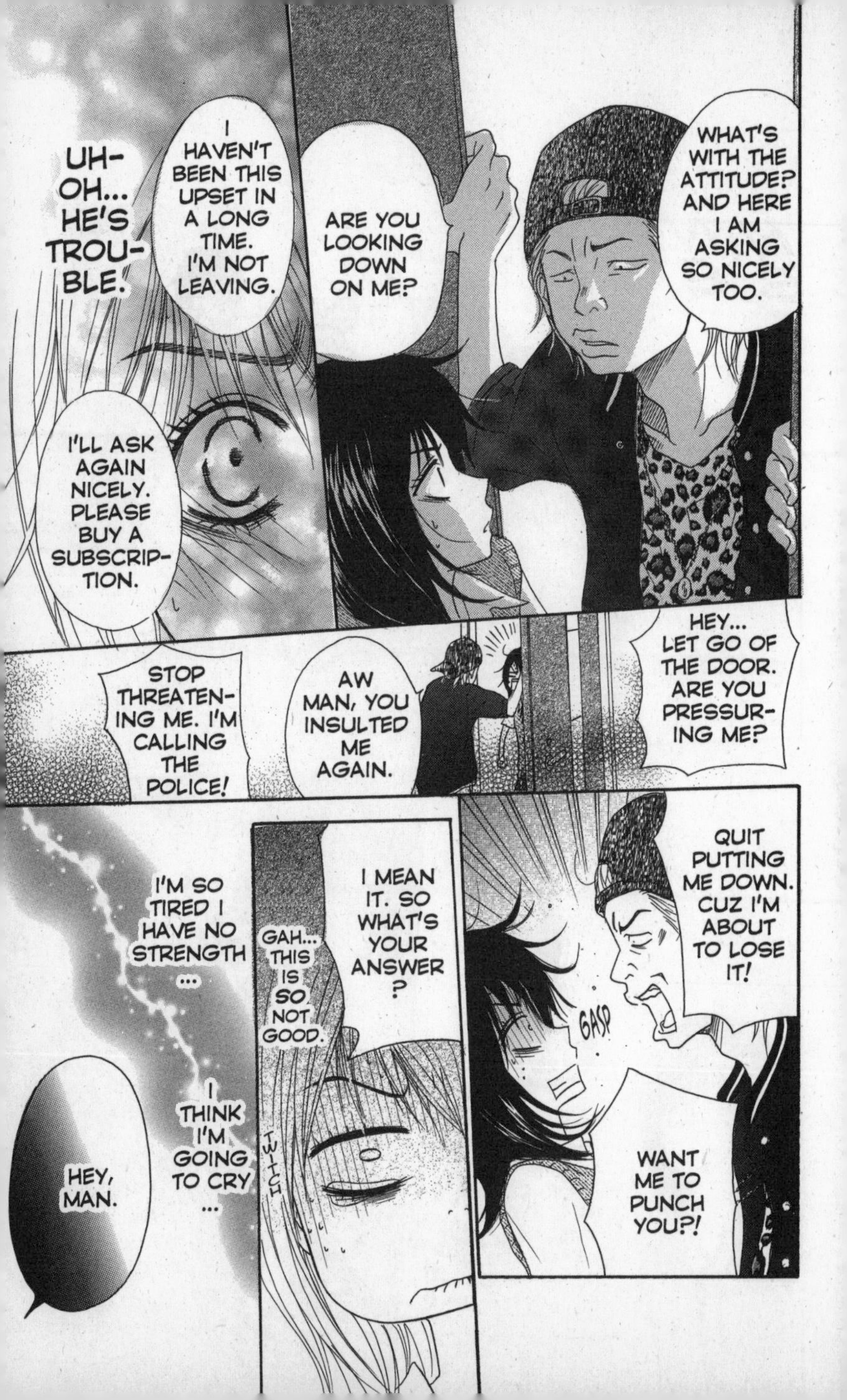
WHAT'S WITH THE ATTITUDE? AND HERE I AM ASKING SO NICELY TOO.
ARE YOU LOOKING DOWN ON ME?
I HAVEN'T BEEN THIS UPSET IN A LONG TIME. I'M NOT LEAVING.
UH-OH... HE'S TROUBLE.
I'LL ASK AGAIN NICELY. PLEASE BUY A SUBSCRIPTION.
HEY... LET GO OF THE DOOR. ARE YOU PRESSURING ME?
AW MAN, YOU INSULTED ME AGAIN.
STOP THREATENING ME. I'M CALLING THE POLICE!
QUIT PUTTING ME DOWN. CUZ I'M ABOUT TO LOSE IT!
GASP
WANT ME TO PUNCH YOU?!
I MEAN IT. SO WHAT'S YOUR ANSWER?
GAH... THIS IS SO NOT GOOD.
TWITCH
I'M SO TIRED I HAVE NO STRENGTH...
I THINK I'M GOING TO CRY...
HEY, MAN.

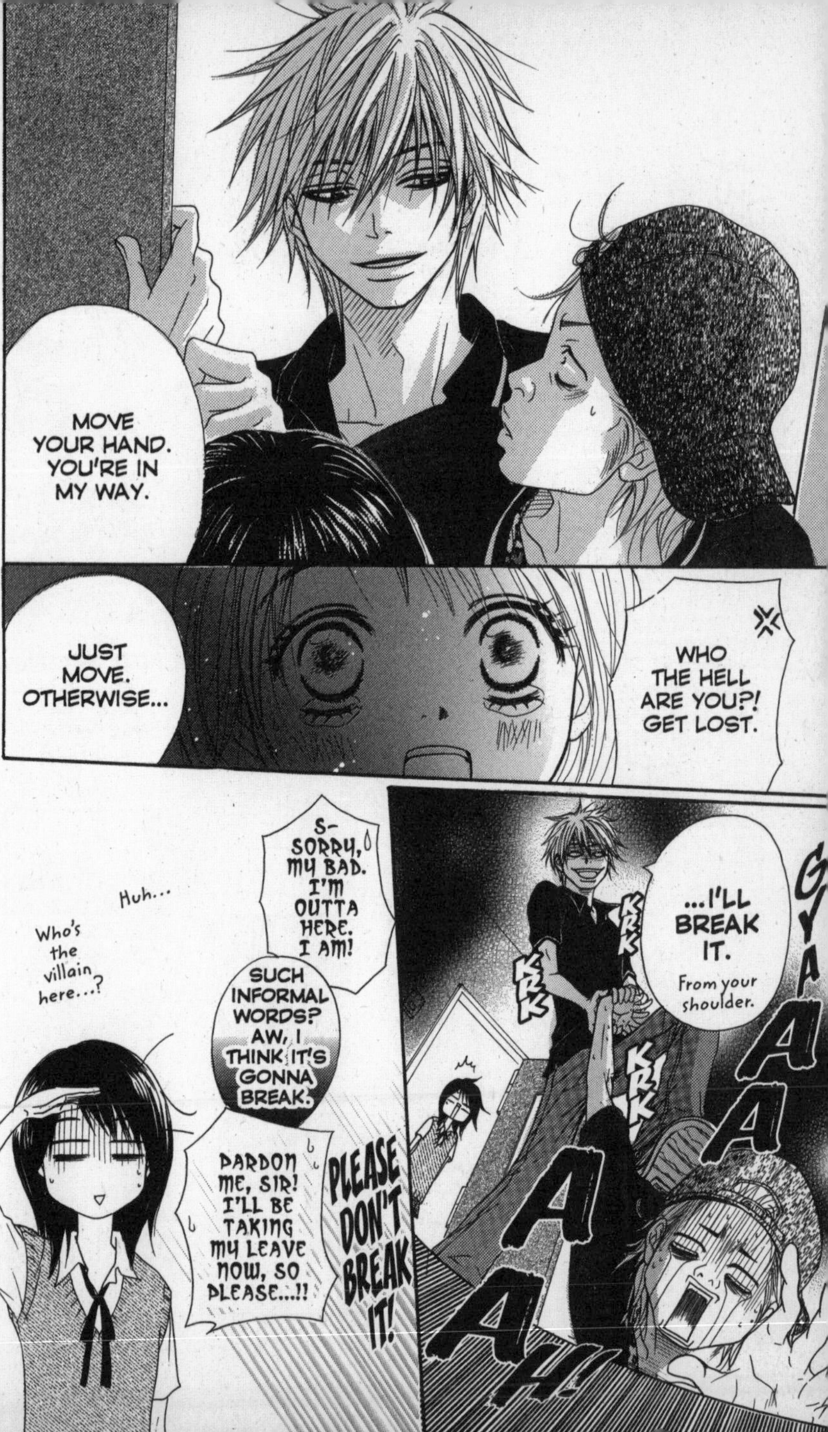
MOVE YOUR HAND. YOU'RE IN MY WAY.
WHO THE HELL ARE YOU?! GET LOST.
JUST MOVE. OTHERWISE...
...I'LL BREAK IT.
From your shoulder.
KRK KRK
KRK KRK
GYAAAAAAAH
S-SORRY, MY BAD. I'M OUTTA HERE. I AM!
SUCH INFORMAL WORDS? AW, I THINK IT'S GONNA BREAK.
PLEASE DON'T BREAK IT!
PARDON ME, SIR! I'LL BE TAKING MY LEAVE NOW, SO PLEASE...!!
Huh...
Who's the villain here...?

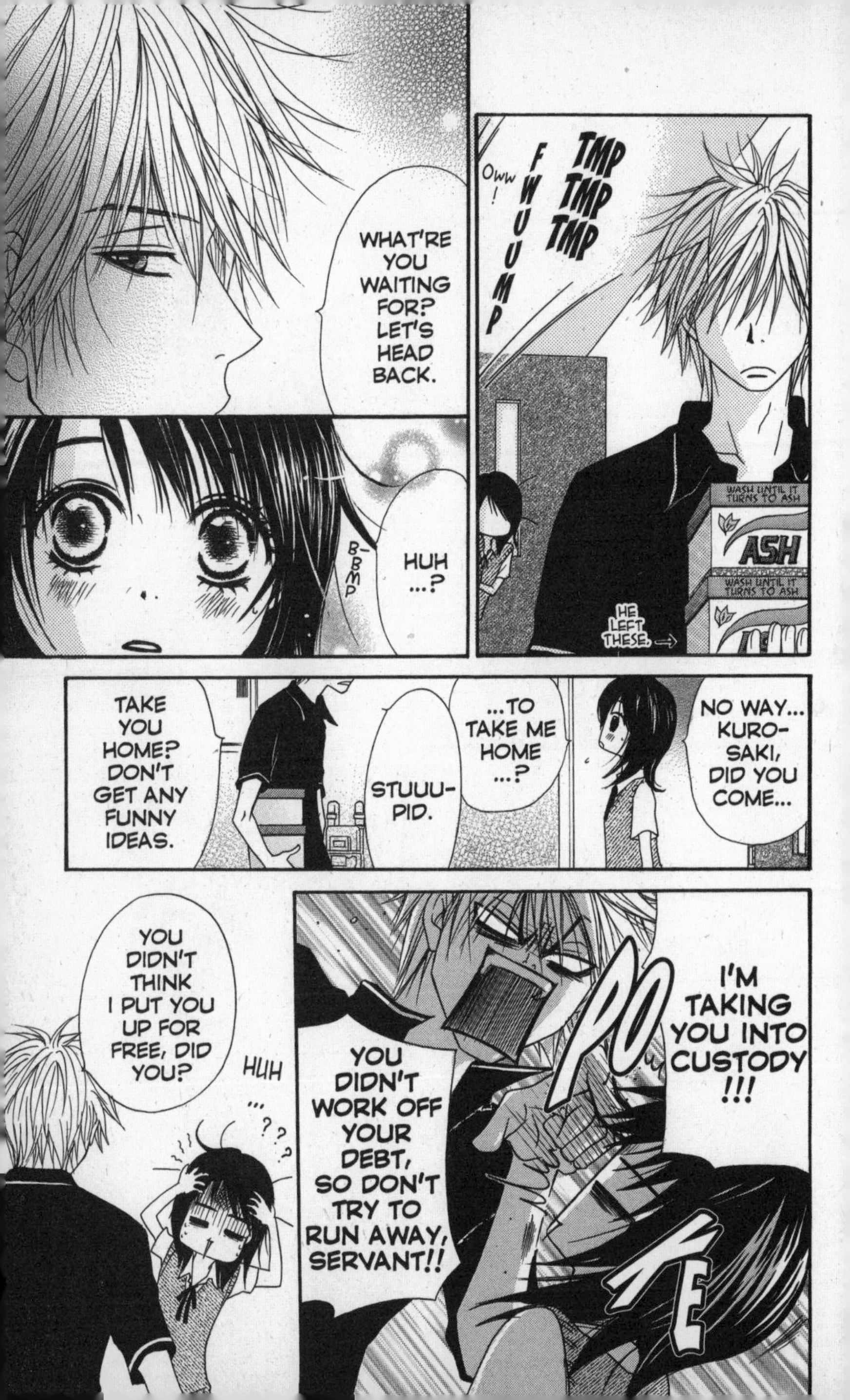
TMP TMP TMP
FWUUUMP
Oww!
WASH UNTIL IT TURNS TO ASH
ASH
WASH UNTIL IT TURNS TO ASH
HE LEFT THESE.
WHAT'RE YOU WAITING FOR? LET'S HEAD BACK.
HUH ...?
B-BMP
NO WAY... KURO-SAKI, DID YOU COME...
...TO TAKE ME HOME ...?
STUUU-PID.
TAKE YOU HOME? DON'T GET ANY FUNNY IDEAS.
I'M TAKING YOU INTO CUSTODY!!!
POKE
YOU DIDN'T WORK OFF YOUR DEBT, SO DON'T TRY TO RUN AWAY, SERVANT!!
YOU DIDN'T THINK I PUT YOU UP FOR FREE, DID YOU?
HUH ...
???

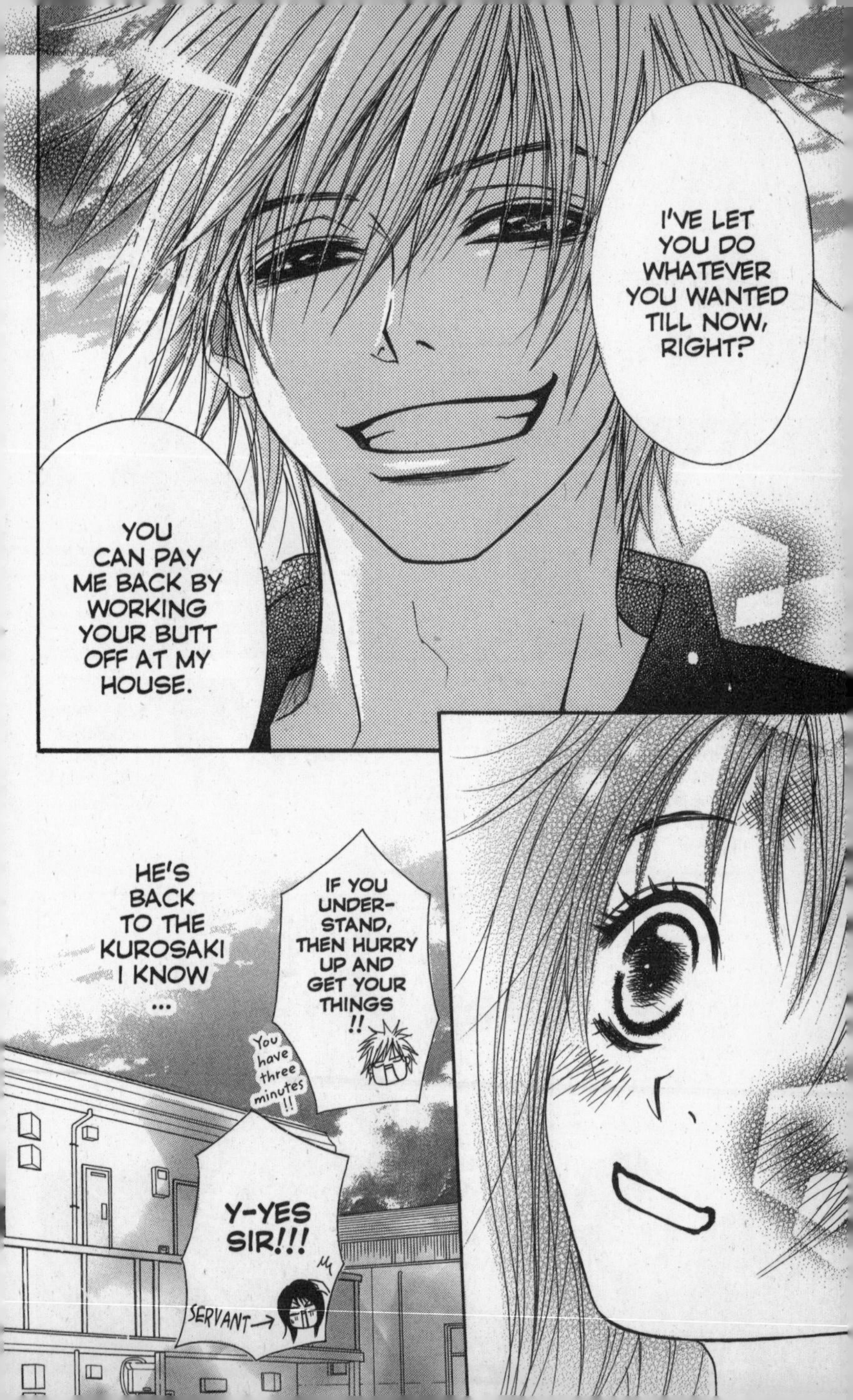
I'VE LET YOU DO WHATEVER YOU WANTED TILL NOW, RIGHT?
YOU CAN PAY ME BACK BY WORKING YOUR BUTT OFF AT MY HOUSE.
IF YOU UNDER-STAND, THEN HURRY UP AND GET YOUR THINGS!!
You have three minutes!!
HE'S BACK TO THE KUROSAKI I KNOW...
Y-YES SIR!!!
SERVANT

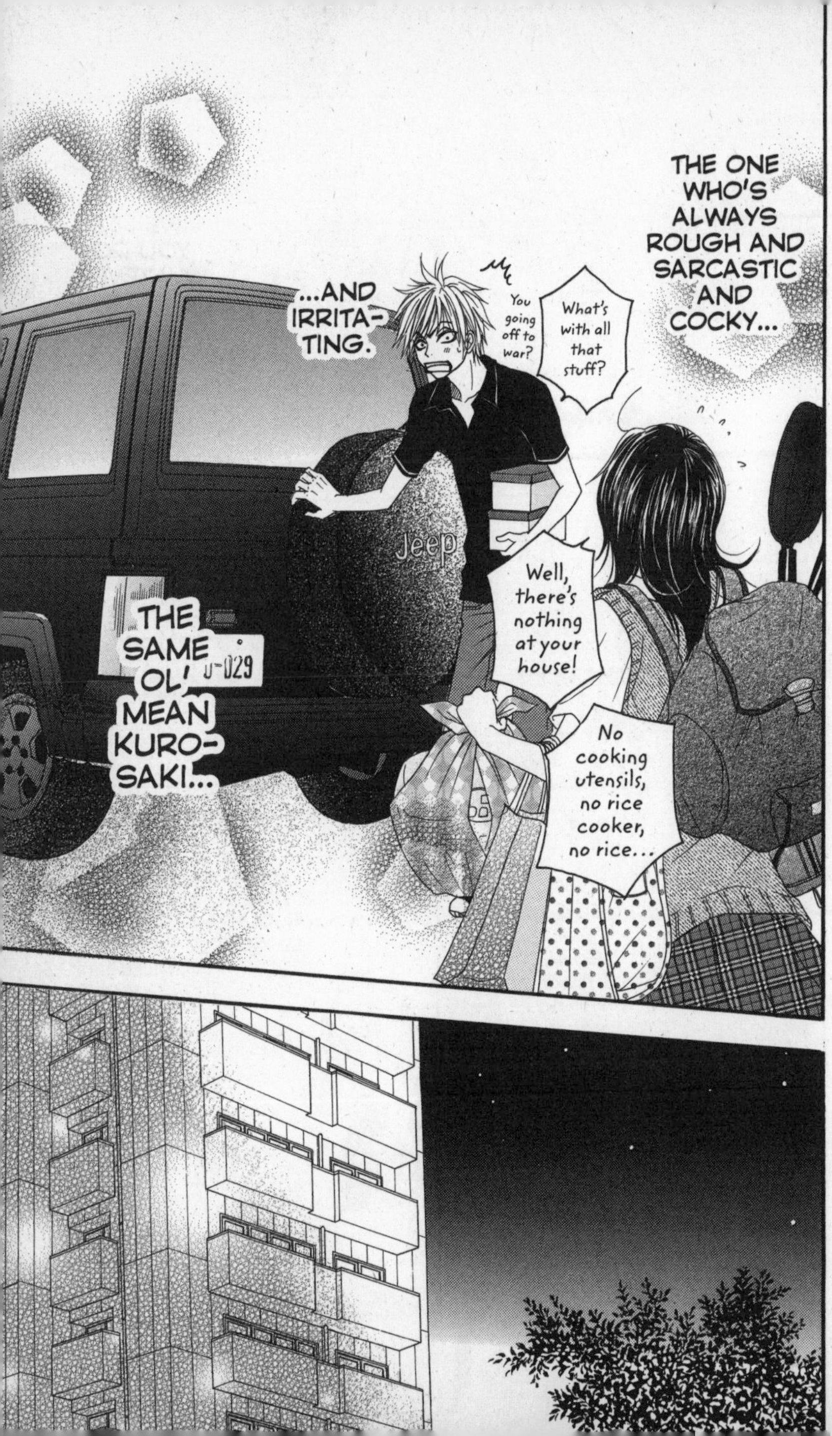
THE ONE WHO'S ALWAYS ROUGH AND SARCASTIC AND COCKY...
What's with all that stuff?
You going off to war?
...AND IRRITA-TING.
Well, there's nothing at your house!
No cooking utensils, no rice cooker, no rice...
THE SAME OL' MEAN KURO-SAKI...

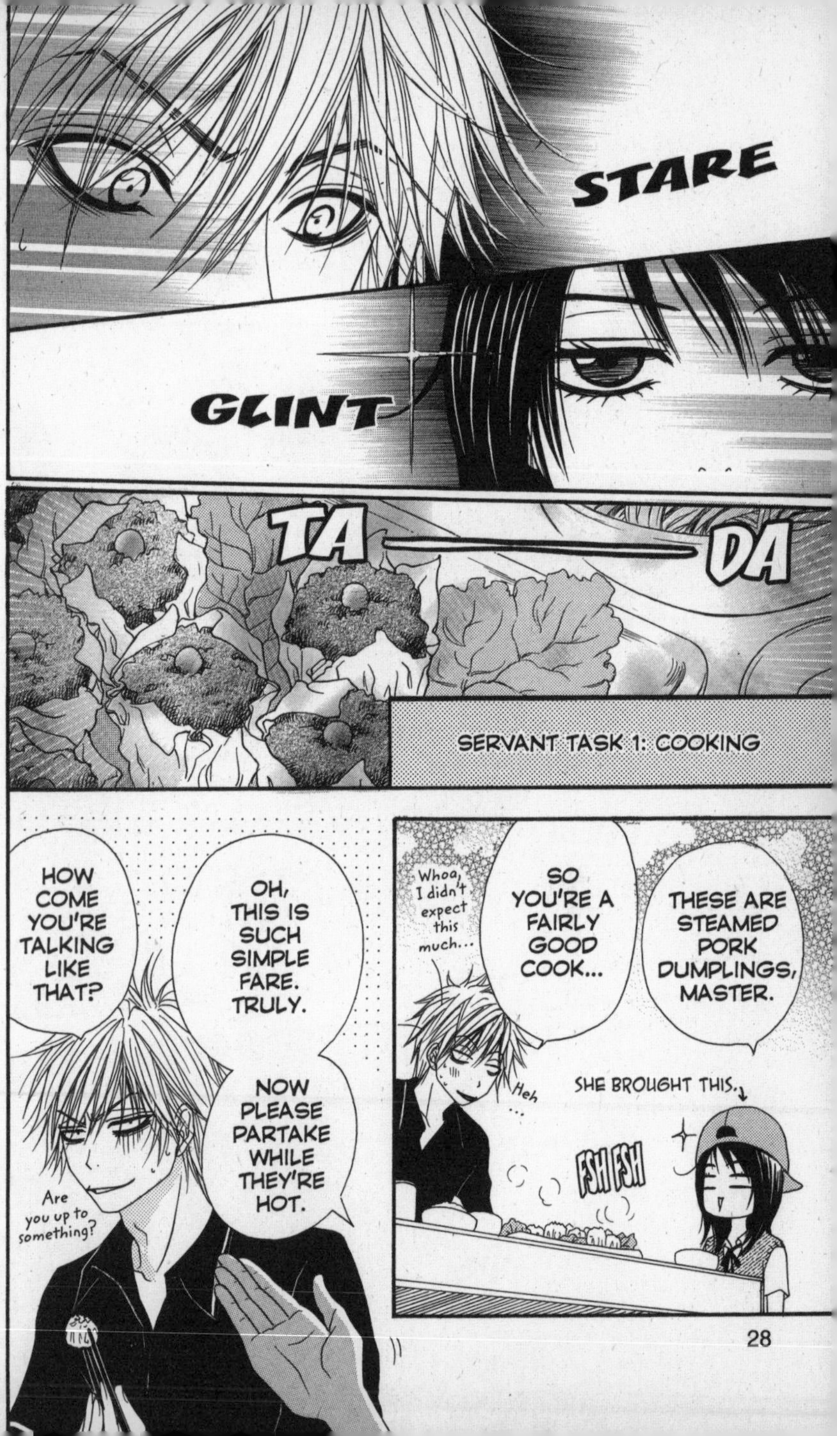
STARE
GLINT
TA—DA
SERVANT TASK 1: COOKING
THESE ARE STEAMED PORK DUMPLINGS, MASTER.
SO YOU'RE A FAIRLY GOOD COOK...
Whoa, I didn't expect this much...
SHE BROUGHT THIS.
FSH FSH
Heh...
OH, THIS IS SUCH SIMPLE FARE. TRULY.
HOW COME YOU'RE TALKING LIKE THAT?
NOW PLEASE PARTAKE WHILE THEY'RE HOT.
Are you up to something?

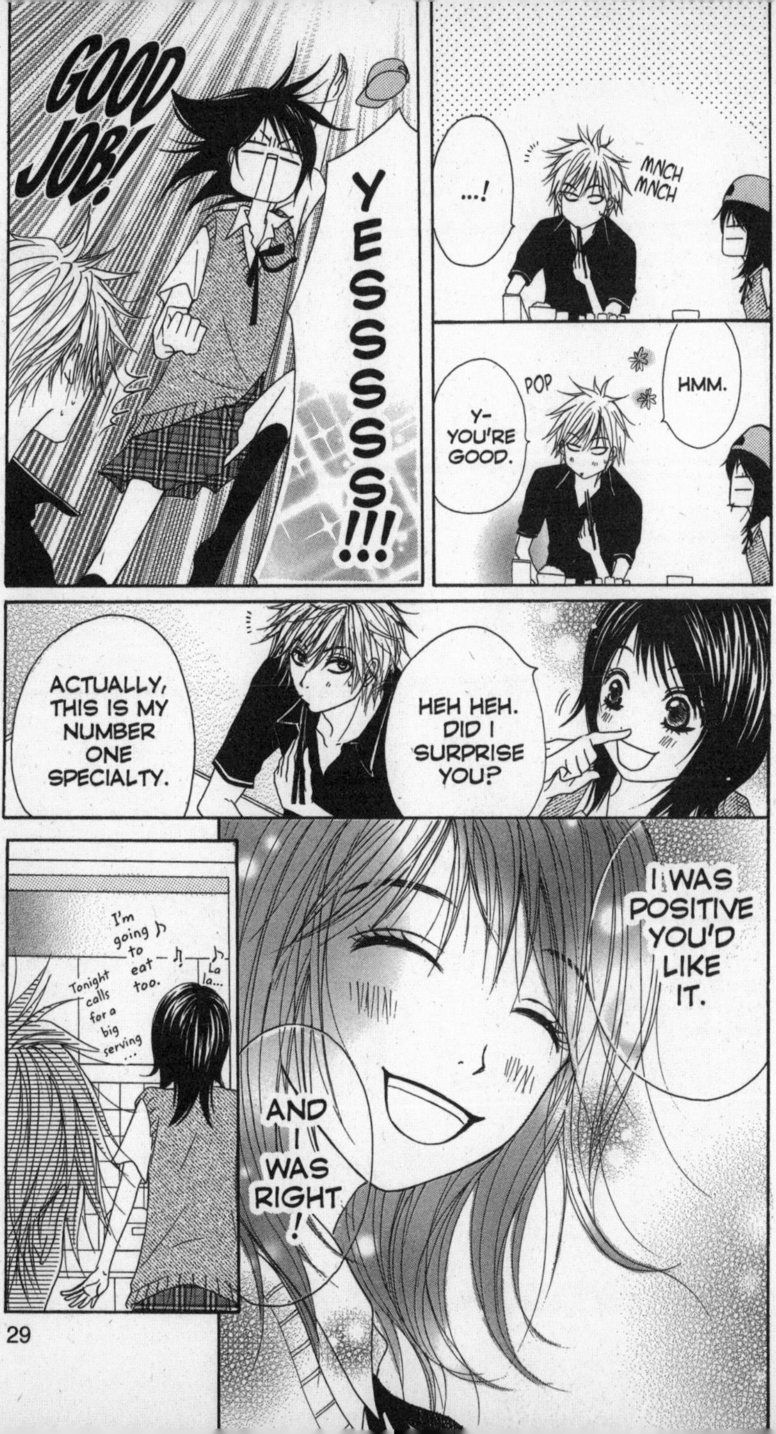
...!
MNCH MNCH
HMM.
POP
Y- YOU'RE GOOD.
YESSSSSS!!!
GOOD JOB!
HEH HEH. DID I SURPRISE YOU?
ACTUALLY, THIS IS MY NUMBER ONE SPECIALTY.
I WAS POSITIVE YOU'D LIKE IT.
AND I WAS RIGHT!
I'm going to eat too.
La la...
Tonight calls for a big serving...

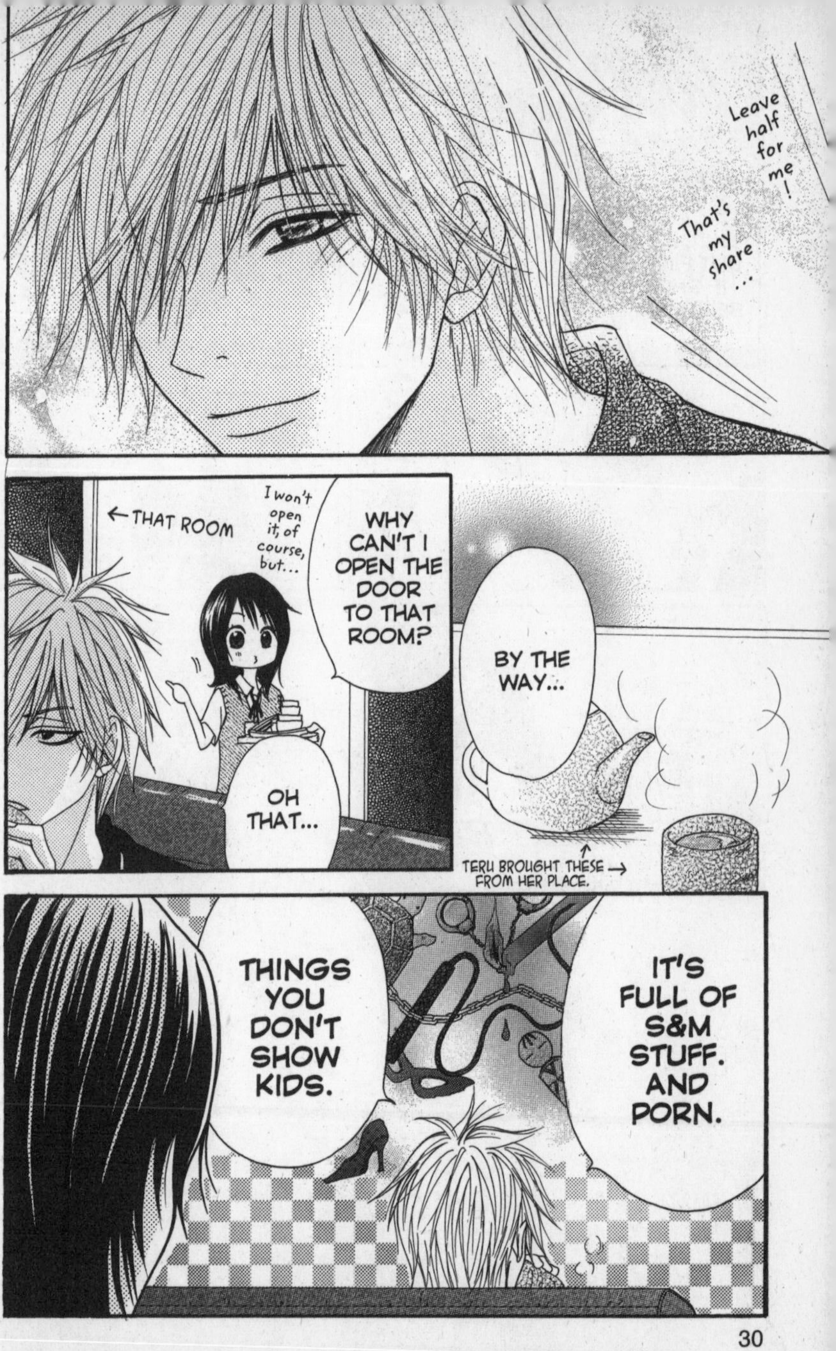
Leave half for me!
That's my share...
BY THE WAY...
TERU BROUGHT THESE FROM HER PLACE. →
WHY CAN'T I OPEN THE DOOR TO THAT ROOM?
I won't open it, of course, but...
← THAT ROOM
OH THAT...
IT'S FULL OF S&M STUFF. AND PORN.
THINGS YOU DON'T SHOW KIDS.

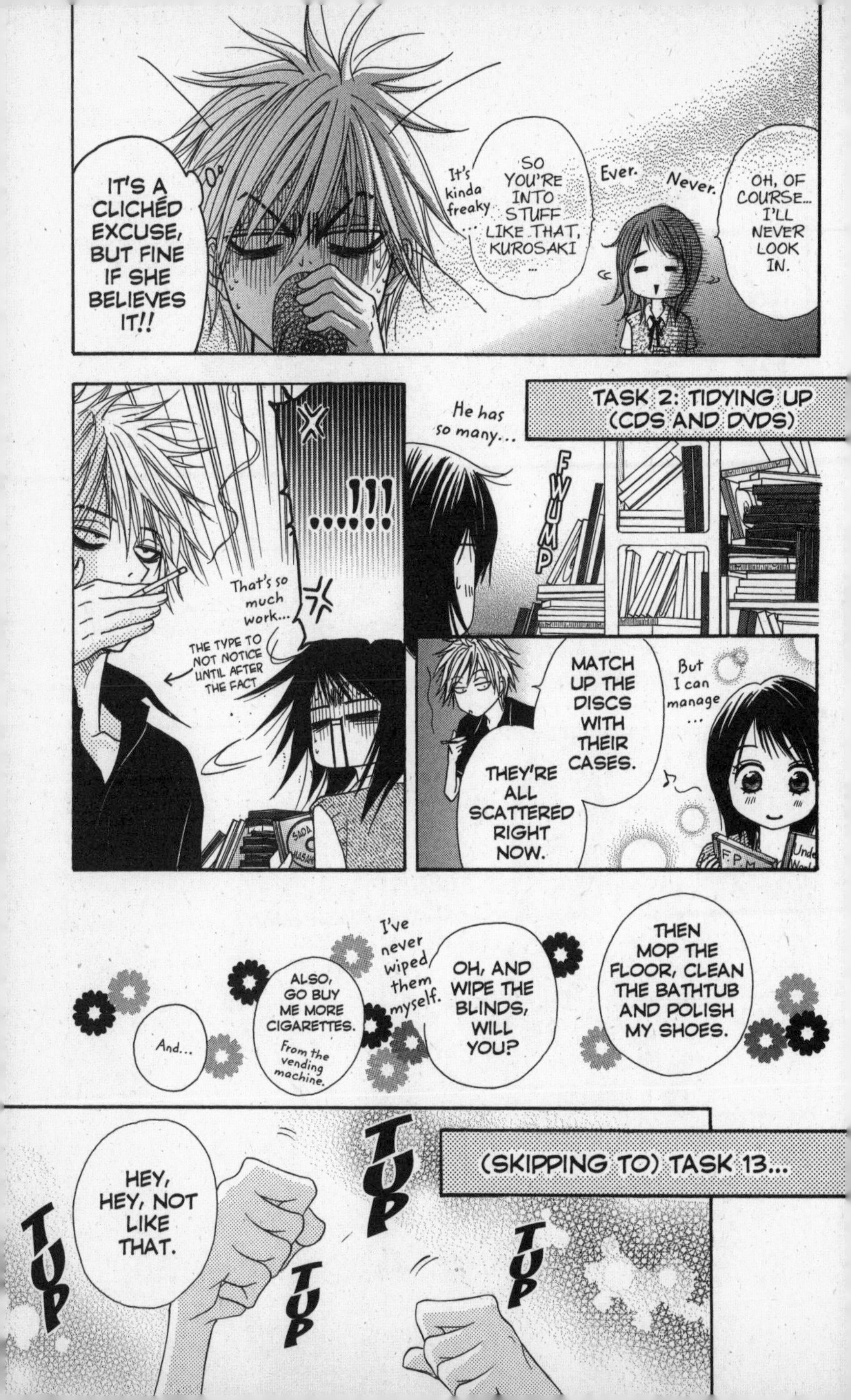

OH, OF COURSE... I'LL NEVER LOOK IN.
Never.
Ever.
SO YOU'RE INTO STUFF LIKE THAT, KUROSAKI...
It's kinda freaky...
IT'S A CLICHÉD EXCUSE, BUT FINE IF SHE BELIEVES IT!!
TASK 2: TIDYING UP (CDS AND DVDS)
He has so many...
FWUMP
But I can manage...
MATCH UP THE DISCS WITH THEIR CASES.
THEY'RE ALL SCATTERED RIGHT NOW.
...!!
That's so much work...
THE TYPE TO NOT NOTICE UNTIL AFTER THE FACT
THEN MOP THE FLOOR, CLEAN THE BATHTUB AND POLISH MY SHOES.
OH, AND WIPE THE BLINDS, WILL YOU?
I've never wiped them myself.
ALSO, GO BUY ME MORE CIGARETTES.
From the vending machine.
And...
(SKIPPING TO) TASK 13...
TUP
TUP
TUP
HEY, HEY, NOT LIKE THAT.
TUP

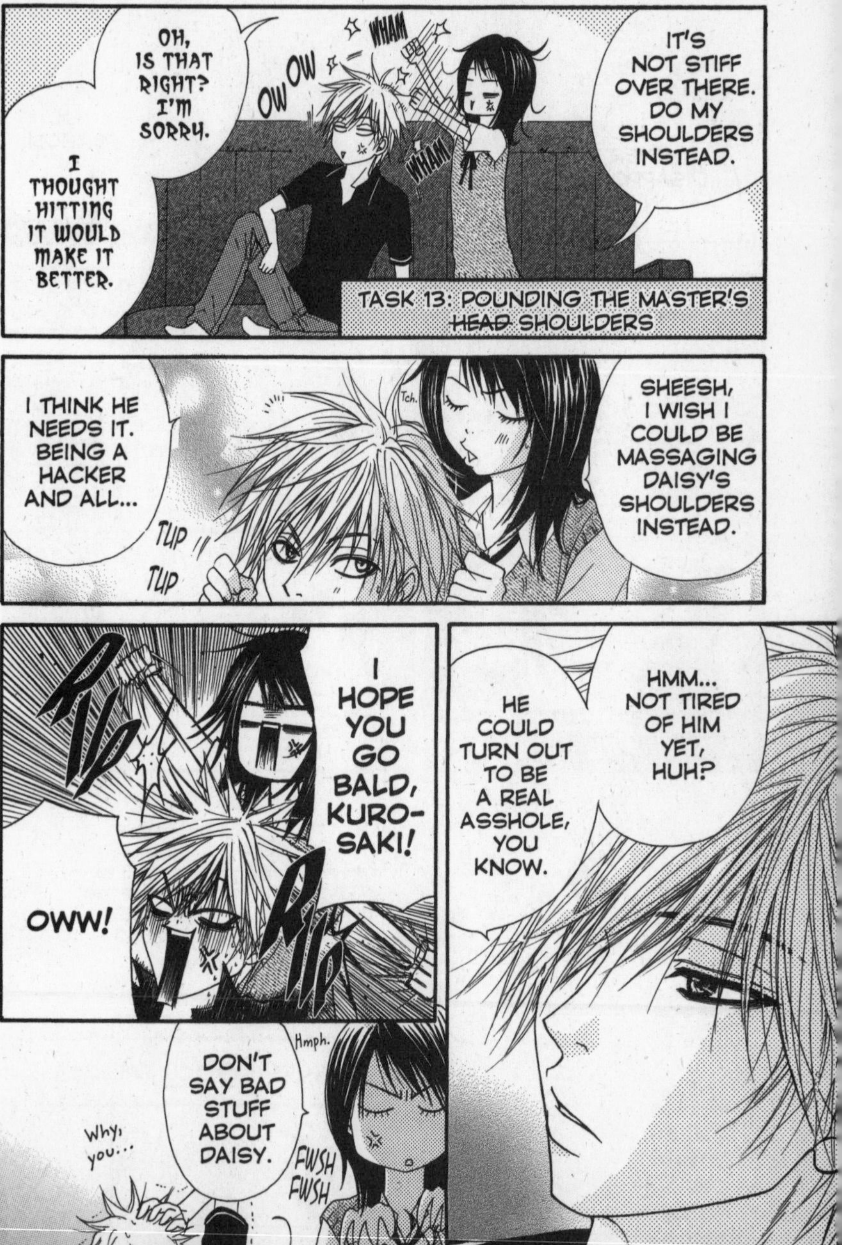
IT'S NOT STIFF OVER THERE. DO MY SHOULDERS INSTEAD.
WHAM
WHAM
OW OW
OH, IS THAT RIGHT? I'M SORRY.
I THOUGHT HITTING IT WOULD MAKE IT BETTER.
TASK 13: POUNDING THE MASTER'S ~~HEAD~~ SHOULDERS
SHEESH, I WISH I COULD BE MASSAGING DAISY'S SHOULDERS INSTEAD.
Tch.
I THINK HE NEEDS IT. BEING A HACKER AND ALL...
TUP
TUP
HMM... NOT TIRED OF HIM YET, HUH?
HE COULD TURN OUT TO BE A REAL ASSHOLE, YOU KNOW.
I HOPE YOU GO BALD, KURO-SAKI!
RIP
RIP
OWW!
Hmph.
DON'T SAY BAD STUFF ABOUT DAISY.
FWSH FWSH
Why, you...

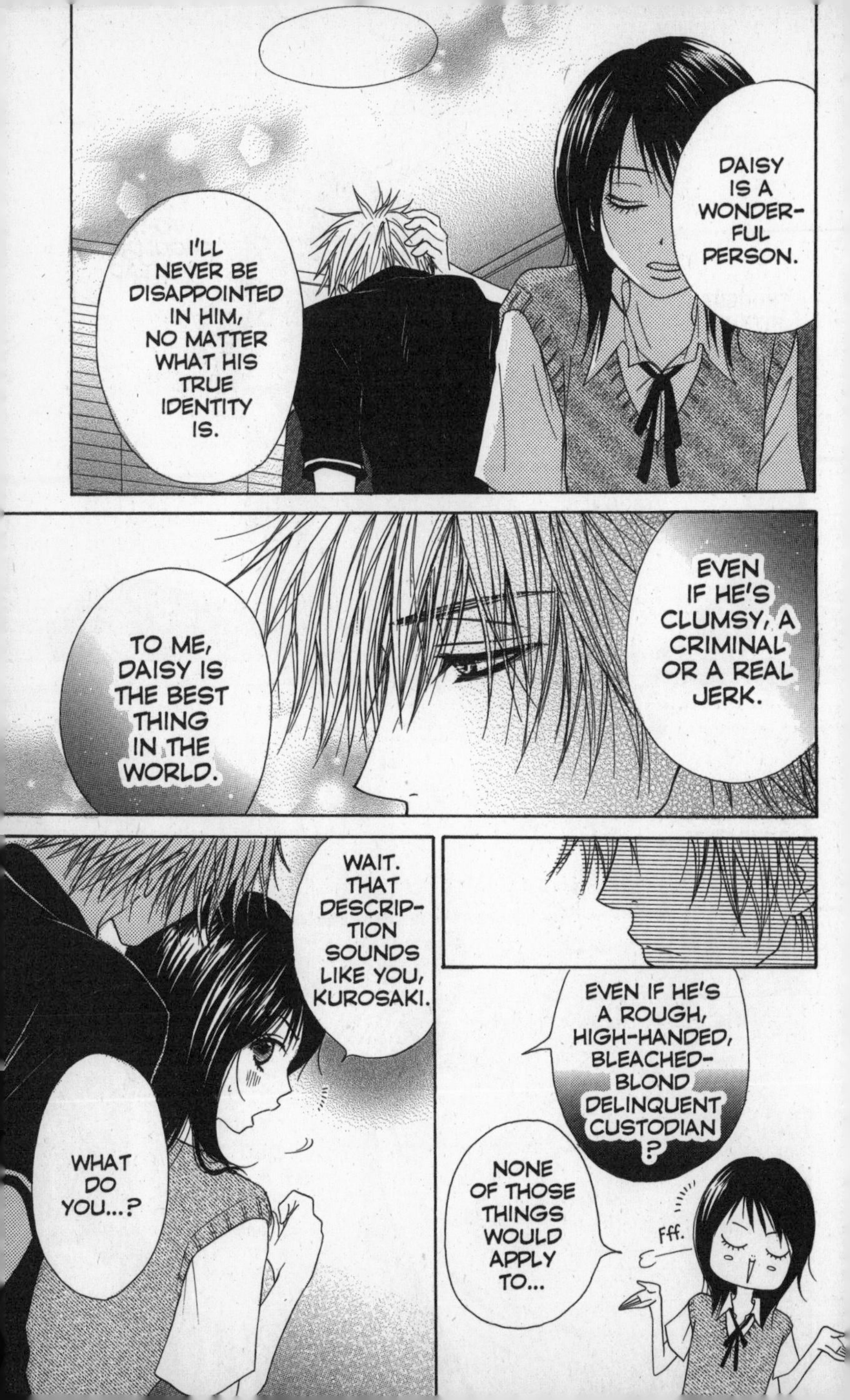
DAISY IS A WONDERFUL PERSON.
I'LL NEVER BE DISAPPOINTED IN HIM, NO MATTER WHAT HIS TRUE IDENTITY IS.
EVEN IF HE'S CLUMSY, A CRIMINAL OR A REAL JERK.
TO ME, DAISY IS THE BEST THING IN THE WORLD.
EVEN IF HE'S A ROUGH, HIGH-HANDED, BLEACHED-BLOND DELINQUENT CUSTODIAN?
NONE OF THOSE THINGS WOULD APPLY TO...
Fff.
WAIT. THAT DESCRIPTION SOUNDS LIKE YOU, KUROSAKI.
WHAT DO YOU...?

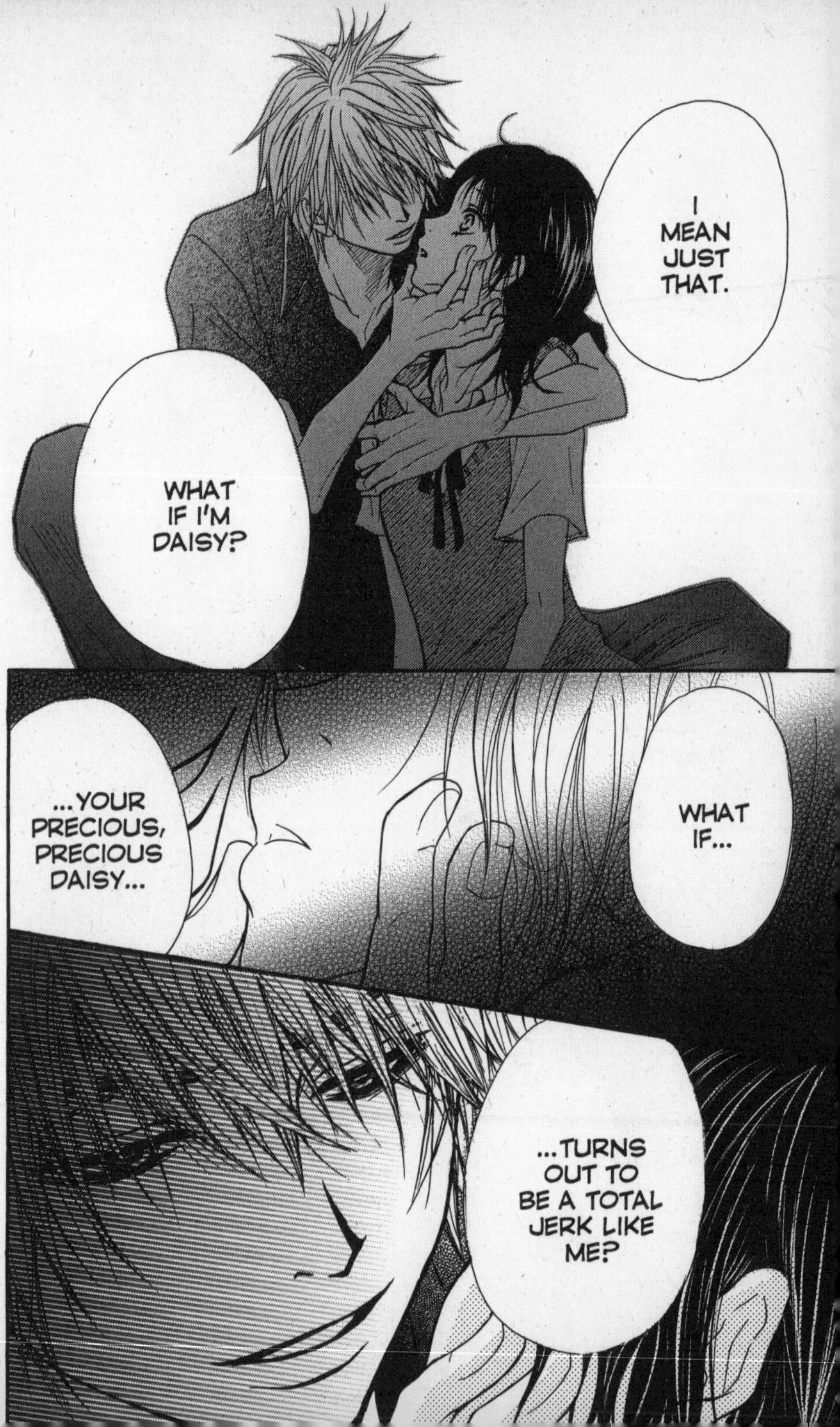
I MEAN JUST THAT.
WHAT IF I'M DAISY?
WHAT IF...
...YOUR PRECIOUS, PRECIOUS DAISY...
...TURNS OUT TO BE A TOTAL JERK LIKE ME?

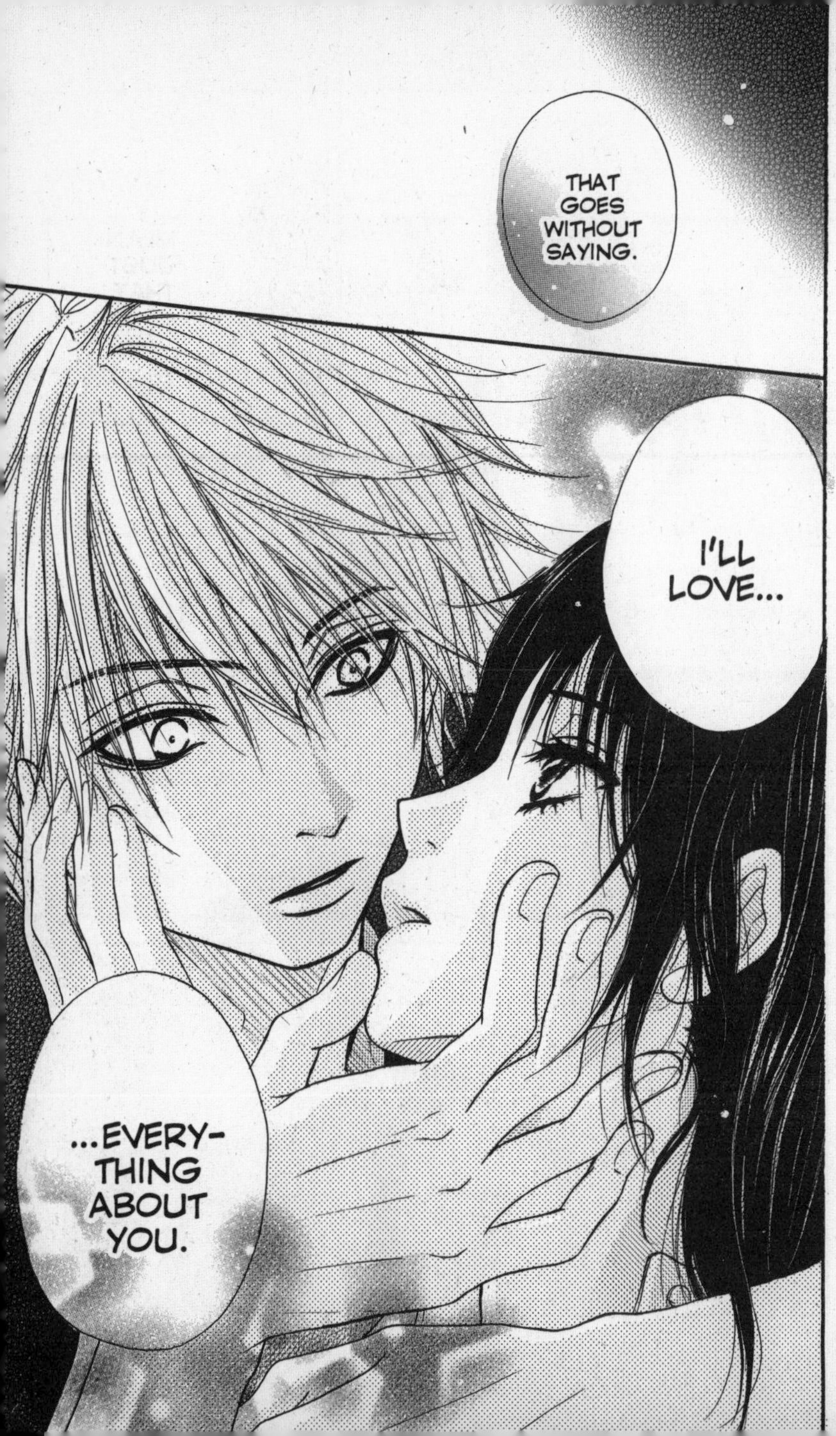
THAT GOES WITHOUT SAYING.
I'LL LOVE...
...EVERY-THING ABOUT YOU.

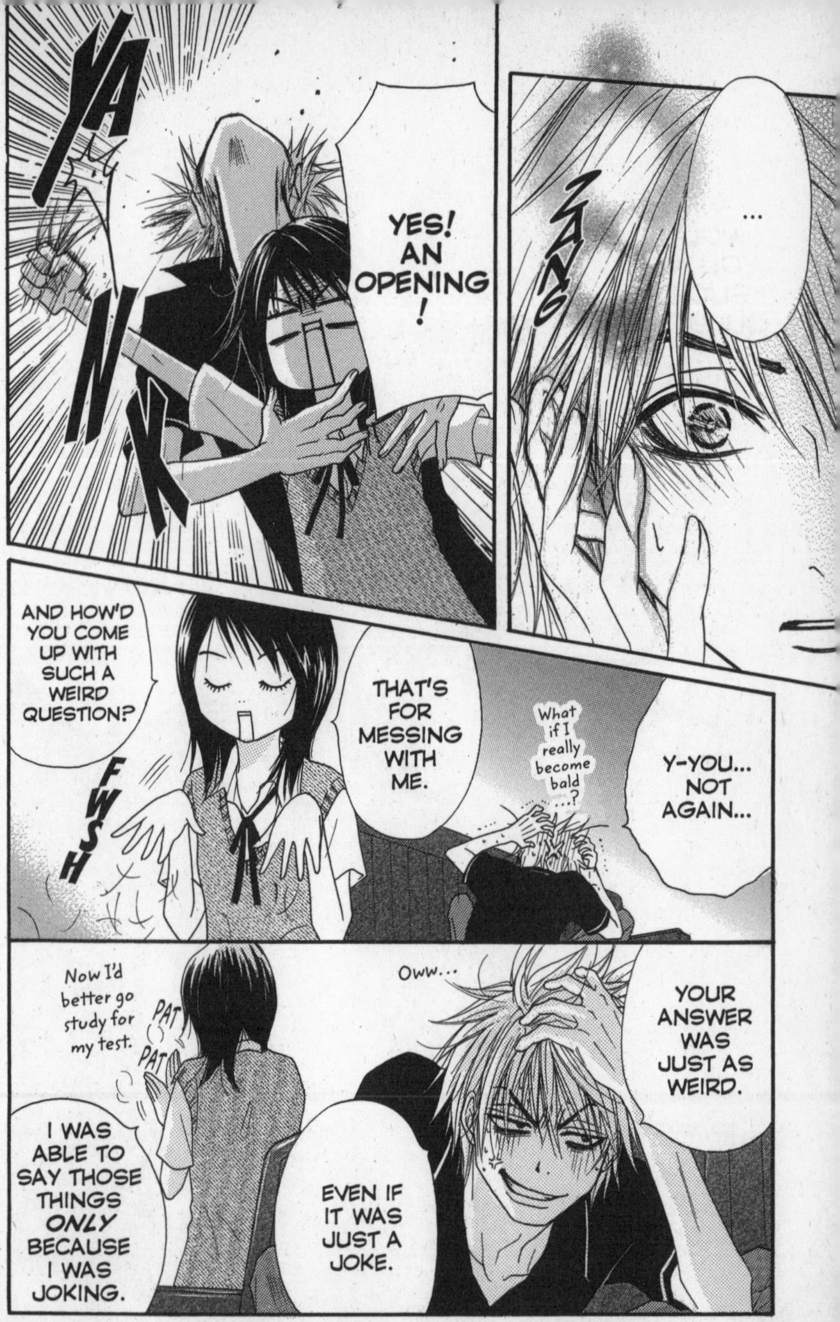
...
ZANG
YANK
YES! AN OPENING!
Y-YOU... NOT AGAIN...
What if I really become bald ...?
THAT'S FOR MESSING WITH ME.
AND HOW'D YOU COME UP WITH SUCH A WEIRD QUESTION?
FWSH
YOUR ANSWER WAS JUST AS WEIRD.
Oww...
EVEN IF IT WAS JUST A JOKE.
Now I'd better go study for my test.
PAT PAT
I WAS ABLE TO SAY THOSE THINGS *ONLY* BECAUSE I WAS JOKING.

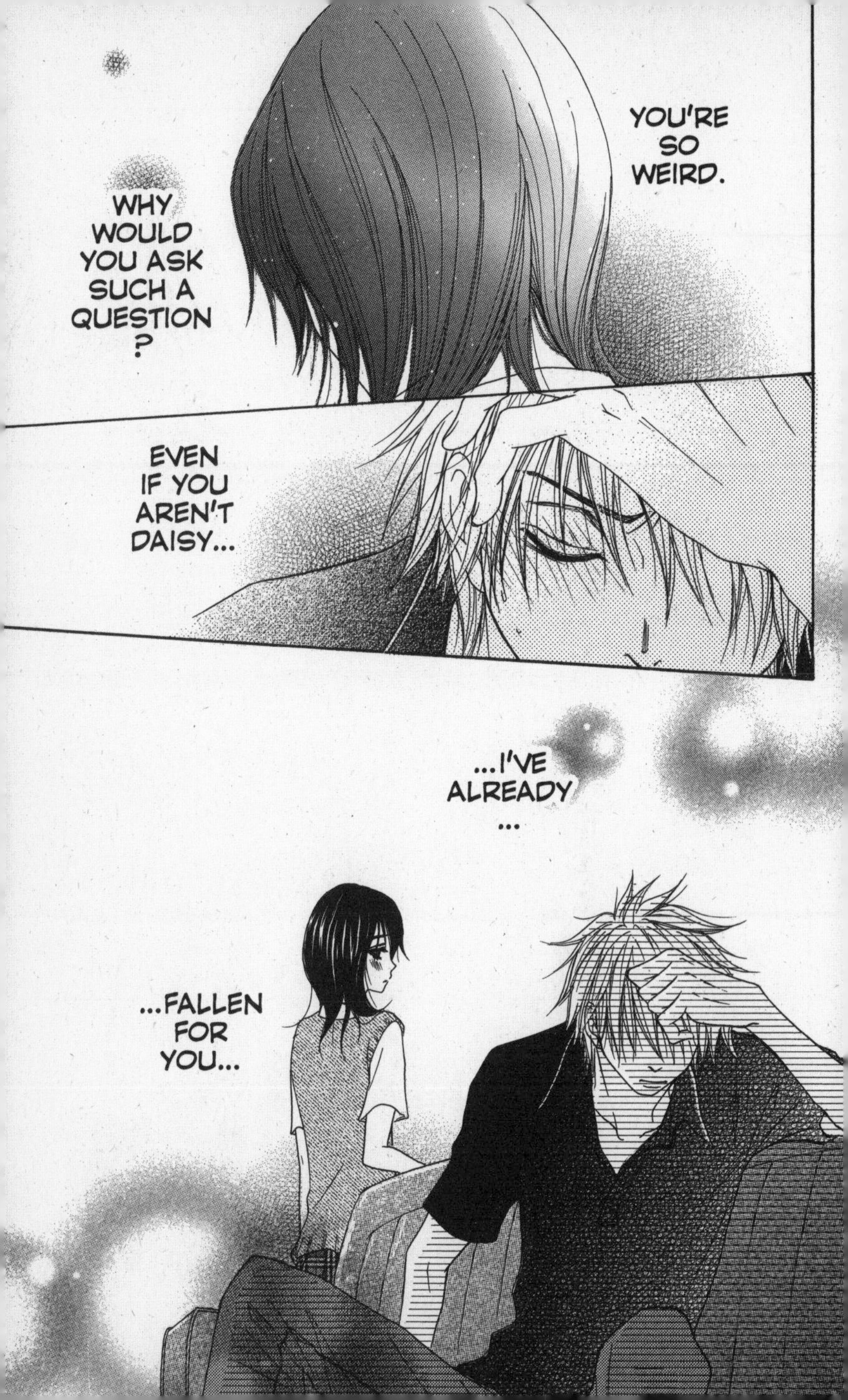
YOU'RE SO WEIRD.
WHY WOULD YOU ASK SUCH A QUESTION?
EVEN IF YOU AREN'T DAISY...
...I'VE ALREADY...
...FALLEN FOR YOU...

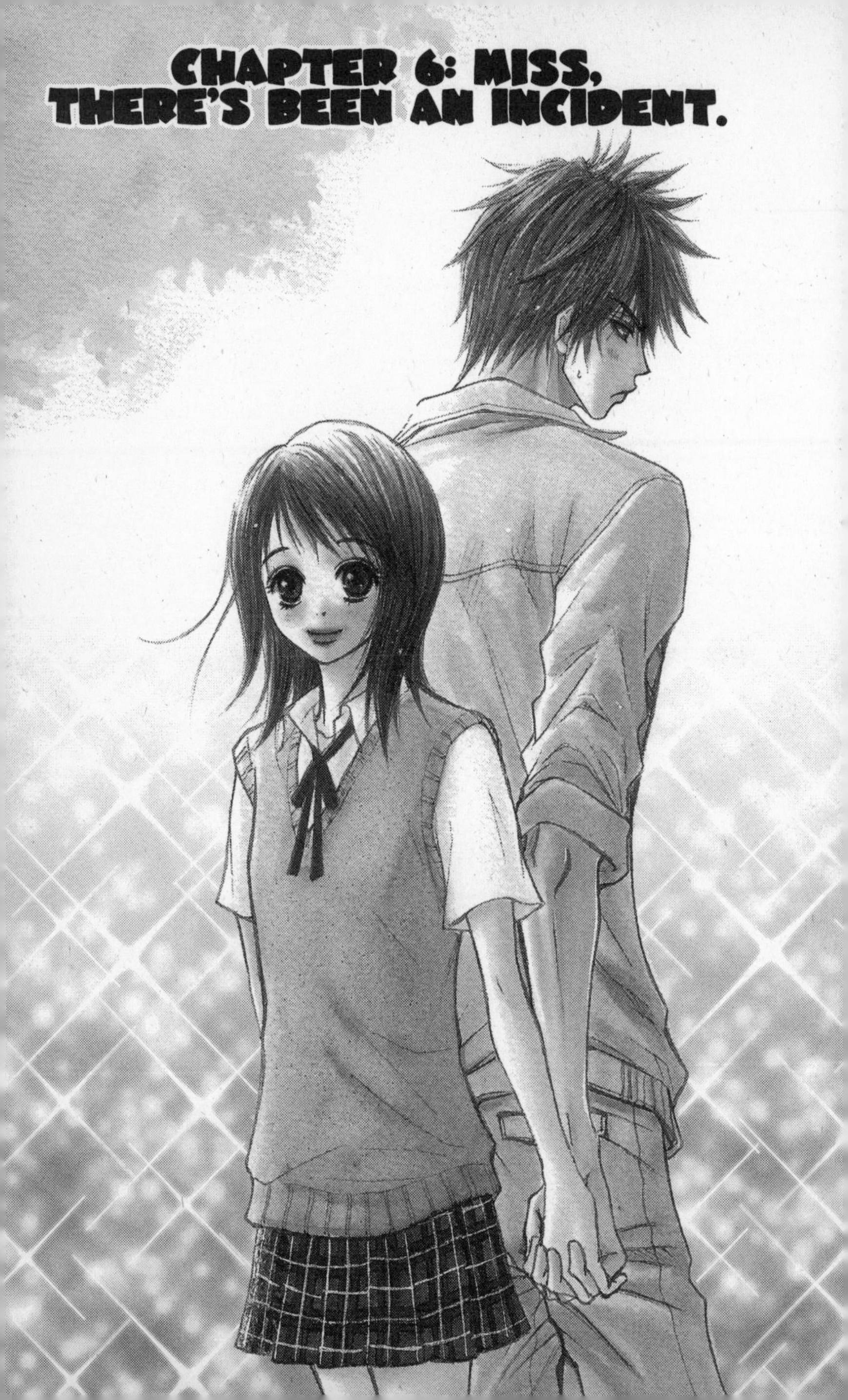
CHAPTER 6: MISS,
THERE'S BEEN AN INCIDENT.

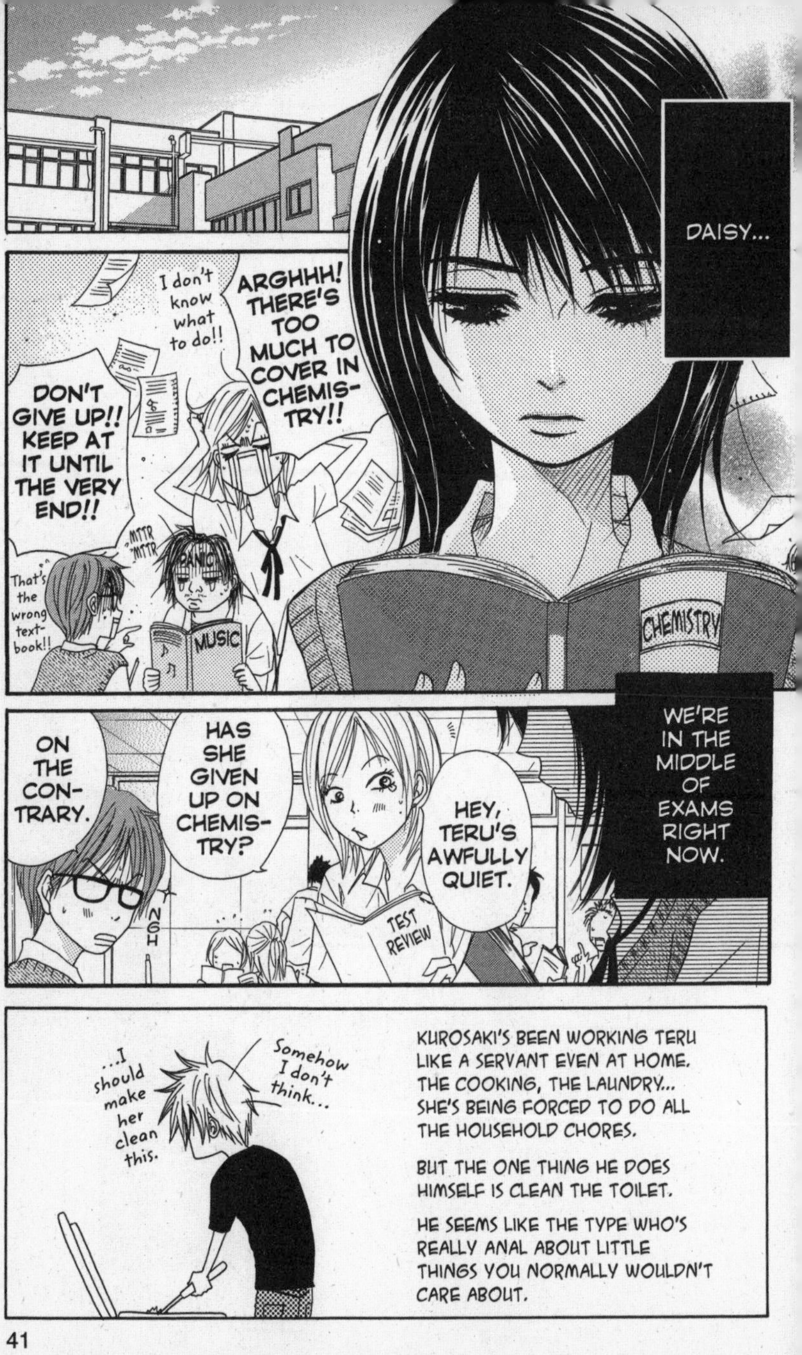
DAISY...
ARGHHH! THERE'S TOO MUCH TO COVER IN CHEMISTRY!!
I don't know what to do!!
DON'T GIVE UP!! KEEP AT IT UNTIL THE VERY END!!
MTTR MTTR
PANIC
That's the wrong textbook!!
MUSIC
CHEMISTRY
WE'RE IN THE MIDDLE OF EXAMS RIGHT NOW.
HEY, TERU'S AWFULLY QUIET.
HAS SHE GIVEN UP ON CHEMISTRY?
ON THE CONTRARY.
NGH
TEST REVIEW
KUROSAKI'S BEEN WORKING TERU LIKE A SERVANT EVEN AT HOME. THE COOKING, THE LAUNDRY... SHE'S BEING FORCED TO DO ALL THE HOUSEHOLD CHORES.
BUT THE ONE THING HE DOES HIMSELF IS CLEAN THE TOILET.
HE SEEMS LIKE THE TYPE WHO'S REALLY ANAL ABOUT LITTLE THINGS YOU NORMALLY WOULDN'T CARE ABOUT.
Somehow I don't think...
...I should make her clean this.

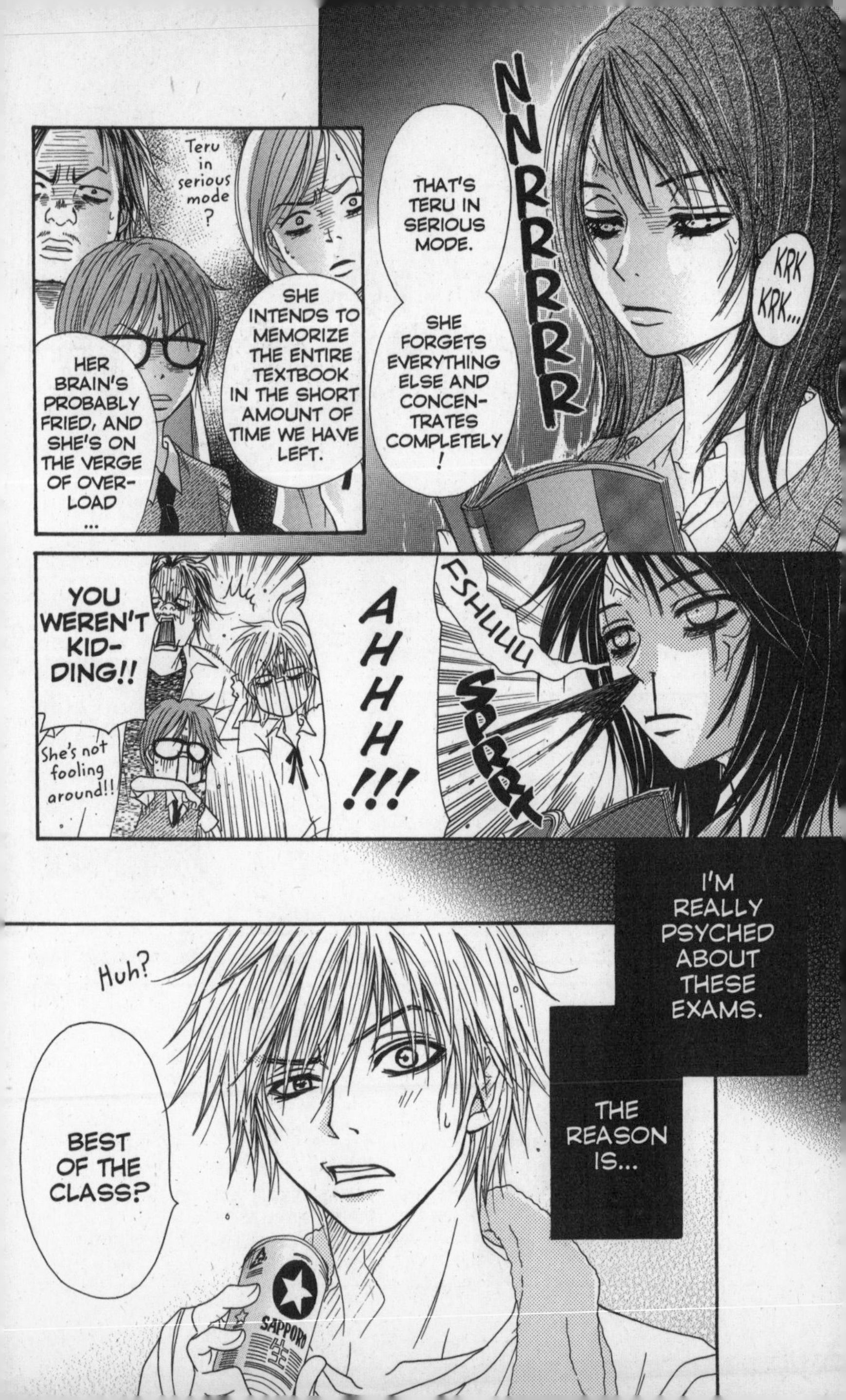
NNRRRRR
KRK KRK...
THAT'S TERU IN SERIOUS MODE.
SHE FORGETS EVERYTHING ELSE AND CONCENTRATES COMPLETELY!
Teru in serious mode?
SHE INTENDS TO MEMORIZE THE ENTIRE TEXTBOOK IN THE SHORT AMOUNT OF TIME WE HAVE LEFT.
HER BRAIN'S PROBABLY FRIED, AND SHE'S ON THE VERGE OF OVERLOAD...
FSHUUU
SPRRT
AHHH!!!
YOU WEREN'T KIDDING!!
She's not fooling around!!
I'M REALLY PSYCHED ABOUT THESE EXAMS.
THE REASON IS...
Huh?
BEST OF THE CLASS?
SAPPORO

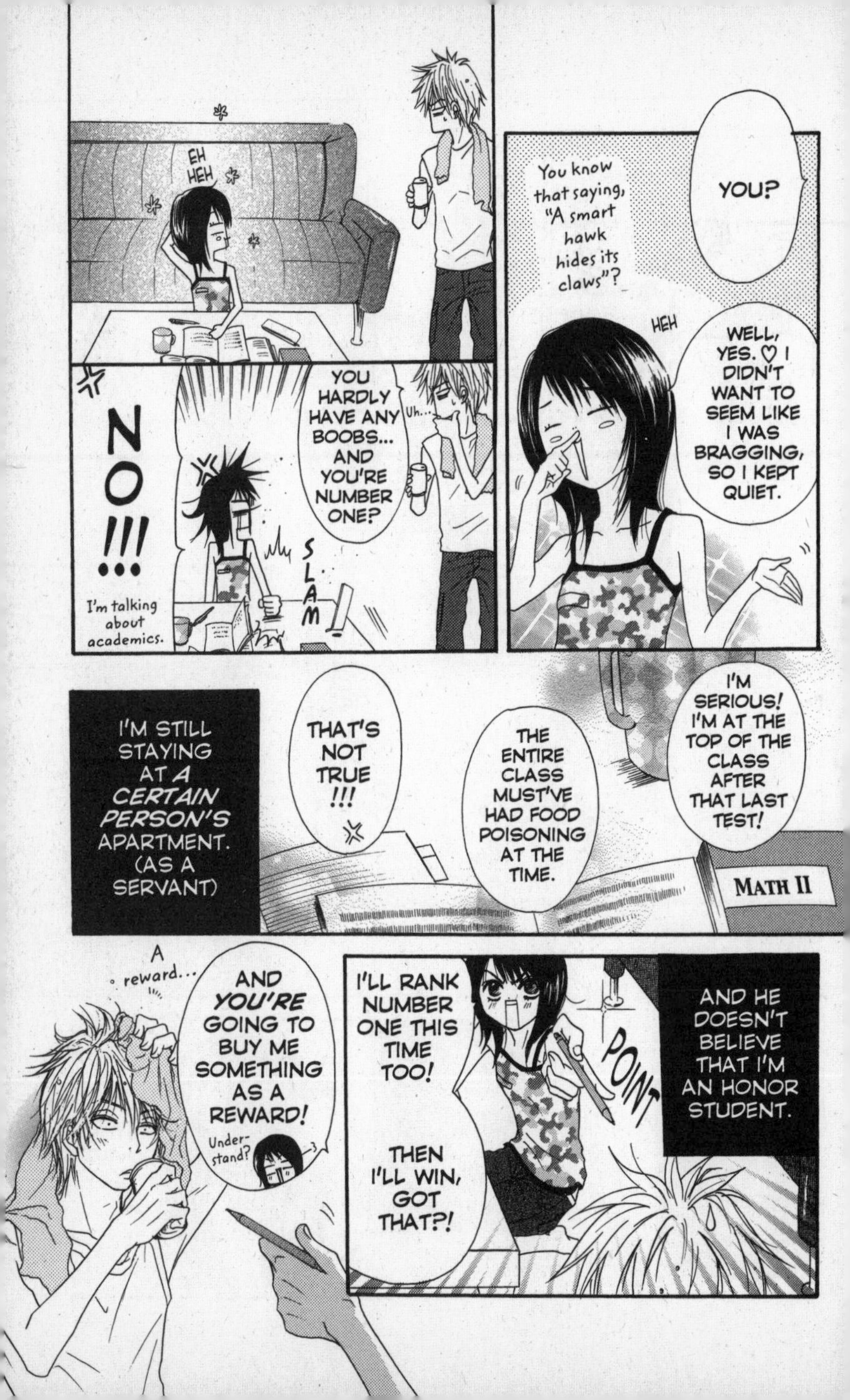
YOU?
You know that saying, "A smart hawk hides its claws"?
HEH
WELL, YES. ♡ I DIDN'T WANT TO SEEM LIKE I WAS BRAGGING, SO I KEPT QUIET.
EH HEH
YOU HARDLY HAVE ANY BOOBS... AND YOU'RE NUMBER ONE?
Uh...
NO!!!
SLAM
I'm talking about academics.
I'M SERIOUS! I'M AT THE TOP OF THE CLASS AFTER THAT LAST TEST!
THE ENTIRE CLASS MUST'VE HAD FOOD POISONING AT THE TIME.
THAT'S NOT TRUE!!!
MATH II
I'M STILL STAYING AT A CERTAIN PERSON'S APARTMENT. (AS A SERVANT)
AND HE DOESN'T BELIEVE THAT I'M AN HONOR STUDENT.
POINT
I'LL RANK NUMBER ONE THIS TIME TOO!
THEN I'LL WIN, GOT THAT?!
A reward...
AND YOU'RE GOING TO BUY ME SOMETHING AS A REWARD!
Understand?

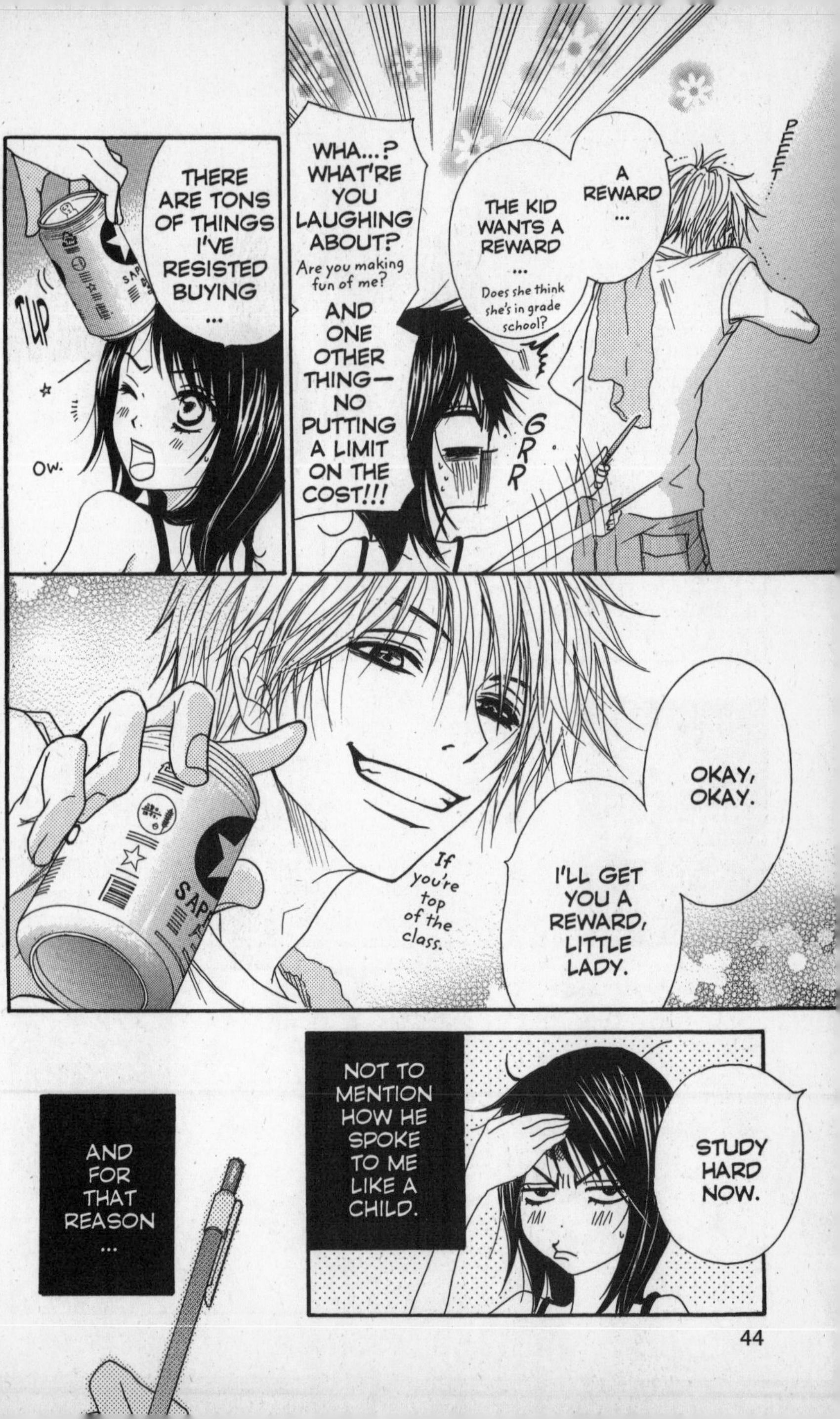
PEEET...
A REWARD...
THE KID WANTS A REWARD...
Does she think she's in grade school?
GRR
WHA...? WHAT'RE YOU LAUGHING ABOUT?
Are you making fun of me?
AND ONE OTHER THING—NO PUTTING A LIMIT ON THE COST!!!
THERE ARE TONS OF THINGS I'VE RESISTED BUYING...
TUP
Ow.
OKAY, OKAY.
I'LL GET YOU A REWARD, LITTLE LADY.
If you're top of the class.
STUDY HARD NOW.
NOT TO MENTION HOW HE SPOKE TO ME LIKE A CHILD.
AND FOR THAT REASON...

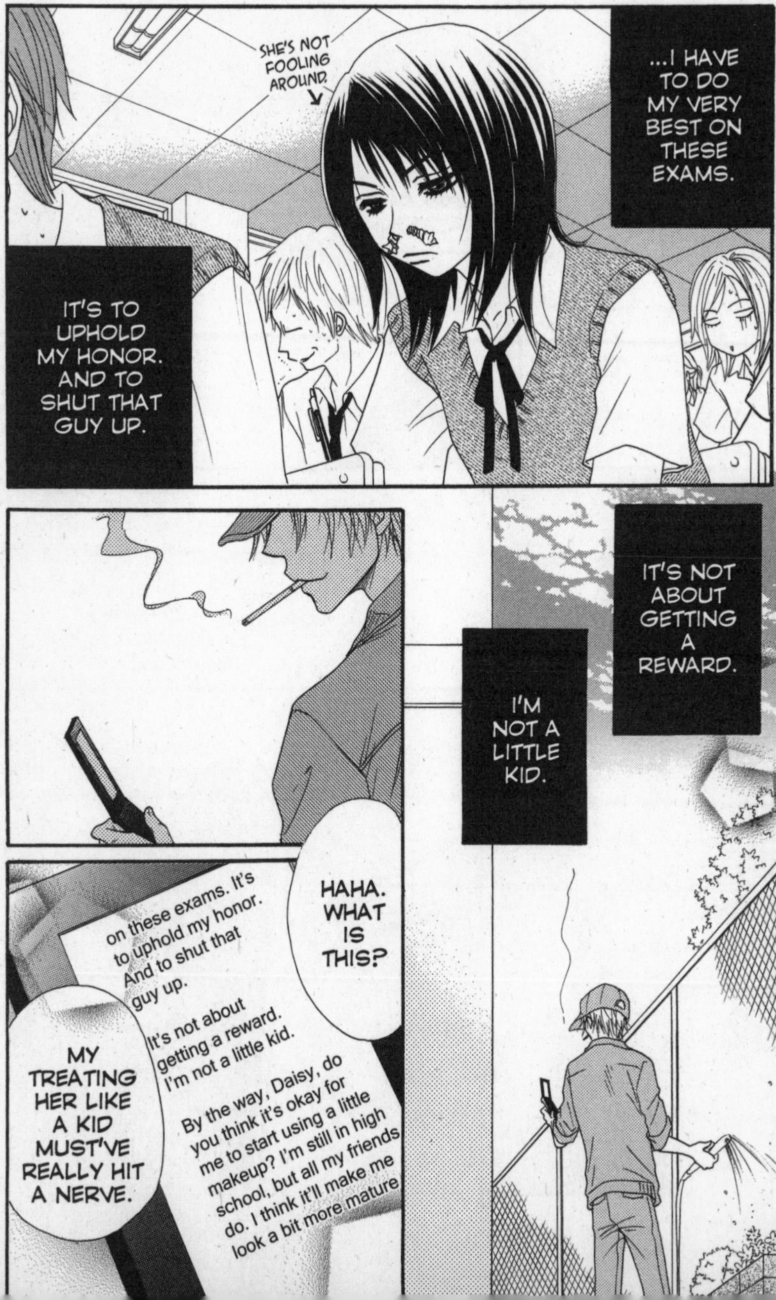
...I HAVE TO DO MY VERY BEST ON THESE EXAMS.
SHE'S NOT FOOLING AROUND.
IT'S TO UPHOLD MY HONOR. AND TO SHUT THAT GUY UP.
IT'S NOT ABOUT GETTING A REWARD.
I'M NOT A LITTLE KID.
HAHA. WHAT IS THIS?
on these exams. It's to uphold my honor. And to shut that guy up.
It's not about getting a reward. I'm not a little kid.
By the way, Daisy, do you think it's okay for me to start using a little makeup? I'm still in high school, but all my friends do. I think it'll make me look a bit more mature
MY TREATING HER LIKE A KID MUST'VE REALLY HIT A NERVE.

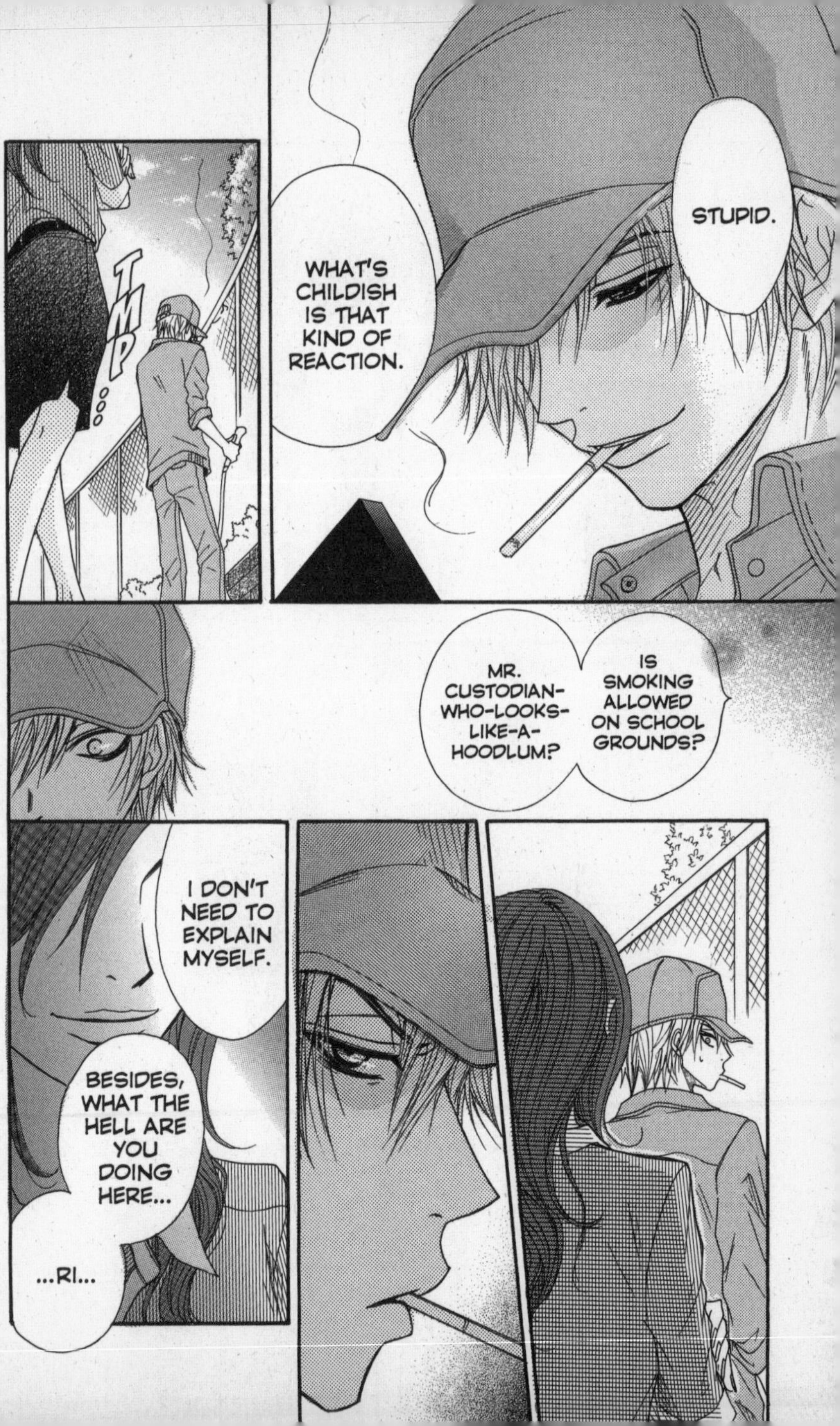
STUPID.
WHAT'S CHILDISH IS THAT KIND OF REACTION.
TMP...
IS SMOKING ALLOWED ON SCHOOL GROUNDS?
MR. CUSTODIAN-WHO-LOOKS-LIKE-A-HOODLUM?
I DON'T NEED TO EXPLAIN MYSELF.
BESIDES, WHAT THE HELL ARE YOU DOING HERE...
...RI...

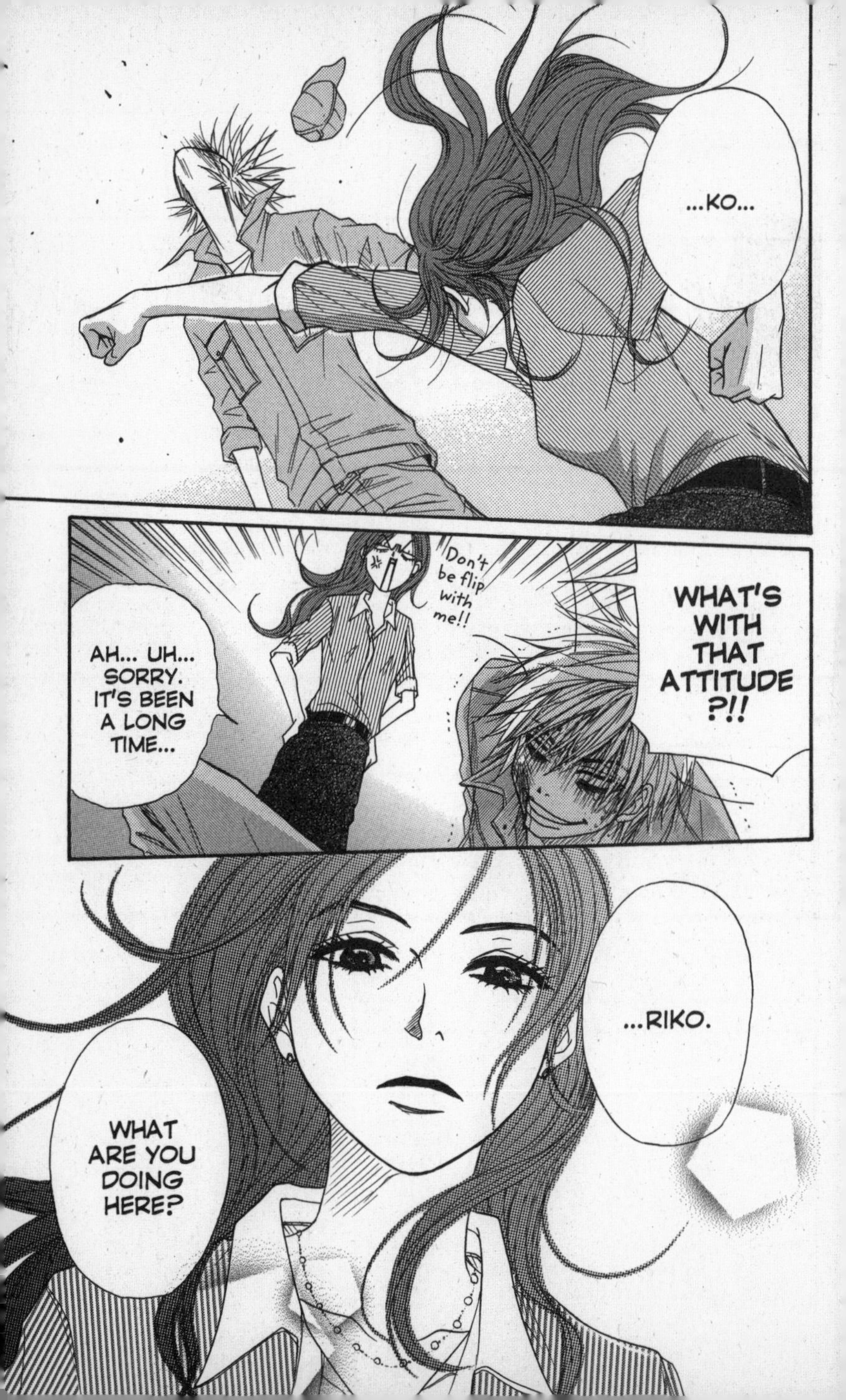
...KO...
WHAT'S WITH THAT ATTITUDE ?!!
Don't be flip with me!!
AH... UH... SORRY. IT'S BEEN A LONG TIME...
...RIKO.
WHAT ARE YOU DOING HERE?

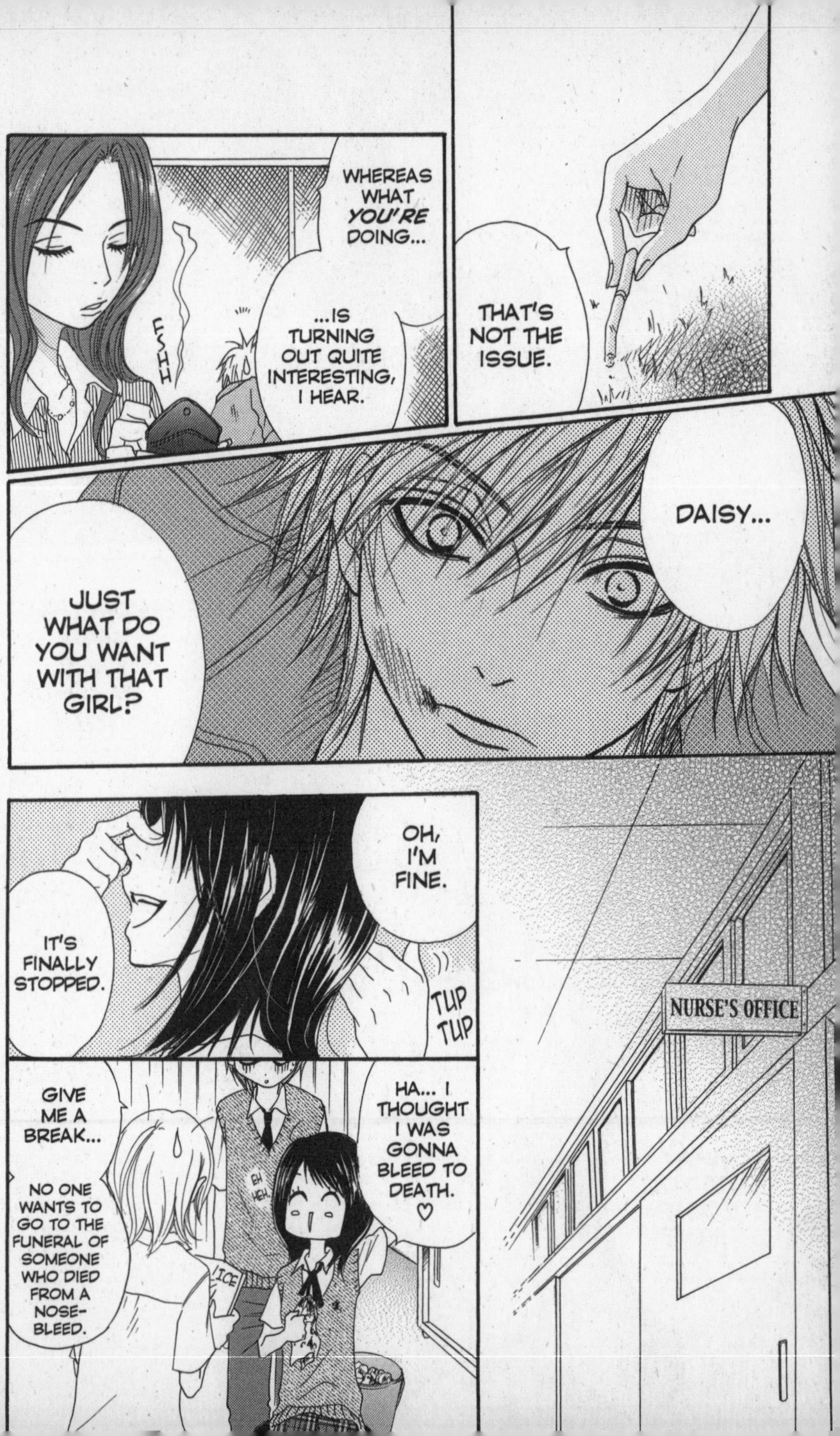
THAT'S NOT THE ISSUE.
WHEREAS WHAT *YOU'RE* DOING...
...IS TURNING OUT QUITE INTERESTING, I HEAR.
FSHH
DAISY...
JUST WHAT DO YOU WANT WITH THAT GIRL?
NURSE'S OFFICE
OH, I'M FINE.
IT'S FINALLY STOPPED.
TUP TUP
HA... I THOUGHT I WAS GONNA BLEED TO DEATH. ♡
EH HEH
GIVE ME A BREAK...
NO ONE WANTS TO GO TO THE FUNERAL OF SOMEONE WHO DIED FROM A NOSE-BLEED.
ICE

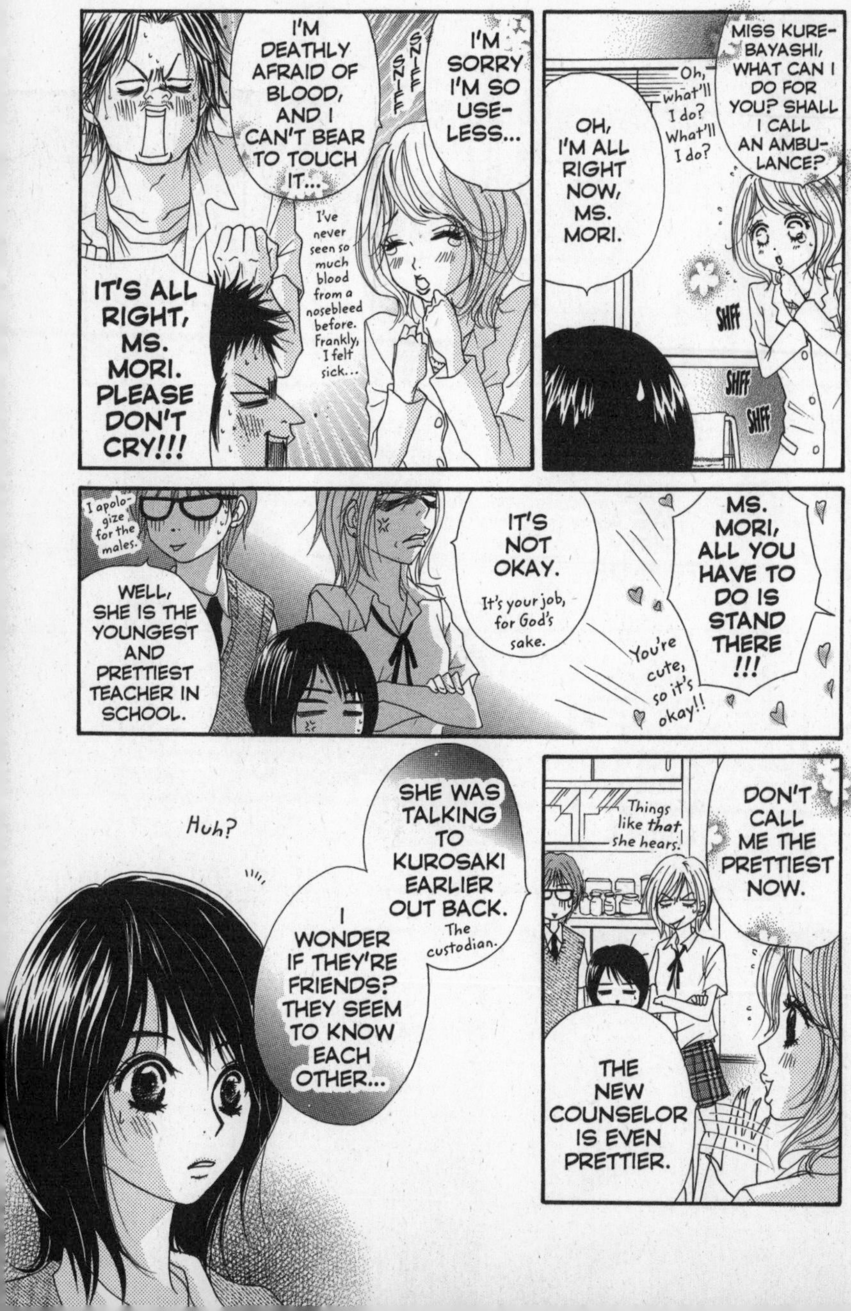
MISS KURE-BAYASHI, WHAT CAN I DO FOR YOU? SHALL I CALL AN AMBULANCE?
Oh, what'll I do? What'll I do?
OH, I'M ALL RIGHT NOW, MS. MORI.
SHFF
SHFF
SHFF
I'M SORRY I'M SO USE-LESS...
SNIFF SNIFF
I'M DEATHLY AFRAID OF BLOOD, AND I CAN'T BEAR TO TOUCH IT...
I've never seen so much blood from a nosebleed before. Frankly, I felt sick...
IT'S ALL RIGHT, MS. MORI. PLEASE DON'T CRY!!!
MS. MORI, ALL YOU HAVE TO DO IS STAND THERE!!!
You're cute, so it's okay!!
IT'S NOT OKAY.
It's your job, for God's sake.
WELL, SHE IS THE YOUNGEST AND PRETTIEST TEACHER IN SCHOOL.
I apolo-gize for the males.
DON'T CALL ME THE PRETTIEST NOW.
Things like that she hears.
THE NEW COUNSELOR IS EVEN PRETTIER.
SHE WAS TALKING TO KUROSAKI EARLIER OUT BACK.
The custodian.
I WONDER IF THEY'RE FRIENDS? THEY SEEM TO KNOW EACH OTHER...
Huh?

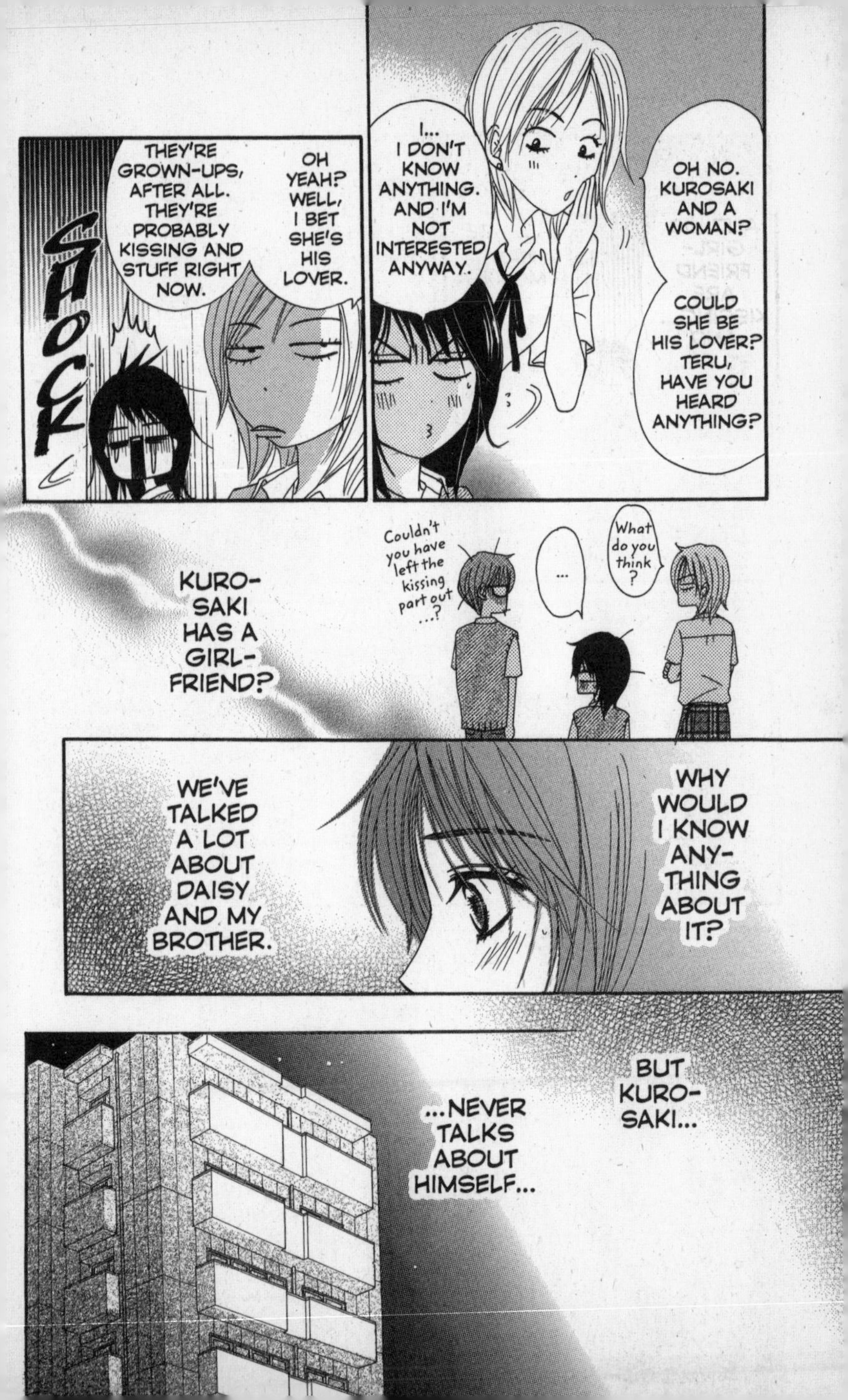
OH NO. KUROSAKI AND A WOMAN?
COULD SHE BE HIS LOVER? TERU, HAVE YOU HEARD ANYTHING?
I... I DON'T KNOW ANYTHING. AND I'M NOT INTERESTED ANYWAY.
OH YEAH? WELL, I BET SHE'S HIS LOVER.
THEY'RE GROWN-UPS, AFTER ALL. THEY'RE PROBABLY KISSING AND STUFF RIGHT NOW.
SHOCK
What do you think?
...
Couldn't you have left the kissing part out...?
KURO-SAKI HAS A GIRL-FRIEND?
WHY WOULD I KNOW ANY-THING ABOUT IT?
WE'VE TALKED A LOT ABOUT DAISY AND MY BROTHER.
BUT KURO-SAKI...
...NEVER TALKS ABOUT HIMSELF...

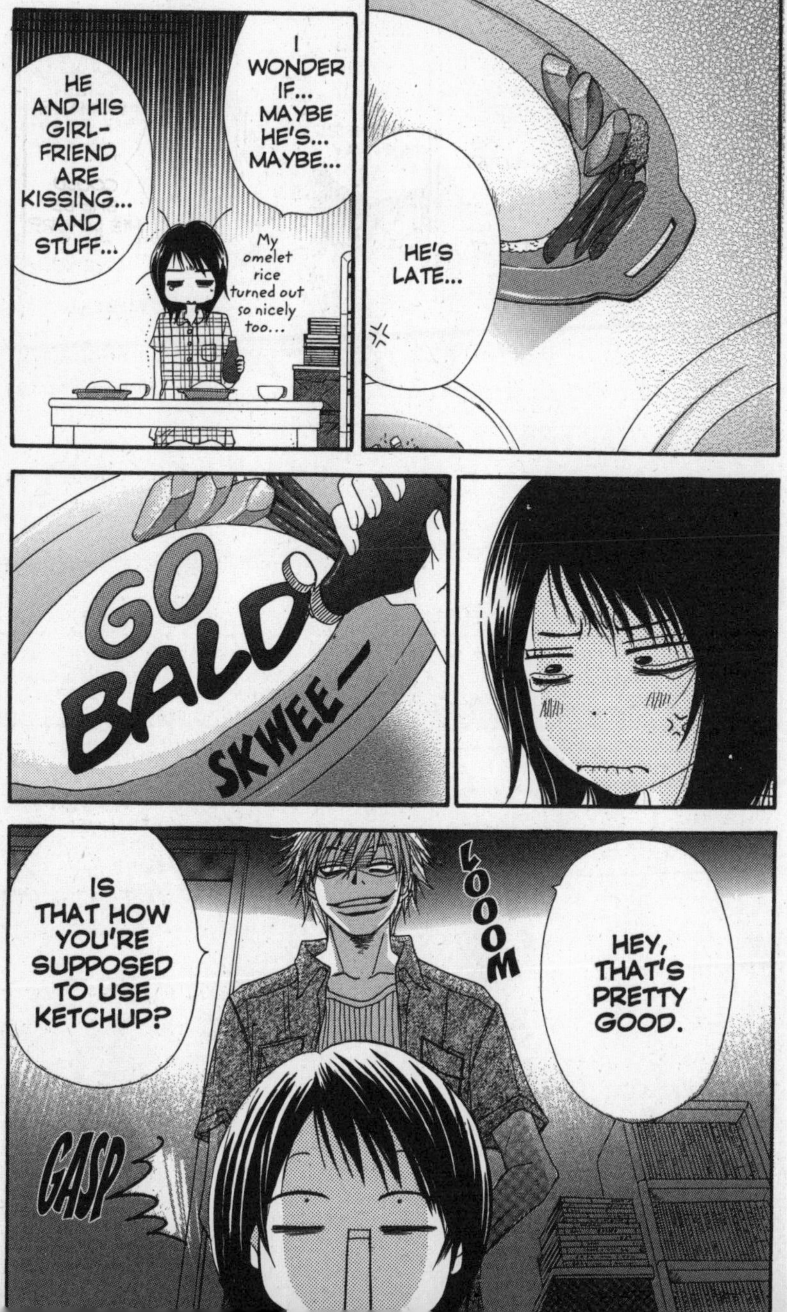
HE'S LATE...
I WONDER IF... MAYBE HE'S... MAYBE...
HE AND HIS GIRLFRIEND ARE KISSING... AND STUFF...
My omelet rice turned out so nicely too...
GO BALD
SKWEE-
HEY, THAT'S PRETTY GOOD.
LOOOOM
IS THAT HOW YOU'RE SUPPOSED TO USE KETCHUP?
GASP

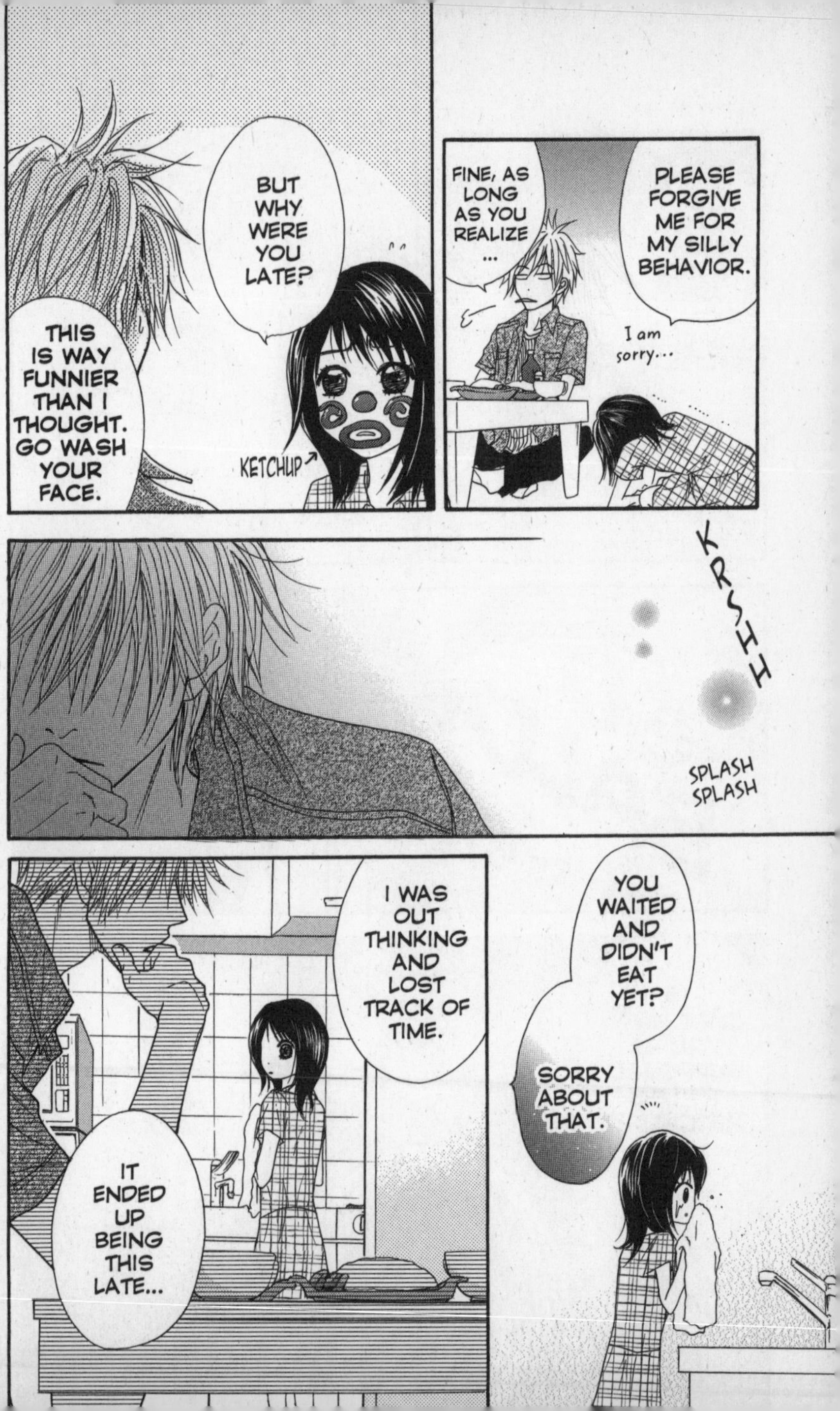
PLEASE FORGIVE ME FOR MY SILLY BEHAVIOR.
FINE, AS LONG AS YOU REALIZE ...
I am sorry...
BUT WHY WERE YOU LATE?
KETCHUP
THIS IS WAY FUNNIER THAN I THOUGHT. GO WASH YOUR FACE.
KRSHH
SPLASH SPLASH
YOU WAITED AND DIDN'T EAT YET?
SORRY ABOUT THAT.
I WAS OUT THINKING AND LOST TRACK OF TIME.
IT ENDED UP BEING THIS LATE...

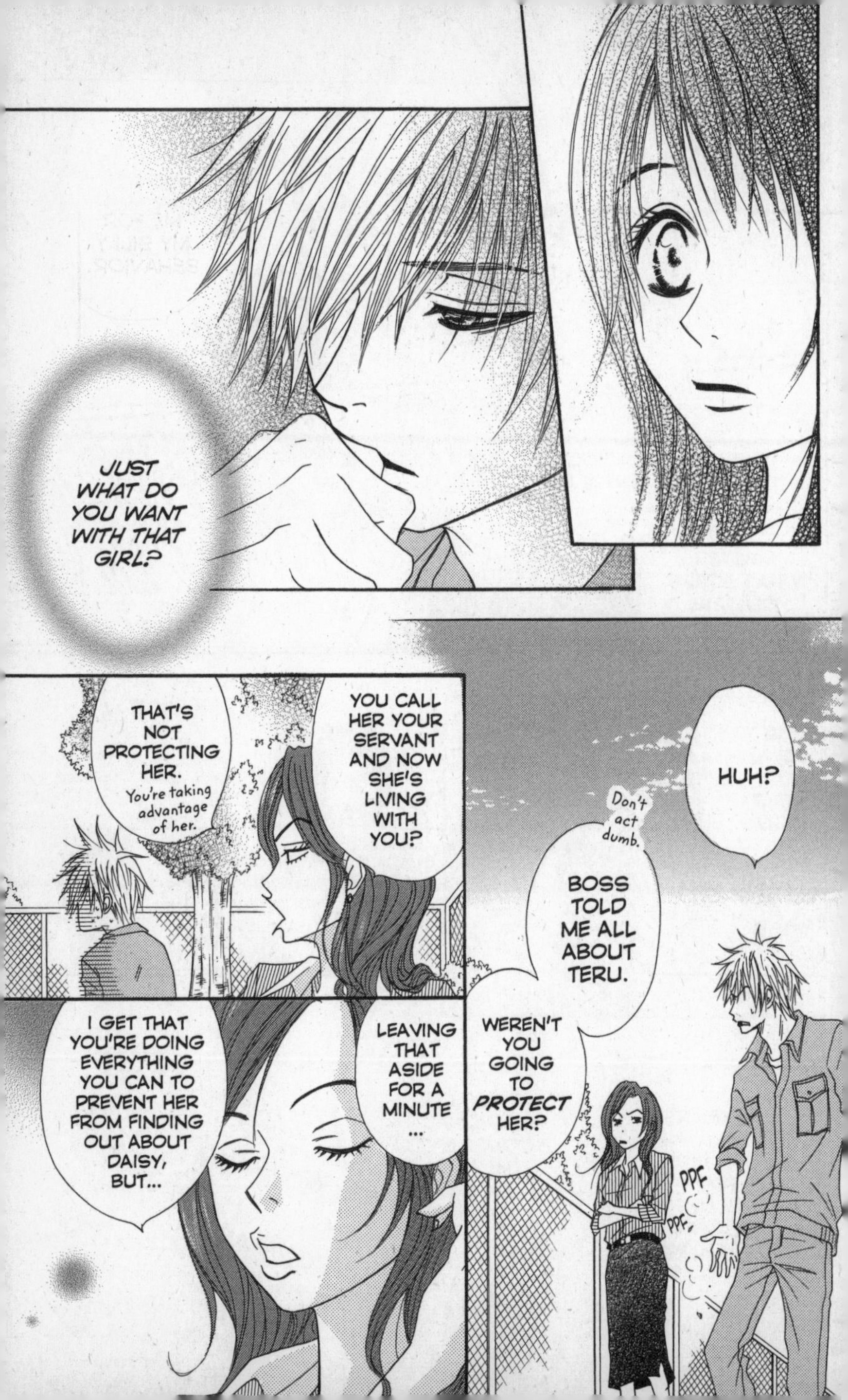
JUST WHAT DO YOU WANT WITH THAT GIRL?
HUH?
Don't act dumb.
BOSS TOLD ME ALL ABOUT TERU.
WEREN'T YOU GOING TO *PROTECT* HER?
PPF
PPF
YOU CALL HER YOUR SERVANT AND NOW SHE'S LIVING WITH YOU?
THAT'S NOT PROTECTING HER.
You're taking advantage of her.
LEAVING THAT ASIDE FOR A MINUTE...
I GET THAT YOU'RE DOING EVERYTHING YOU CAN TO PREVENT HER FROM FINDING OUT ABOUT DAISY, BUT...

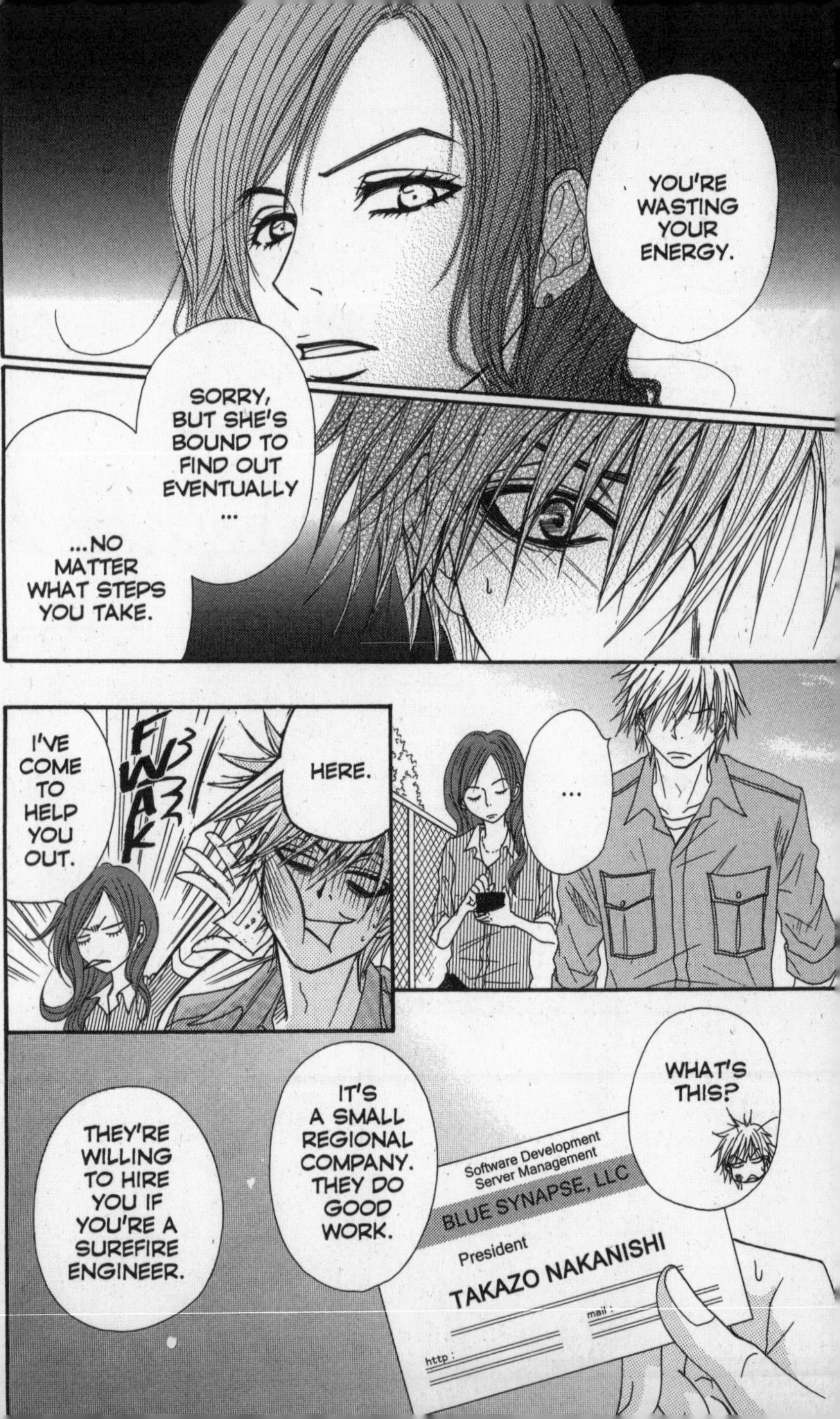
YOU'RE WASTING YOUR ENERGY.
SORRY, BUT SHE'S BOUND TO FIND OUT EVENTUALLY ...
...NO MATTER WHAT STEPS YOU TAKE.
...
HERE.
FWAK
I'VE COME TO HELP YOU OUT.
WHAT'S THIS?
Software Development
Server Management
BLUE SYNAPSE, LLC
President
TAKAZO NAKANISHI
mail :
http :
IT'S A SMALL REGIONAL COMPANY. THEY DO GOOD WORK.
THEY'RE WILLING TO HIRE YOU IF YOU'RE A SUREFIRE ENGINEER.

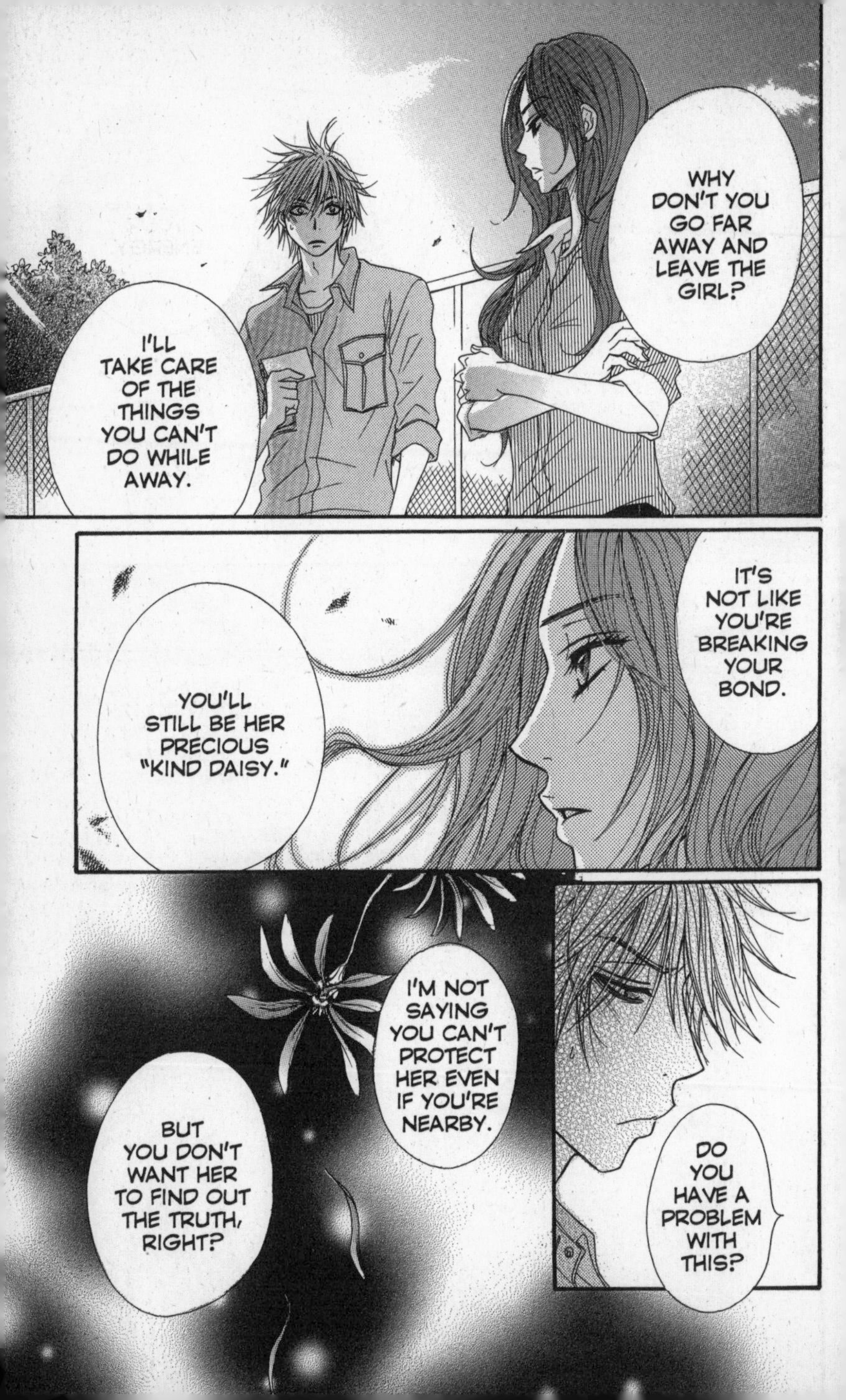
WHY DON'T YOU GO FAR AWAY AND LEAVE THE GIRL?
I'LL TAKE CARE OF THE THINGS YOU CAN'T DO WHILE AWAY.
IT'S NOT LIKE YOU'RE BREAKING YOUR BOND.
YOU'LL STILL BE HER PRECIOUS "KIND DAISY."
DO YOU HAVE A PROBLEM WITH THIS?
I'M NOT SAYING YOU CAN'T PROTECT HER EVEN IF YOU'RE NEARBY.
BUT YOU DON'T WANT HER TO FIND OUT THE TRUTH, RIGHT?

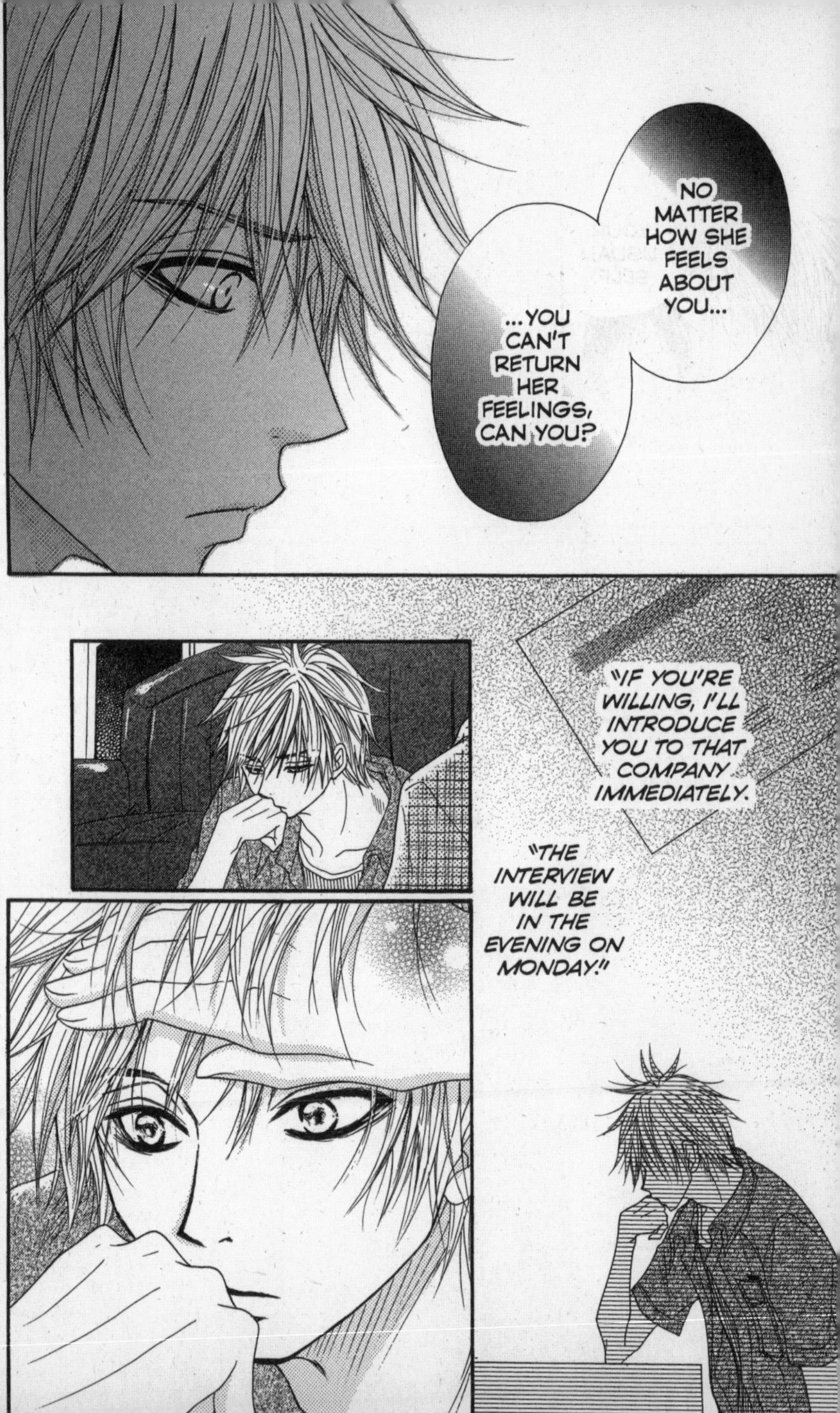
NO MATTER HOW SHE FEELS ABOUT YOU...
...YOU CAN'T RETURN HER FEELINGS, CAN YOU?
"IF YOU'RE WILLING, I'LL INTRODUCE YOU TO THAT COMPANY IMMEDIATELY.
"THE INTERVIEW WILL BE IN THE EVENING ON MONDAY!"

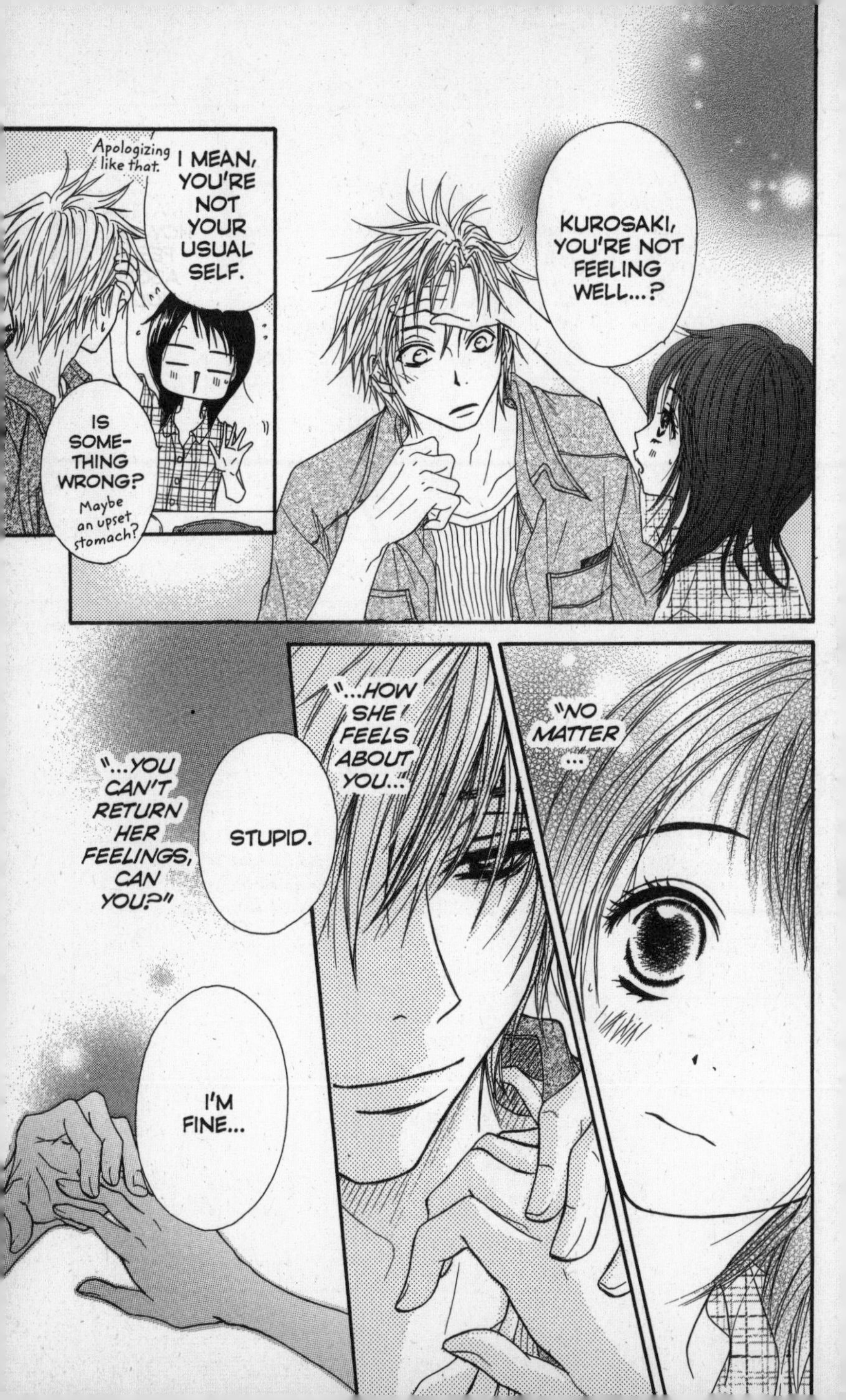
KUROSAKI, YOU'RE NOT FEELING WELL...?
I MEAN, YOU'RE NOT YOUR USUAL SELF.
Apologizing like that.
IS SOME-THING WRONG?
Maybe an upset stomach?
"NO MATTER...
"...HOW SHE FEELS ABOUT YOU...
"...YOU CAN'T RETURN HER FEELINGS, CAN YOU?"
STUPID.
I'M FINE...

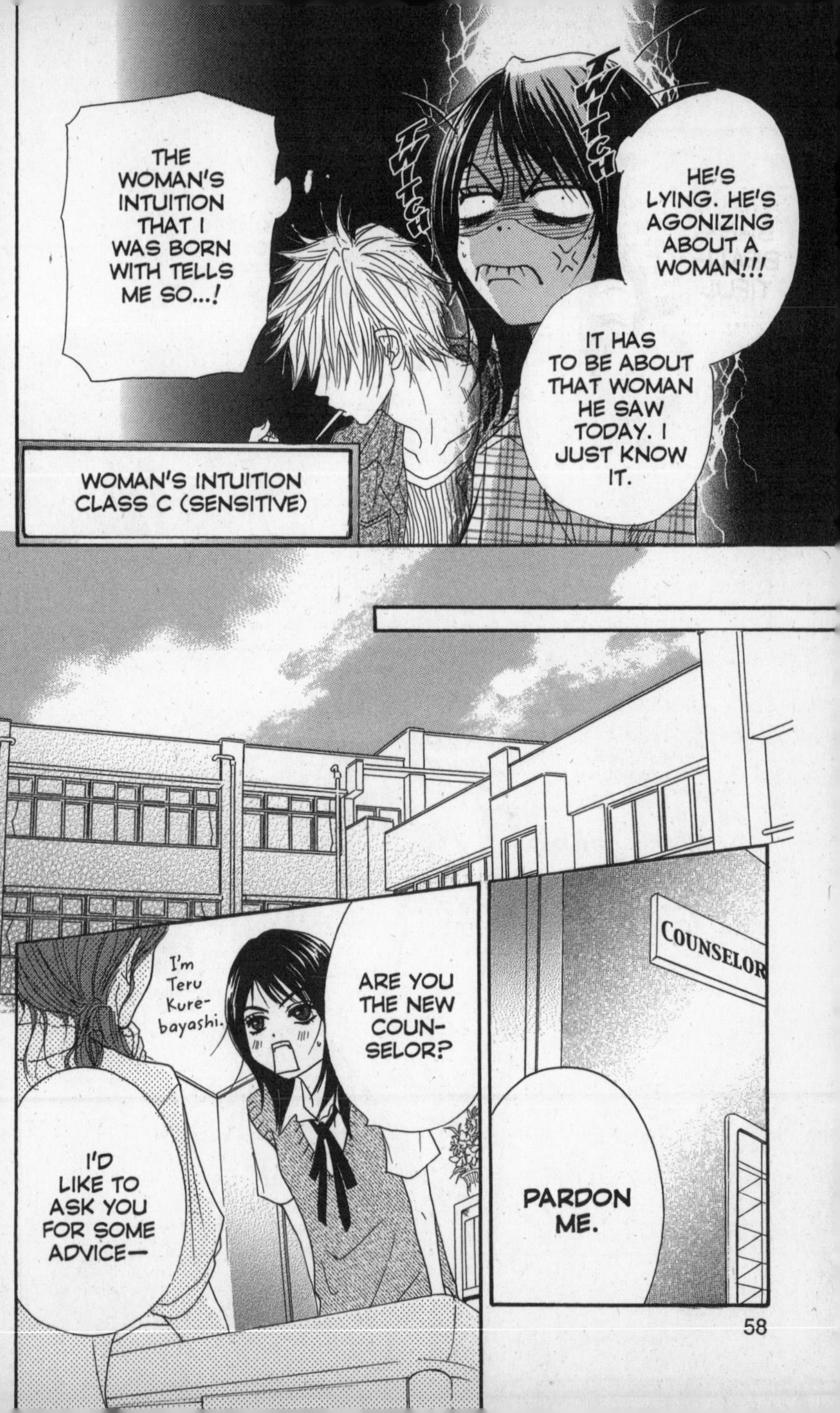
TWITCH
TWITCH
HE'S LYING. HE'S AGONIZING ABOUT A WOMAN!!!
IT HAS TO BE ABOUT THAT WOMAN HE SAW TODAY. I JUST KNOW IT.
THE WOMAN'S INTUITION THAT I WAS BORN WITH TELLS ME SO...!
WOMAN'S INTUITION CLASS C (SENSITIVE)
COUNSELOR
PARDON ME.
ARE YOU THE NEW COUN-SELOR?
I'm Teru Kure-bayashi.
I'D LIKE TO ASK YOU FOR SOME ADVICE—

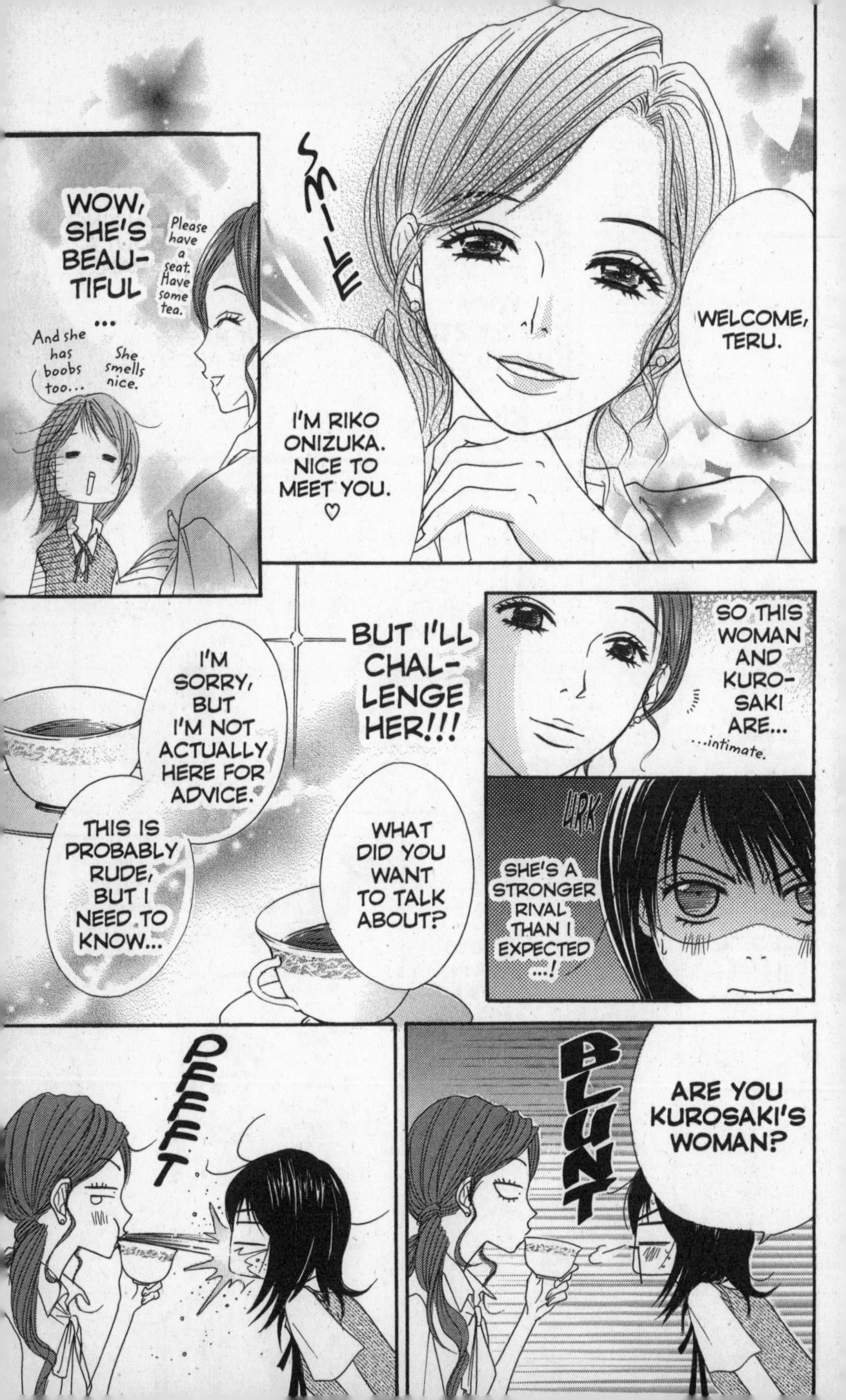
WELCOME, TERU.
SMILE
I'M RIKO ONIZUKA. NICE TO MEET YOU. ♡
Please have a seat. Have some tea.
WOW, SHE'S BEAUTIFUL...
She smells nice.
And she has boobs too...
SO THIS WOMAN AND KUROSAKI ARE...
...intimate.
URK
SHE'S A STRONGER RIVAL THAN I EXPECTED...!
BUT I'LL CHALLENGE HER!!!
WHAT DID YOU WANT TO TALK ABOUT?
I'M SORRY, BUT I'M NOT ACTUALLY HERE FOR ADVICE.
THIS IS PROBABLY RUDE, BUT I NEED TO KNOW...
ARE YOU KUROSAKI'S WOMAN?
BLUNT
PFFFT

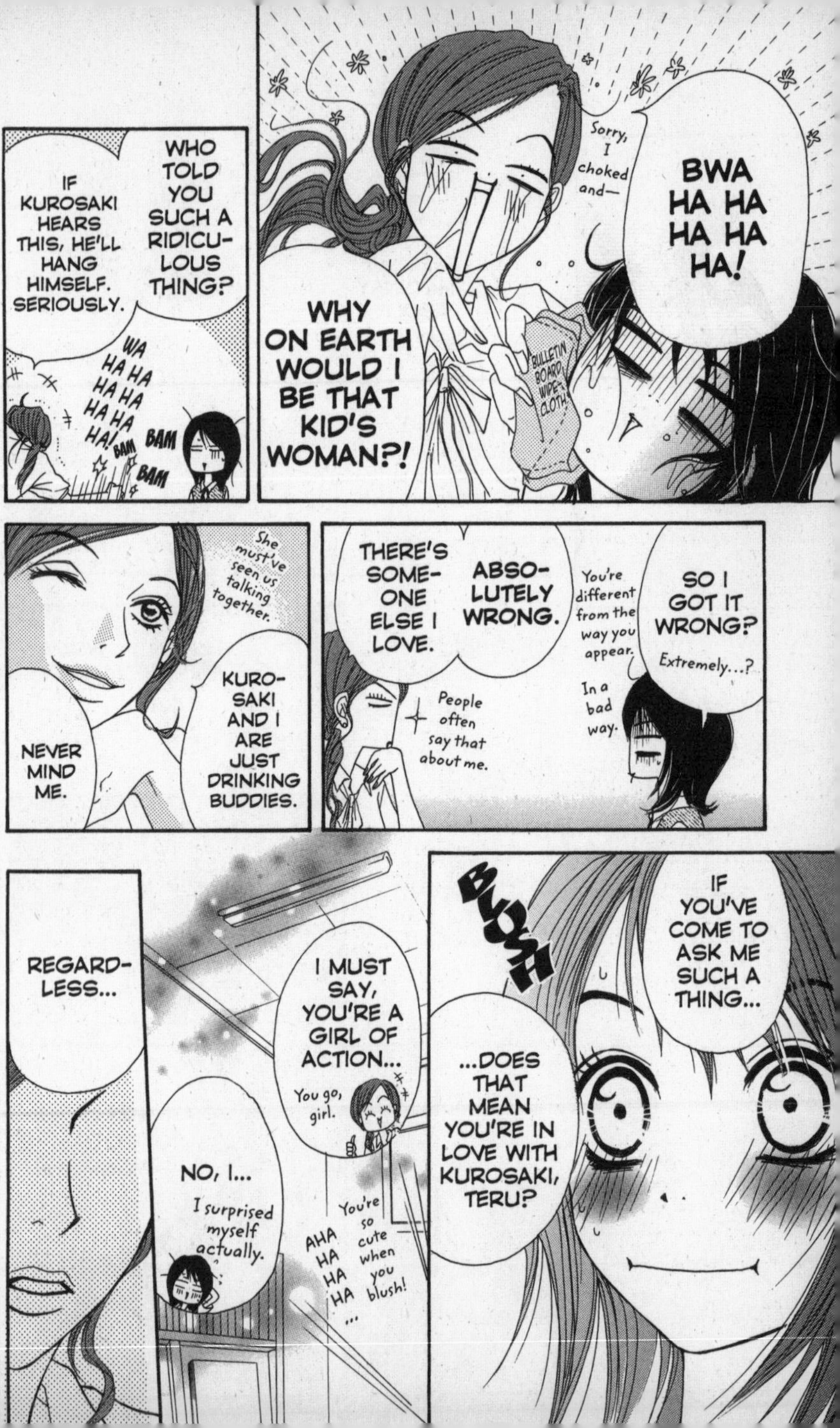
Sorry, I choked and—
BWA HA HA HA HA HA!
WHY ON EARTH WOULD I BE THAT KID'S WOMAN?!
BULLETIN BOARD WIPE-CLOTH
WHO TOLD YOU SUCH A RIDICULOUS THING?
IF KUROSAKI HEARS THIS, HE'LL HANG HIMSELF. SERIOUSLY.
WA HA HA HA HA HA HA HA!
BAM BAM BAM
SO I GOT IT WRONG?
Extremely...?
In a bad way.
You're different from the way you appear.
ABSOLUTELY WRONG.
THERE'S SOMEONE ELSE I LOVE.
People often say that about me.
She must've seen us talking together.
KUROSAKI AND I ARE JUST DRINKING BUDDIES.
NEVER MIND ME.
BLUSH
IF YOU'VE COME TO ASK ME SUCH A THING...
...DOES THAT MEAN YOU'RE IN LOVE WITH KUROSAKI, TERU?
I MUST SAY, YOU'RE A GIRL OF ACTION...
You go, girl.
You're so cute when you blush!
AHA HA HA HA...
NO, I...
I surprised myself actually.
REGARDLESS...

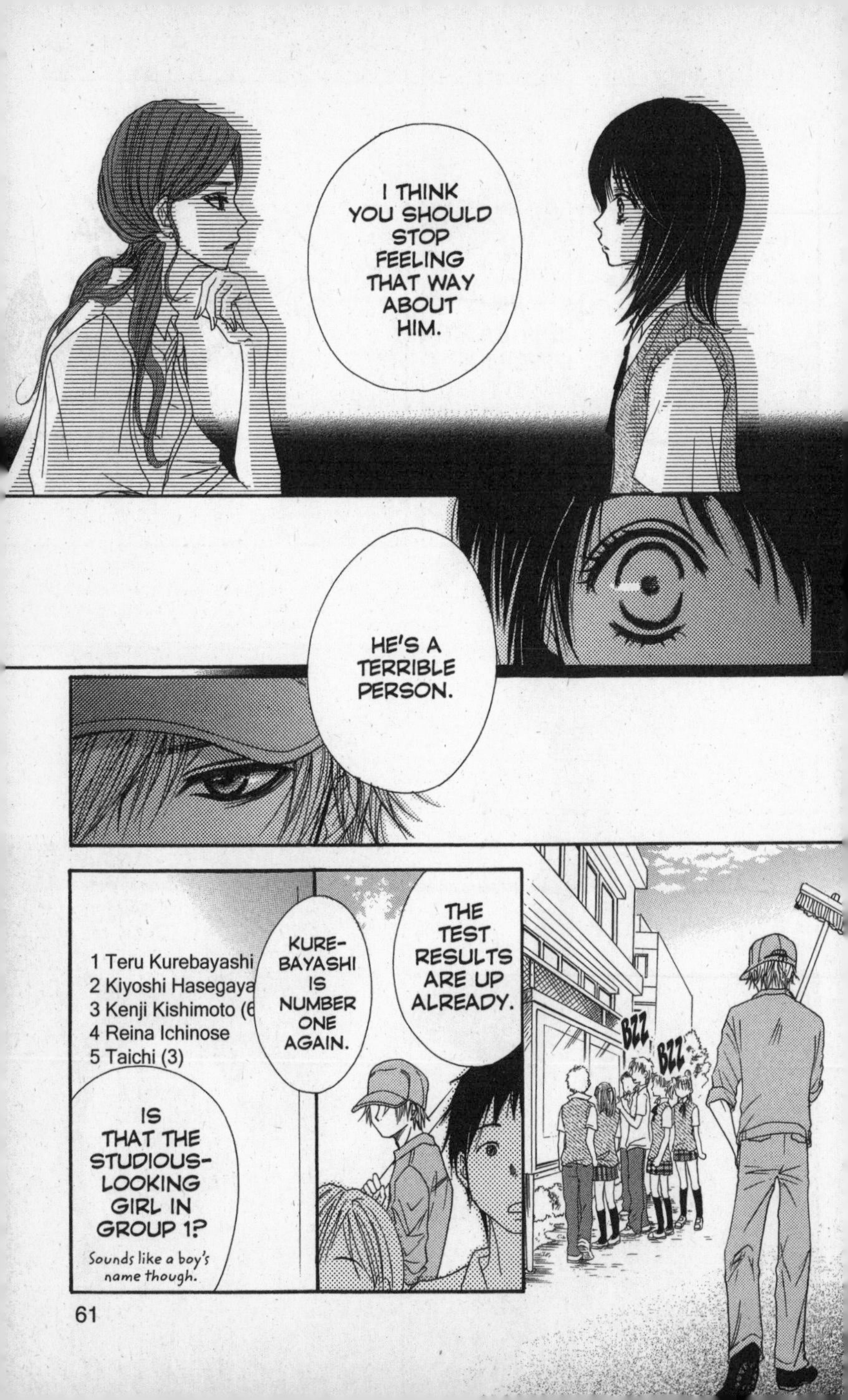
I THINK YOU SHOULD STOP FEELING THAT WAY ABOUT HIM.
HE'S A TERRIBLE PERSON.
THE TEST RESULTS ARE UP ALREADY.
KURE-BAYASHI IS NUMBER ONE AGAIN.
BZZ
BZZ
1 Teru Kurebayashi
2 Kiyoshi Hasegaya
3 Kenji Kishimoto (6
4 Reina Ichinose
5 Taichi (3)
IS THAT THE STUDIOUS-LOOKING GIRL IN GROUP 1?
Sounds like a boy's name though.

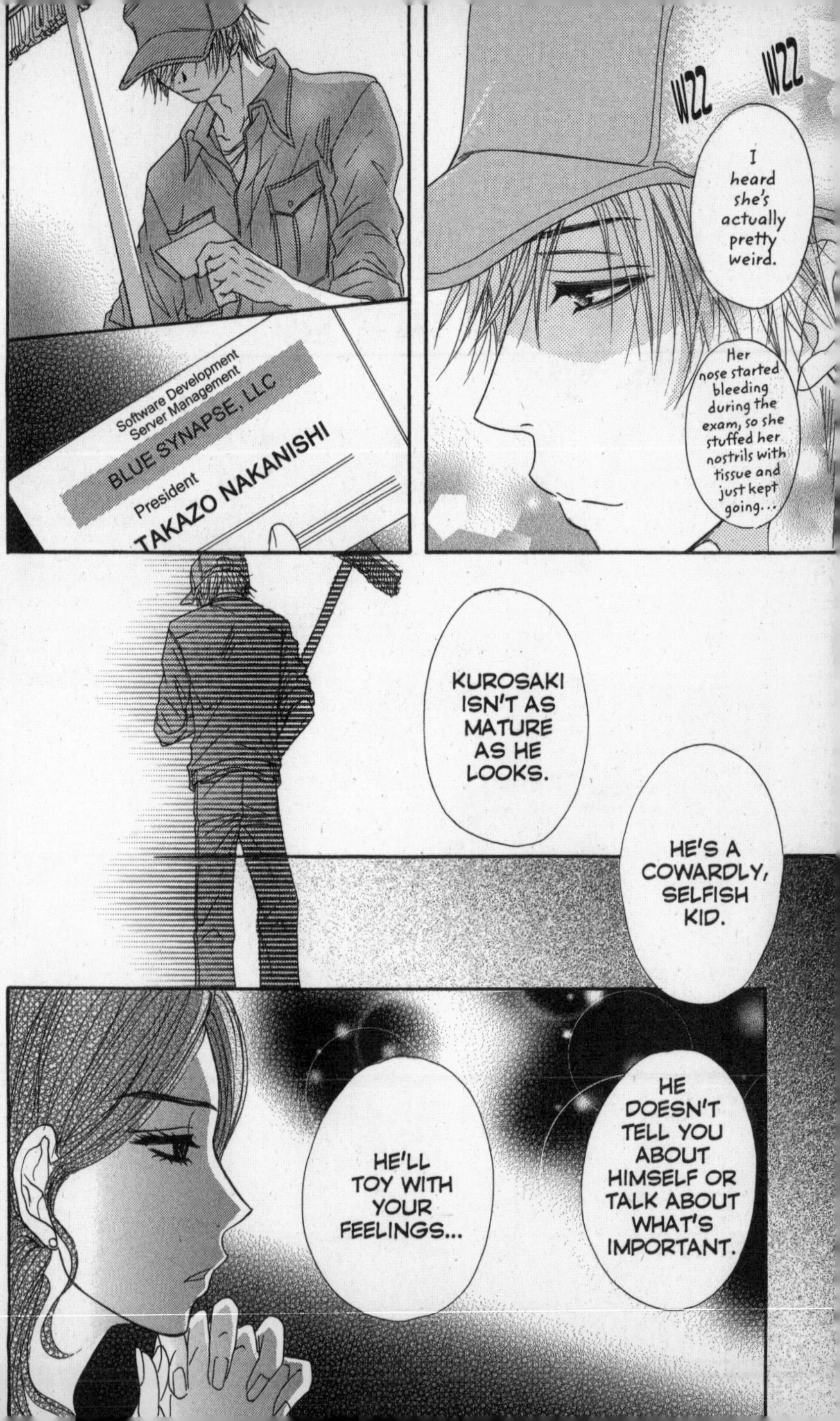
WZZ WZZ
I heard she's actually pretty weird.
Her nose started bleeding during the exam, so she stuffed her nostrils with tissue and just kept going...
Software Development
Server Management
BLUE SYNAPSE, LLC
President
TAKAZO NAKANISHI
KUROSAKI ISN'T AS MATURE AS HE LOOKS.
HE'S A COWARDLY, SELFISH KID.
HE DOESN'T TELL YOU ABOUT HIMSELF OR TALK ABOUT WHAT'S IMPORTANT.
HE'LL TOY WITH YOUR FEELINGS...

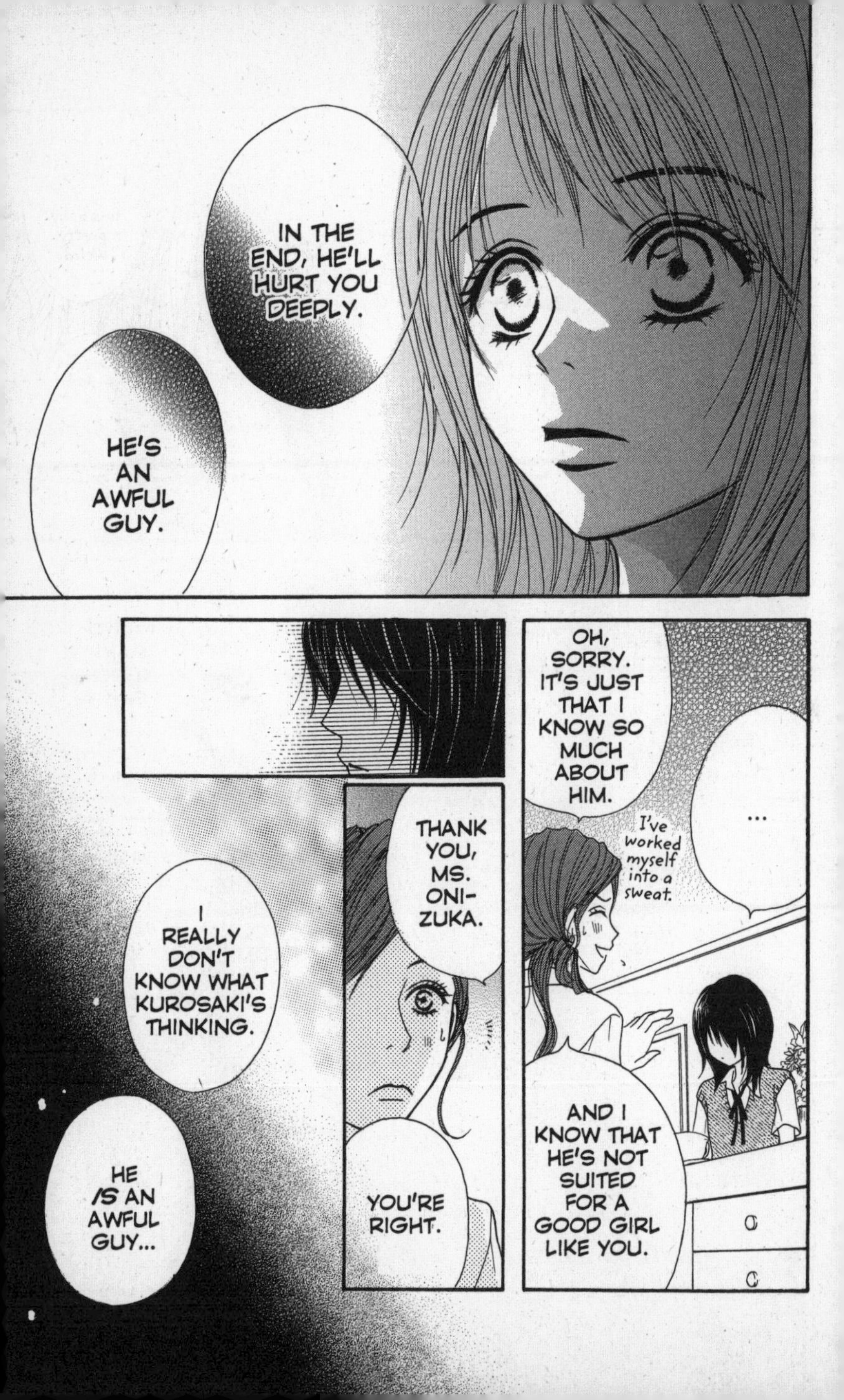
IN THE END, HE'LL HURT YOU DEEPLY.
HE'S AN AWFUL GUY.
...
OH, SORRY. IT'S JUST THAT I KNOW SO MUCH ABOUT HIM.
I've worked myself into a sweat.
AND I KNOW THAT HE'S NOT SUITED FOR A GOOD GIRL LIKE YOU.
THANK YOU, MS. ONI-ZUKA.
YOU'RE RIGHT.
I REALLY DON'T KNOW WHAT KUROSAKI'S THINKING.
HE *IS* AN AWFUL GUY...

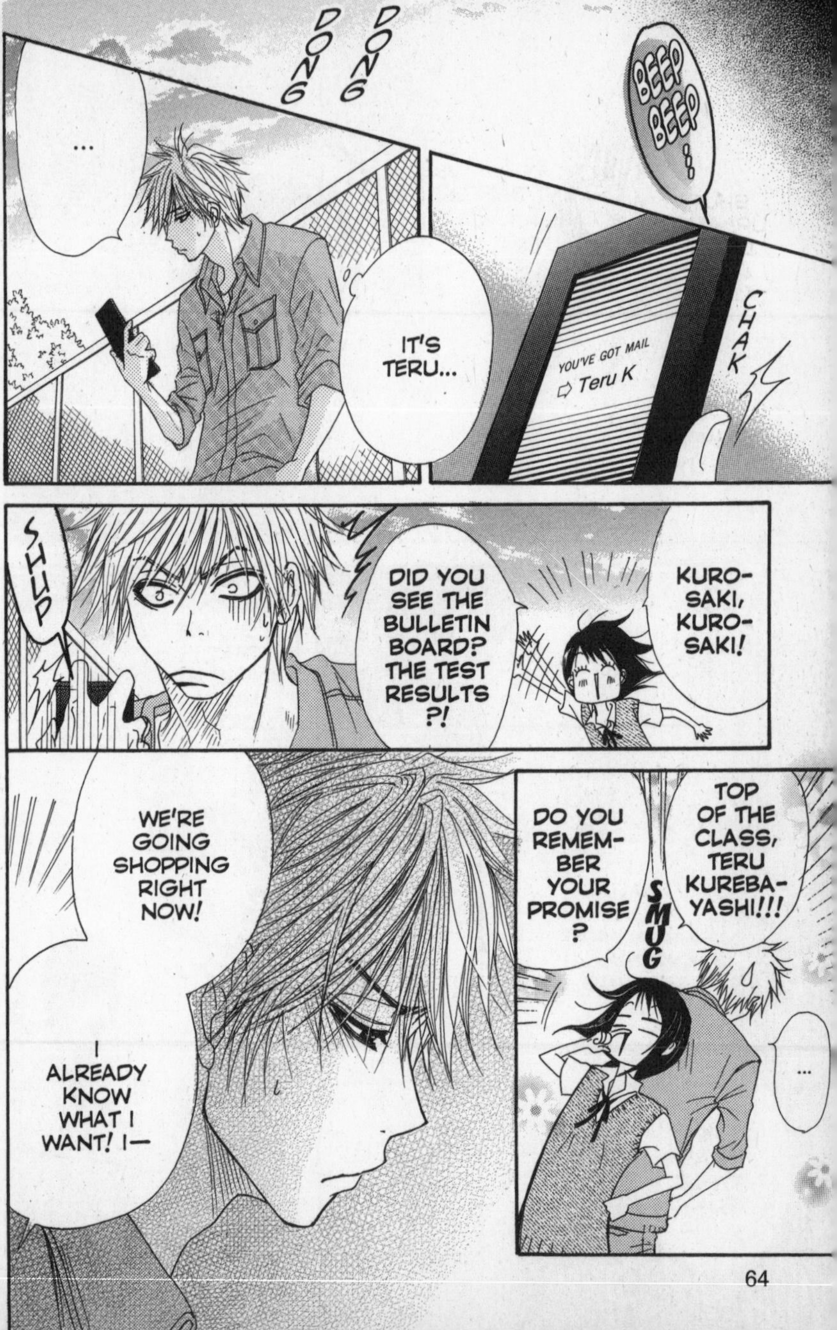
BEEP BEEP...
YOU'VE GOT MAIL
⇨ Teru K
CHAK
DONG DONG
IT'S TERU...
...
KURO-SAKI, KURO-SAKI!
DID YOU SEE THE BULLETIN BOARD? THE TEST RESULTS?!
SHUP
TOP OF THE CLASS, TERU KUREBA-YASHI!!!
SMUG
DO YOU REMEM-BER YOUR PROMISE?
...
WE'RE GOING SHOPPING RIGHT NOW!
I ALREADY KNOW WHAT I WANT! I—

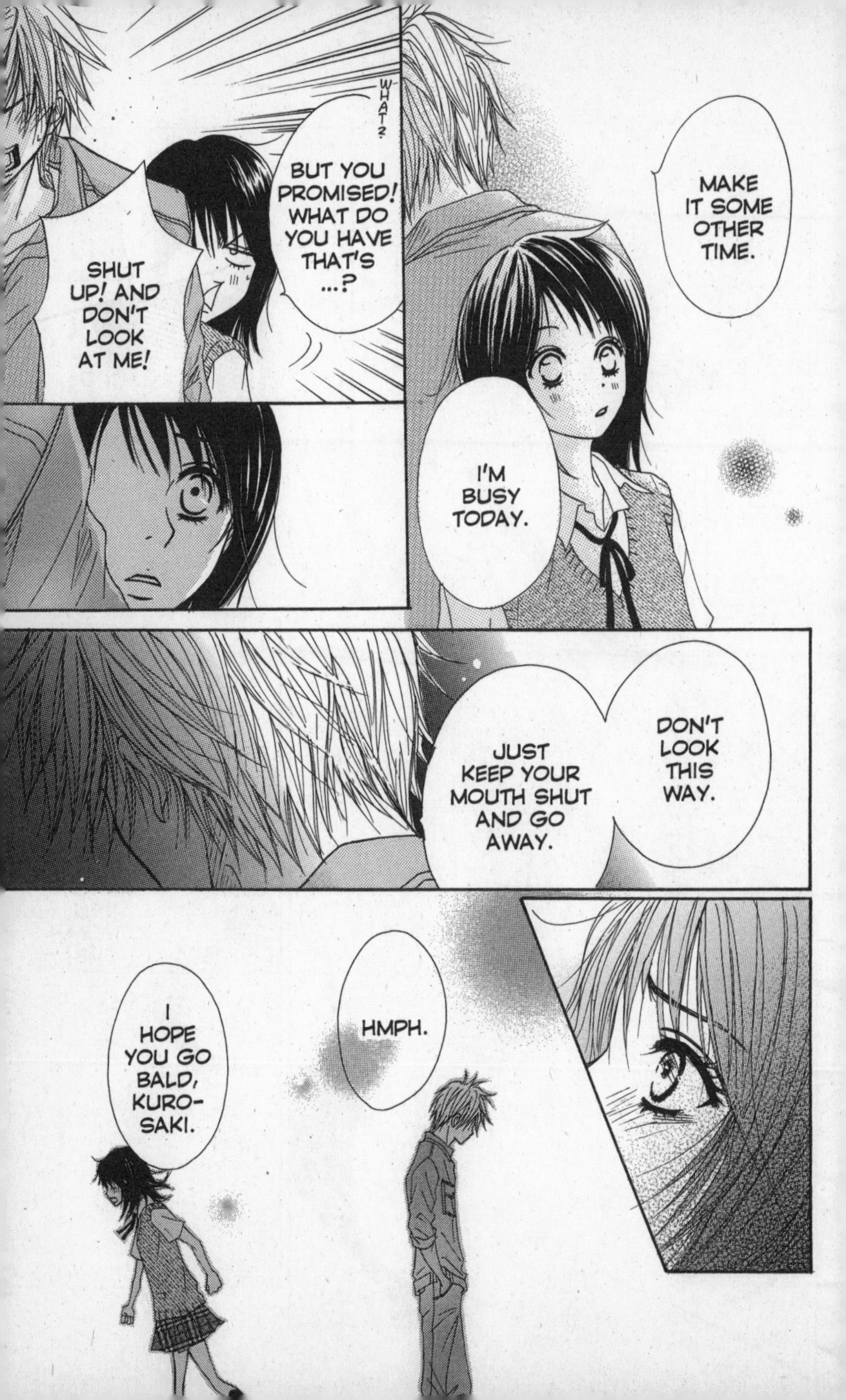
MAKE IT SOME OTHER TIME.
I'M BUSY TODAY.
WHAT?
BUT YOU PROMISED! WHAT DO YOU HAVE THAT'S ...?
SHUT UP! AND DON'T LOOK AT ME!
DON'T LOOK THIS WAY.
JUST KEEP YOUR MOUTH SHUT AND GO AWAY.
HMPH.
I HOPE YOU GO BALD, KURO-SAKI.

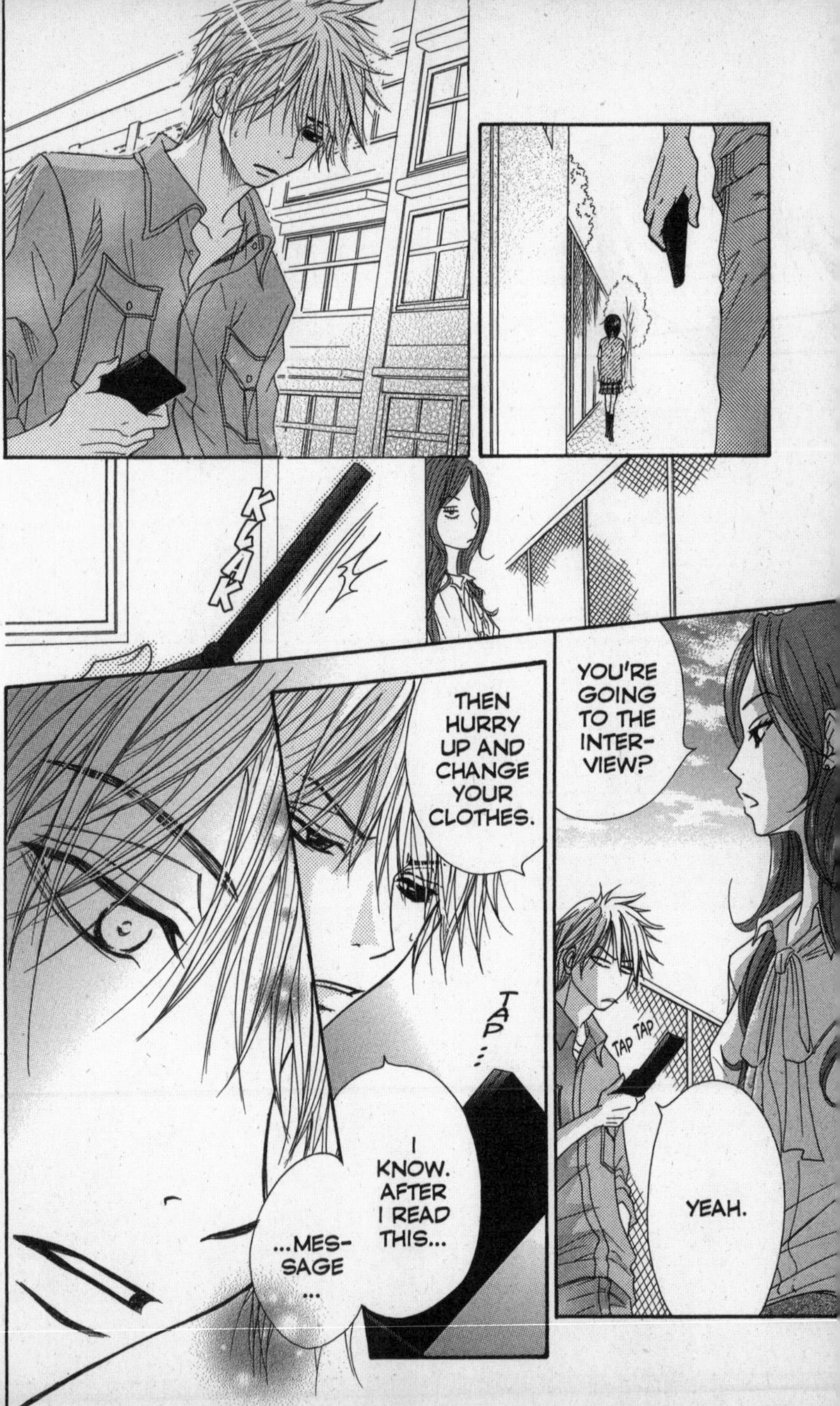
KLAK
YOU'RE GOING TO THE INTER-VIEW?
TAP TAP
YEAH.
THEN HURRY UP AND CHANGE YOUR CLOTHES.
TAP...
I KNOW. AFTER I READ THIS...
...MES-SAGE...

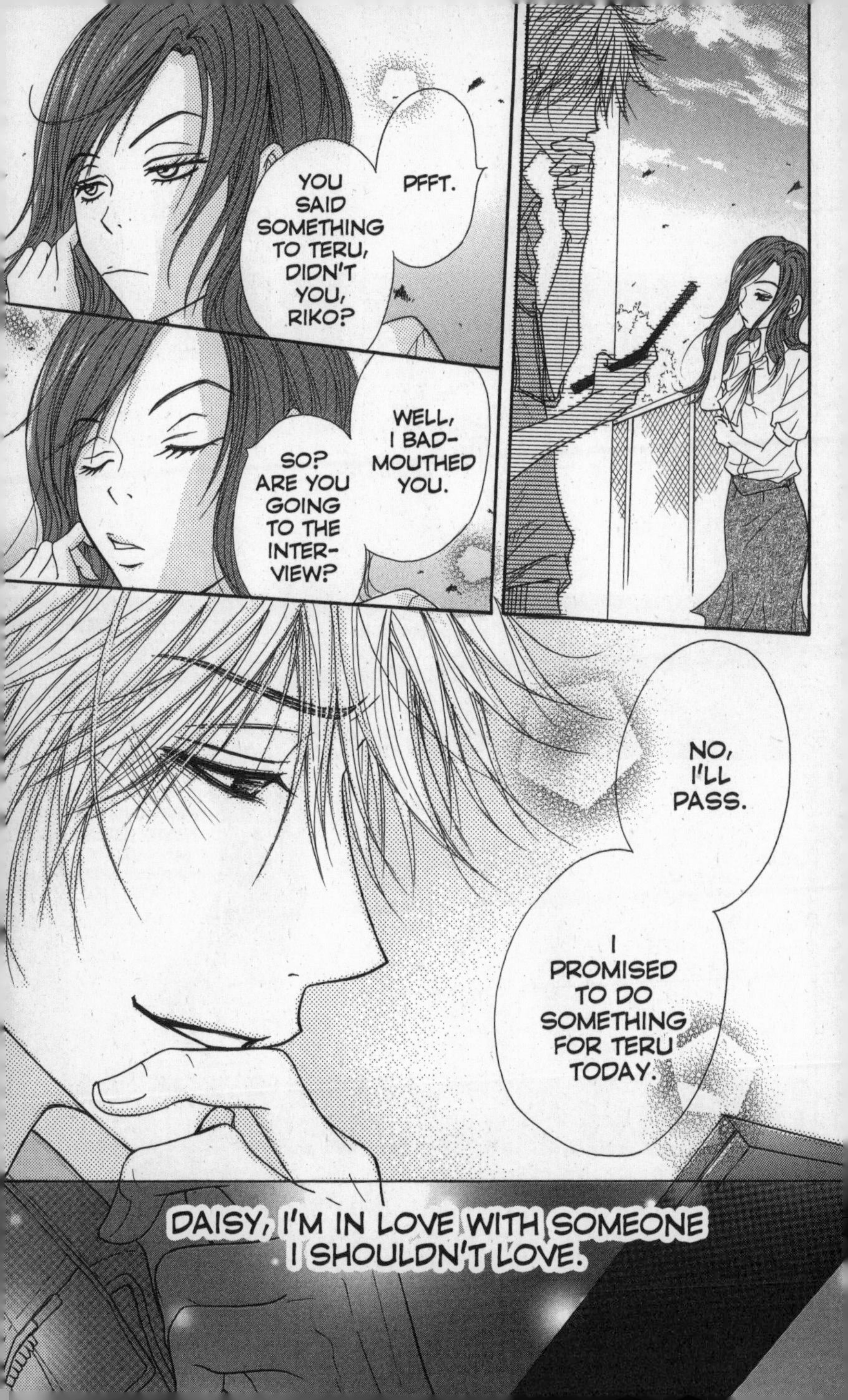
PFFT.
YOU SAID SOMETHING TO TERU, DIDN'T YOU, RIKO?
WELL, I BAD-MOUTHED YOU.
SO? ARE YOU GOING TO THE INTER-VIEW?
NO, I'LL PASS.
I PROMISED TO DO SOMETHING FOR TERU TODAY.
DAISY, I'M IN LOVE WITH SOMEONE I SHOULDN'T LOVE.

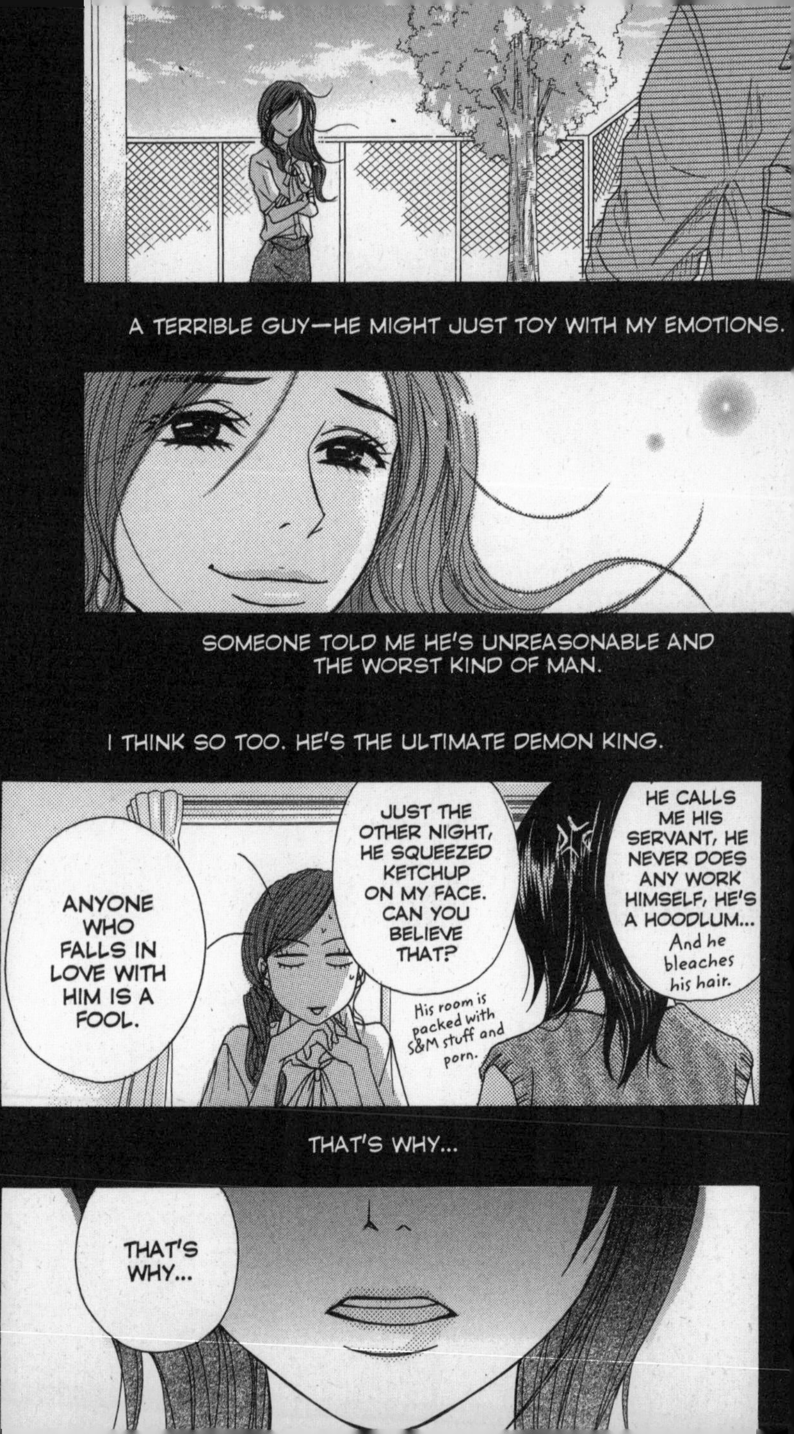
A TERRIBLE GUY—HE MIGHT JUST TOY WITH MY EMOTIONS.
SOMEONE TOLD ME HE'S UNREASONABLE AND THE WORST KIND OF MAN.
I THINK SO TOO. HE'S THE ULTIMATE DEMON KING.
HE CALLS ME HIS SERVANT, HE NEVER DOES ANY WORK HIMSELF, HE'S A HOODLUM...
And he bleaches his hair.
JUST THE OTHER NIGHT, HE SQUEEZED KETCHUP ON MY FACE. CAN YOU BELIEVE THAT?
His room is packed with S&M stuff and porn.
ANYONE WHO FALLS IN LOVE WITH HIM IS A FOOL.
THAT'S WHY...
THAT'S WHY...

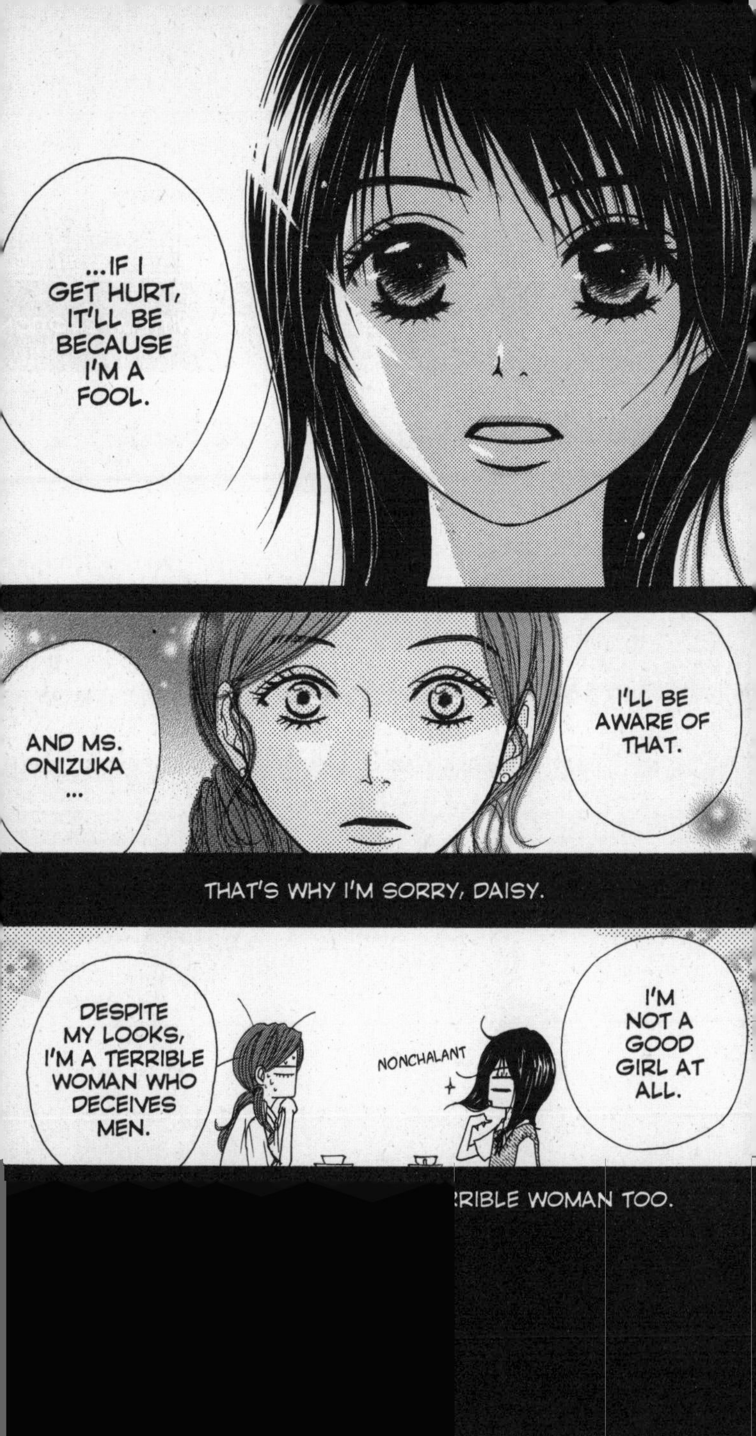
...IF I GET HURT, IT'LL BE BECAUSE I'M A FOOL.
I'LL BE AWARE OF THAT.
AND MS. ONIZUKA ...
THAT'S WHY I'M SORRY, DAISY.
I'M NOT A GOOD GIRL AT ALL.
NONCHALANT
DESPITE MY LOOKS, I'M A TERRIBLE WOMAN WHO DECEIVES MEN.
[redacted]RIBLE WOMAN TOO.

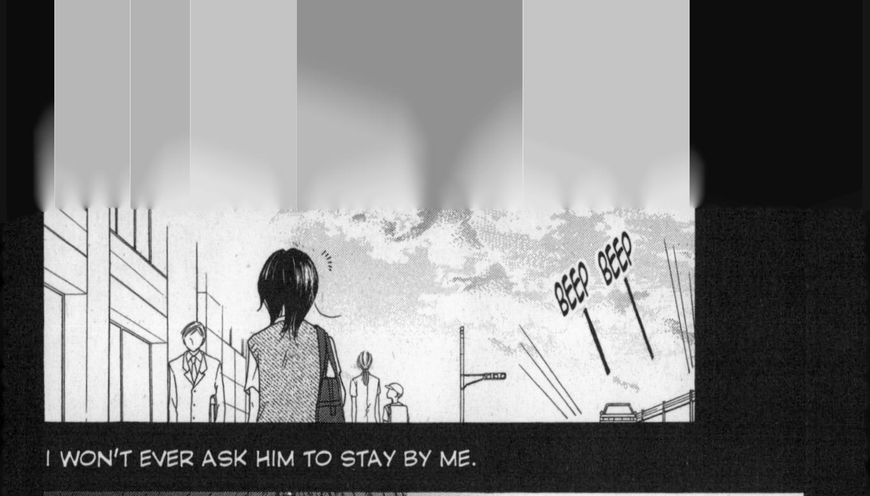
BEEP
BEEP

I WON'T EVER ASK HIM TO STAY BY ME.

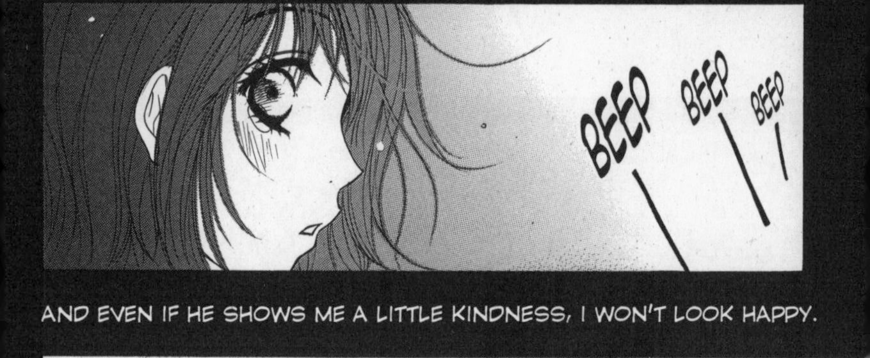
BEEP
BEEP
BEEP

AND EVEN IF HE SHOWS ME A LITTLE KINDNESS, I WON'T LOOK HAPPY.

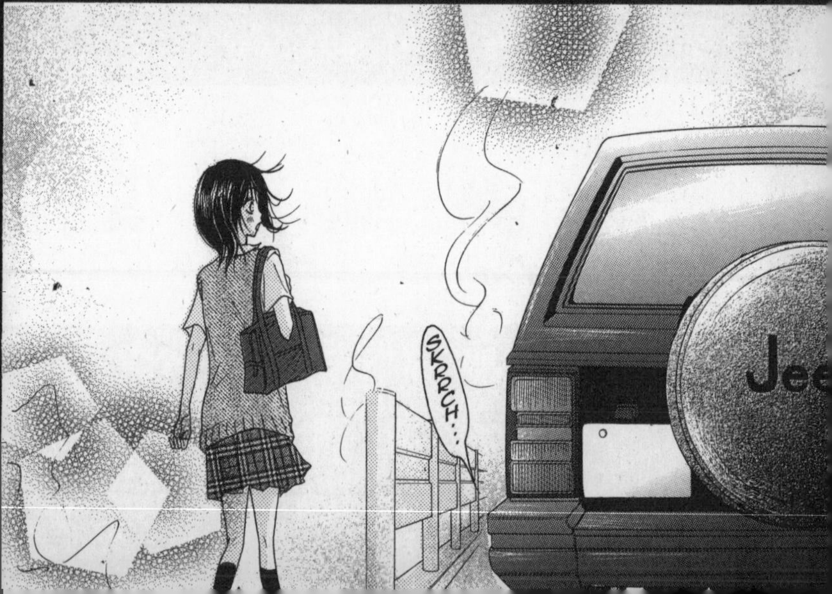
SKRRCH...

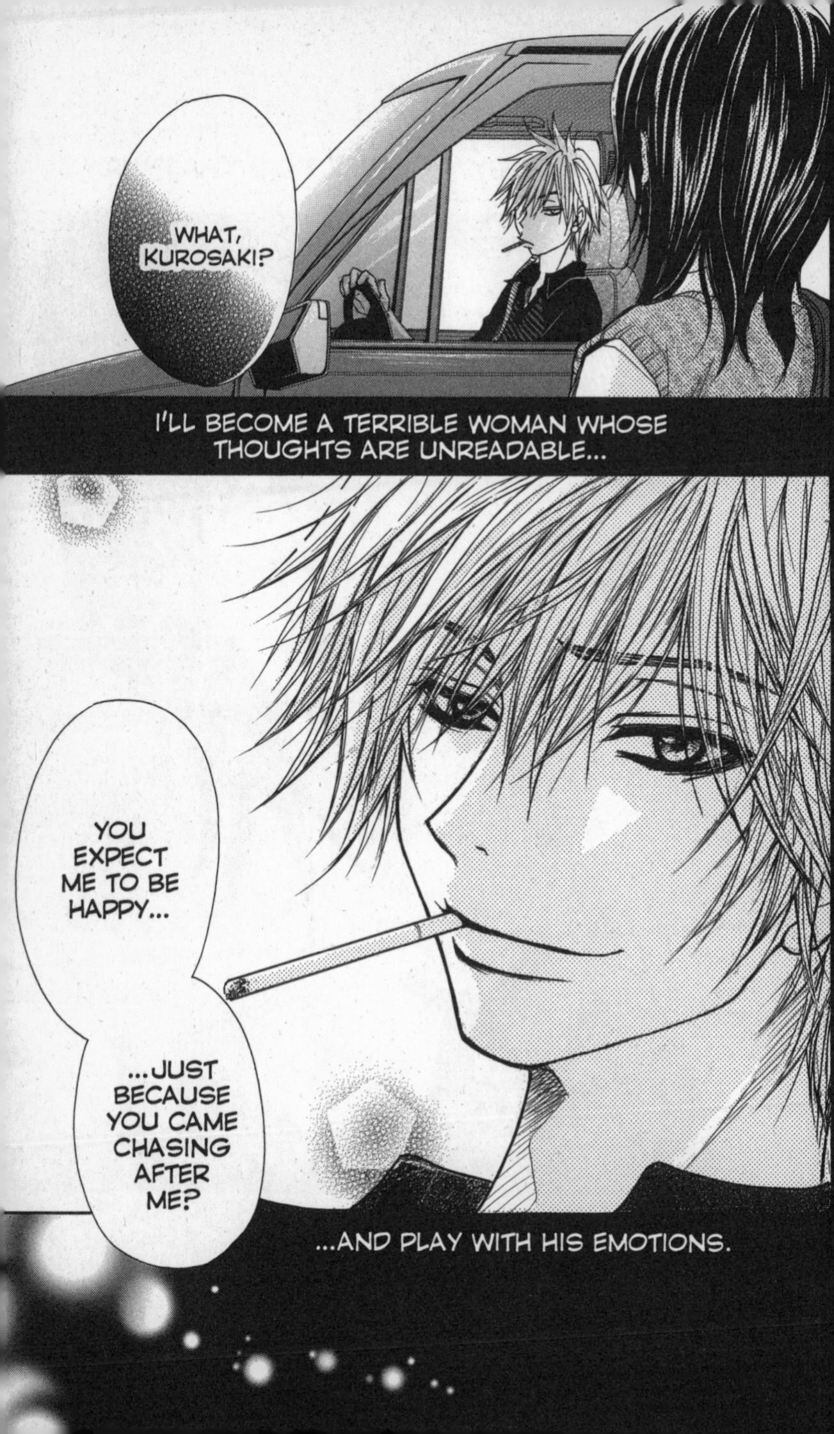
WHAT, KUROSAKI?
I'LL BECOME A TERRIBLE WOMAN WHOSE THOUGHTS ARE UNREADABLE...
YOU EXPECT ME TO BE HAPPY...
...JUST BECAUSE YOU CAME CHASING AFTER ME?
...AND PLAY WITH HIS EMOTIONS.

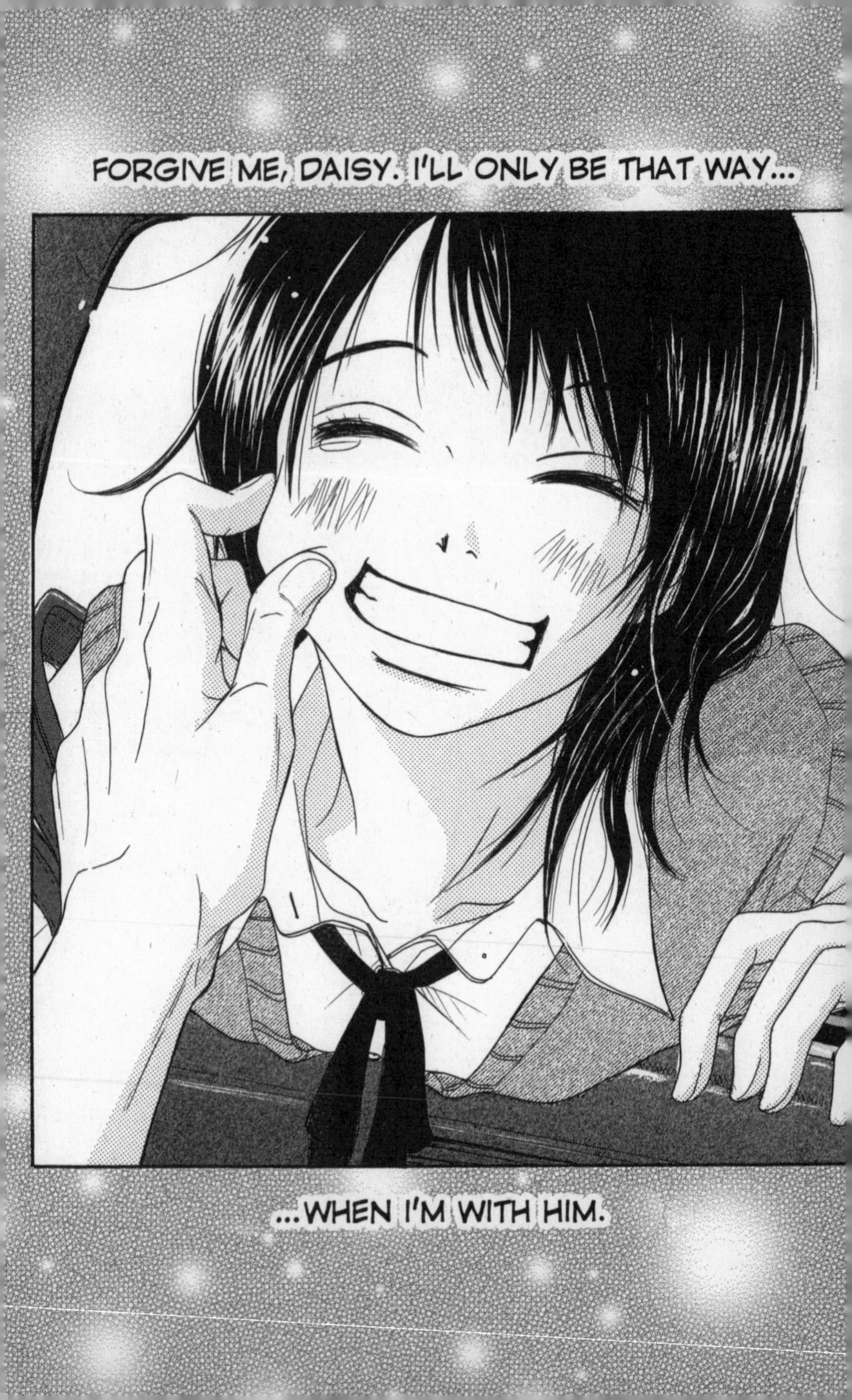
FORGIVE ME, DAISY. I'LL ONLY BE THAT WAY...
...WHEN I'M WITH HIM.

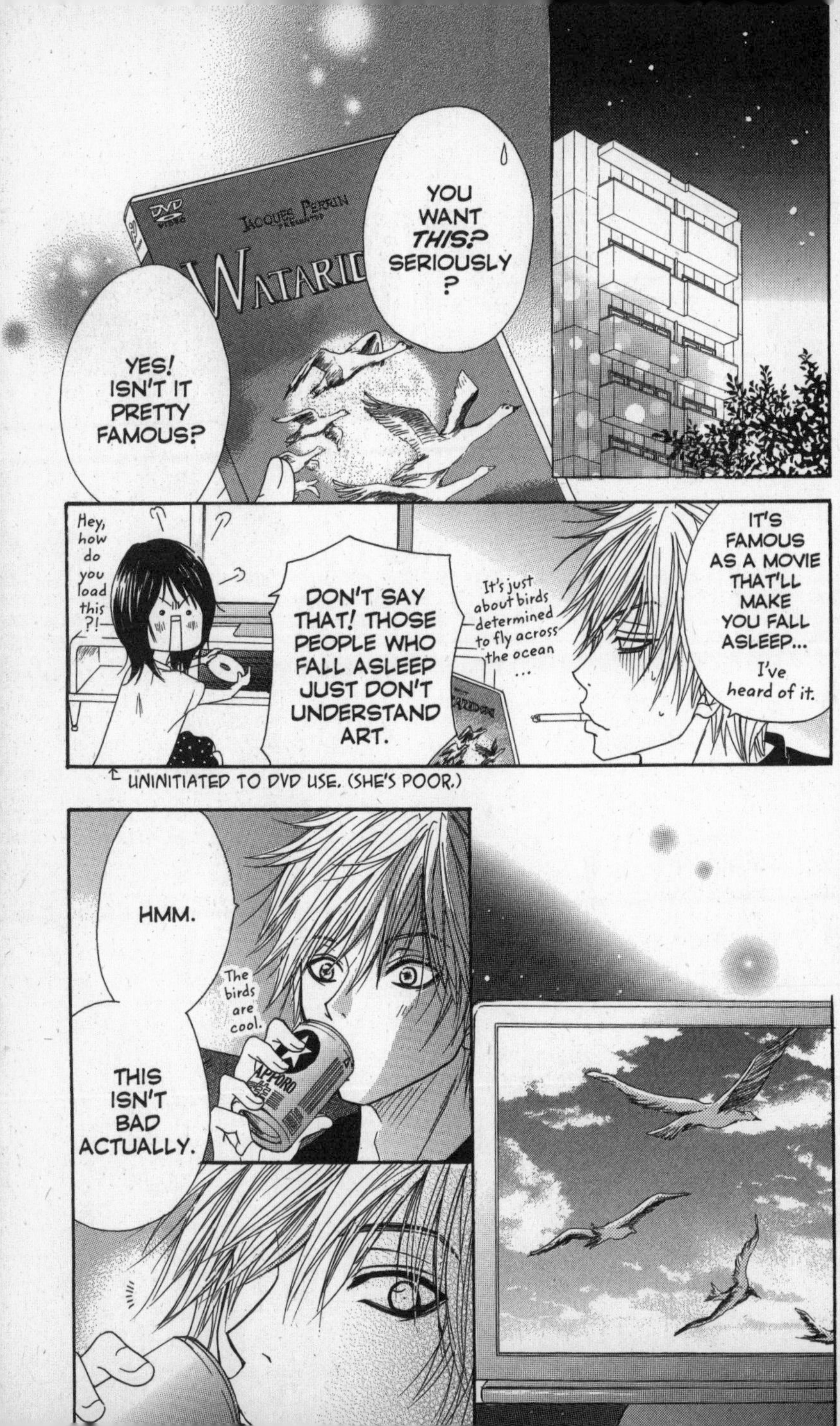
YOU WANT THIS? SERIOUSLY?
JACQUES PERRIN
YES! ISN'T IT PRETTY FAMOUS?
IT'S FAMOUS AS A MOVIE THAT'LL MAKE YOU FALL ASLEEP...
I've heard of it.
It's just about birds determined to fly across the ocean ...
DON'T SAY THAT! THOSE PEOPLE WHO FALL ASLEEP JUST DON'T UNDERSTAND ART.
Hey, how do you load this?!
UNINITIATED TO DVD USE. (SHE'S POOR.)
HMM.
The birds are cool.
THIS ISN'T BAD ACTUALLY.

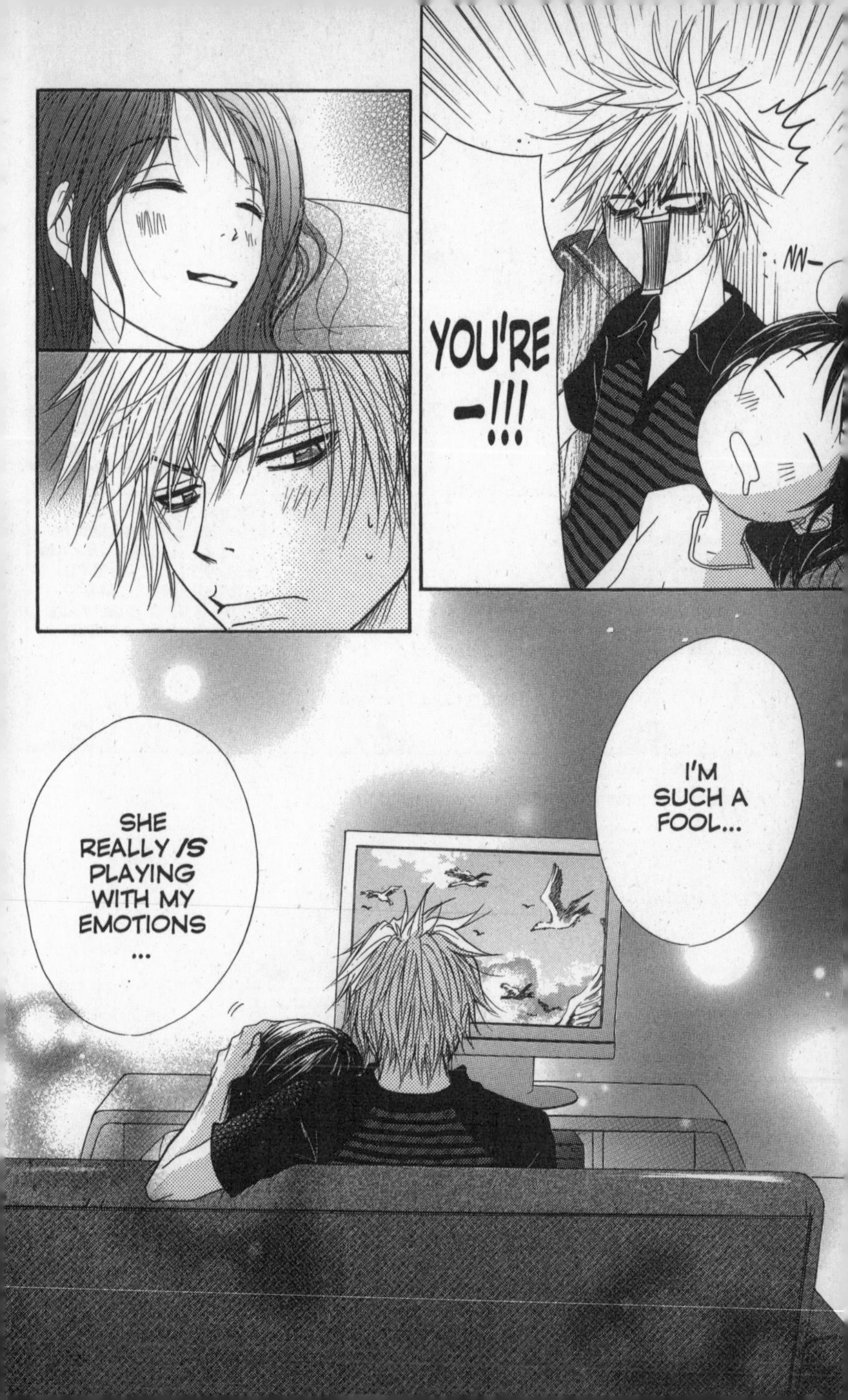
NN–
YOU'RE –!!!
I'M SUCH A FOOL...
SHE REALLY *IS* PLAYING WITH MY EMOTIONS ...

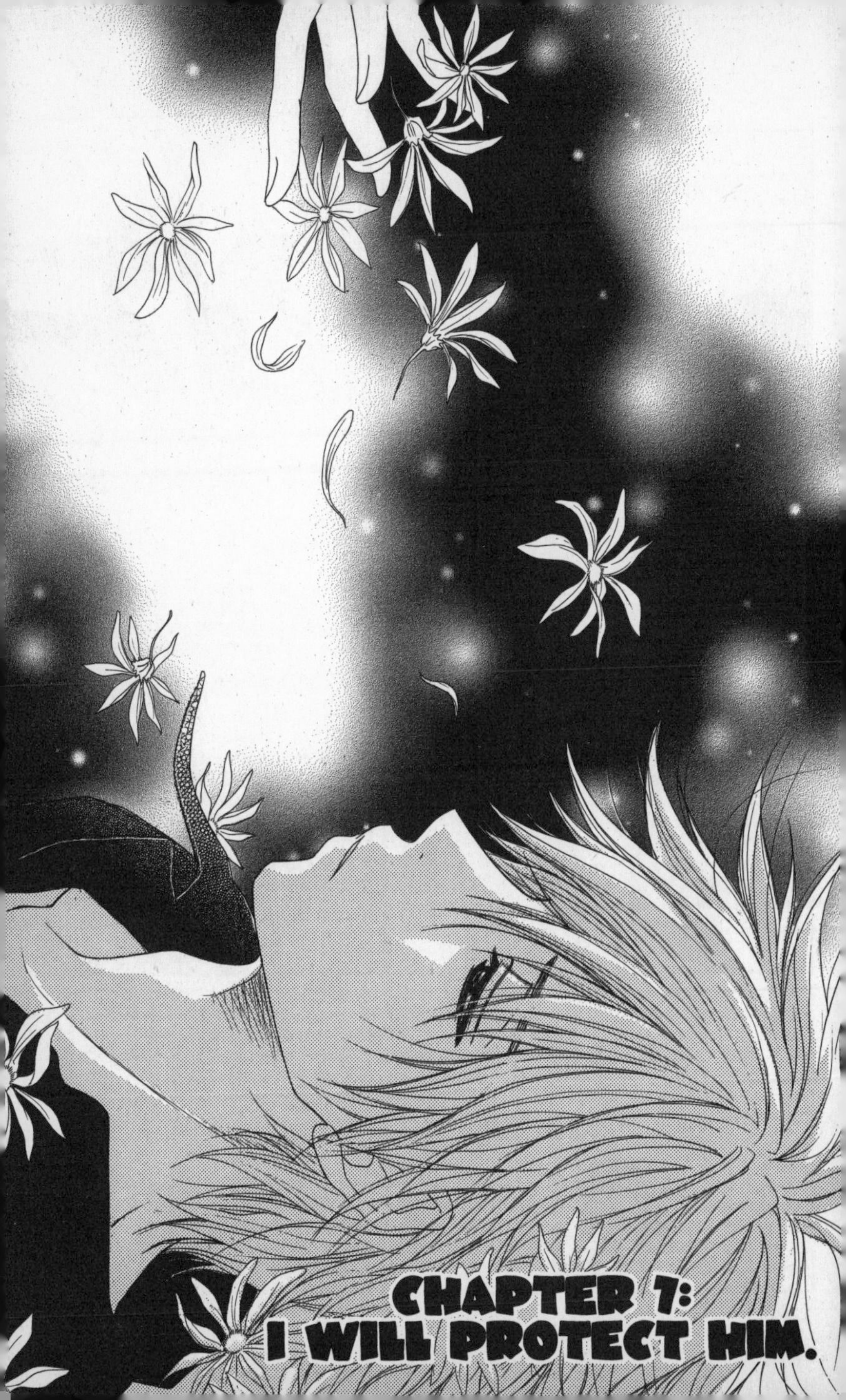
CHAPTER 7:
I WILL PROTECT HIM.

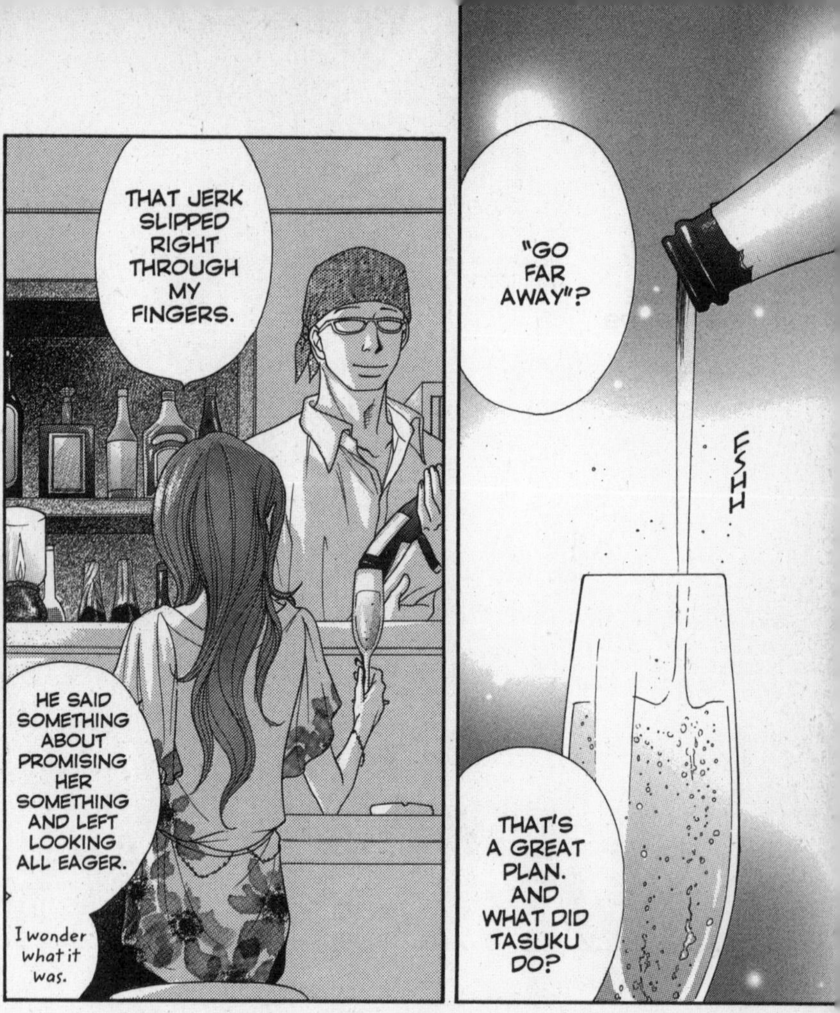
"GO FAR AWAY"?
FSHH
THAT'S A GREAT PLAN. AND WHAT DID TASUKU DO?
THAT JERK SLIPPED RIGHT THROUGH MY FINGERS.
HE SAID SOMETHING ABOUT PROMISING HER SOMETHING AND LEFT LOOKING ALL EAGER.
I wonder what it was.

TERU GOT A NOSEBLEED, SO SHE WIPED HER FACE, STUFFED TISSUES IN HER NOSTRILS AND TOOK HER TEST. AS FOR REACTIONS TO A SHOJO MANGA HEROINE DOING THAT, I DIDN'T REALLY GET THAT MANY COMMENTS. (BE THAT AS IT MAY...)

ONE READER DID WRITE THIS: "IF HER NOSTRILS WERE PLUGGED AND SHE KEPT HER MOUTH SHUT DURING THE EXAM, TERU WOULD'VE DIED OF SUFFOCATION INSTEAD OF HEMORRHAGING TO DEATH."

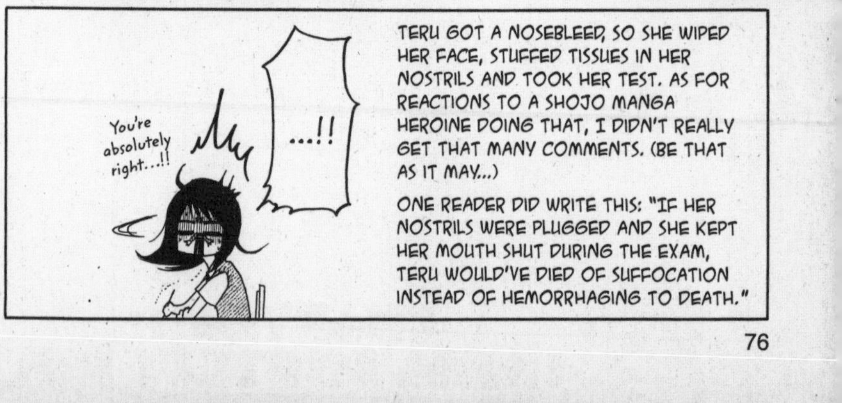
...!!
You're absolutely right...!!

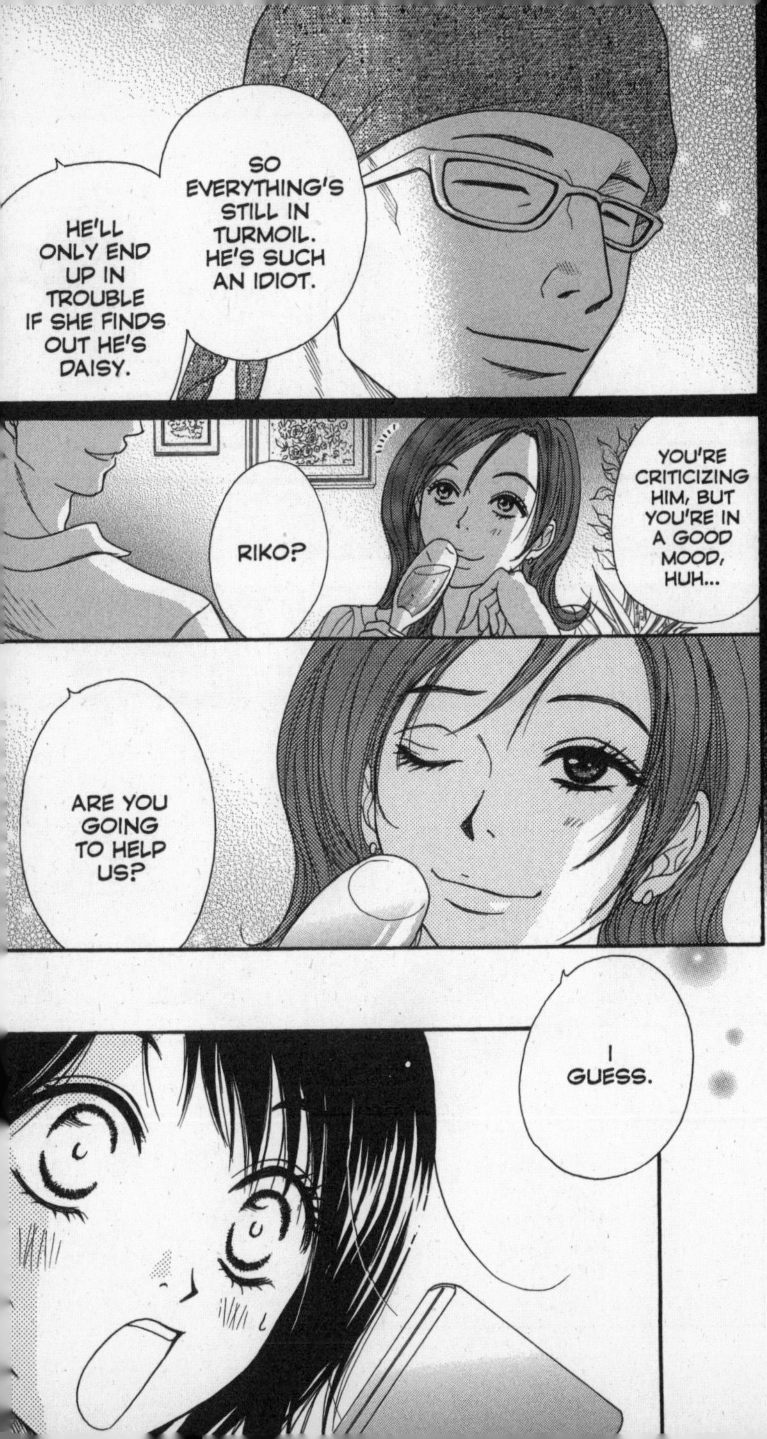
SO EVERYTHING'S STILL IN TURMOIL. HE'S SUCH AN IDIOT.
HE'LL ONLY END UP IN TROUBLE IF SHE FINDS OUT HE'S DAISY.
YOU'RE CRITICIZING HIM, BUT YOU'RE IN A GOOD MOOD, HUH...
RIKO?
ARE YOU GOING TO HELP US?
I GUESS.

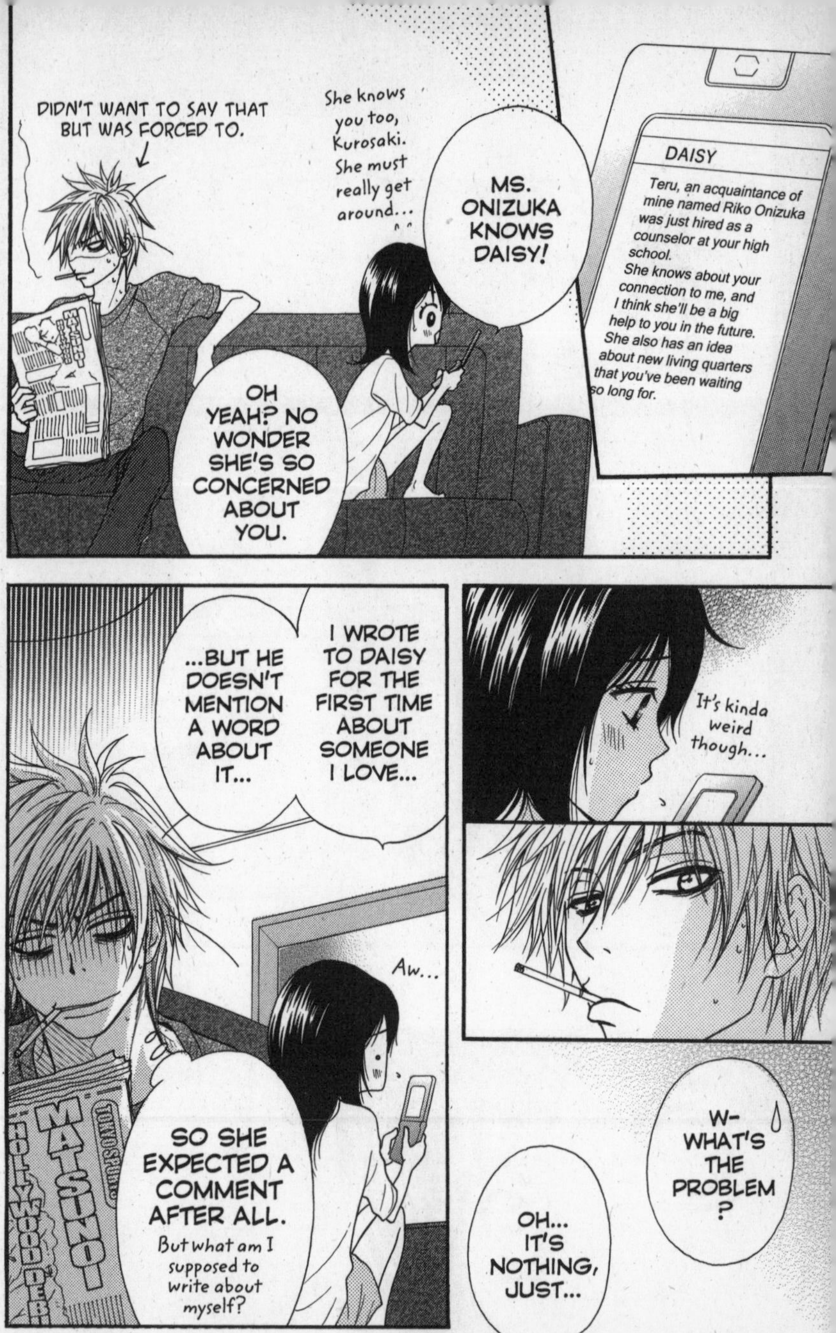
DAISY
Teru, an acquaintance of mine named Riko Onizuka was just hired as a counselor at your high school.
She knows about your connection to me, and I think she'll be a big help to you in the future.
She also has an idea about new living quarters that you've been waiting so long for.
MS. ONIZUKA KNOWS DAISY!
She knows you too, Kurosaki. She must really get around...
DIDN'T WANT TO SAY THAT BUT WAS FORCED TO.
OH YEAH? NO WONDER SHE'S SO CONCERNED ABOUT YOU.
It's kinda weird though...
W-WHAT'S THE PROBLEM?
OH... IT'S NOTHING, JUST...
I WROTE TO DAISY FOR THE FIRST TIME ABOUT SOMEONE I LOVE...
...BUT HE DOESN'T MENTION A WORD ABOUT IT...
Aw...
SO SHE EXPECTED A COMMENT AFTER ALL.
But what am I supposed to write about myself?

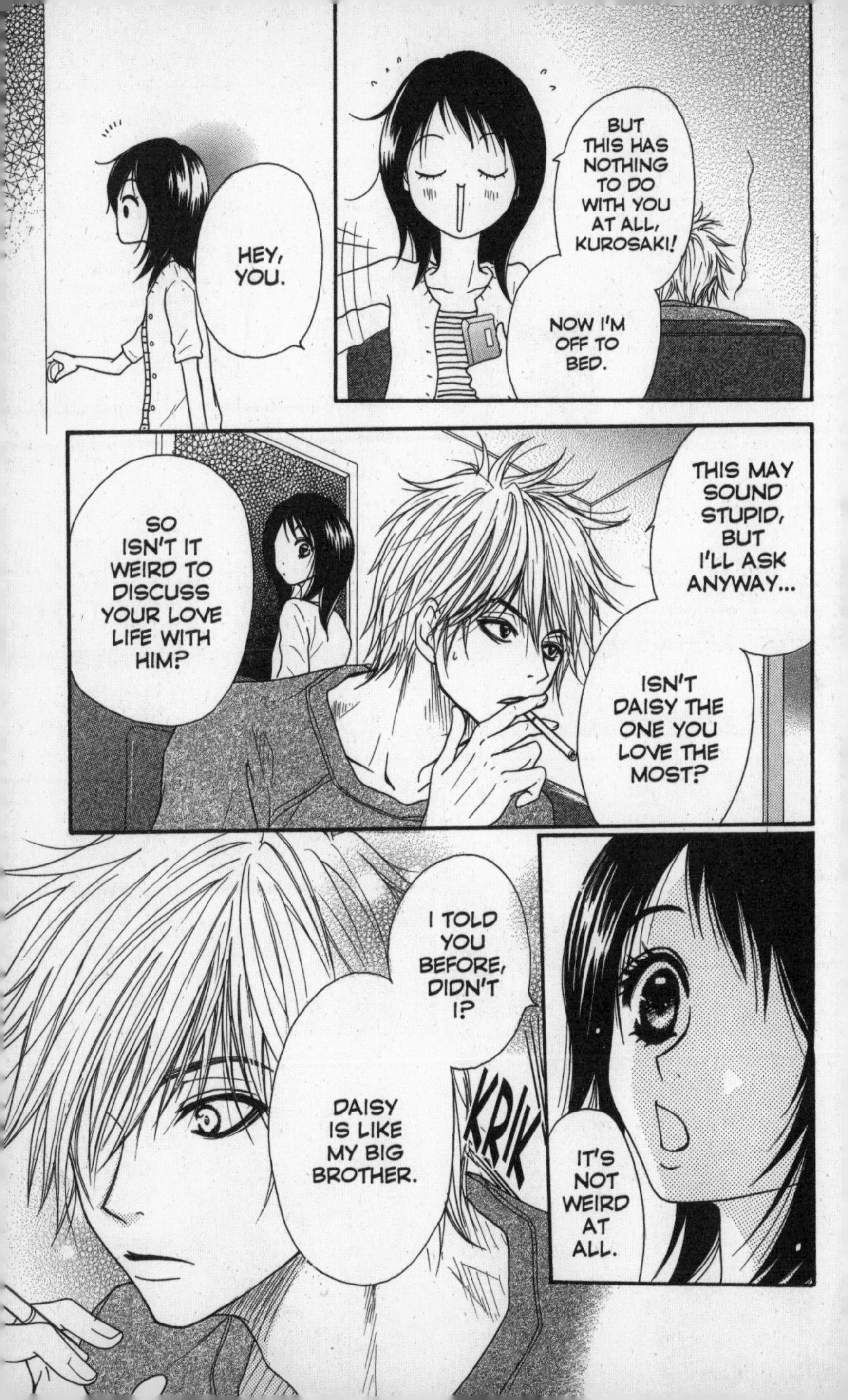
BUT THIS HAS NOTHING TO DO WITH YOU AT ALL, KUROSAKI!
NOW I'M OFF TO BED.
HEY, YOU.
THIS MAY SOUND STUPID, BUT I'LL ASK ANYWAY...
ISN'T DAISY THE ONE YOU LOVE THE MOST?
SO ISN'T IT WEIRD TO DISCUSS YOUR LOVE LIFE WITH HIM?
IT'S NOT WEIRD AT ALL.
KRIK
I TOLD YOU BEFORE, DIDN'T I?
DAISY IS LIKE MY BIG BROTHER.

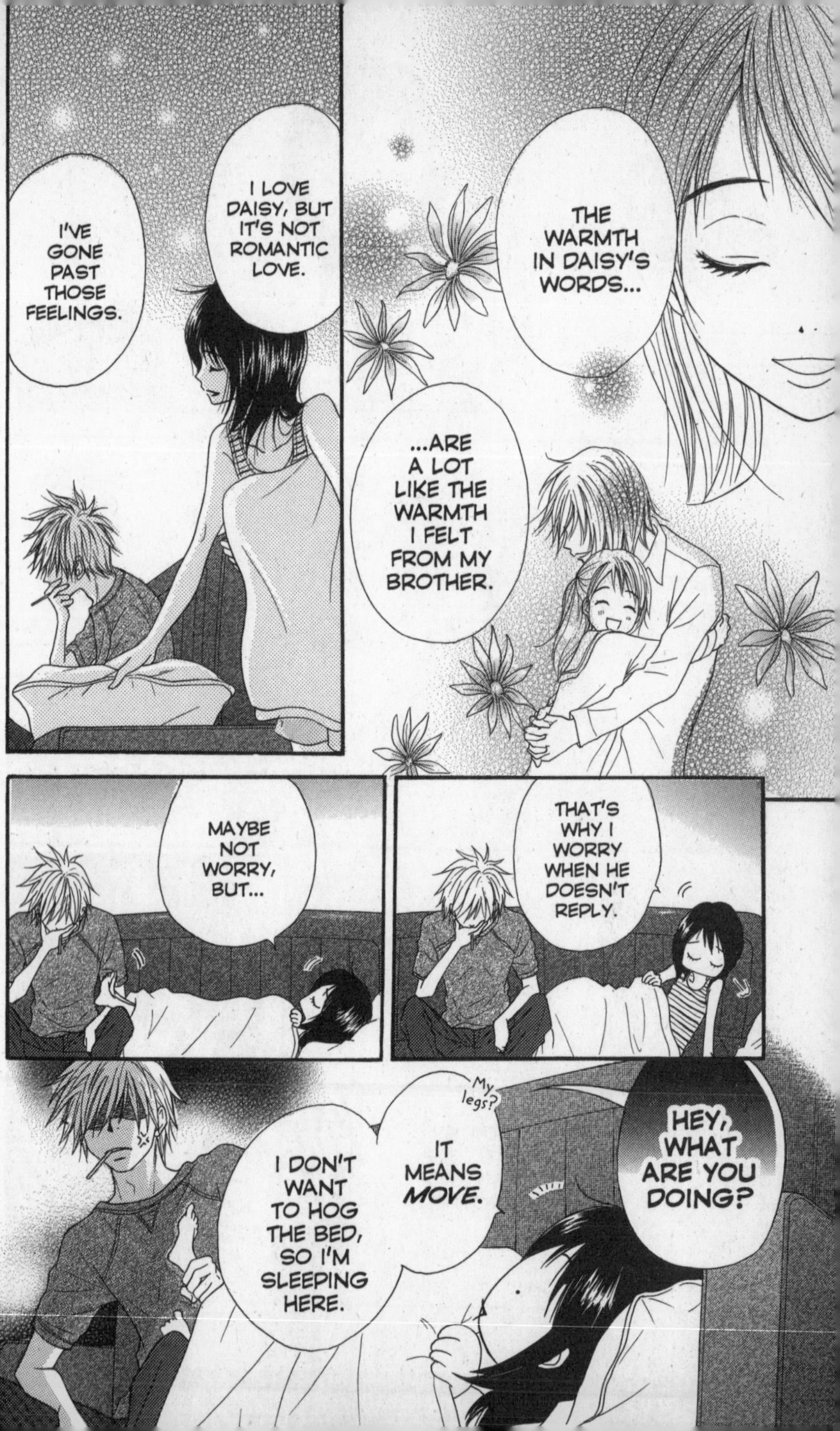
THE WARMTH IN DAISY'S WORDS...
...ARE A LOT LIKE THE WARMTH I FELT FROM MY BROTHER.
I LOVE DAISY, BUT IT'S NOT ROMANTIC LOVE.
I'VE GONE PAST THOSE FEELINGS.
THAT'S WHY I WORRY WHEN HE DOESN'T REPLY.
MAYBE NOT WORRY, BUT...
HEY, WHAT ARE YOU DOING?
My legs?
IT MEANS *MOVE*.
I DON'T WANT TO HOG THE BED, SO I'M SLEEPING HERE.

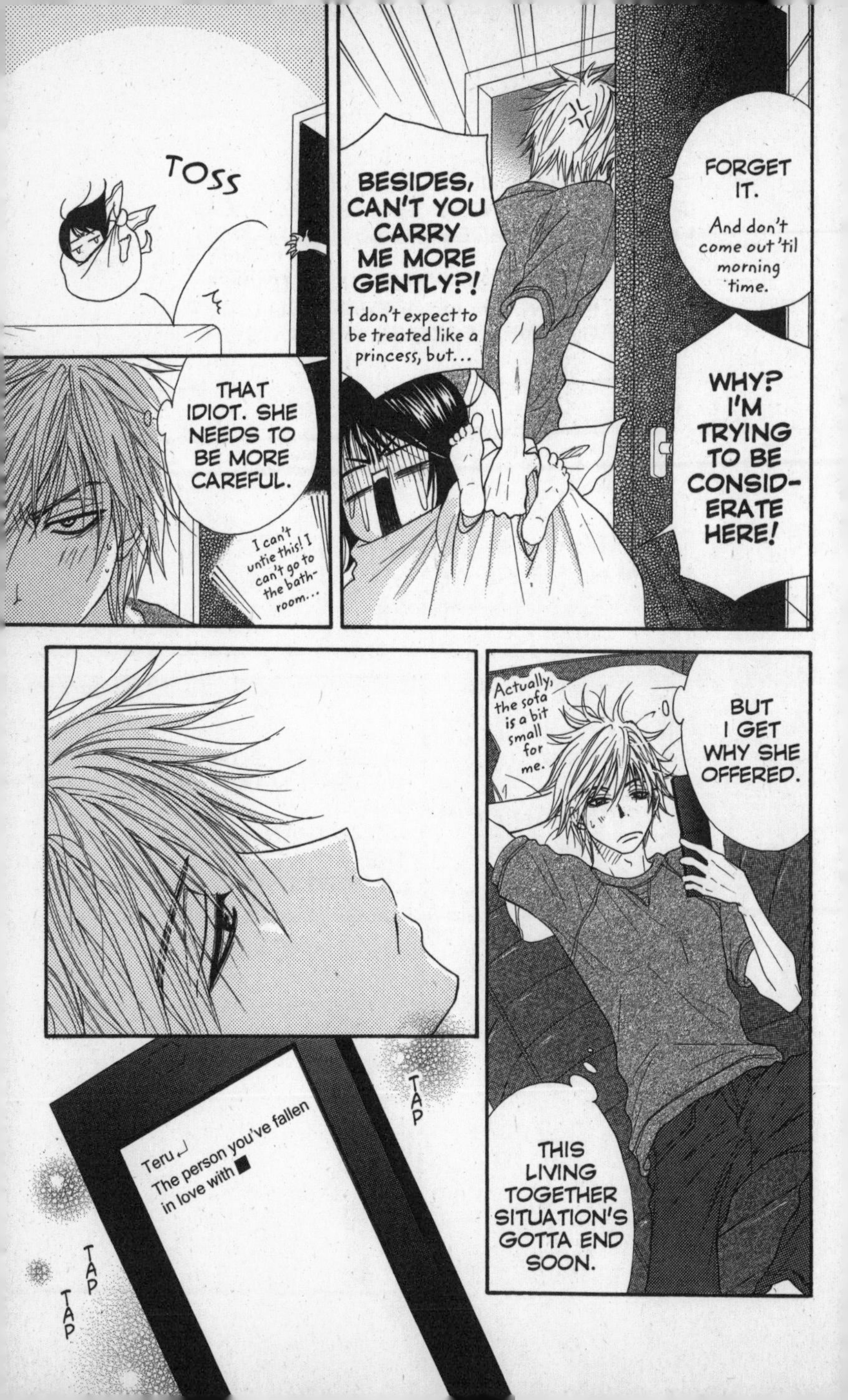

FORGET IT.
And don't come out 'til morning time.
BESIDES, CAN'T YOU CARRY ME MORE GENTLY?!
I don't expect to be treated like a princess, but...
WHY? I'M TRYING TO BE CONSID-ERATE HERE!
TOSS
THAT IDIOT. SHE NEEDS TO BE MORE CAREFUL.
I can't untie this! I can't go to the bath-room...
Actually, the sofa is a bit small for me.
BUT I GET WHY SHE OFFERED.
THIS LIVING TOGETHER SITUATION'S GOTTA END SOON.
TAP
Teru↲
The person you've fallen in love with ■
TAP
TAP

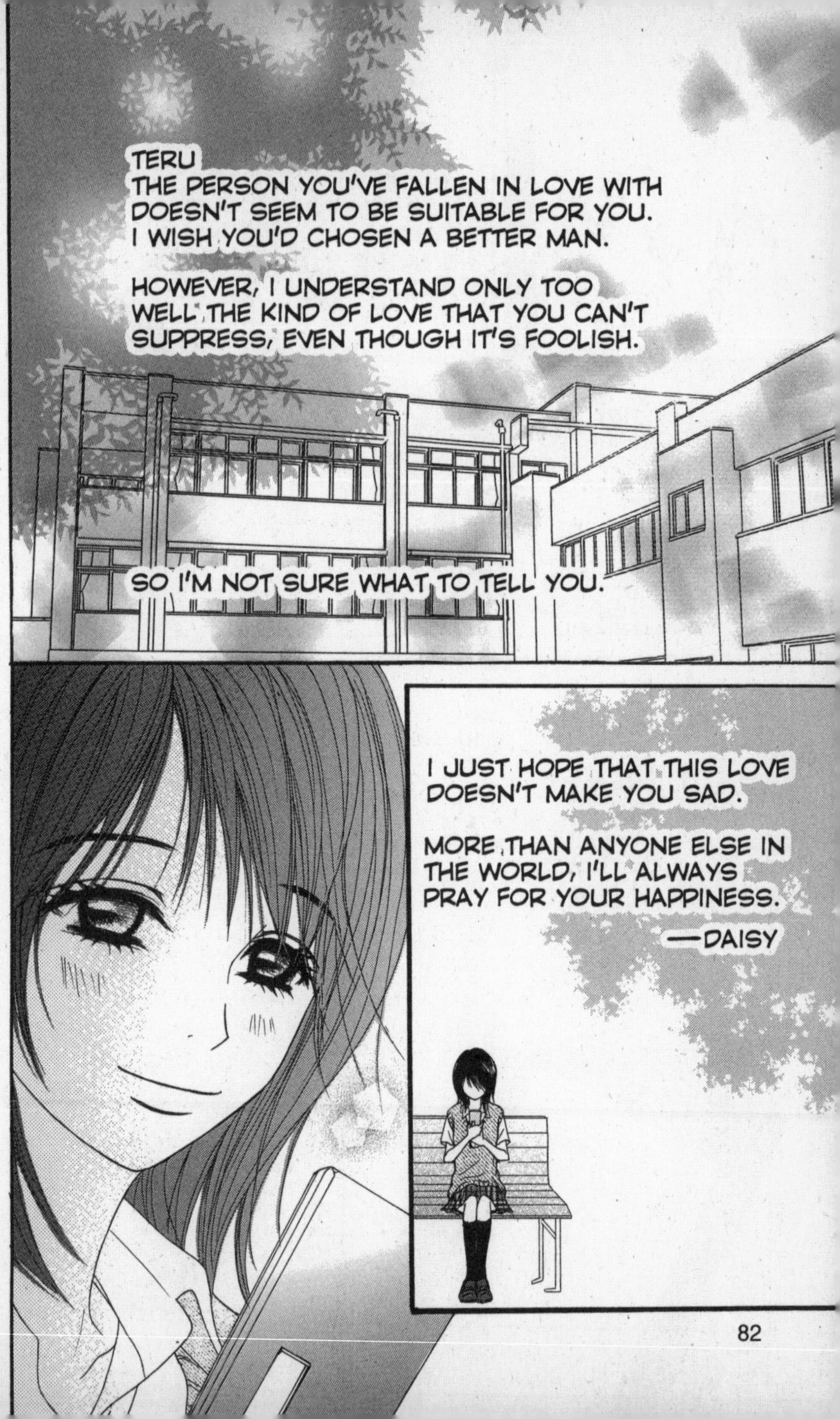
TERU
THE PERSON YOU'VE FALLEN IN LOVE WITH DOESN'T SEEM TO BE SUITABLE FOR YOU. I WISH YOU'D CHOSEN A BETTER MAN.
HOWEVER, I UNDERSTAND ONLY TOO WELL THE KIND OF LOVE THAT YOU CAN'T SUPPRESS, EVEN THOUGH IT'S FOOLISH.
SO I'M NOT SURE WHAT TO TELL YOU.
I JUST HOPE THAT THIS LOVE DOESN'T MAKE YOU SAD.
MORE THAN ANYONE ELSE IN THE WORLD, I'LL ALWAYS PRAY FOR YOUR HAPPINESS.
—DAISY

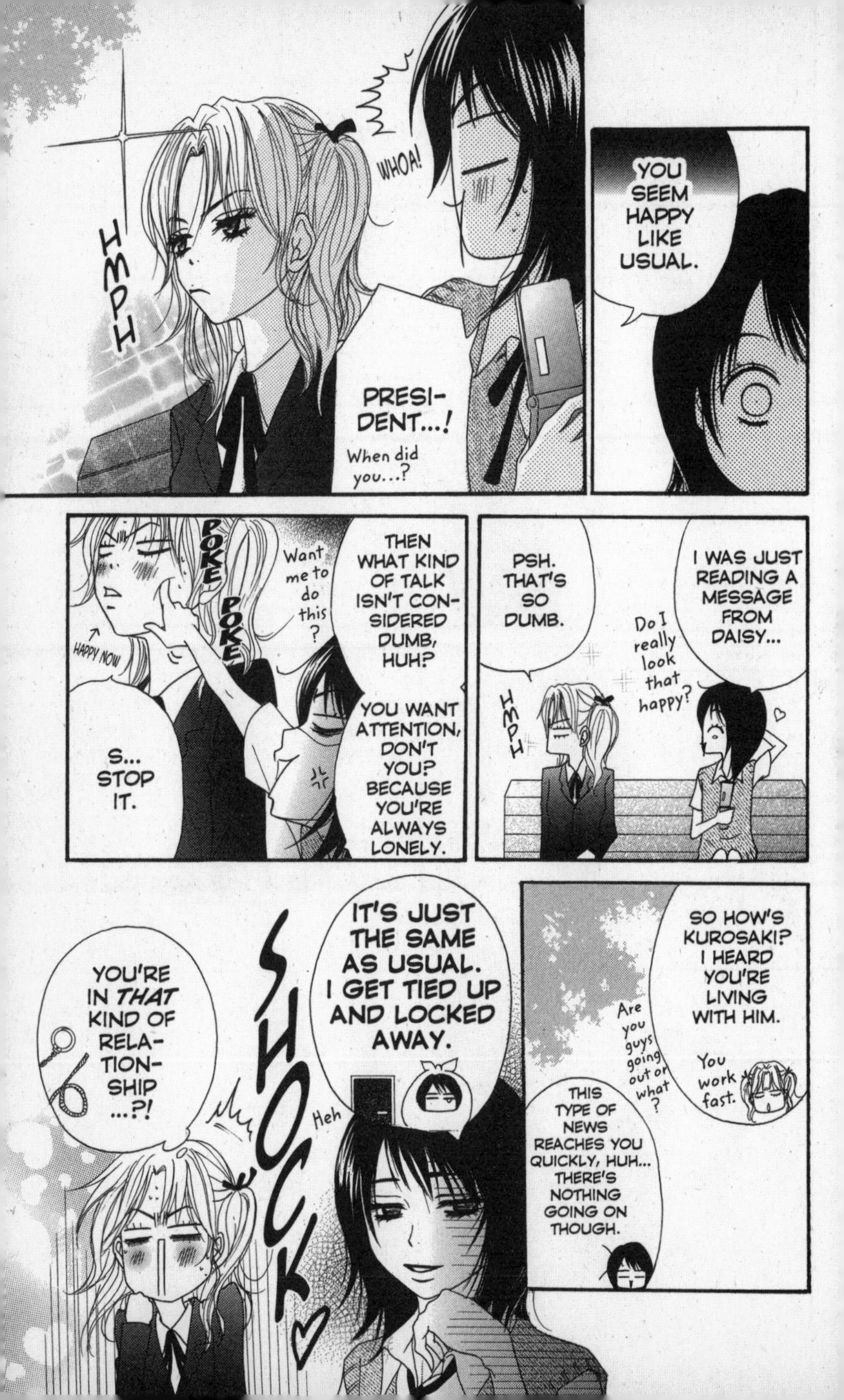
YOU SEEM HAPPY LIKE USUAL.
WHOA!
PRESI-DENT...!
When did you...?
HMPH
I WAS JUST READING A MESSAGE FROM DAISY...
Do I really look that happy?
PSH. THAT'S SO DUMB.
HMPH
THEN WHAT KIND OF TALK ISN'T CON-SIDERED DUMB, HUH?
Want me to do this?
POKE
POKE
YOU WANT ATTENTION, DON'T YOU? BECAUSE YOU'RE ALWAYS LONELY.
HAPPY NOW
S... STOP IT.
SO HOW'S KUROSAKI? I HEARD YOU'RE LIVING WITH HIM.
You work fast.
Are you guys going out or what?
THIS TYPE OF NEWS REACHES YOU QUICKLY, HUH... THERE'S NOTHING GOING ON THOUGH.
IT'S JUST THE SAME AS USUAL. I GET TIED UP AND LOCKED AWAY.
Heh
SHOCK
YOU'RE IN *THAT* KIND OF RELA-TION-SHIP...?!

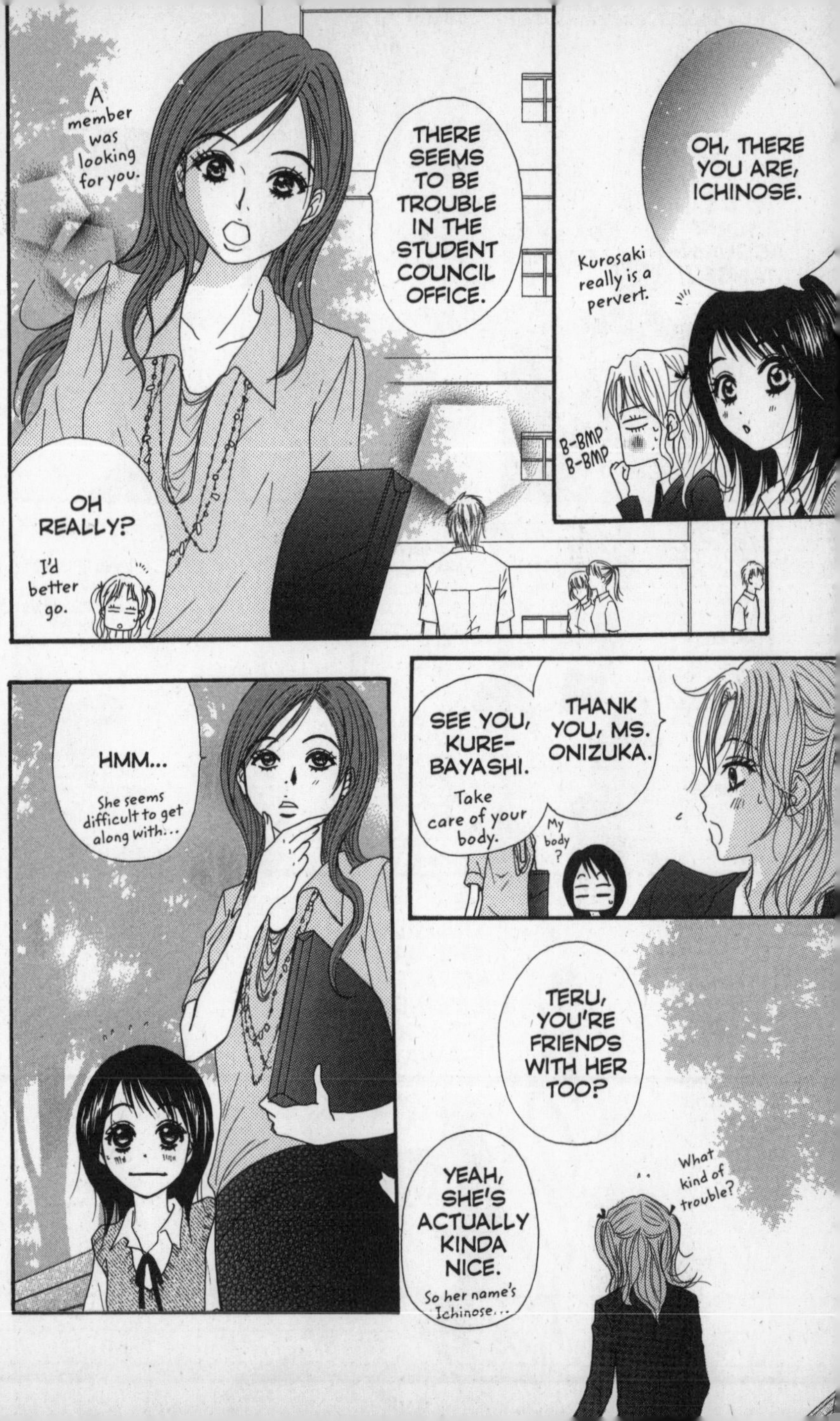
OH, THERE YOU ARE, ICHINOSE.
Kurosaki really is a pervert.
B-BMP B-BMP
THERE SEEMS TO BE TROUBLE IN THE STUDENT COUNCIL OFFICE.
A member was looking for you.
OH REALLY?
I'd better go.
THANK YOU, MS. ONIZUKA.
SEE YOU, KURE-BAYASHI.
Take care of your body.
My body?
TERU, YOU'RE FRIENDS WITH HER TOO?
YEAH, SHE'S ACTUALLY KINDA NICE.
So her name's Ichinose...
What kind of trouble?
HMM...
She seems difficult to get along with...

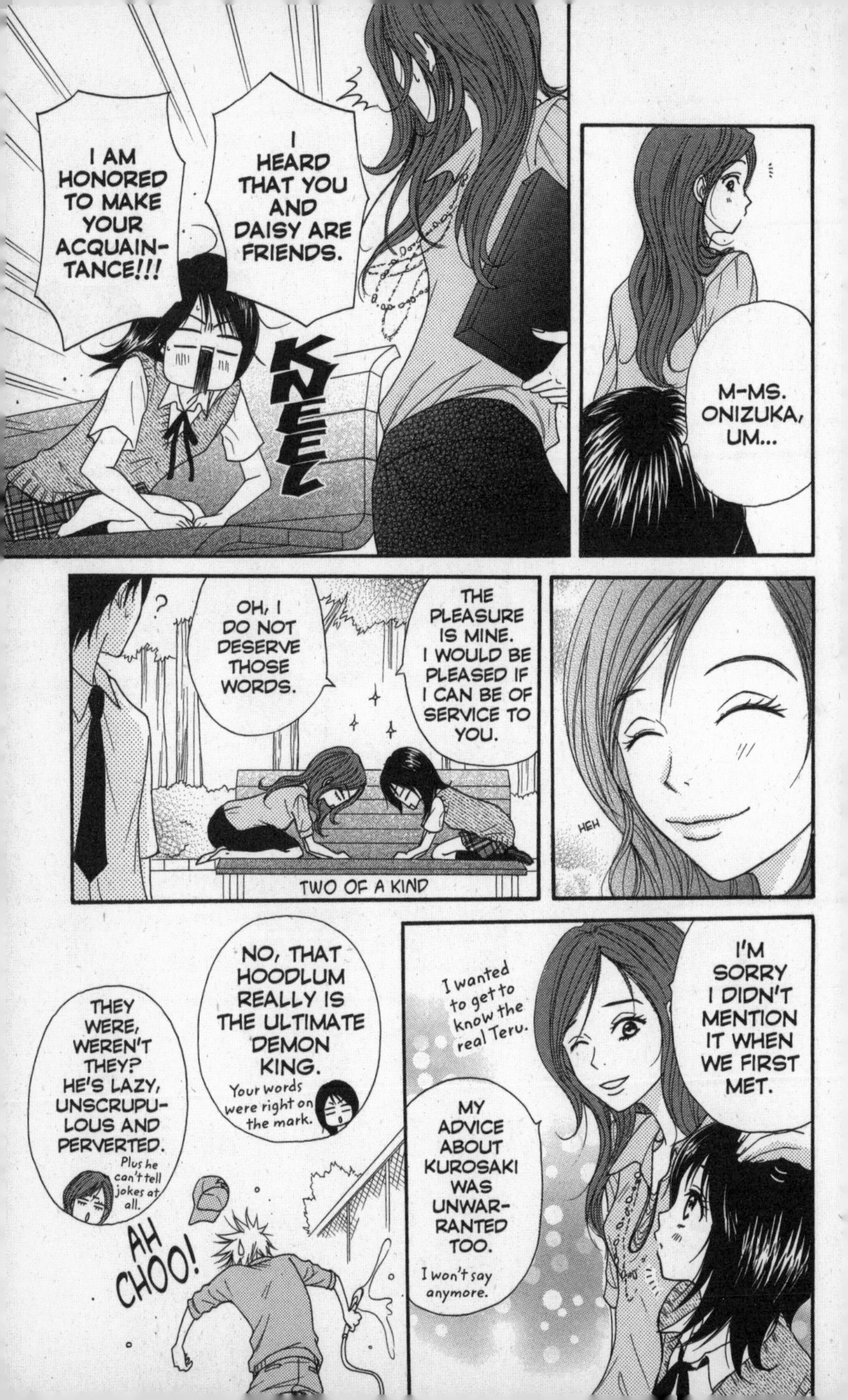
M-MS. ONIZUKA, UM...
I HEARD THAT YOU AND DAISY ARE FRIENDS.
I AM HONORED TO MAKE YOUR ACQUAINTANCE!!!
KNEEL
HEH
THE PLEASURE IS MINE. I WOULD BE PLEASED IF I CAN BE OF SERVICE TO YOU.
OH, I DO NOT DESERVE THOSE WORDS.
?
TWO OF A KIND
I'M SORRY I DIDN'T MENTION IT WHEN WE FIRST MET.
I wanted to get to know the real Teru.
MY ADVICE ABOUT KUROSAKI WAS UNWARRANTED TOO.
I won't say anymore.
NO, THAT HOODLUM REALLY IS THE ULTIMATE DEMON KING.
Your words were right on the mark.
THEY WERE, WEREN'T THEY? HE'S LAZY, UNSCRUPULOUS AND PERVERTED.
Plus he can't tell jokes at all.
AH CHOO!

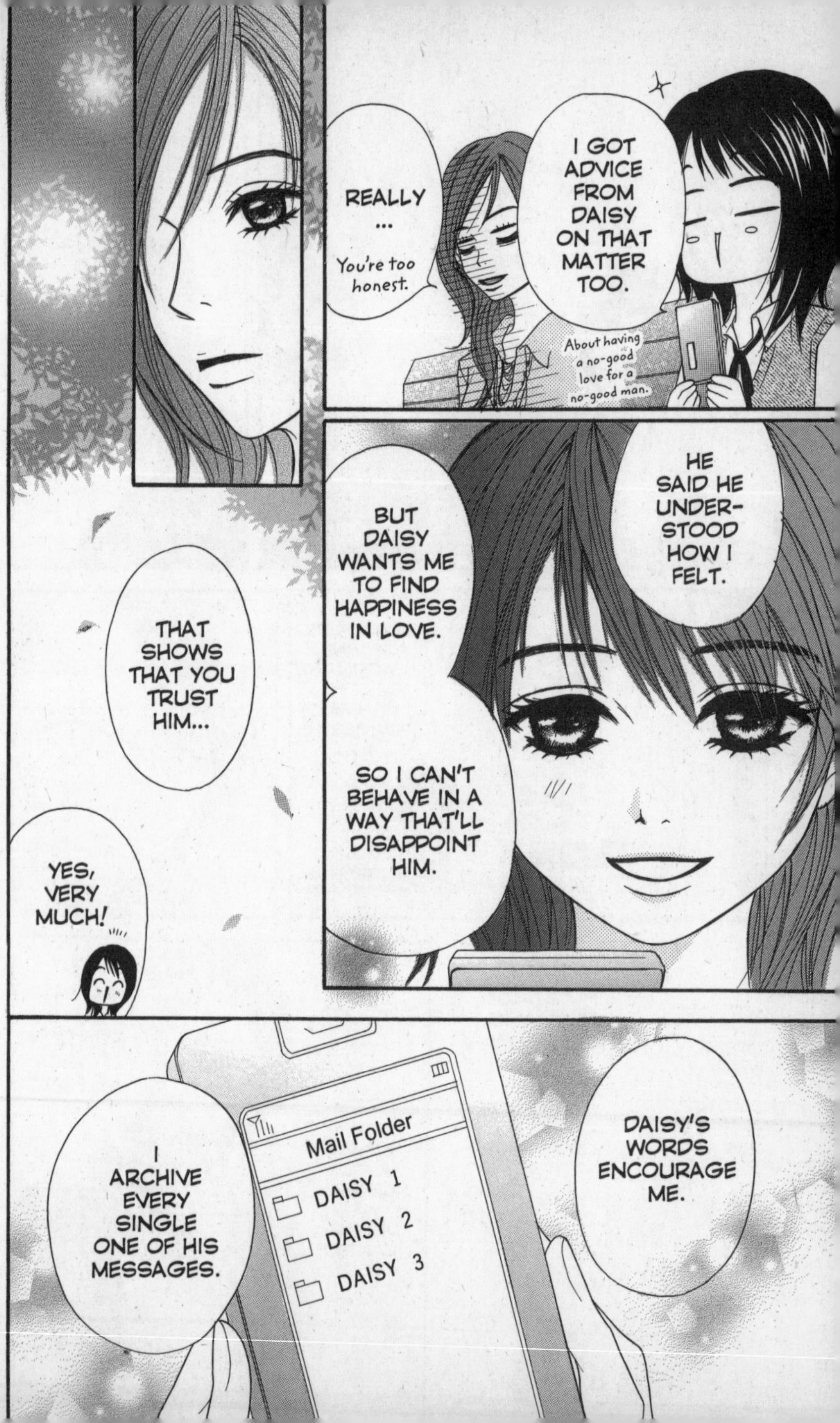
I GOT ADVICE FROM DAISY ON THAT MATTER TOO.
About having a no-good love for a no-good man.
REALLY ...
You're too honest.
HE SAID HE UNDER-STOOD HOW I FELT.
BUT DAISY WANTS ME TO FIND HAPPINESS IN LOVE.
SO I CAN'T BEHAVE IN A WAY THAT'LL DISAPPOINT HIM.
THAT SHOWS THAT YOU TRUST HIM...
YES, VERY MUCH!
DAISY'S WORDS ENCOURAGE ME.
Mail Folder
DAISY 1
DAISY 2
DAISY 3
I ARCHIVE EVERY SINGLE ONE OF HIS MESSAGES.

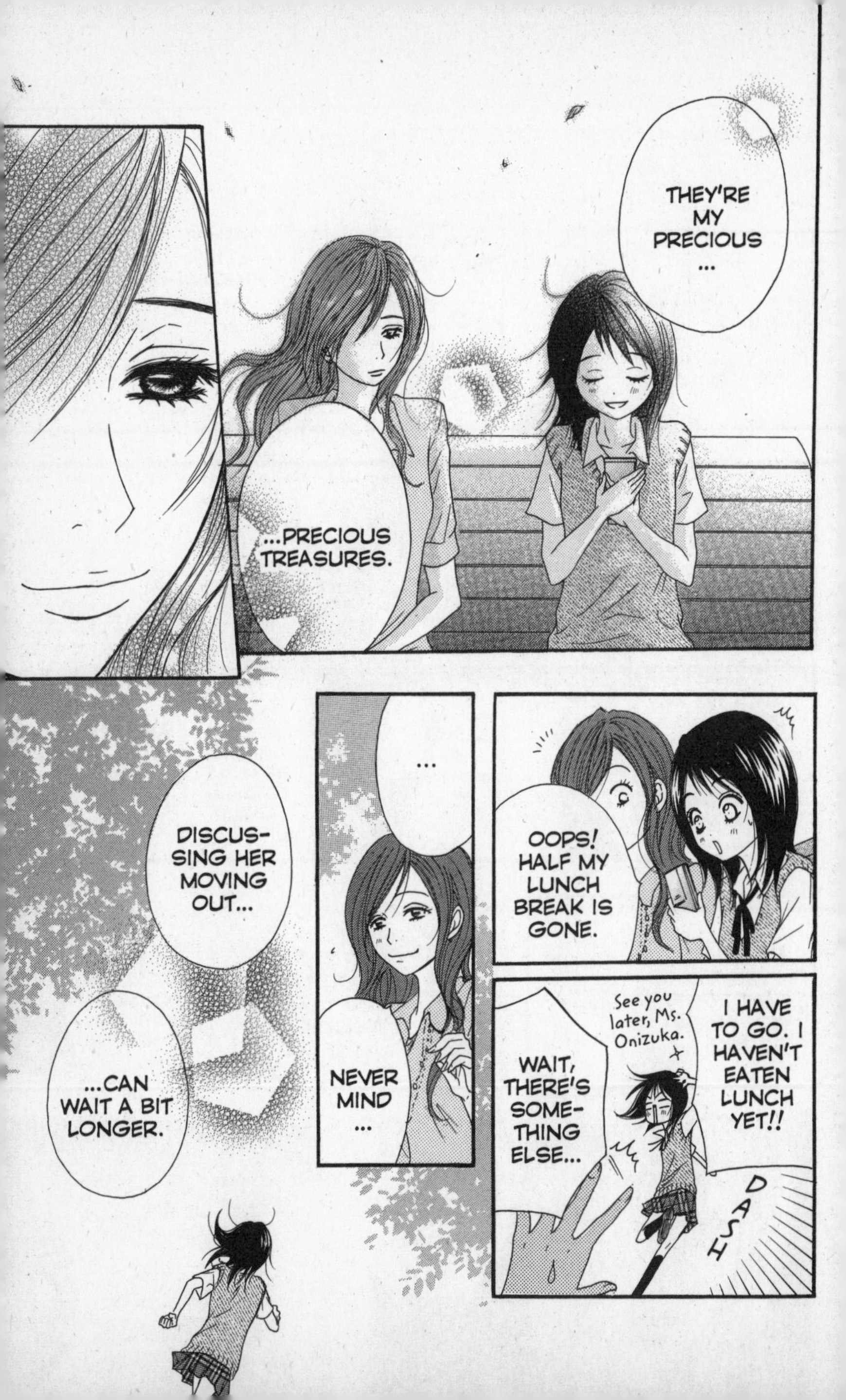
THEY'RE MY PRECIOUS ...
...PRECIOUS TREASURES.
OOPS! HALF MY LUNCH BREAK IS GONE.
I HAVE TO GO. I HAVEN'T EATEN LUNCH YET!!
See you later, Ms. Onizuka.
WAIT, THERE'S SOME-THING ELSE...
DASH
...
NEVER MIND ...
DISCUS-SING HER MOVING OUT...
...CAN WAIT A BIT LONGER.

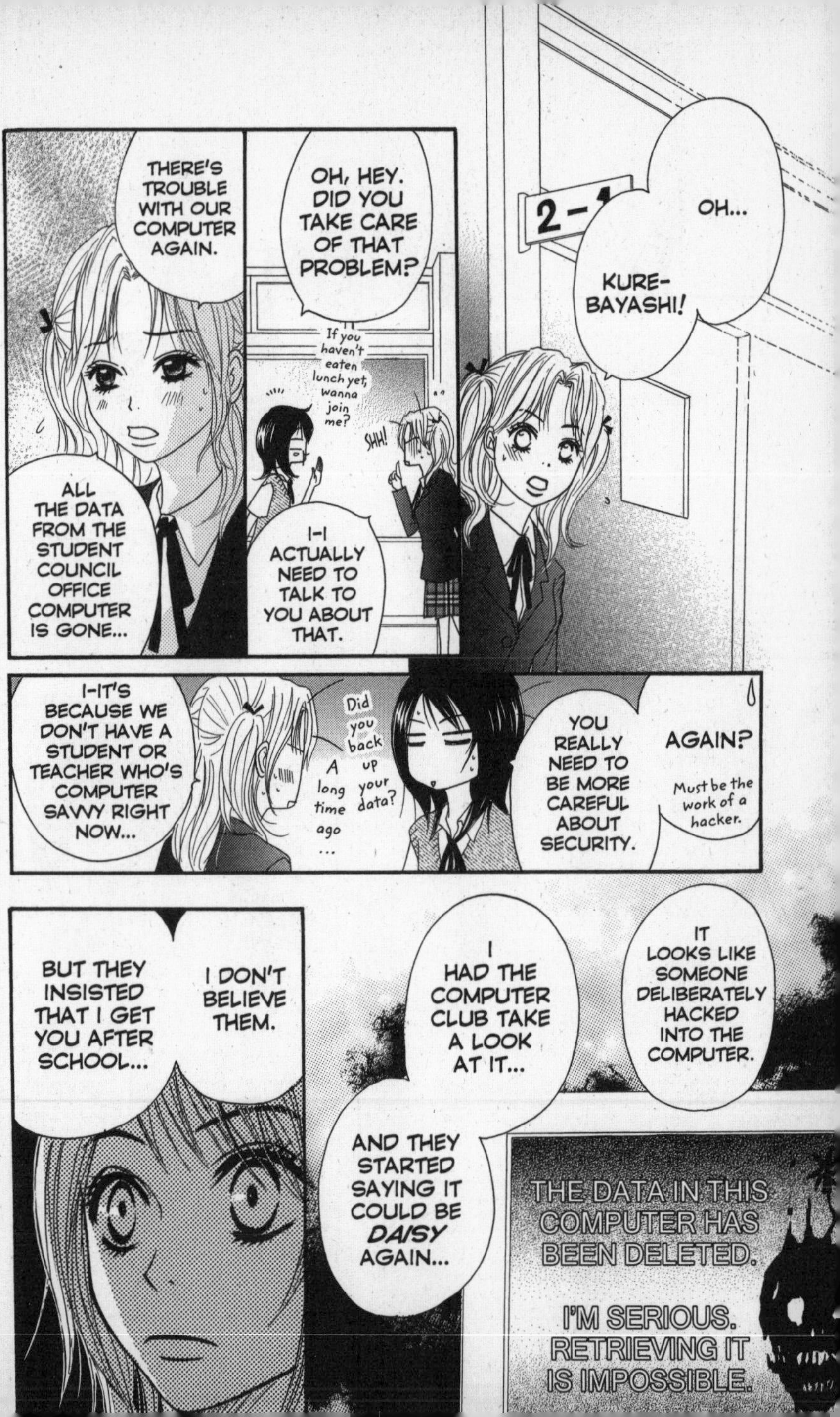
2-1
OH...
KURE-BAYASHI!
OH, HEY. DID YOU TAKE CARE OF THAT PROBLEM?
If you haven't eaten lunch yet, wanna join me?
SHH!
I-I ACTUALLY NEED TO TALK TO YOU ABOUT THAT.
THERE'S TROUBLE WITH OUR COMPUTER AGAIN.
ALL THE DATA FROM THE STUDENT COUNCIL OFFICE COMPUTER IS GONE...
AGAIN?
Must be the work of a hacker.
YOU REALLY NEED TO BE MORE CAREFUL ABOUT SECURITY.
Did you back up your data?
A long time ago...
I-IT'S BECAUSE WE DON'T HAVE A STUDENT OR TEACHER WHO'S COMPUTER SAVVY RIGHT NOW...
IT LOOKS LIKE SOMEONE DELIBERATELY HACKED INTO THE COMPUTER.
I HAD THE COMPUTER CLUB TAKE A LOOK AT IT...
AND THEY STARTED SAYING IT COULD BE *DAISY* AGAIN...
THE DATA IN THIS COMPUTER HAS BEEN DELETED.
I'M SERIOUS. RETRIEVING IT IS IMPOSSIBLE.
I DON'T BELIEVE THEM.
BUT THEY INSISTED THAT I GET YOU AFTER SCHOOL...

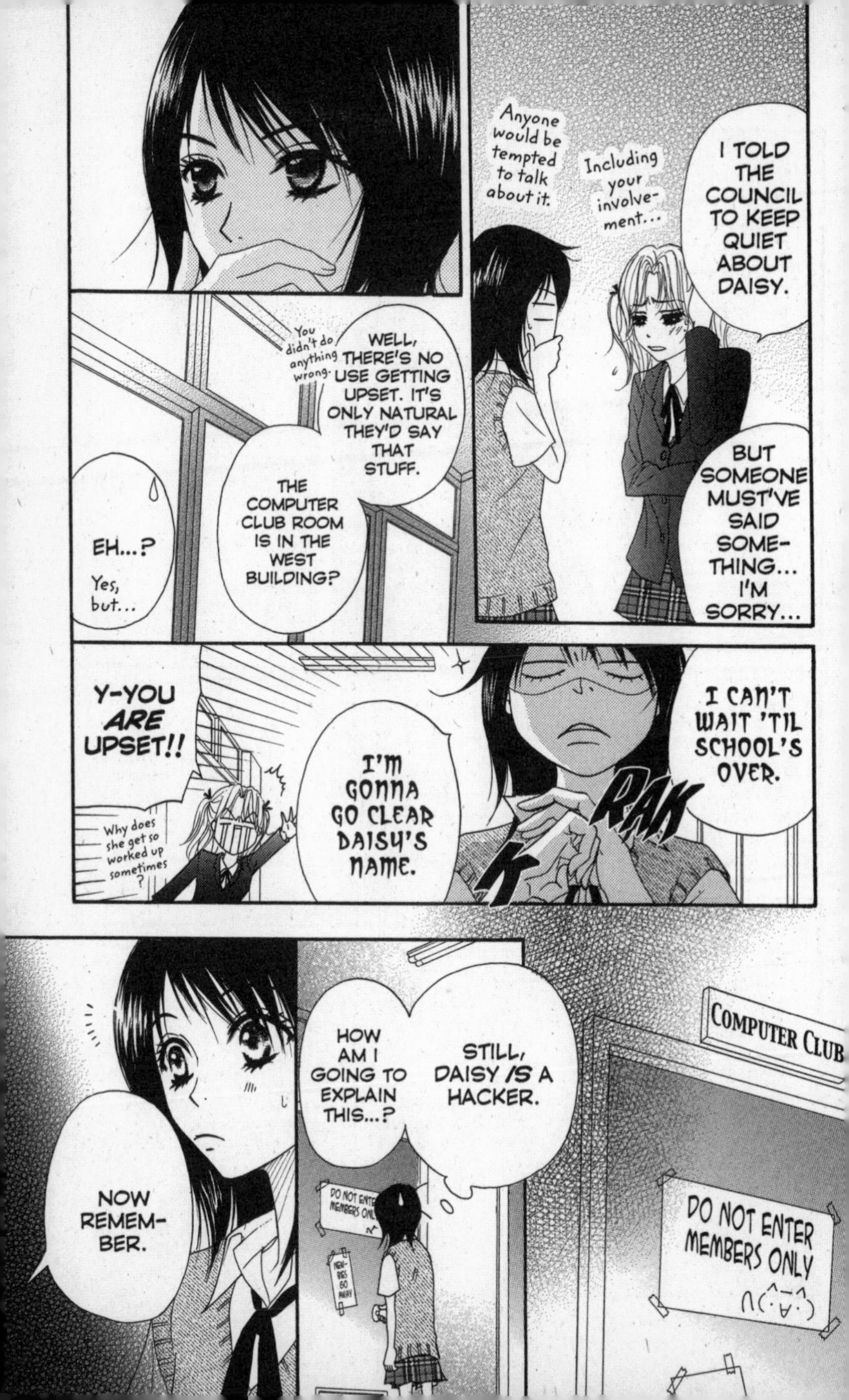
I TOLD THE COUNCIL TO KEEP QUIET ABOUT DAISY.
BUT SOMEONE MUST'VE SAID SOMETHING... I'M SORRY...
Including your involvement...
Anyone would be tempted to talk about it.
WELL, THERE'S NO USE GETTING UPSET. IT'S ONLY NATURAL THEY'D SAY THAT STUFF.
You didn't do anything wrong.
THE COMPUTER CLUB ROOM IS IN THE WEST BUILDING?
EH...?
Yes, but...
I CAN'T WAIT 'TIL SCHOOL'S OVER.
KRAK
I'M GONNA GO CLEAR DAISY'S NAME.
Y-YOU ARE UPSET!!
Why does she get so worked up sometimes?
COMPUTER CLUB
STILL, DAISY IS A HACKER.
HOW AM I GOING TO EXPLAIN THIS...?
DO NOT ENTER MEMBERS ONLY
NOW REMEMBER.

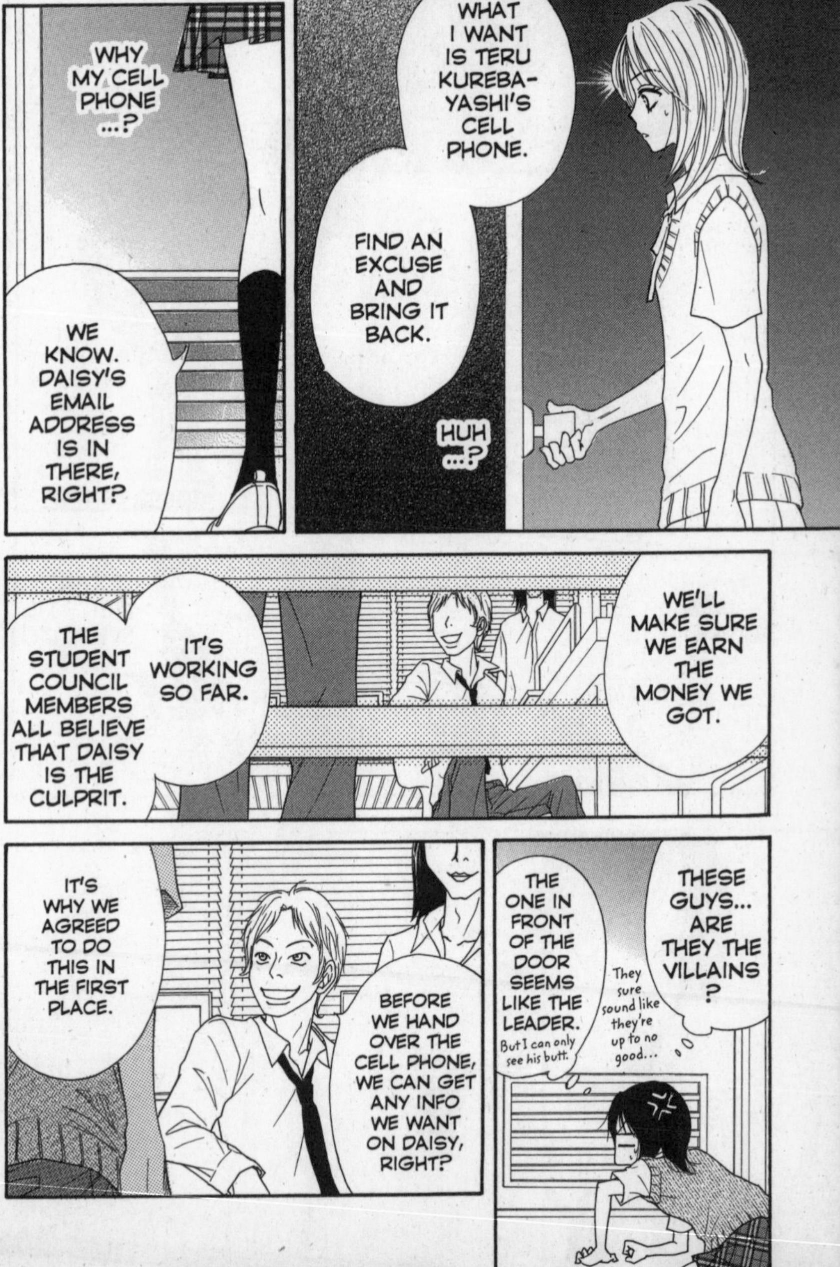
WHAT I WANT IS TERU KUREBAYASHI'S CELL PHONE.
FIND AN EXCUSE AND BRING IT BACK.
HUH...?
WHY MY CELL PHONE...?
WE KNOW. DAISY'S EMAIL ADDRESS IS IN THERE, RIGHT?
WE'LL MAKE SURE WE EARN THE MONEY WE GOT.
IT'S WORKING SO FAR.
THE STUDENT COUNCIL MEMBERS ALL BELIEVE THAT DAISY IS THE CULPRIT.
THESE GUYS... ARE THEY THE VILLAINS?
They sure sound like they're up to no good...
THE ONE IN FRONT OF THE DOOR SEEMS LIKE THE LEADER.
But I can only see his butt.
BEFORE WE HAND OVER THE CELL PHONE, WE CAN GET ANY INFO WE WANT ON DAISY, RIGHT?
IT'S WHY WE AGREED TO DO THIS IN THE FIRST PLACE.

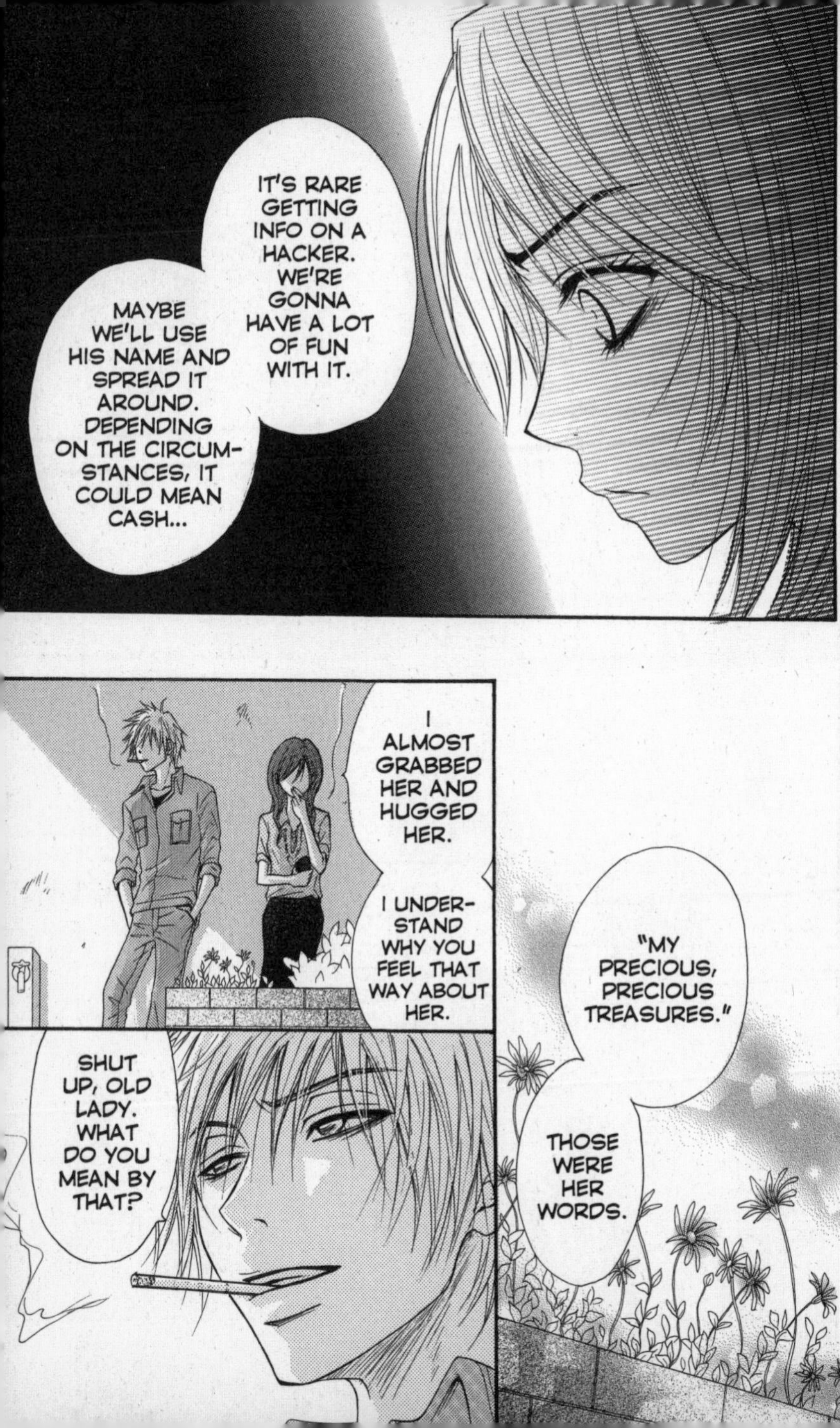
IT'S RARE GETTING INFO ON A HACKER. WE'RE GONNA HAVE A LOT OF FUN WITH IT.
MAYBE WE'LL USE HIS NAME AND SPREAD IT AROUND. DEPENDING ON THE CIRCUMSTANCES, IT COULD MEAN CASH...
"MY PRECIOUS, PRECIOUS TREASURES."
THOSE WERE HER WORDS.
I ALMOST GRABBED HER AND HUGGED HER.
I UNDERSTAND WHY YOU FEEL THAT WAY ABOUT HER.
SHUT UP, OLD LADY. WHAT DO YOU MEAN BY THAT?

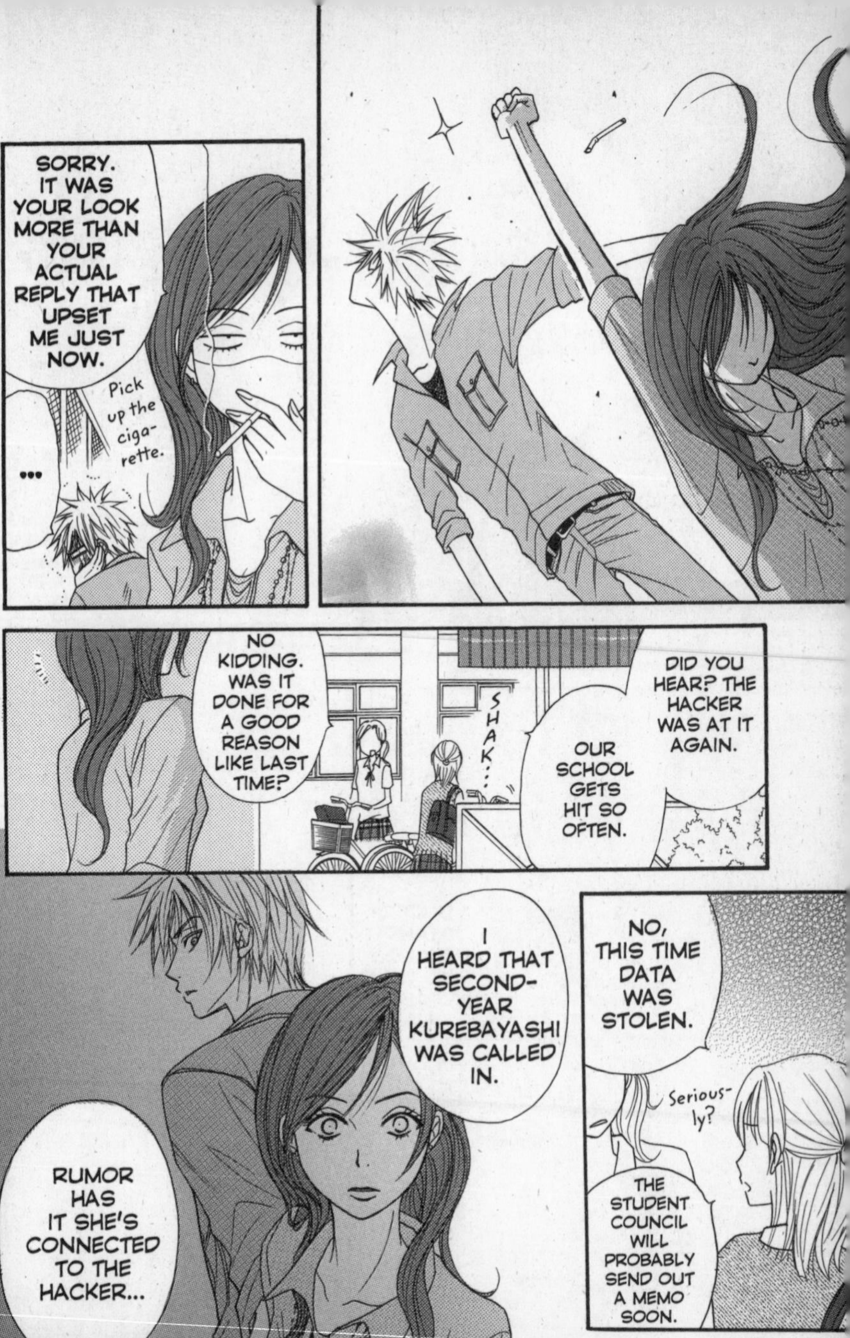
SORRY. IT WAS YOUR LOOK MORE THAN YOUR ACTUAL REPLY THAT UPSET ME JUST NOW.
Pick up the ciga-rette.
...
DID YOU HEAR? THE HACKER WAS AT IT AGAIN.
OUR SCHOOL GETS HIT SO OFTEN.
SHAK...
NO KIDDING. WAS IT DONE FOR A GOOD REASON LIKE LAST TIME?
NO, THIS TIME DATA WAS STOLEN.
Serious-ly?
THE STUDENT COUNCIL WILL PROBABLY SEND OUT A MEMO SOON.
I HEARD THAT SECOND-YEAR KUREBAYASHI WAS CALLED IN.
RUMOR HAS IT SHE'S CONNECTED TO THE HACKER...

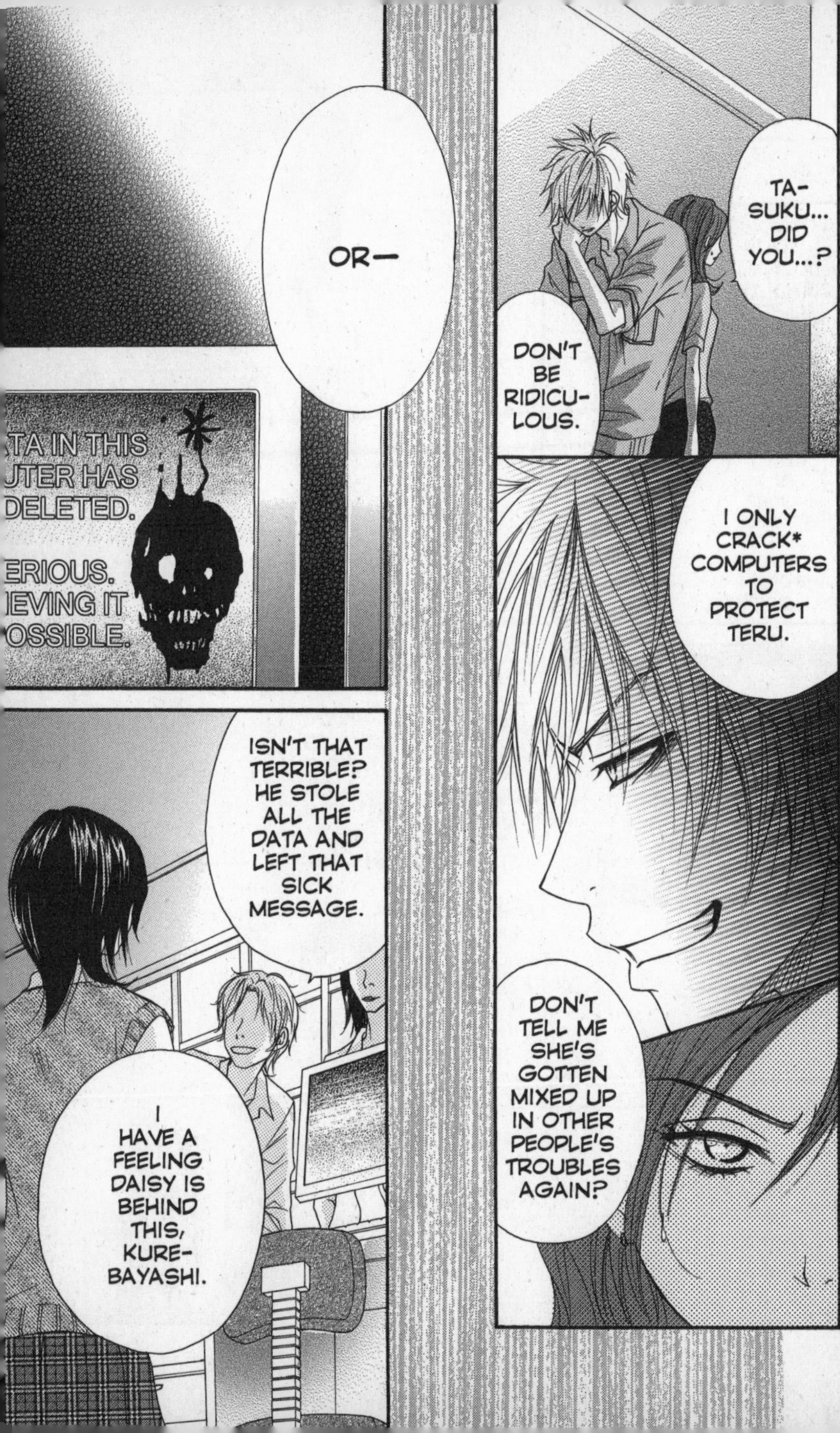
TA-SUKU... DID YOU...?
DON'T BE RIDICULOUS.
I ONLY CRACK* COMPUTERS TO PROTECT TERU.
DON'T TELL ME SHE'S GOTTEN MIXED UP IN OTHER PEOPLE'S TROUBLES AGAIN?
OR—
TA IN THIS
UTER HAS
DELETED.
ERIOUS.
IEVING IT
OSSIBLE.
ISN'T THAT TERRIBLE? HE STOLE ALL THE DATA AND LEFT THAT SICK MESSAGE.
I HAVE A FEELING DAISY IS BEHIND THIS, KURE-BAYASHI.

*CRACK: TO INFILTRATE A COMPUTER SYSTEM FOR THE PURPOSE OF ALTERING AND DESTROYING DATA.

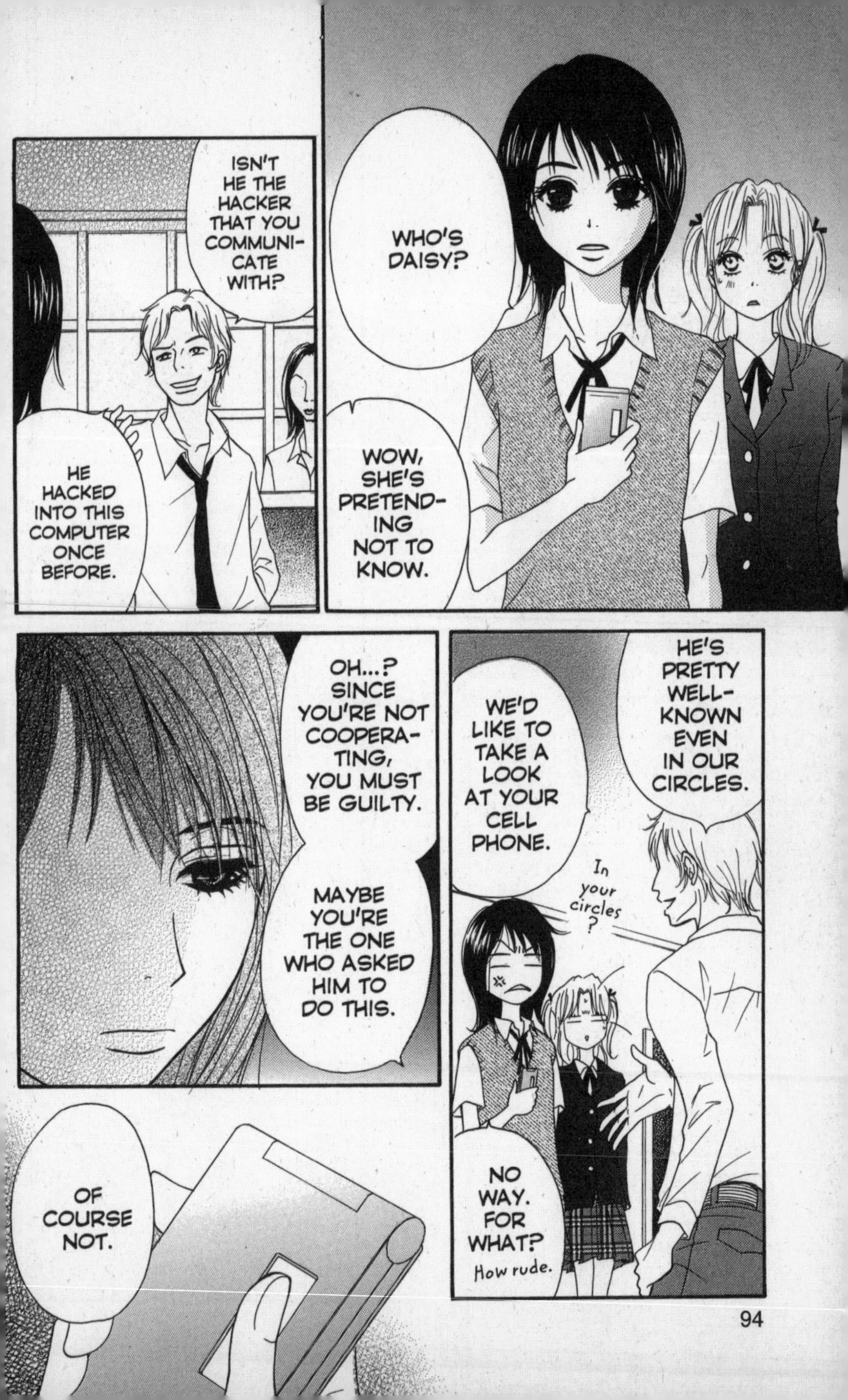
WHO'S DAISY?
WOW, SHE'S PRETENDING NOT TO KNOW.
ISN'T HE THE HACKER THAT YOU COMMUNICATE WITH?
HE HACKED INTO THIS COMPUTER ONCE BEFORE.
HE'S PRETTY WELL-KNOWN EVEN IN OUR CIRCLES.
WE'D LIKE TO TAKE A LOOK AT YOUR CELL PHONE.
In your circles?
NO WAY. FOR WHAT?
How rude.
OH...? SINCE YOU'RE NOT COOPERATING, YOU MUST BE GUILTY.
MAYBE YOU'RE THE ONE WHO ASKED HIM TO DO THIS.
OF COURSE NOT.

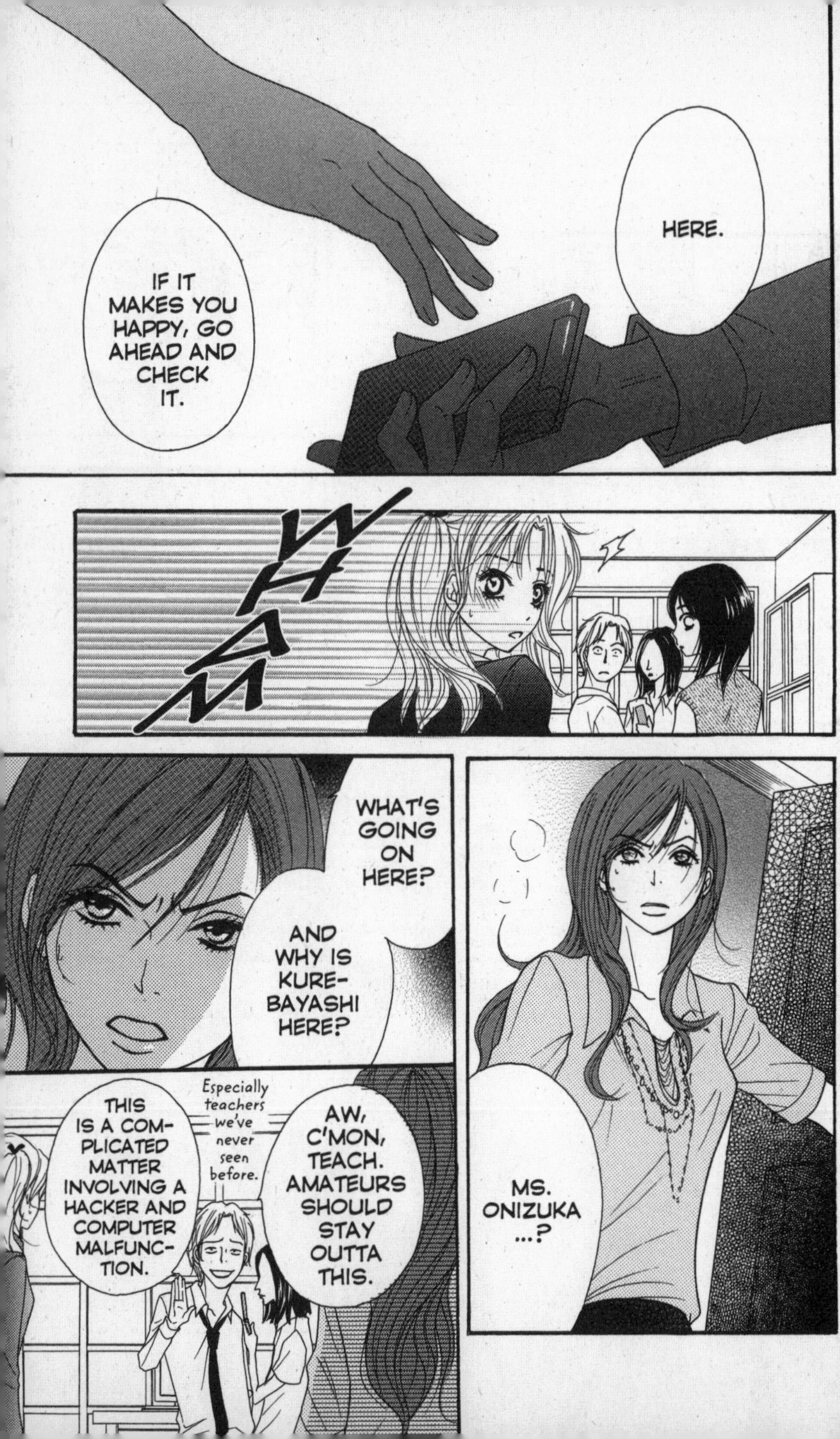
HERE.
IF IT MAKES YOU HAPPY, GO AHEAD AND CHECK IT.
WHAM
MS. ONIZUKA ...?
WHAT'S GOING ON HERE?
AND WHY IS KURE-BAYASHI HERE?
AW, C'MON, TEACH. AMATEURS SHOULD STAY OUTTA THIS.
Especially teachers we've never seen before.
THIS IS A COMPLICATED MATTER INVOLVING A HACKER AND COMPUTER MALFUNCTION.

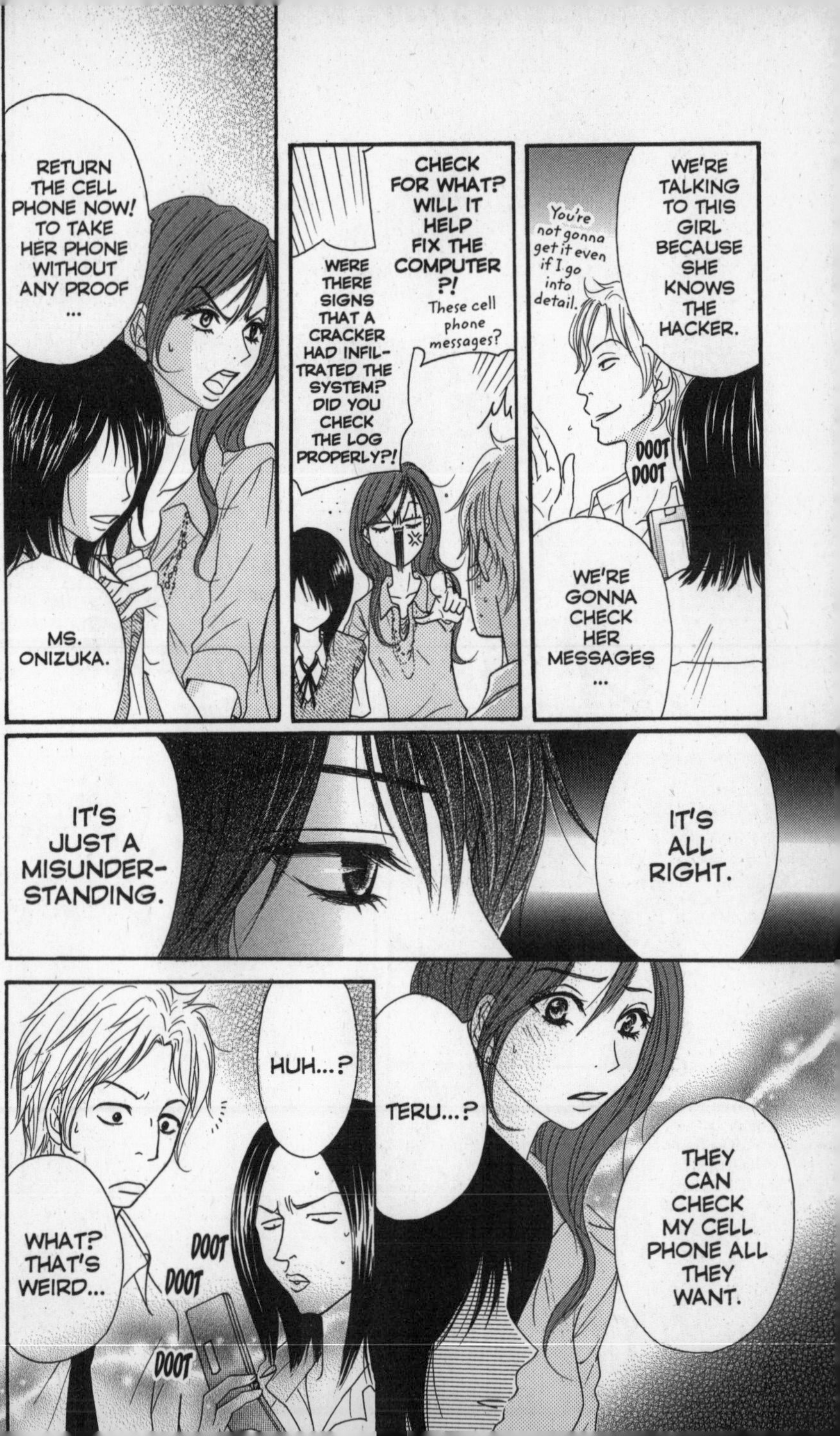
WE'RE TALKING TO THIS GIRL BECAUSE SHE KNOWS THE HACKER.
You're not gonna get it even if I go into detail.
DOOT DOOT
WE'RE GONNA CHECK HER MESSAGES ...
CHECK FOR WHAT? WILL IT HELP FIX THE COMPUTER ?!
These cell phone messages?
WERE THERE SIGNS THAT A CRACKER HAD INFILTRATED THE SYSTEM? DID YOU CHECK THE LOG PROPERLY?!
RETURN THE CELL PHONE NOW! TO TAKE HER PHONE WITHOUT ANY PROOF ...
MS. ONIZUKA.
IT'S ALL RIGHT.
IT'S JUST A MISUNDERSTANDING.
THEY CAN CHECK MY CELL PHONE ALL THEY WANT.
TERU...?
HUH...?
DOOT DOOT
DOOT
WHAT? THAT'S WEIRD...

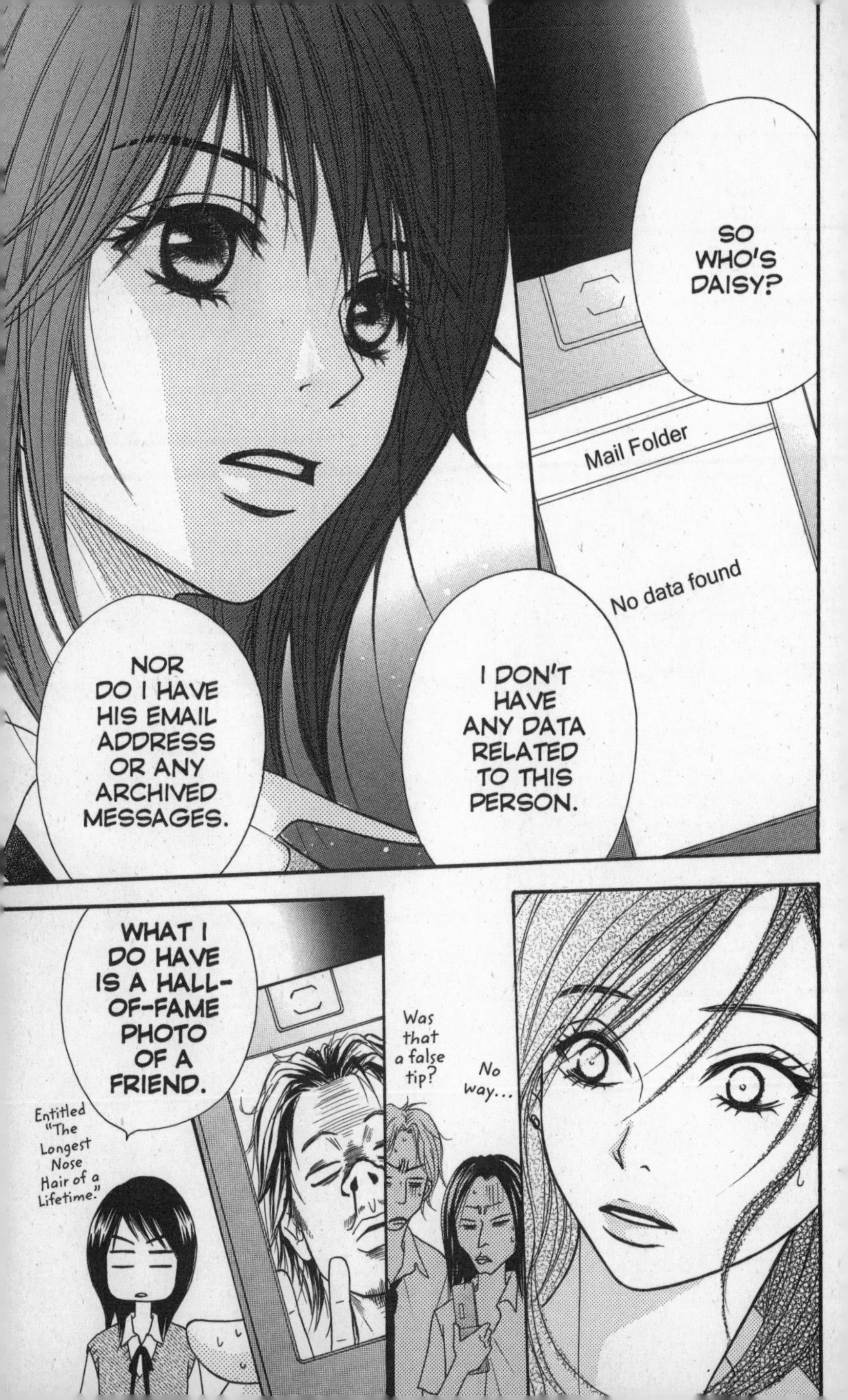
SO WHO'S DAISY?
Mail Folder
No data found
I DON'T HAVE ANY DATA RELATED TO THIS PERSON.
NOR DO I HAVE HIS EMAIL ADDRESS OR ANY ARCHIVED MESSAGES.
Was that a false tip?
No way...
WHAT I DO HAVE IS A HALL-OF-FAME PHOTO OF A FRIEND.
Entitled "The Longest Nose Hair of a Lifetime."

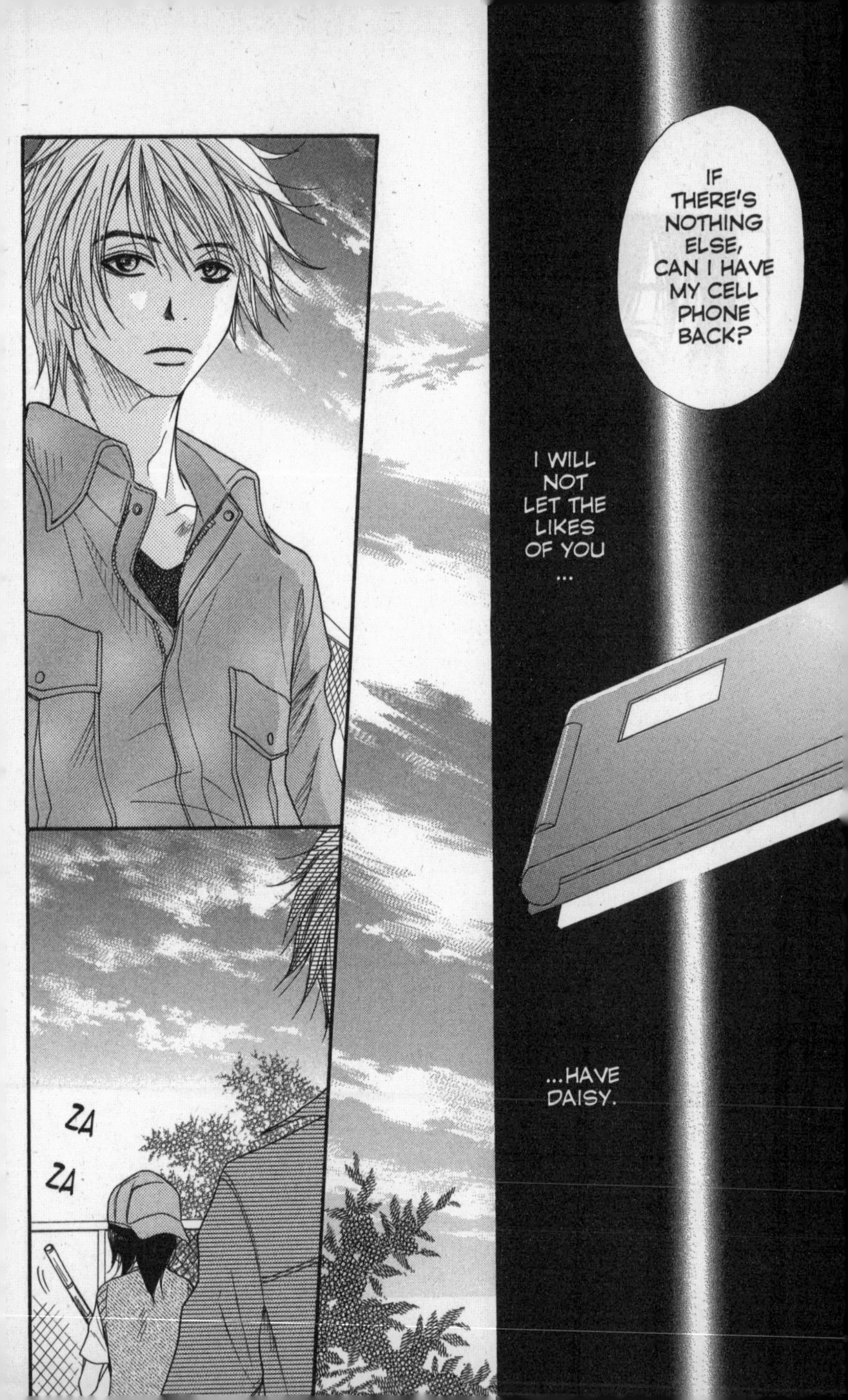
IF THERE'S NOTHING ELSE, CAN I HAVE MY CELL PHONE BACK?
I WILL NOT LET THE LIKES OF YOU ...
...HAVE DAISY.
ZA
ZA

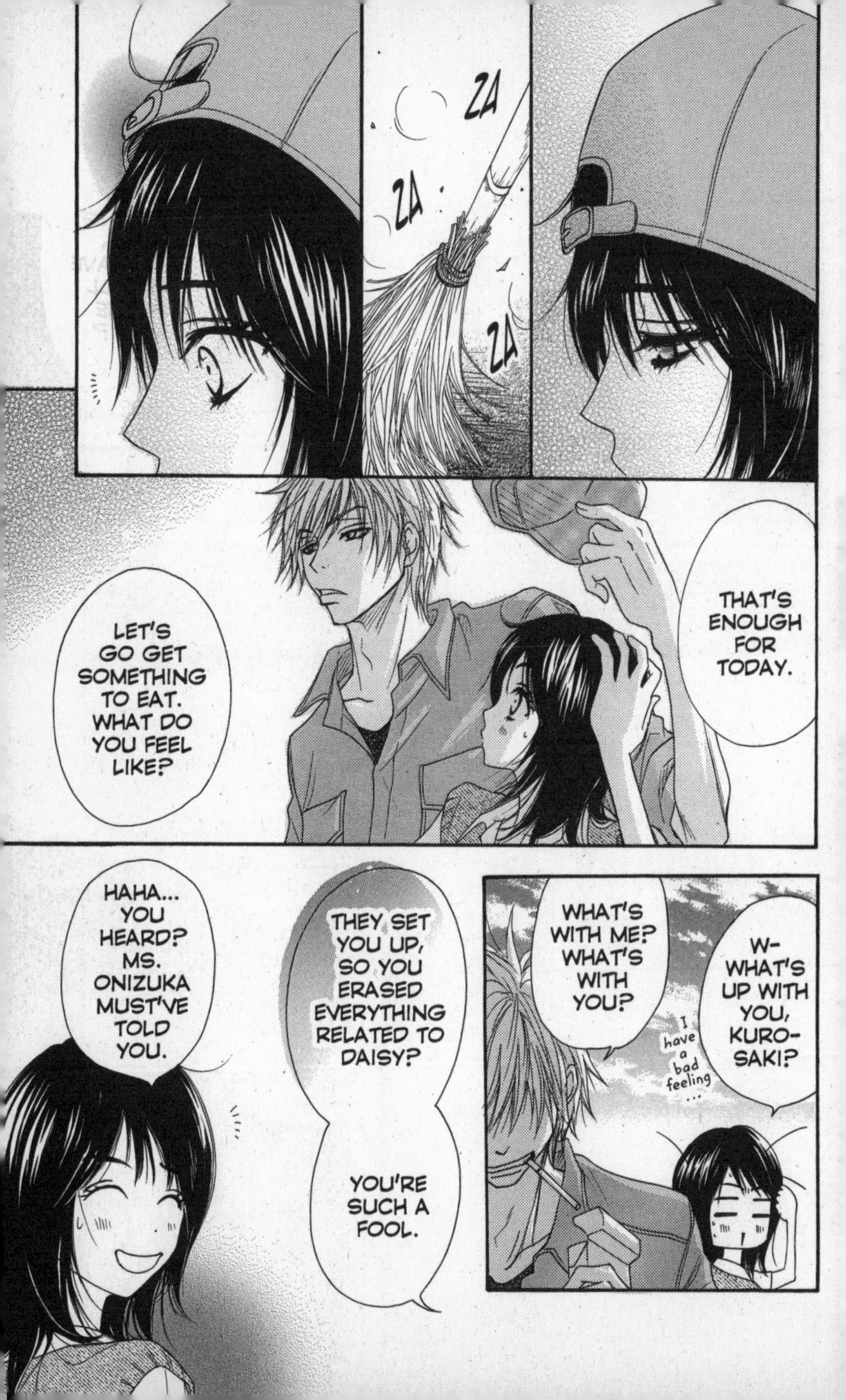

ZA
ZA
ZA
THAT'S ENOUGH FOR TODAY.
LET'S GO GET SOMETHING TO EAT. WHAT DO YOU FEEL LIKE?
W-WHAT'S UP WITH YOU, KURO-SAKI?
I have a bad feeling...
WHAT'S WITH ME? WHAT'S WITH YOU?
THEY SET YOU UP, SO YOU ERASED EVERYTHING RELATED TO DAISY?
YOU'RE SUCH A FOOL.
HAHA... YOU HEARD? MS. ONIZUKA MUST'VE TOLD YOU.

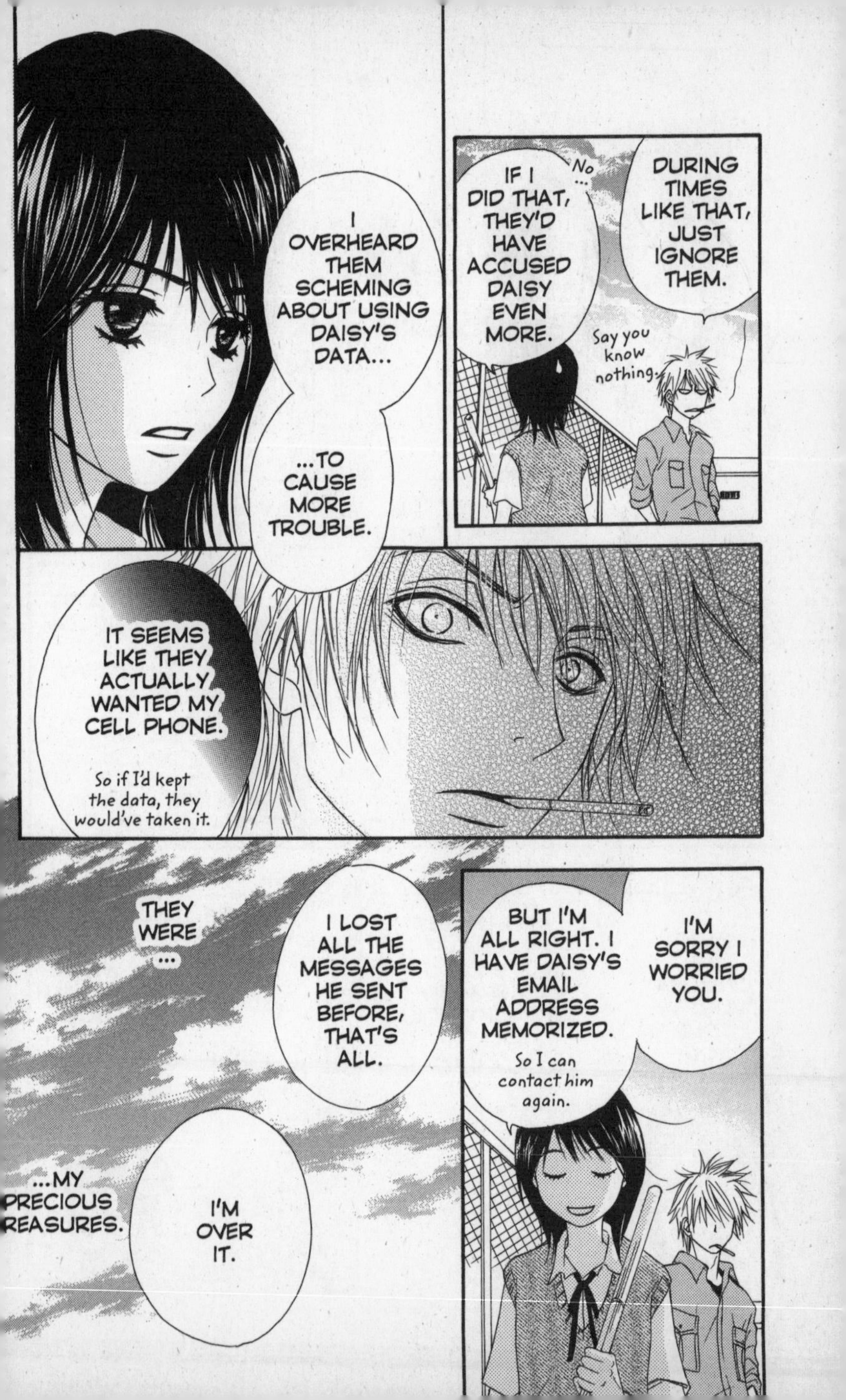
DURING TIMES LIKE THAT, JUST IGNORE THEM.
Say you know nothing.
No...
IF I DID THAT, THEY'D HAVE ACCUSED DAISY EVEN MORE.
I OVERHEARD THEM SCHEMING ABOUT USING DAISY'S DATA...
...TO CAUSE MORE TROUBLE.
IT SEEMS LIKE THEY ACTUALLY WANTED MY CELL PHONE.
So if I'd kept the data, they would've taken it.
I'M SORRY I WORRIED YOU.
BUT I'M ALL RIGHT. I HAVE DAISY'S EMAIL ADDRESS MEMORIZED.
So I can contact him again.
I LOST ALL THE MESSAGES HE SENT BEFORE, THAT'S ALL.
THEY WERE...
...MY PRECIOUS REASURES.
I'M OVER IT.

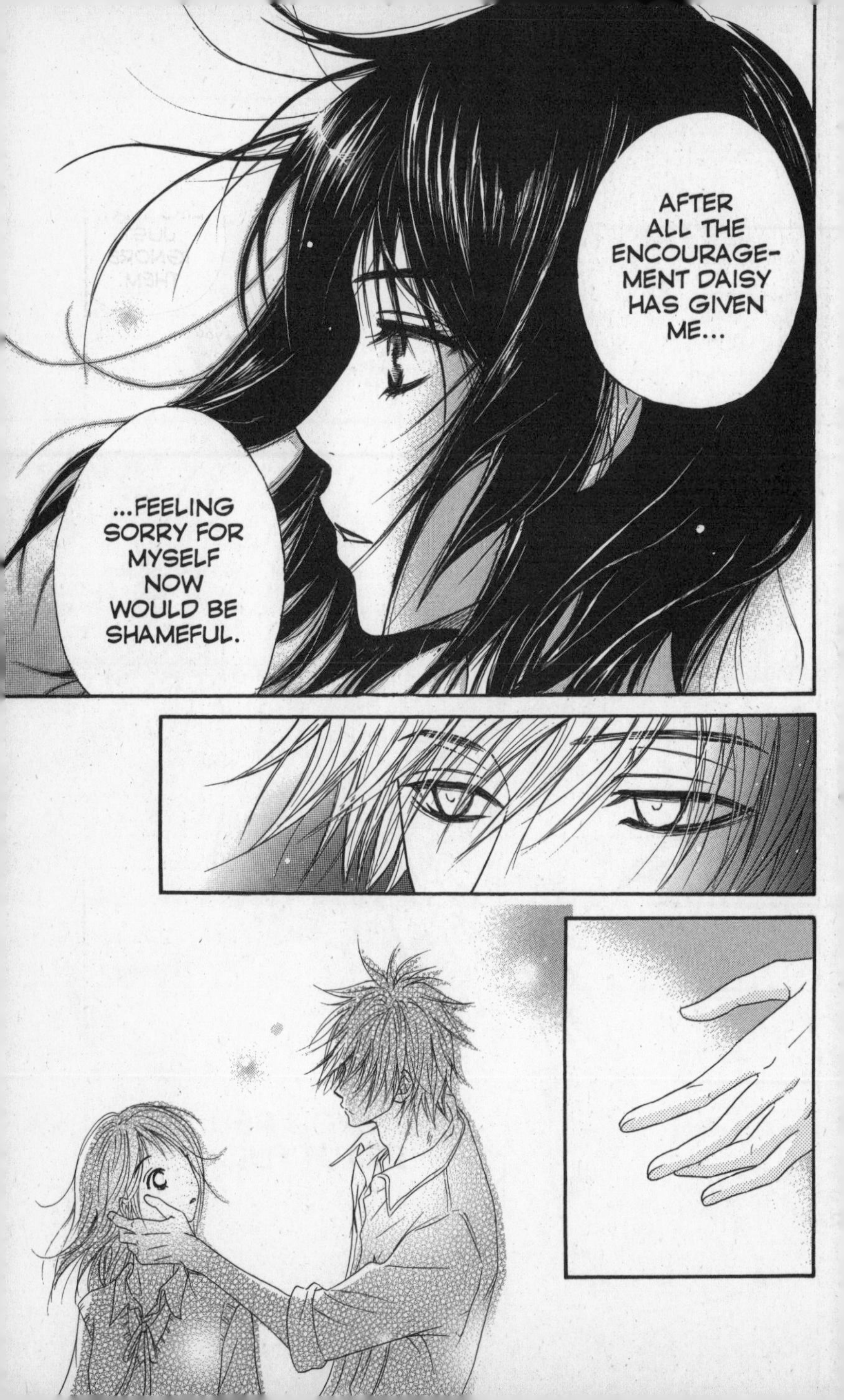
AFTER ALL THE ENCOURAGE-MENT DAISY HAS GIVEN ME...
...FEELING SORRY FOR MYSELF NOW WOULD BE SHAMEFUL.

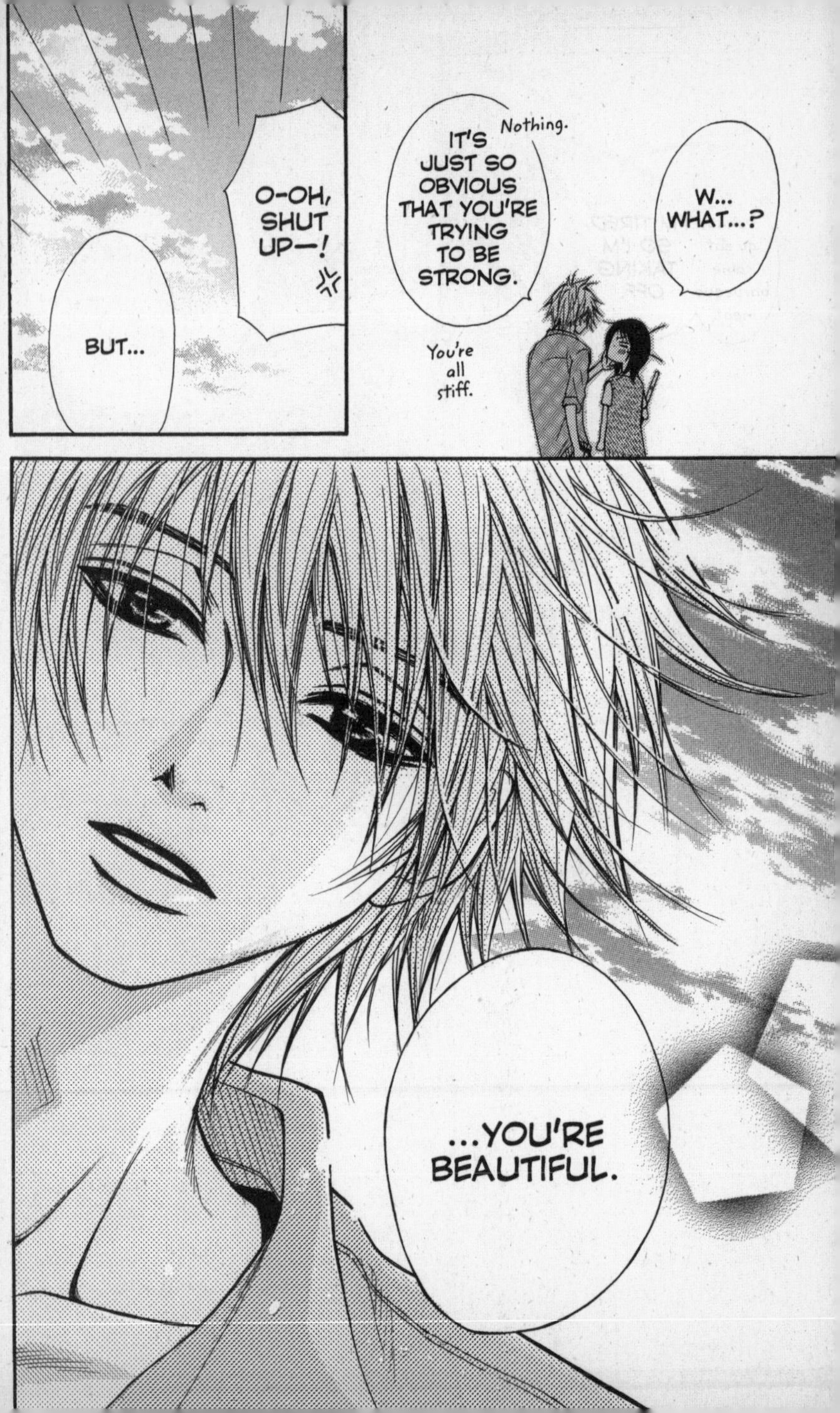
W... WHAT...?
Nothing.
IT'S JUST SO OBVIOUS THAT YOU'RE TRYING TO BE STRONG.
You're all stiff.
O-OH, SHUT UP—!
BUT...
...YOU'RE BEAUTIFUL.

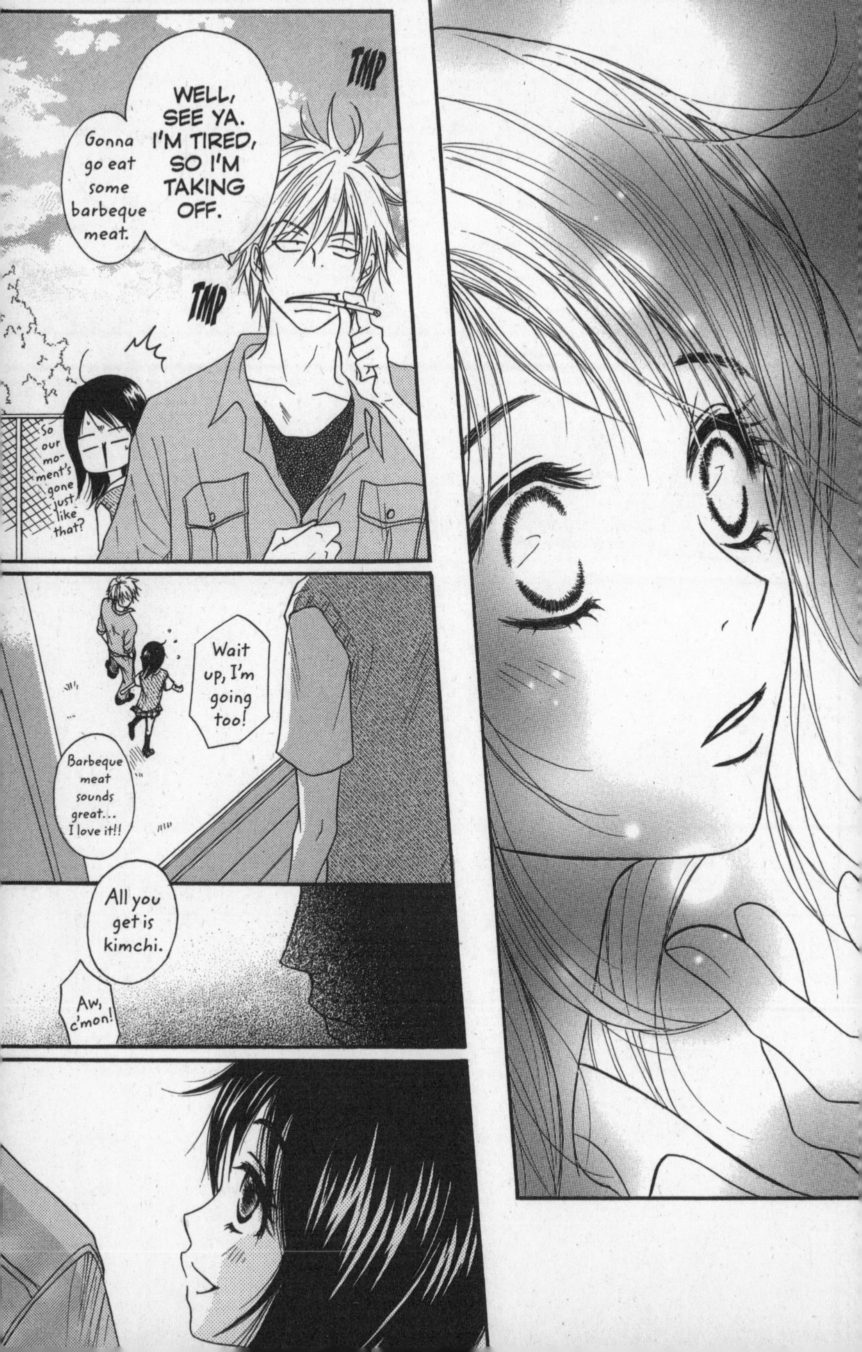
TMP
WELL, SEE YA. I'M TIRED, SO I'M TAKING OFF.
Gonna go eat some barbeque meat.
TMP
So our moment's gone just like that?
Wait up, I'm going too!
Barbeque meat sounds great... I love it!!
All you get is kimchi.
Aw, c'mon!

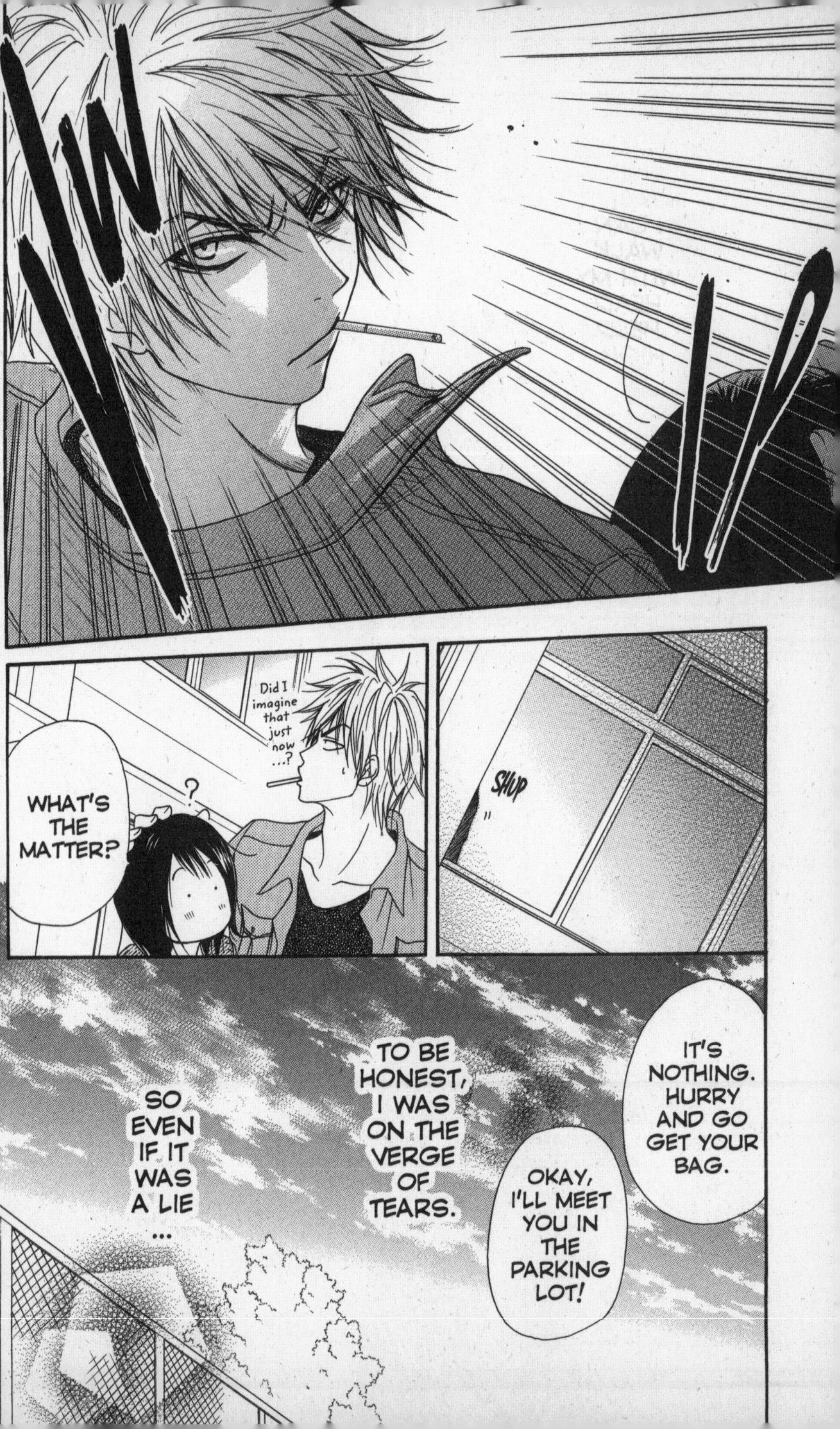
SHUP
Did I imagine that just now ...?
WHAT'S THE MATTER?
IT'S NOTHING. HURRY AND GO GET YOUR BAG.
OKAY, I'LL MEET YOU IN THE PARKING LOT!
TO BE HONEST, I WAS ON THE VERGE OF TEARS.
SO EVEN IF IT WAS A LIE ...

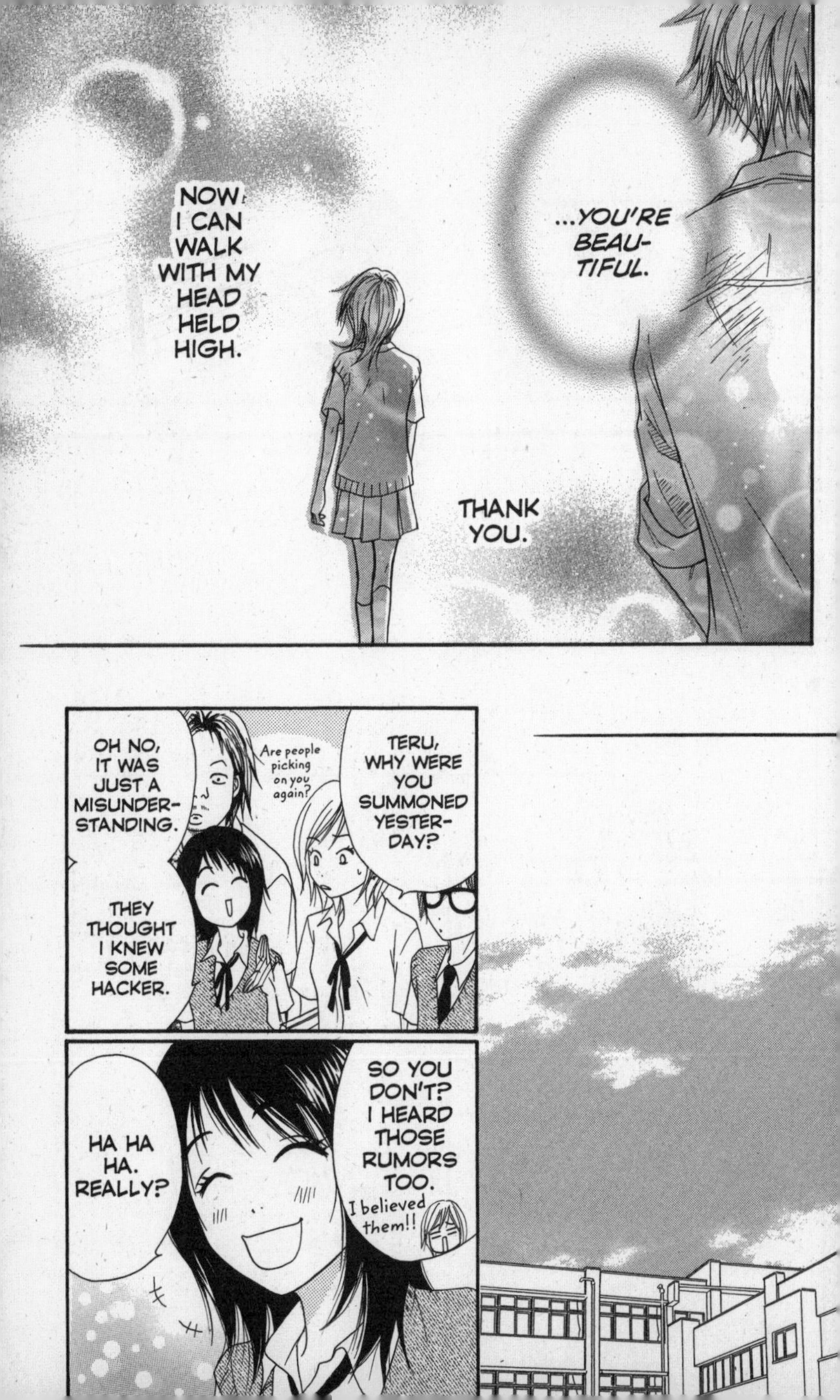
...YOU'RE BEAU-TIFUL.
NOW I CAN WALK WITH MY HEAD HELD HIGH.
THANK YOU.
TERU, WHY WERE YOU SUMMONED YESTER-DAY?
Are people picking on you again?
OH NO, IT WAS JUST A MISUNDER-STANDING.
THEY THOUGHT I KNEW SOME HACKER.
SO YOU DON'T? I HEARD THOSE RUMORS TOO.
I believed them!!
HA HA HA. REALLY?

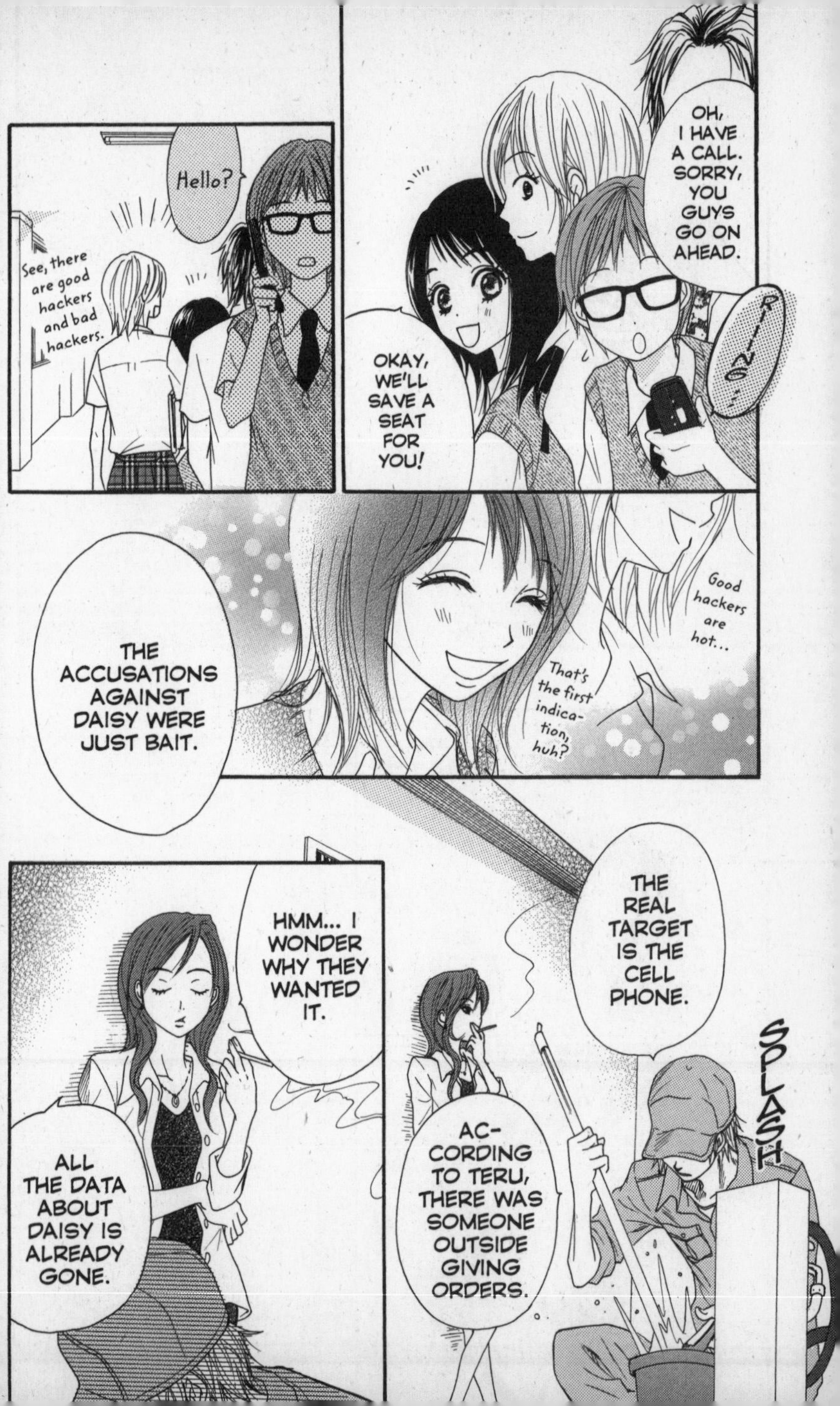
OH, I HAVE A CALL. SORRY, YOU GUYS GO ON AHEAD.
RIING..
OKAY, WE'LL SAVE A SEAT FOR YOU!
Hello?
See, there are good hackers and bad hackers.
Good hackers are hot...
That's the first indica-tion, huh?
THE ACCUSATIONS AGAINST DAISY WERE JUST BAIT.
THE REAL TARGET IS THE CELL PHONE.
SPLASH
AC-CORDING TO TERU, THERE WAS SOMEONE OUTSIDE GIVING ORDERS.
HMM... I WONDER WHY THEY WANTED IT.
ALL THE DATA ABOUT DAISY IS ALREADY GONE.

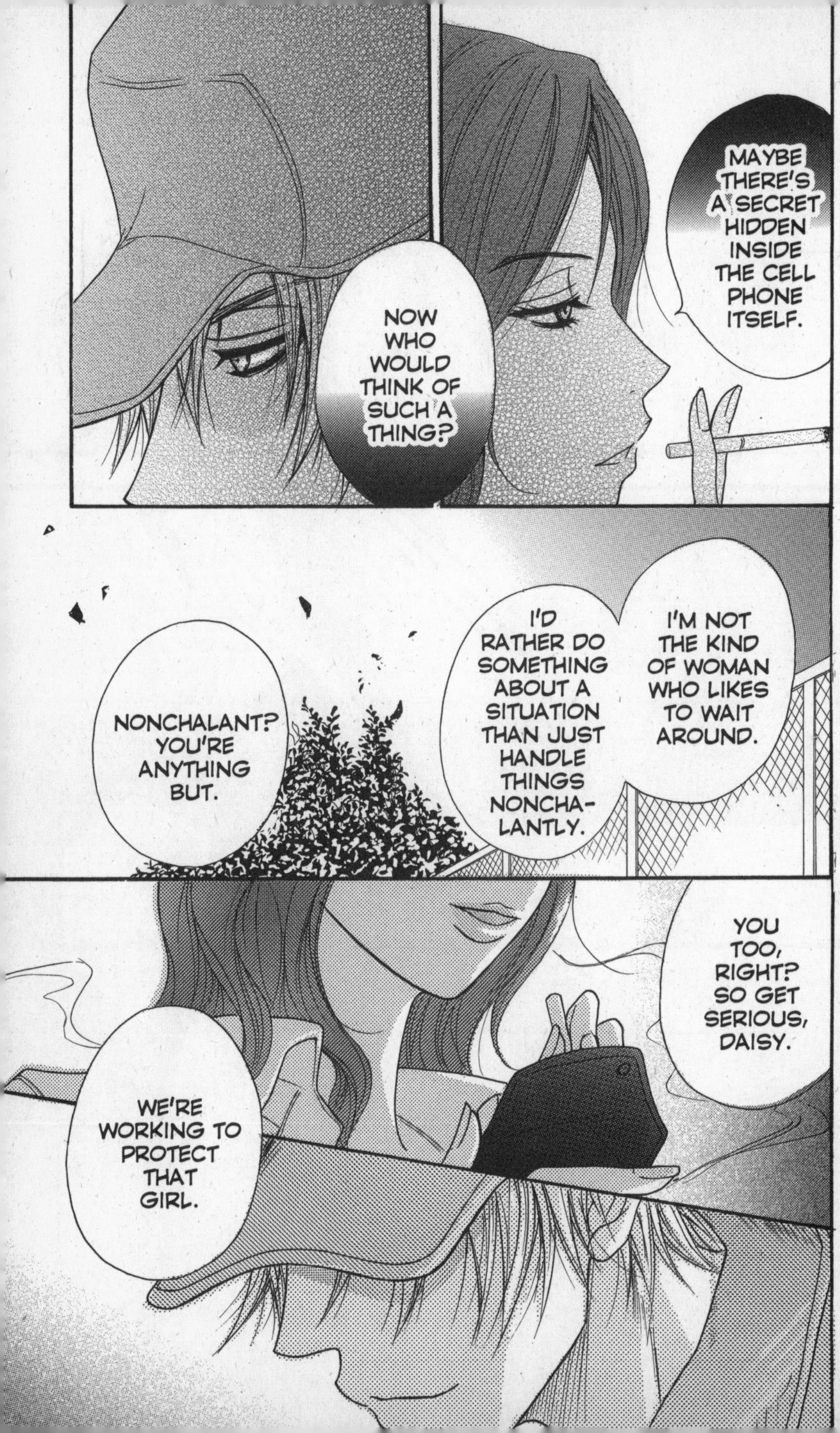
MAYBE THERE'S A SECRET HIDDEN INSIDE THE CELL PHONE ITSELF.
NOW WHO WOULD THINK OF SUCH A THING?
I'M NOT THE KIND OF WOMAN WHO LIKES TO WAIT AROUND.
I'D RATHER DO SOMETHING ABOUT A SITUATION THAN JUST HANDLE THINGS NONCHA-LANTLY.
NONCHALANT? YOU'RE ANYTHING BUT.
YOU TOO, RIGHT? SO GET SERIOUS, DAISY.
WE'RE WORKING TO PROTECT THAT GIRL.

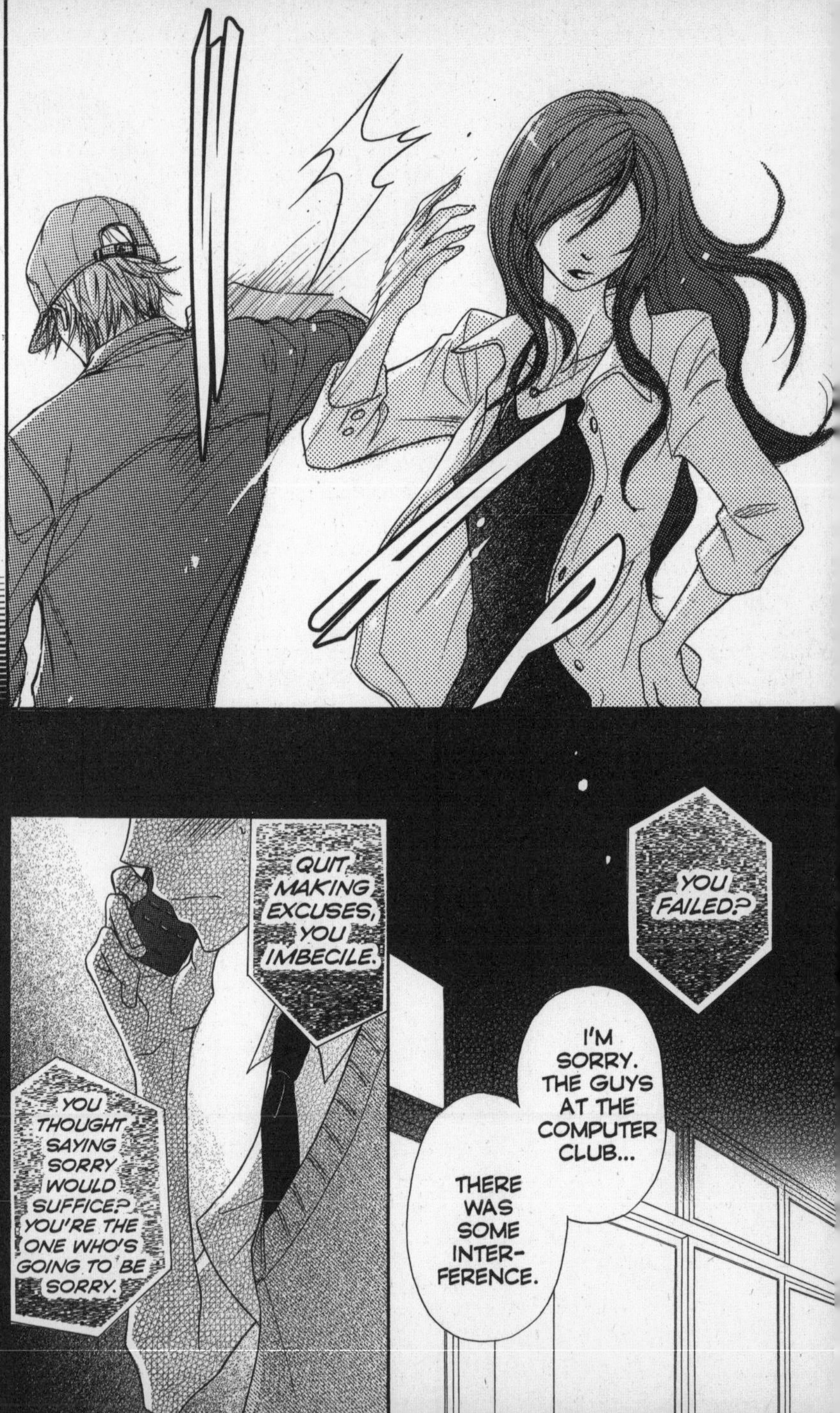
YOU FAILED?
I'M SORRY. THE GUYS AT THE COMPUTER CLUB...
THERE WAS SOME INTER-FERENCE.
QUIT MAKING EXCUSES, YOU IMBECILE.
YOU THOUGHT SAYING SORRY WOULD SUFFICE? YOU'RE THE ONE WHO'S GOING TO BE SORRY.

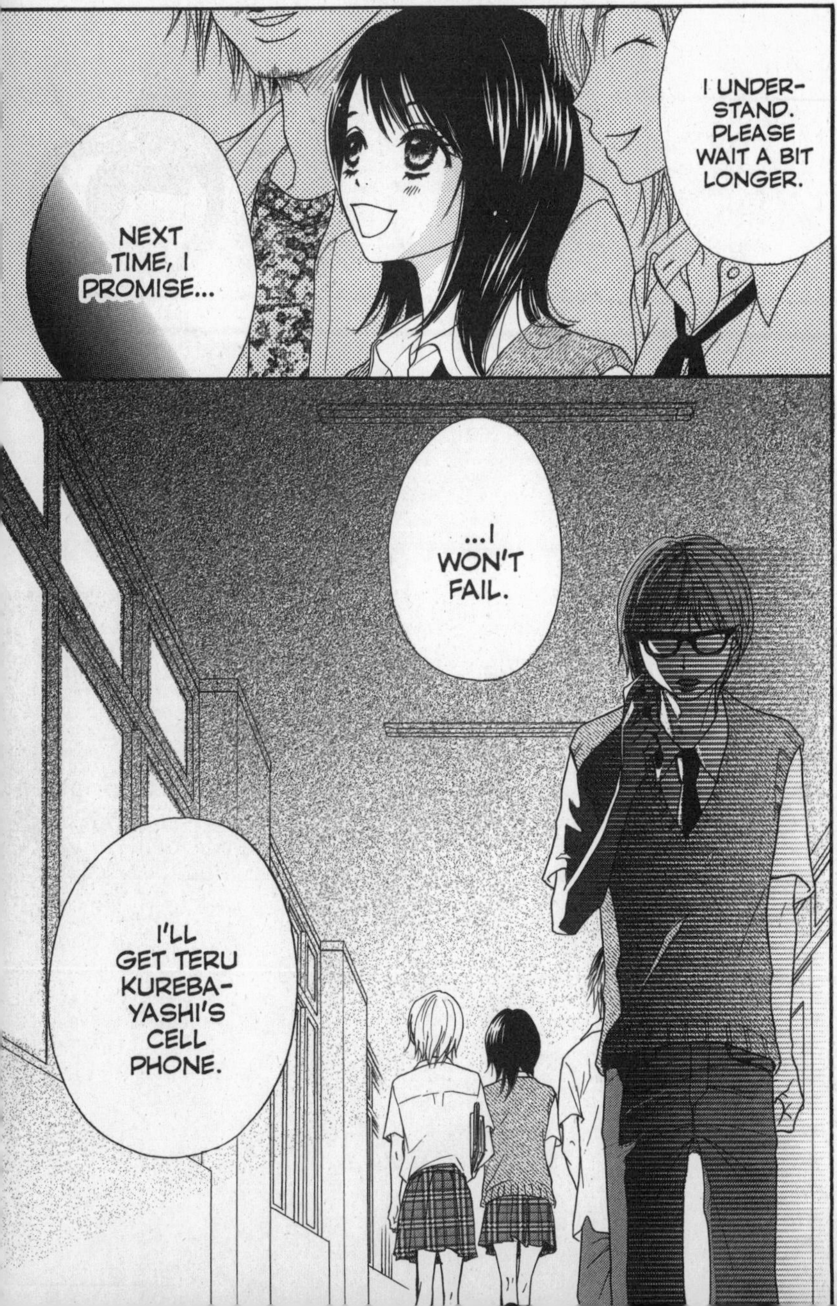
I UNDER-STAND. PLEASE WAIT A BIT LONGER.
NEXT TIME, I PROMISE...
...I WON'T FAIL.
I'LL GET TERU KUREBA-YASHI'S CELL PHONE.

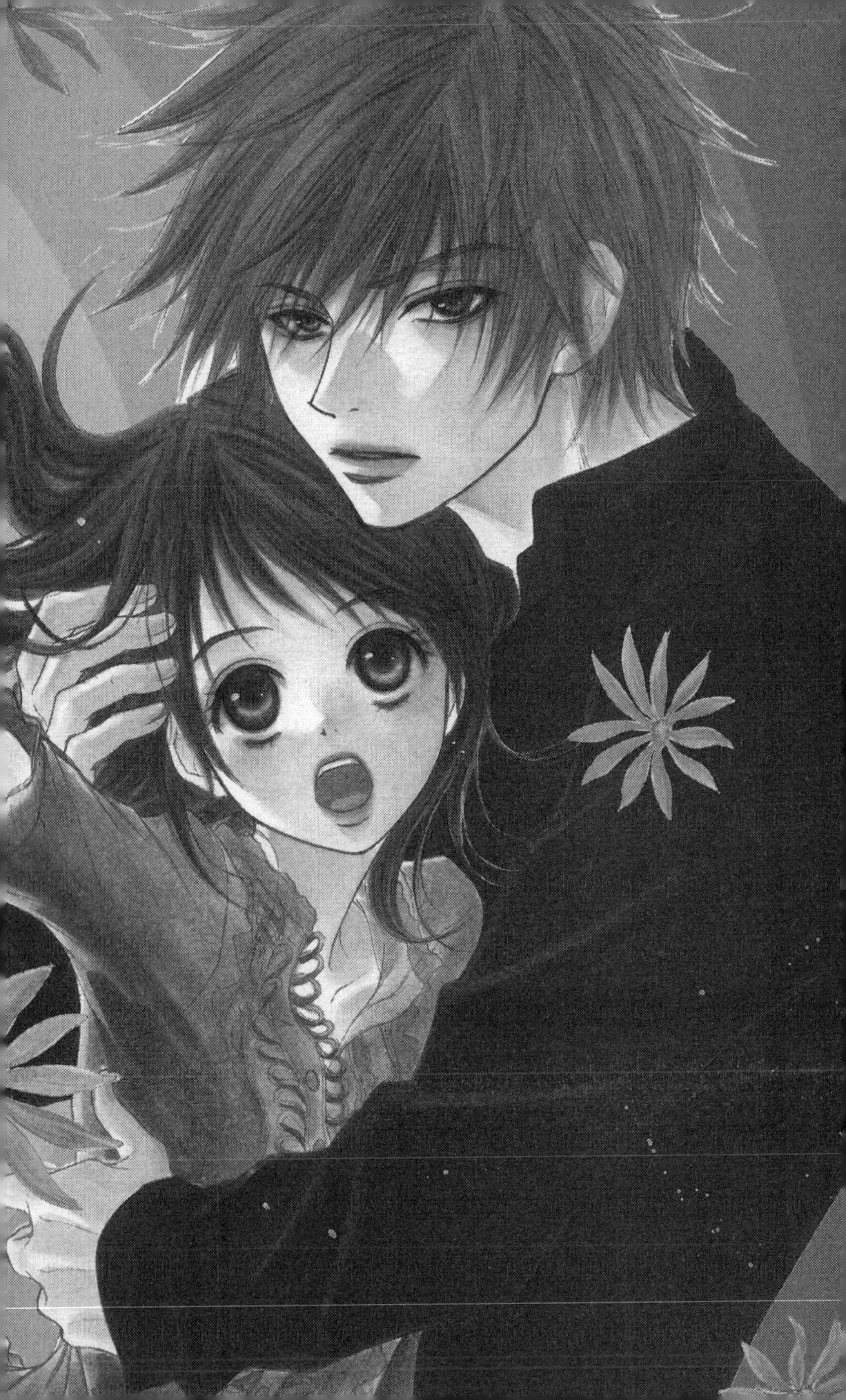

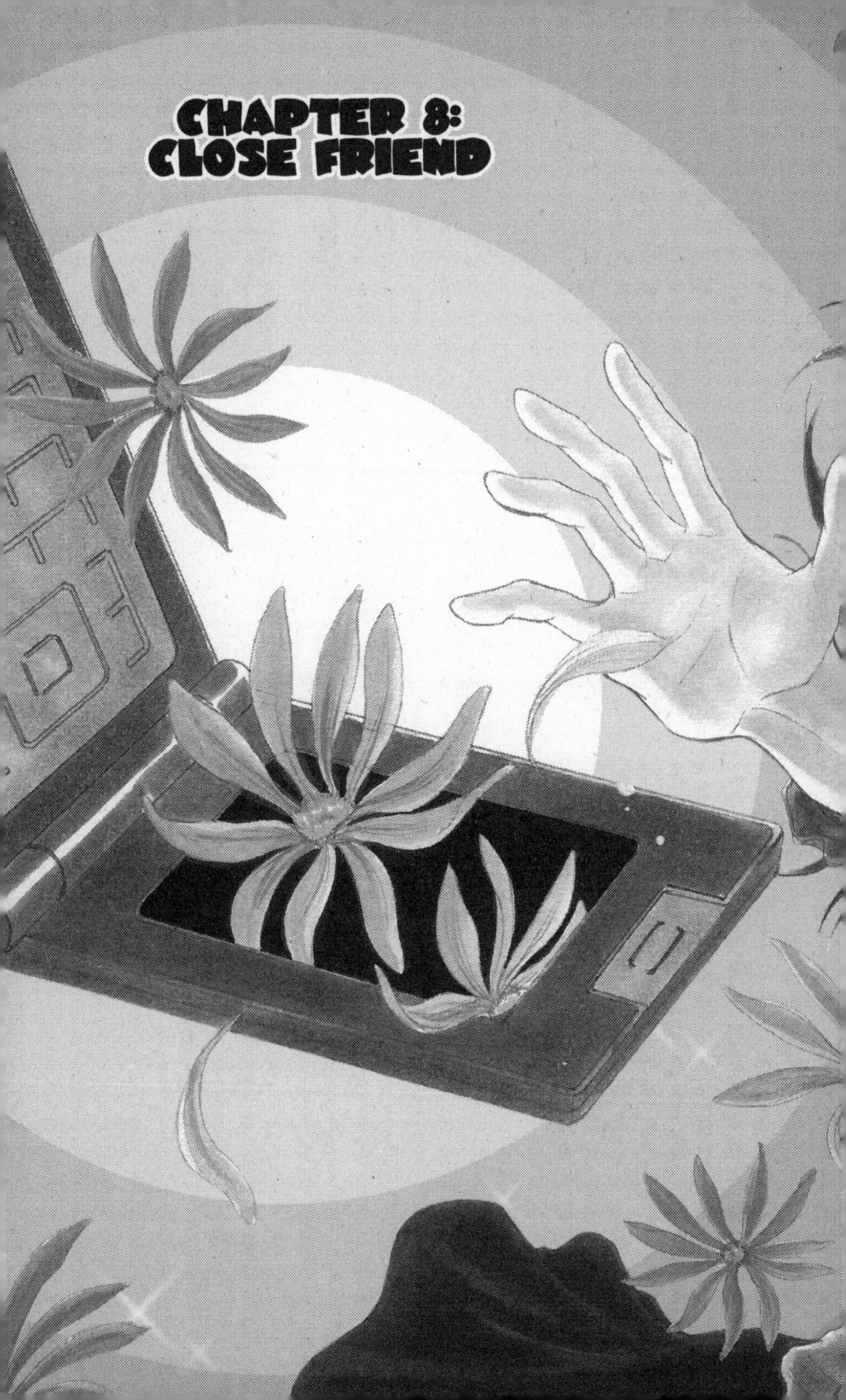
CHAPTER 8:
CLOSE FRIEND

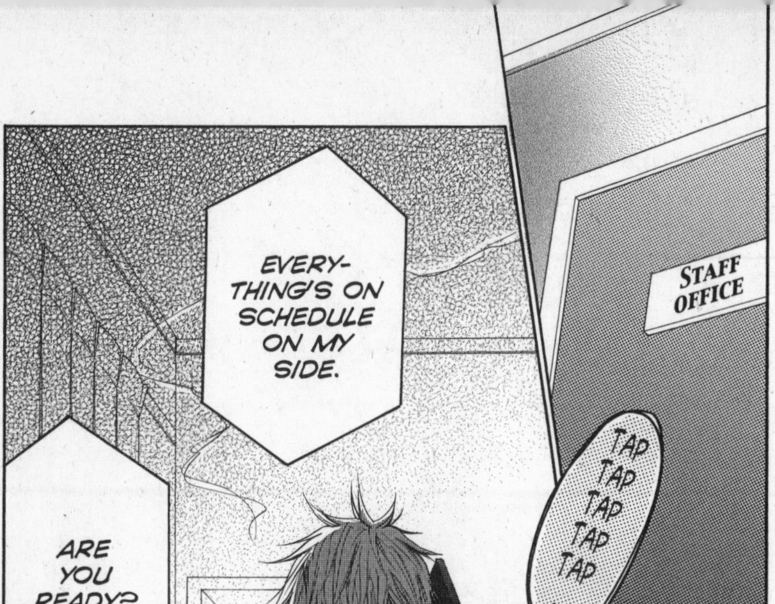
STAFF OFFICE
EVERY-THING'S ON SCHEDULE ON MY SIDE.
TAP TAP TAP TAP TAP ...
ARE YOU READY?
TAP TAP TAP TAP TAP ...

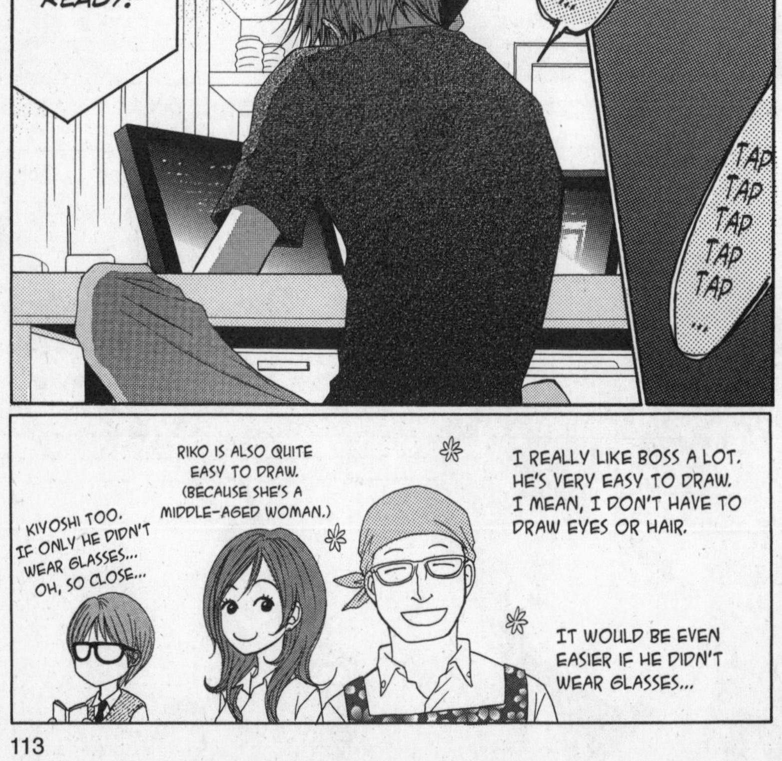
I REALLY LIKE BOSS A LOT. HE'S VERY EASY TO DRAW. I MEAN, I DON'T HAVE TO DRAW EYES OR HAIR.
IT WOULD BE EVEN EASIER IF HE DIDN'T WEAR GLASSES...
RIKO IS ALSO QUITE EASY TO DRAW. (BECAUSE SHE'S A MIDDLE-AGED WOMAN.)
KIYOSHI TOO. IF ONLY HE DIDN'T WEAR GLASSES... OH, SO CLOSE...

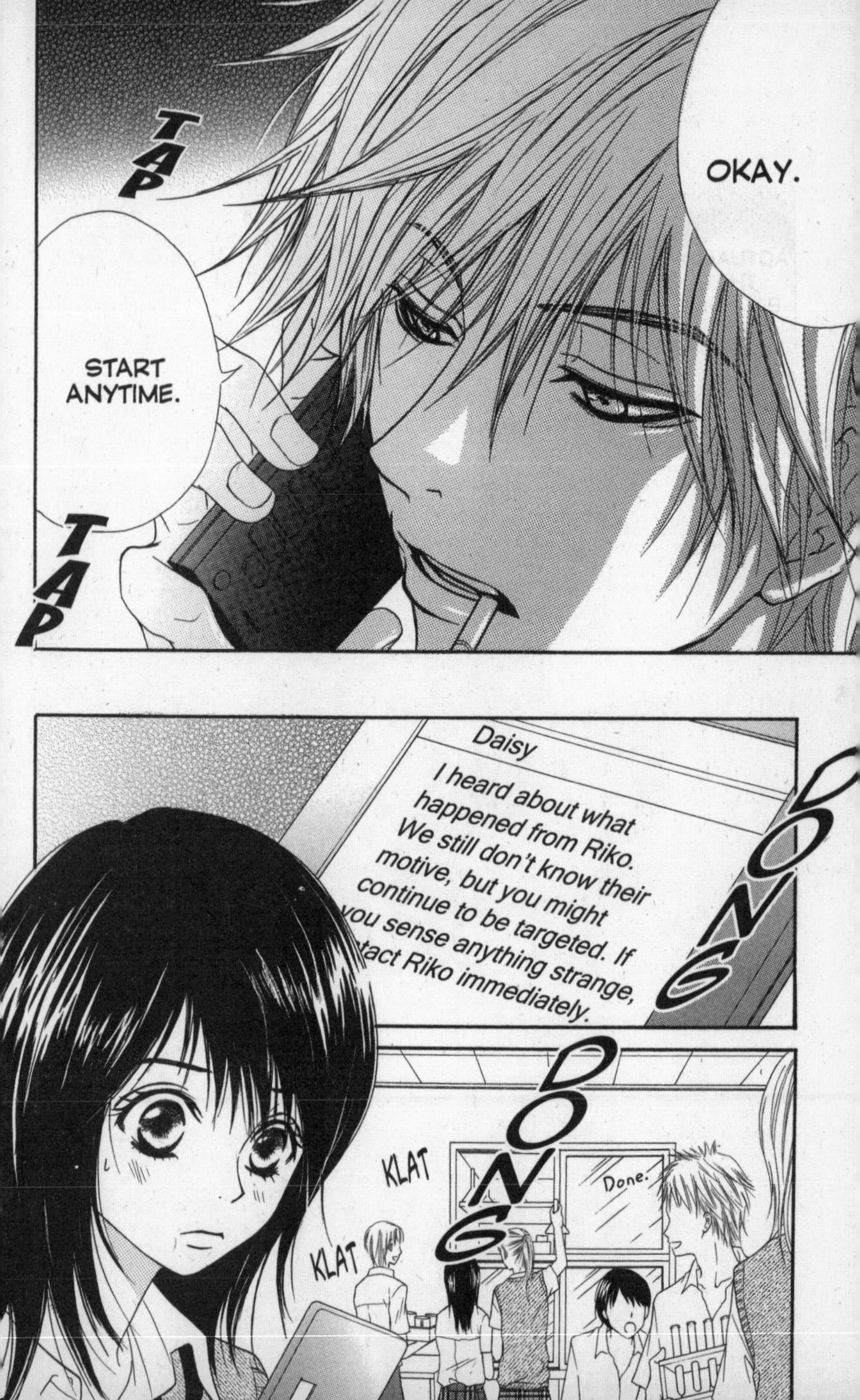
OKAY.
TAP
START ANYTIME.
TAP
Daisy
I heard about what happened from Riko. We still don't know their motive, but you might continue to be targeted. If ou sense anything strange, tact Riko immediately.
DONG
DONG
Done.
KLAT
KLAT

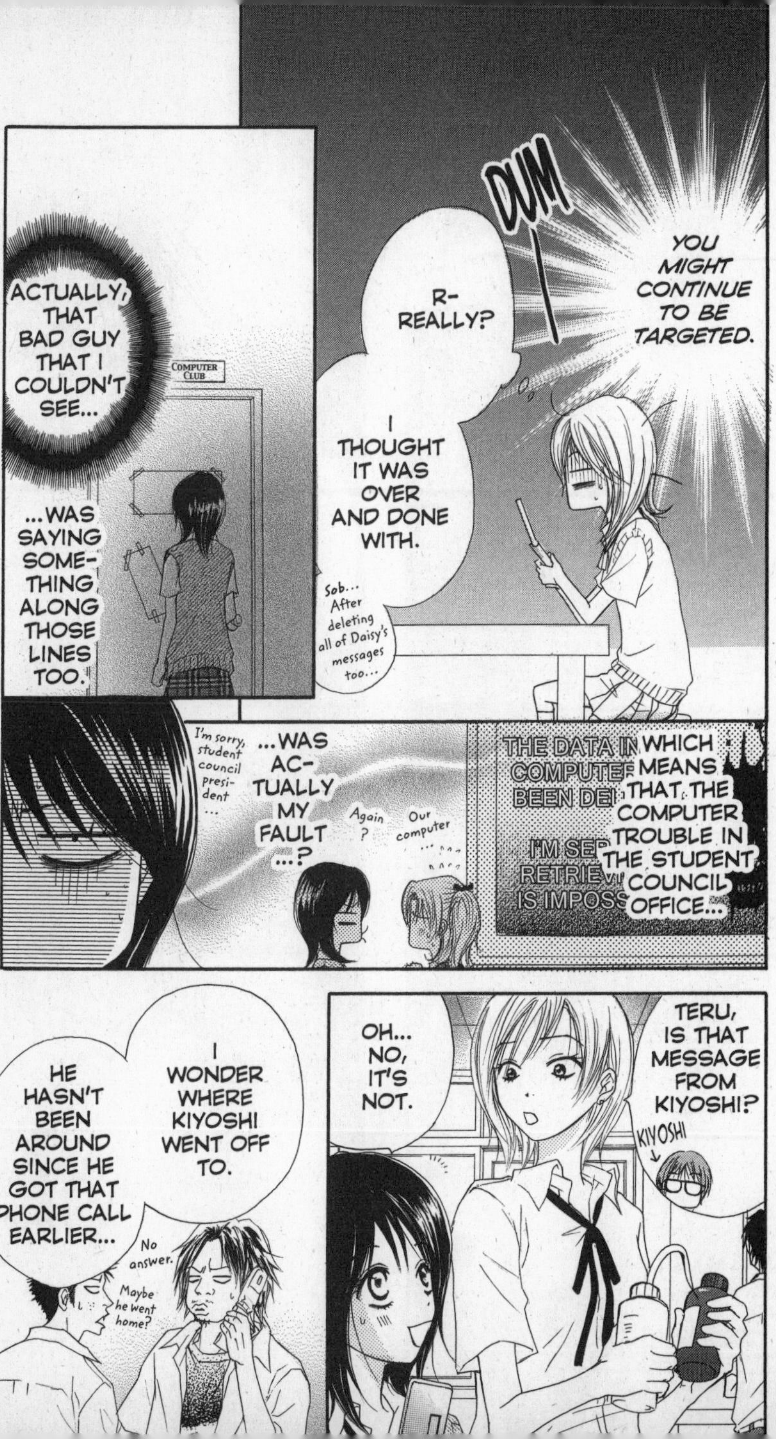
DUM
YOU MIGHT CONTINUE TO BE TARGETED.
R-REALLY?
I THOUGHT IT WAS OVER AND DONE WITH.
Sob... After deleting all of Daisy's messages too...
ACTUALLY, THAT BAD GUY THAT I COULDN'T SEE...
COMPUTER CLUB
...WAS SAYING SOMETHING ALONG THOSE LINES TOO.
WHICH MEANS THAT THE COMPUTER TROUBLE IN THE STUDENT COUNCIL OFFICE...
Our computer...
Again?
...WAS ACTUALLY MY FAULT...?
I'm sorry, student council president...
TERU, IS THAT MESSAGE FROM KIYOSHI?
KIYOSHI
OH... NO, IT'S NOT.
I WONDER WHERE KIYOSHI WENT OFF TO.
HE HASN'T BEEN AROUND SINCE HE GOT THAT PHONE CALL EARLIER...
No answer.
Maybe he went home?

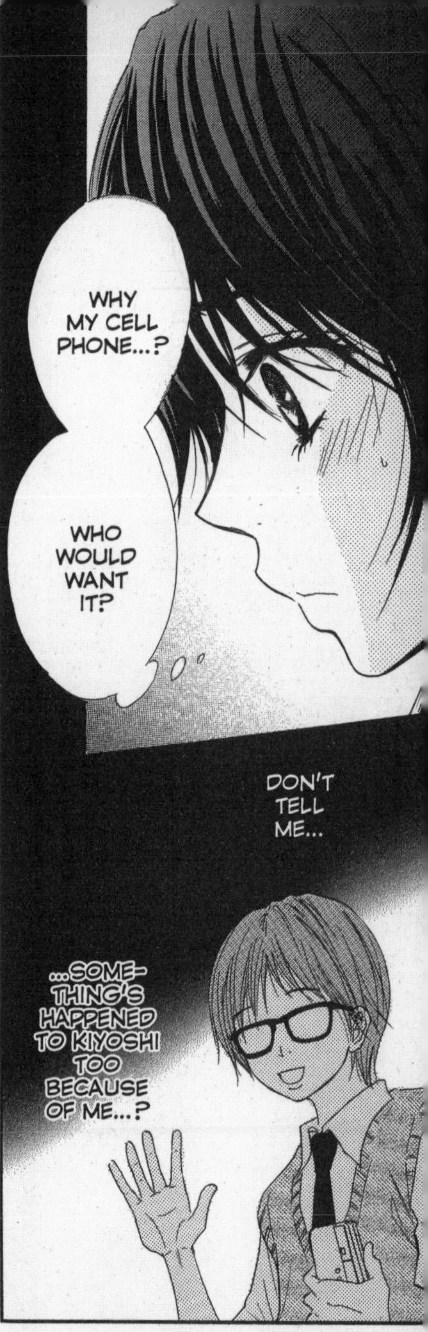
WHY MY CELL PHONE...?
WHO WOULD WANT IT?
DON'T TELL ME...
...SOME-THING'S HAPPENED TO KIYOSHI TOO BECAUSE OF ME...?

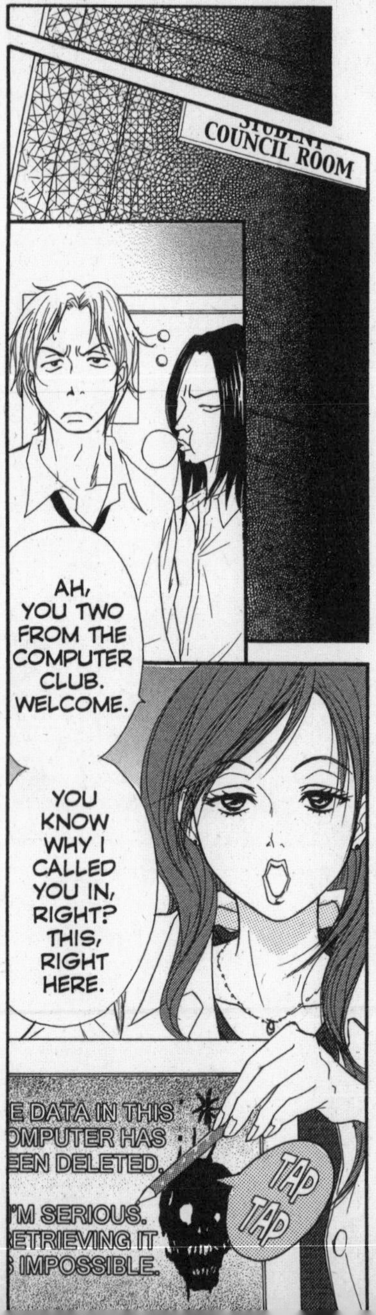
STUDENT COUNCIL ROOM
AH, YOU TWO FROM THE COMPUTER CLUB. WELCOME.
YOU KNOW WHY I CALLED YOU IN, RIGHT? THIS, RIGHT HERE.
E DATA IN THIS OMPUTER HAS EEN DELETED.
TAP TAP
I'M SERIOUS. ETRIEVING IT S IMPOSSIBLE.

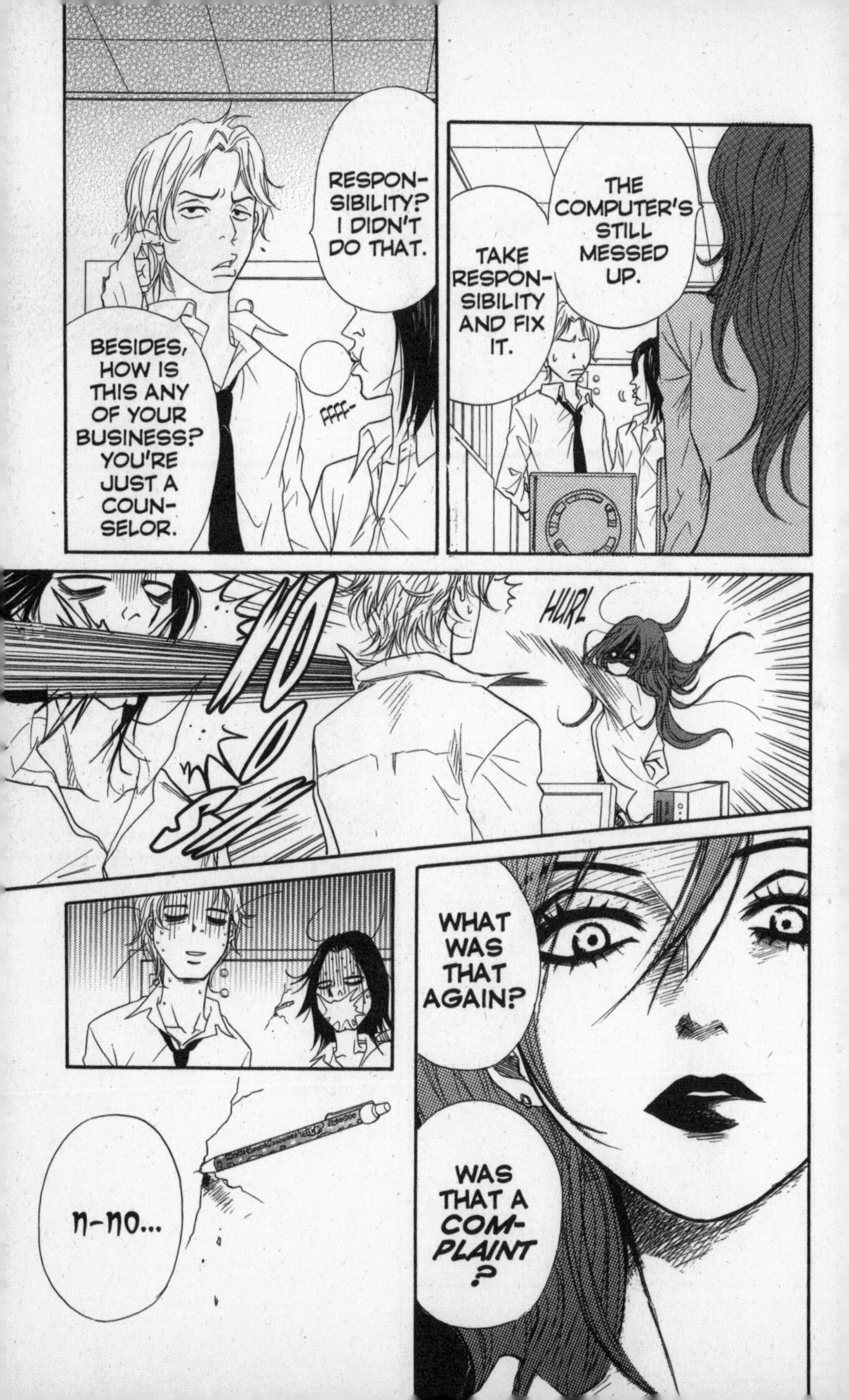
THE COMPUTER'S STILL MESSED UP.
TAKE RESPON-SIBILITY AND FIX IT.
RESPON-SIBILITY? I DIDN'T DO THAT.
FFFF-
BESIDES, HOW IS THIS ANY OF YOUR BUSINESS? YOU'RE JUST A COUN-SELOR.
HURL
WHAT WAS THAT AGAIN?
WAS THAT A *COM-PLAINT*?
n-no...

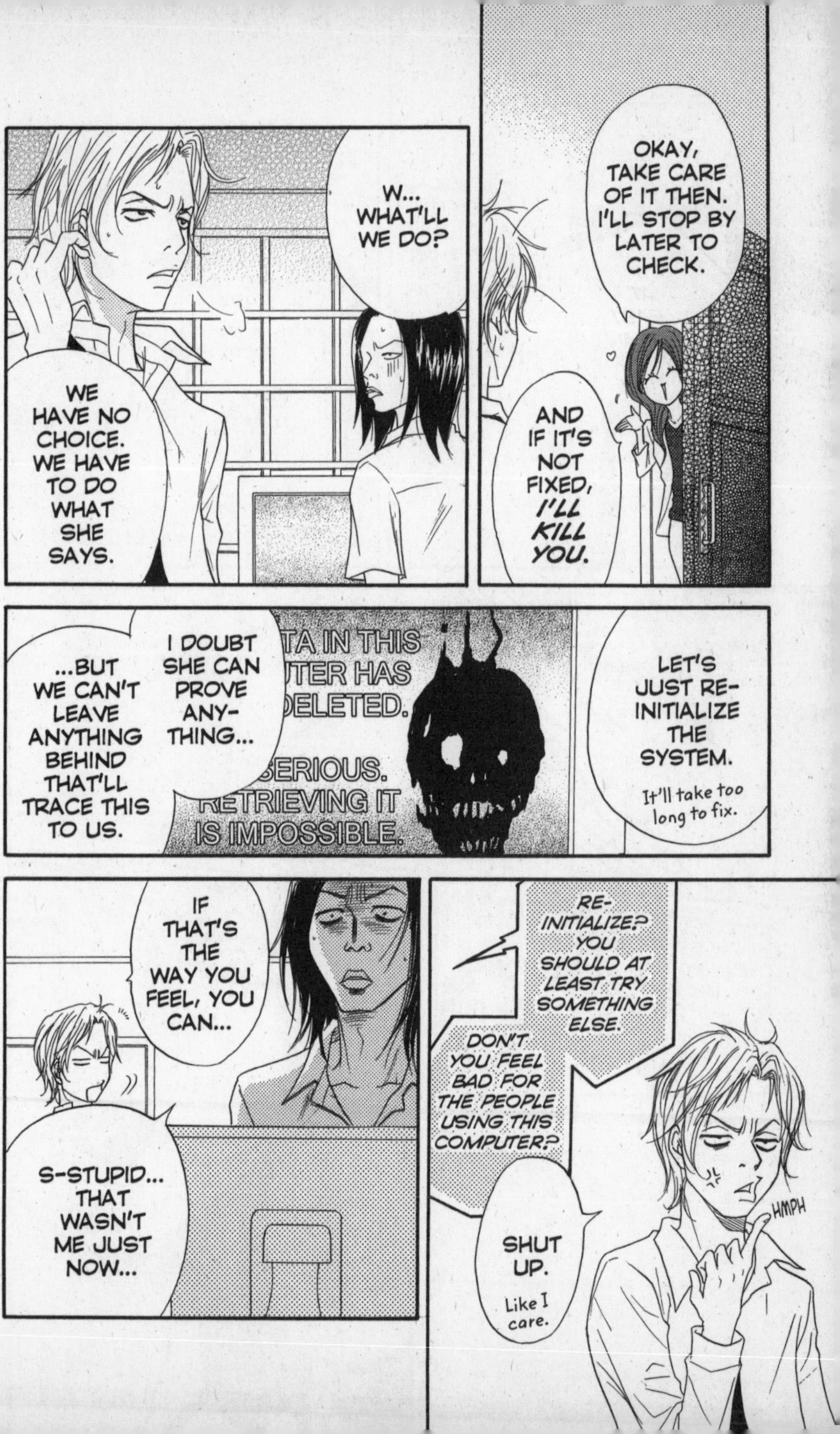
OKAY, TAKE CARE OF IT THEN. I'LL STOP BY LATER TO CHECK.
AND IF IT'S NOT FIXED, *I'LL KILL YOU.*
W... WHAT'LL WE DO?
WE HAVE NO CHOICE. WE HAVE TO DO WHAT SHE SAYS.
LET'S JUST RE-INITIALIZE THE SYSTEM.
It'll take too long to fix.
TA IN THIS
UTER HAS
DELETED.
SERIOUS.
RETRIEVING IT IS IMPOSSIBLE.
I DOUBT SHE CAN PROVE ANY-THING...
...BUT WE CAN'T LEAVE ANYTHING BEHIND THAT'LL TRACE THIS TO US.
RE-INITIALIZE? YOU SHOULD AT LEAST TRY SOMETHING ELSE.
DON'T YOU FEEL BAD FOR THE PEOPLE USING THIS COMPUTER?
SHUT UP.
Like I care.
HMPH
IF THAT'S THE WAY YOU FEEL, YOU CAN...
S-STUPID... THAT WASN'T ME JUST NOW...

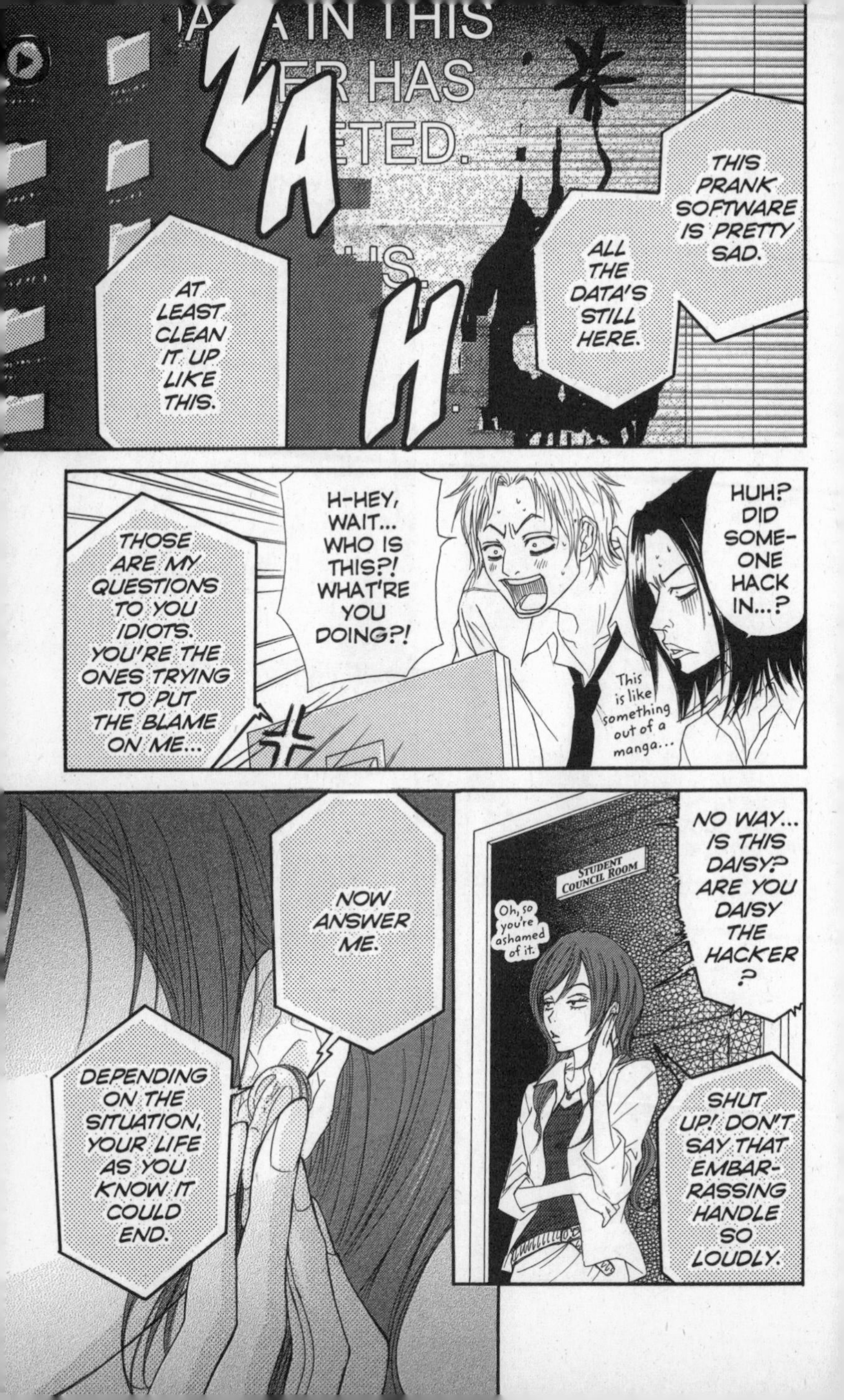
THIS PRANK SOFTWARE IS PRETTY SAD.
ALL THE DATA'S STILL HERE.
AT LEAST CLEAN IT UP LIKE THIS.
HUH? DID SOME-ONE HACK IN...?
This is like something out of a manga...
H-HEY, WAIT... WHO IS THIS?! WHAT'RE YOU DOING?!
THOSE ARE MY QUESTIONS TO YOU IDIOTS. YOU'RE THE ONES TRYING TO PUT THE BLAME ON ME...
NO WAY... IS THIS DAISY? ARE YOU DAISY THE HACKER?
STUDENT COUNCIL ROOM
Oh, so you're ashamed of it.
SHUT UP! DON'T SAY THAT EMBARRASSING HANDLE SO LOUDLY.
NOW ANSWER ME.
DEPENDING ON THE SITUATION, YOUR LIFE AS YOU KNOW IT COULD END.

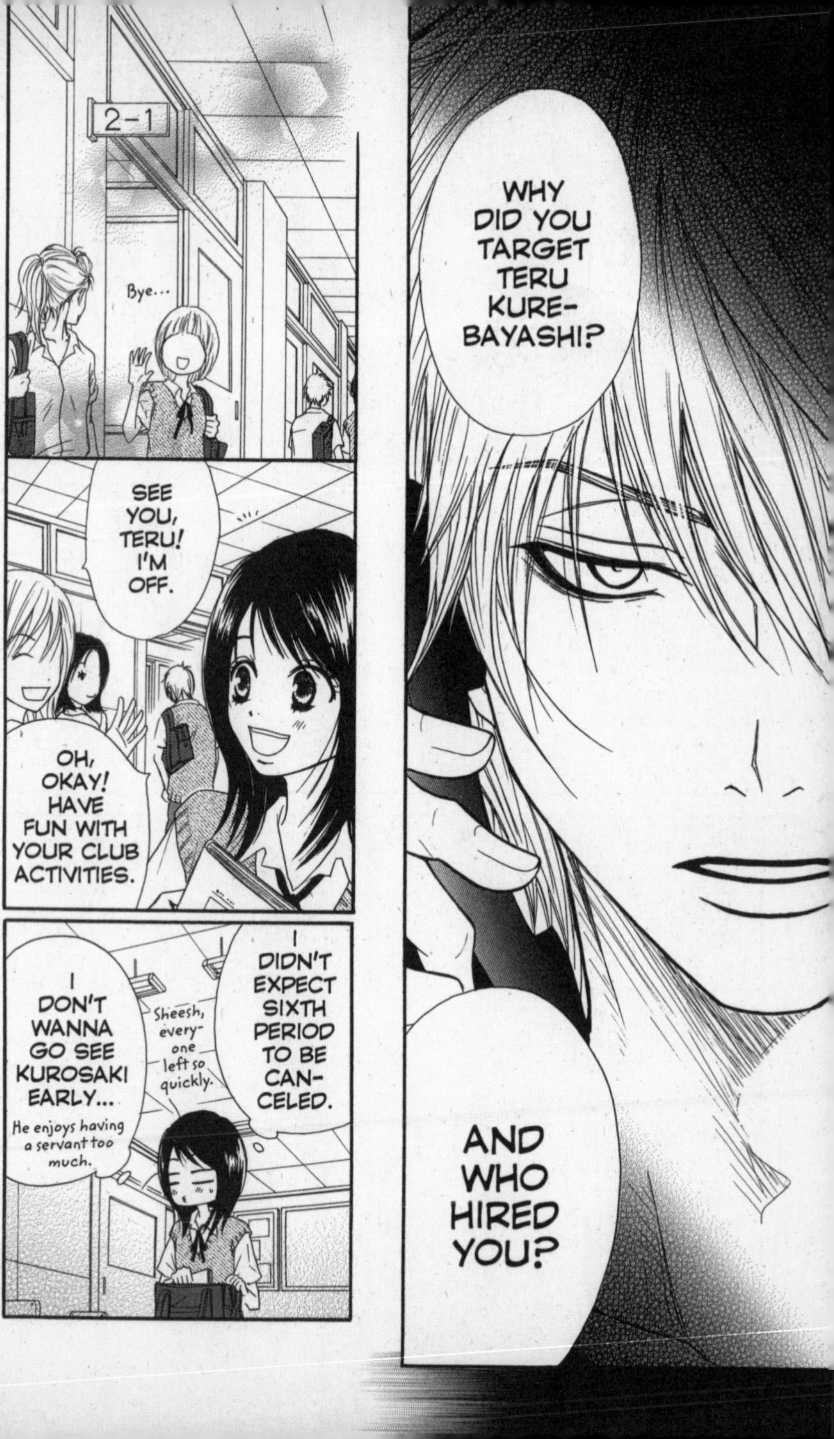
WHY DID YOU TARGET TERU KURE-BAYASHI?
AND WHO HIRED YOU?
Bye...
SEE YOU, TERU! I'M OFF.
OH, OKAY! HAVE FUN WITH YOUR CLUB ACTIVITIES.
I DIDN'T EXPECT SIXTH PERIOD TO BE CAN-CELED.
Sheesh, every-one left so quickly.
I DON'T WANNA GO SEE KUROSAKI EARLY...
He enjoys having a servant too much.

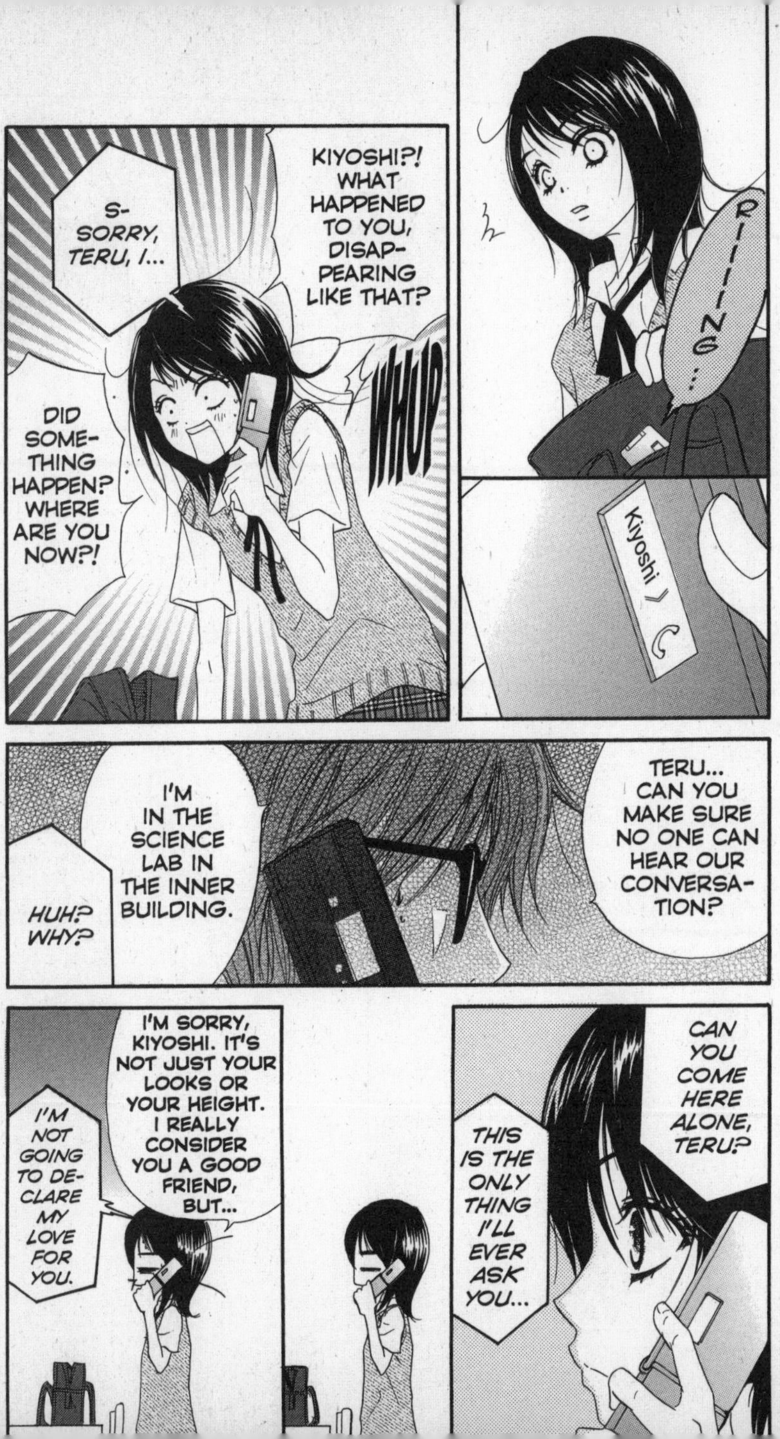
RIIIING...
Kiyoshi
KIYOSHI?! WHAT HAPPENED TO YOU, DISAPPEARING LIKE THAT?
WHUP
S-SORRY, TERU, I...
DID SOMETHING HAPPEN? WHERE ARE YOU NOW?!
TERU... CAN YOU MAKE SURE NO ONE CAN HEAR OUR CONVERSATION?
I'M IN THE SCIENCE LAB IN THE INNER BUILDING.
HUH? WHY?
CAN YOU COME HERE ALONE, TERU?
THIS IS THE ONLY THING I'LL EVER ASK YOU...
I'M SORRY, KIYOSHI. IT'S NOT JUST YOUR LOOKS OR YOUR HEIGHT. I REALLY CONSIDER YOU A GOOD FRIEND, BUT...
I'M NOT GOING TO DECLARE MY LOVE FOR YOU.

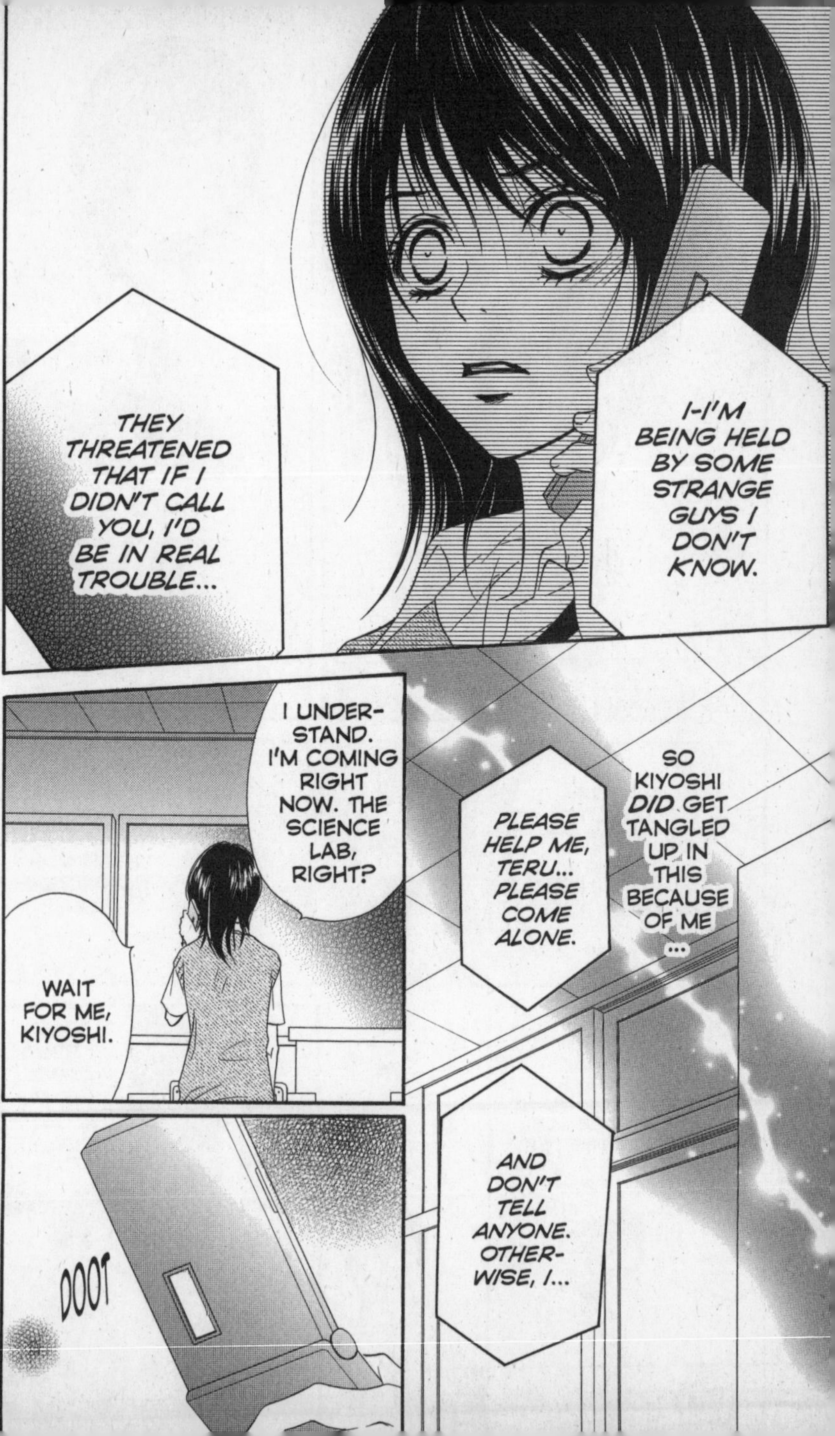

I-I'M BEING HELD BY SOME STRANGE GUYS I DON'T KNOW.
THEY THREATENED THAT IF I DIDN'T CALL YOU, I'D BE IN REAL TROUBLE...
SO KIYOSHI DID GET TANGLED UP IN THIS BECAUSE OF ME...
PLEASE HELP ME, TERU... PLEASE COME ALONE.
AND DON'T TELL ANYONE. OTHER-WISE, I...
I UNDER-STAND. I'M COMING RIGHT NOW. THE SCIENCE LAB, RIGHT?
WAIT FOR ME, KIYOSHI.
DOOT

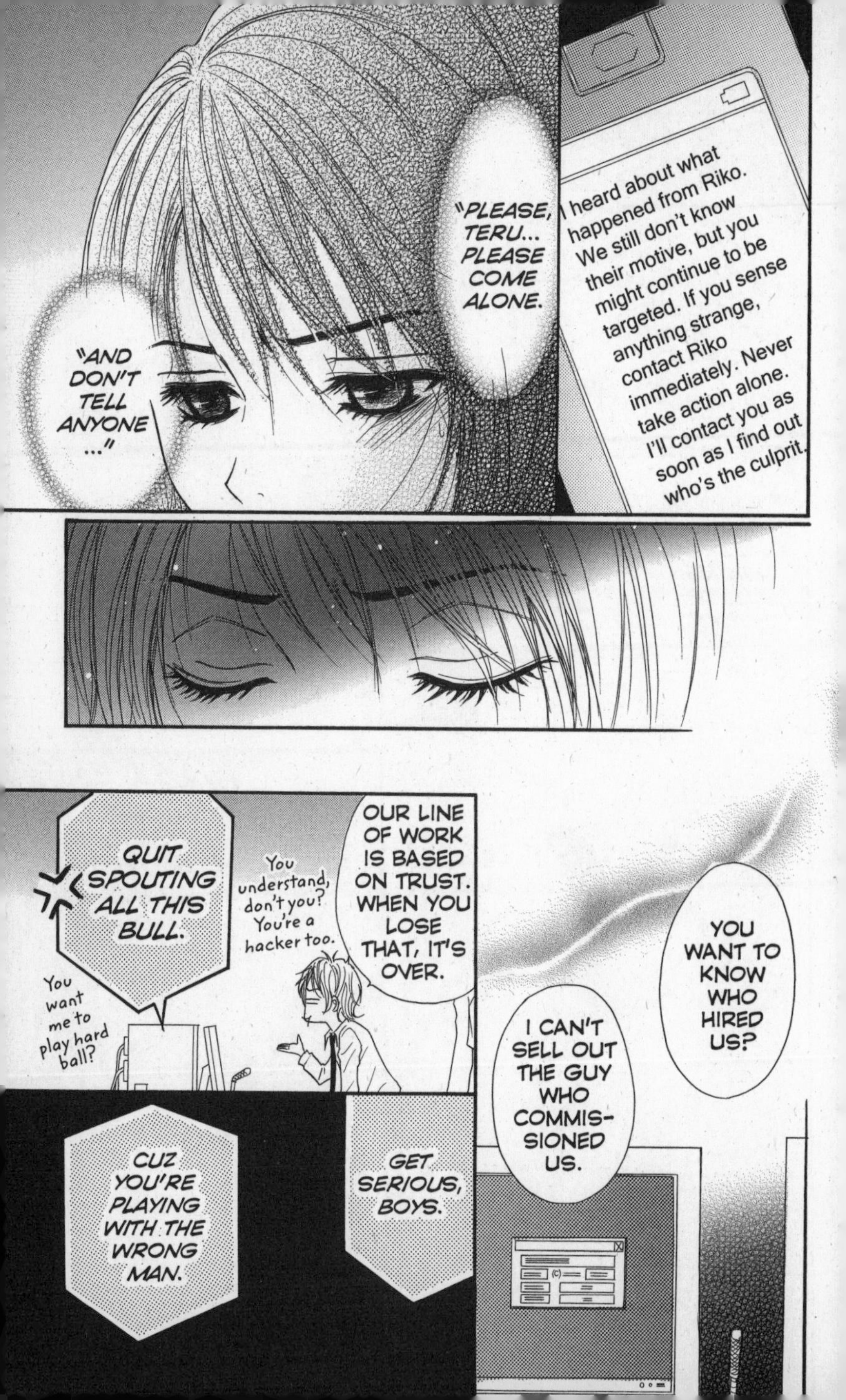

I heard about what happened from Riko. We still don't know their motive, but you might continue to be targeted. If you sense anything strange, contact Riko immediately. Never take action alone. I'll contact you as soon as I find out who's the culprit.
"PLEASE, TERU... PLEASE COME ALONE.
"AND DON'T TELL ANYONE..."
YOU WANT TO KNOW WHO HIRED US?
I CAN'T SELL OUT THE GUY WHO COMMISSIONED US.
OUR LINE OF WORK IS BASED ON TRUST. WHEN YOU LOSE THAT, IT'S OVER.
You understand, don't you? You're a hacker too.
QUIT SPOUTING ALL THIS BULL.
You want me to play hard ball?
GET SERIOUS, BOYS.
CUZ YOU'RE PLAYING WITH THE WRONG MAN.

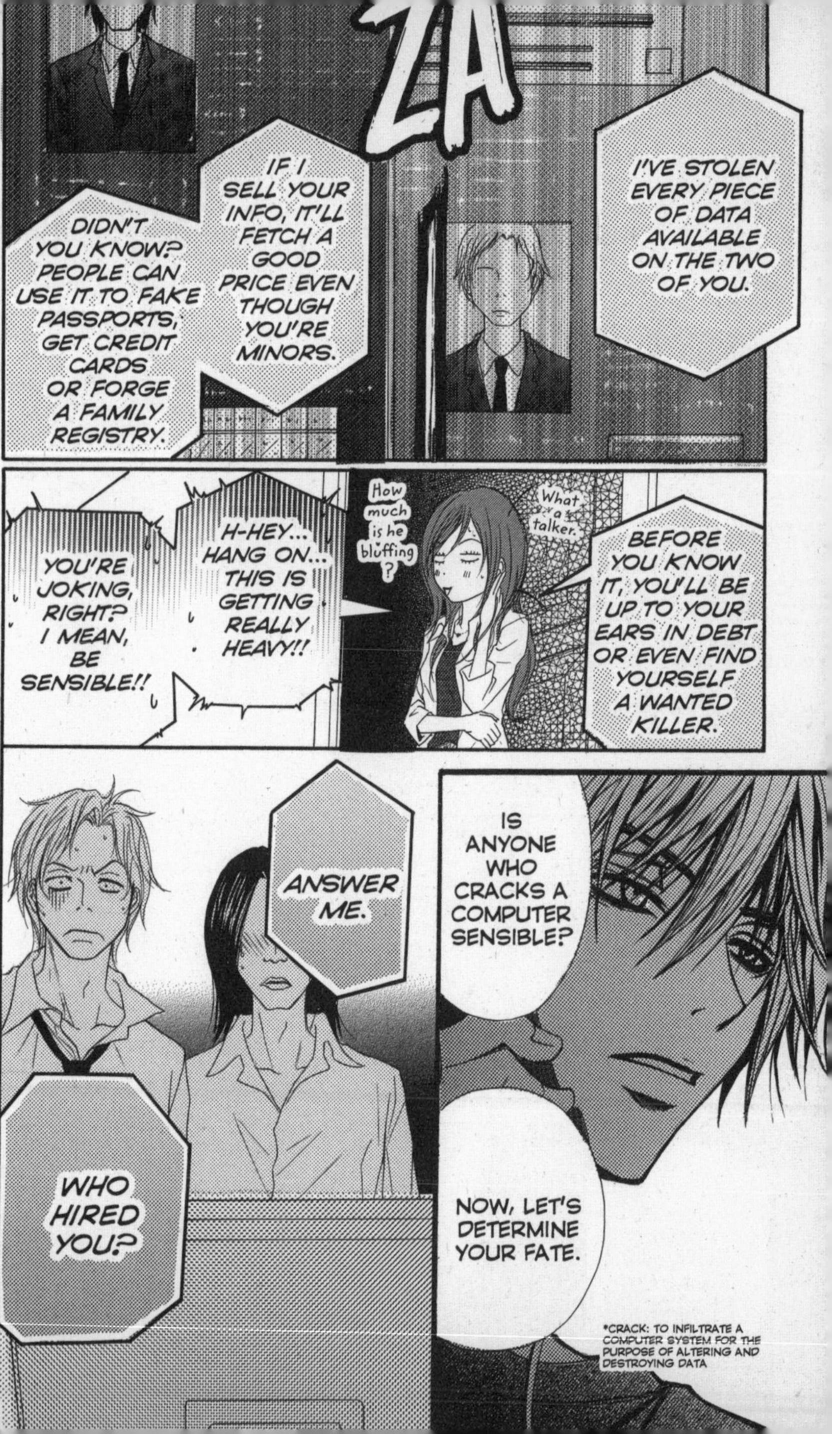
ZA
I'VE STOLEN EVERY PIECE OF DATA AVAILABLE ON THE TWO OF YOU.
IF I SELL YOUR INFO, IT'LL FETCH A GOOD PRICE EVEN THOUGH YOU'RE MINORS.
DIDN'T YOU KNOW? PEOPLE CAN USE IT TO FAKE PASSPORTS, GET CREDIT CARDS OR FORGE A FAMILY REGISTRY.
What a talker.
BEFORE YOU KNOW IT, YOU'LL BE UP TO YOUR EARS IN DEBT OR EVEN FIND YOURSELF A WANTED KILLER.
How much is he bluffing?
H-HEY... HANG ON... THIS IS GETTING REALLY HEAVY!!
YOU'RE JOKING, RIGHT? I MEAN, BE SENSIBLE!!
IS ANYONE WHO CRACKS A COMPUTER SENSIBLE?
NOW, LET'S DETERMINE YOUR FATE.
*CRACK: TO INFILTRATE A COMPUTER SYSTEM FOR THE PURPOSE OF ALTERING AND DESTROYING DATA
ANSWER ME.
WHO HIRED YOU?

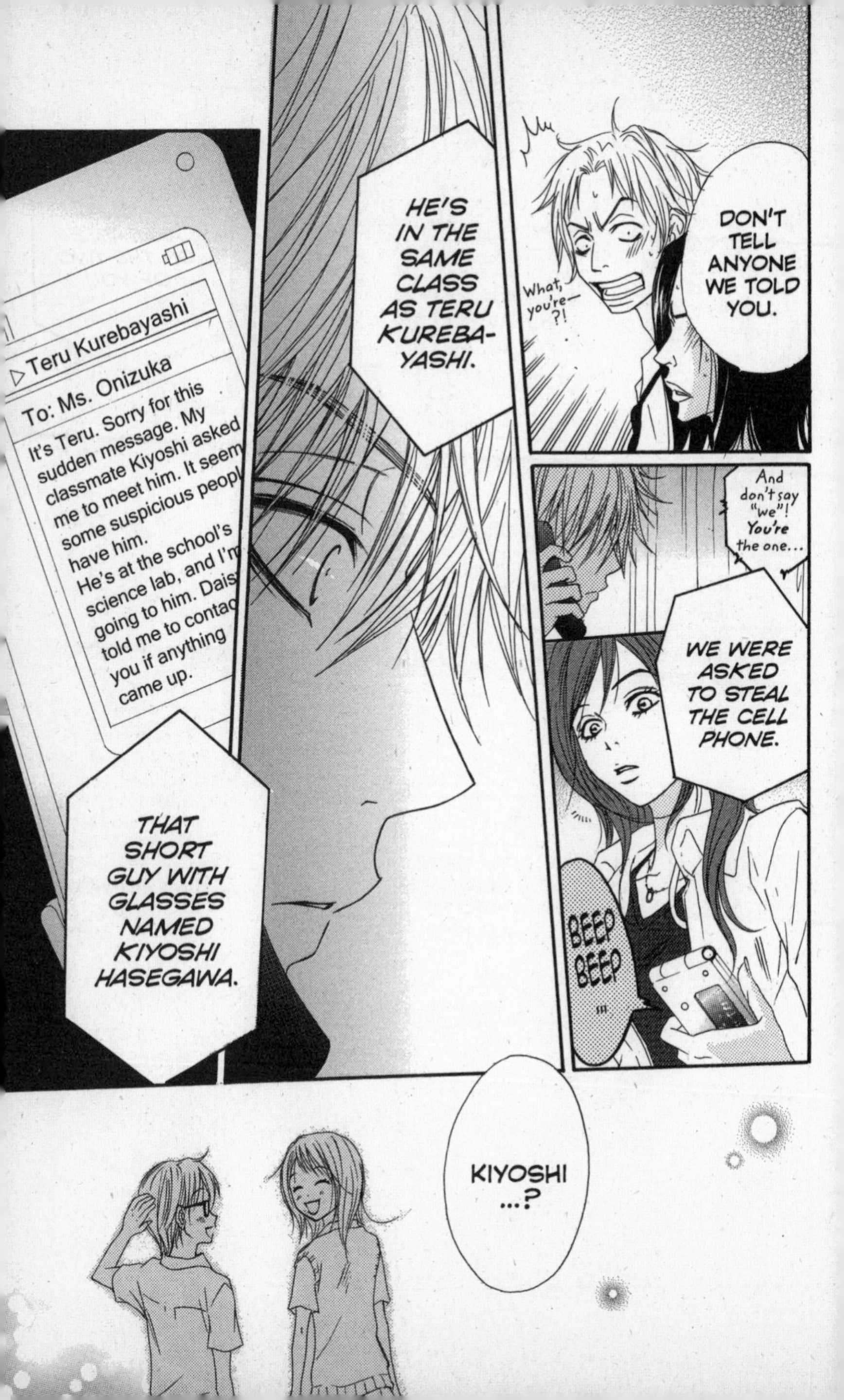

DON'T TELL ANYONE WE TOLD YOU.
What, you're—?!
And don't say "we"! You're the one...
WE WERE ASKED TO STEAL THE CELL PHONE.
BEEP BEEP
HE'S IN THE SAME CLASS AS TERU KUREBAYASHI.
Teru Kurebayashi
To: Ms. Onizuka
It's Teru. Sorry for this sudden message. My classmate Kiyoshi asked me to meet him. It seem some suspicious peopl have him.
He's at the school's science lab, and I'r going to him. Dais told me to contac you if anything came up.
THAT SHORT GUY WITH GLASSES NAMED KIYOSHI HASEGAWA.
KIYOSHI ...?

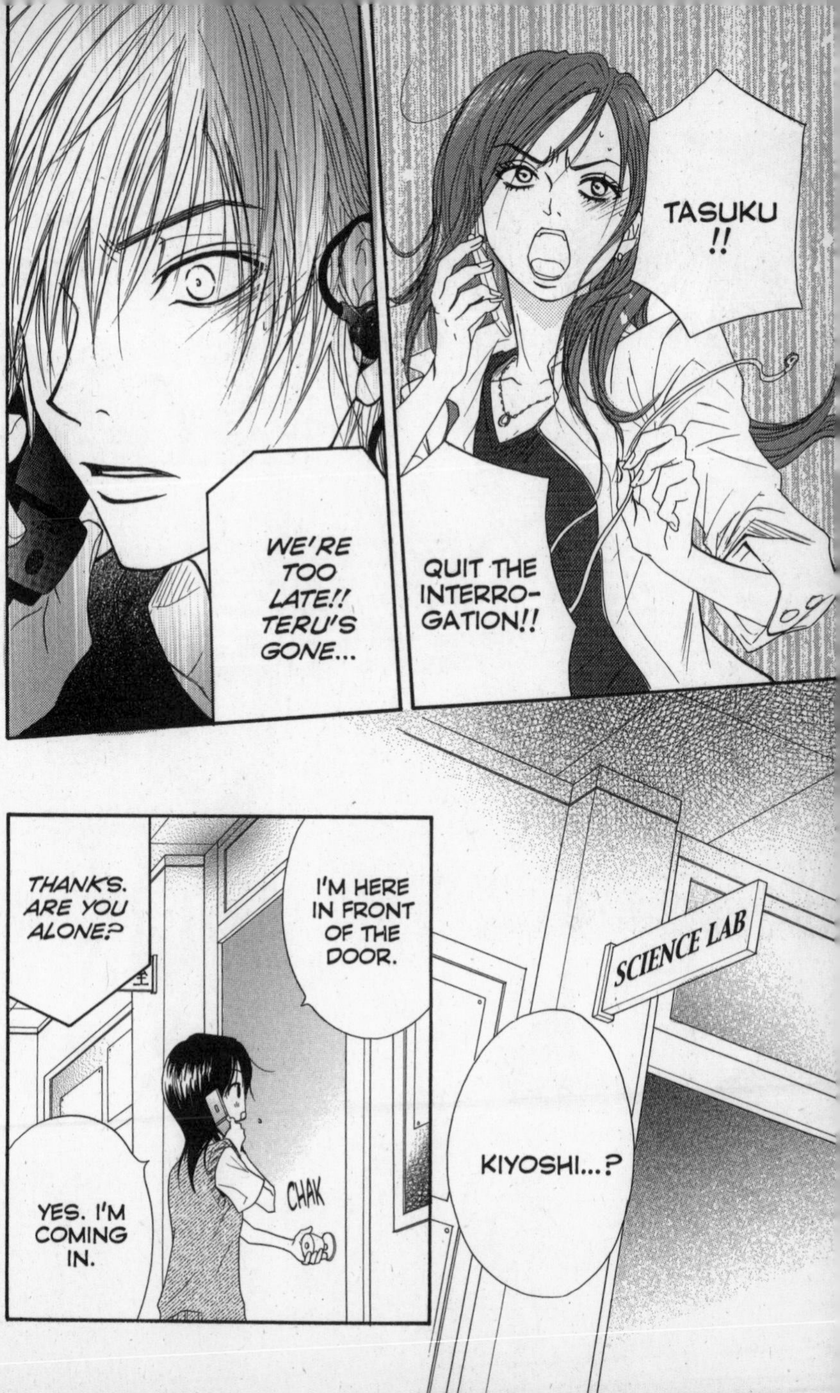
TASUKU !!
QUIT THE INTERROGATION!!
WE'RE TOO LATE!! TERU'S GONE...
SCIENCE LAB
KIYOSHI...?
I'M HERE IN FRONT OF THE DOOR.
THANKS. ARE YOU ALONE?
CHAK
YES. I'M COMING IN.

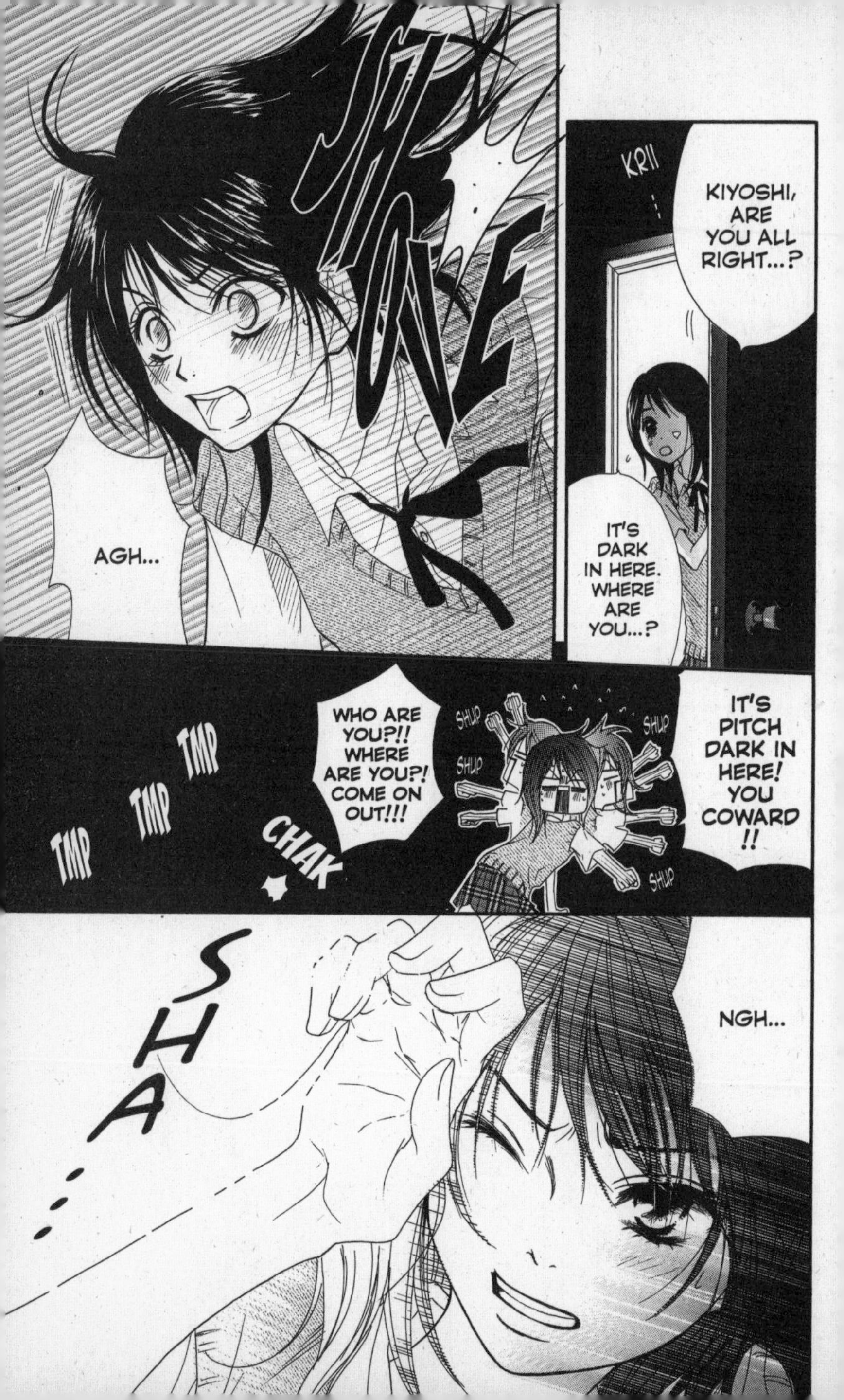
KRII
KIYOSHI, ARE YOU ALL RIGHT...?
IT'S DARK IN HERE. WHERE ARE YOU...?
SHOVE
AGH...
IT'S PITCH DARK IN HERE! YOU COWARD!!
SHUP
SHUP
SHUP
SHUP
WHO ARE YOU?!! WHERE ARE YOU?! COME ON OUT!!!
CHAK
TMP
TMP
TMP
NGH...
SHA...

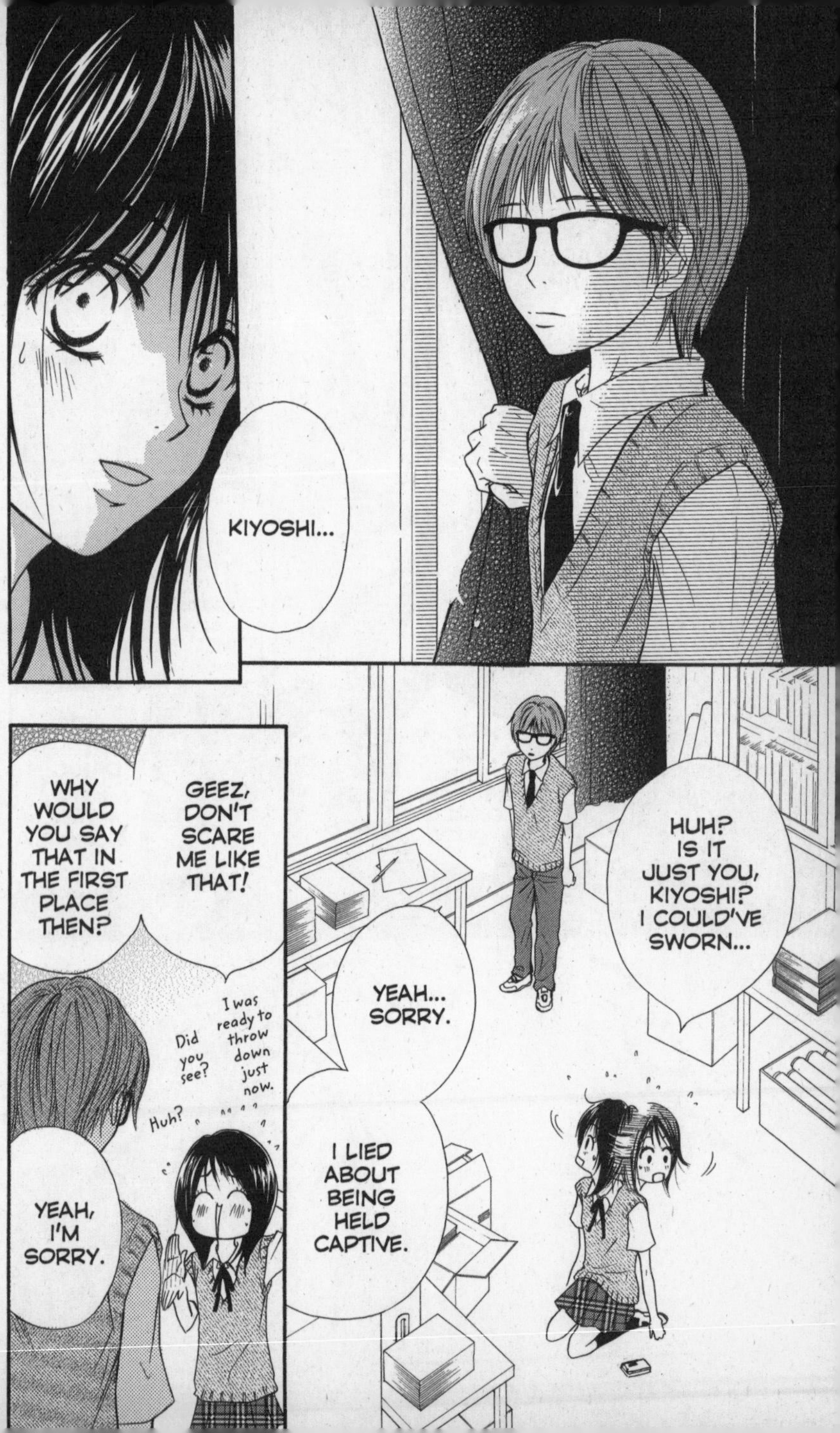
KIYOSHI...
HUH? IS IT JUST YOU, KIYOSHI? I COULD'VE SWORN...
YEAH... SORRY.
I LIED ABOUT BEING HELD CAPTIVE.
GEEZ, DON'T SCARE ME LIKE THAT!
WHY WOULD YOU SAY THAT IN THE FIRST PLACE THEN?
I was ready to throw down just now.
Did you see?
Huh?
YEAH, I'M SORRY.

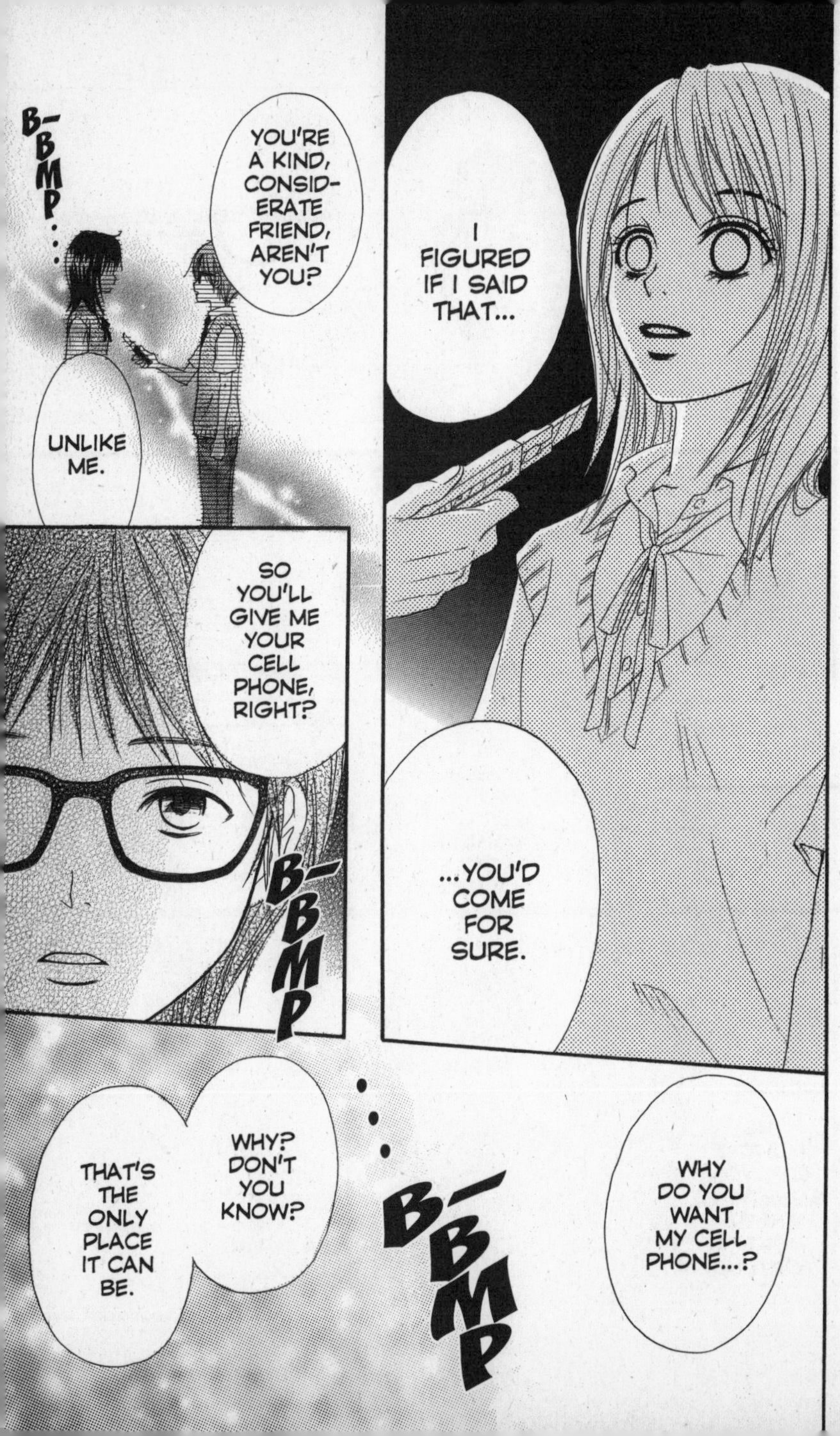

I FIGURED IF I SAID THAT...
...YOU'D COME FOR SURE.
YOU'RE A KIND, CONSID-ERATE FRIEND, AREN'T YOU?
B-BMP...
UNLIKE ME.
SO YOU'LL GIVE ME YOUR CELL PHONE, RIGHT?
B-BMP
WHY DO YOU WANT MY CELL PHONE...?
B-BMP
...
WHY? DON'T YOU KNOW?
THAT'S THE ONLY PLACE IT CAN BE.

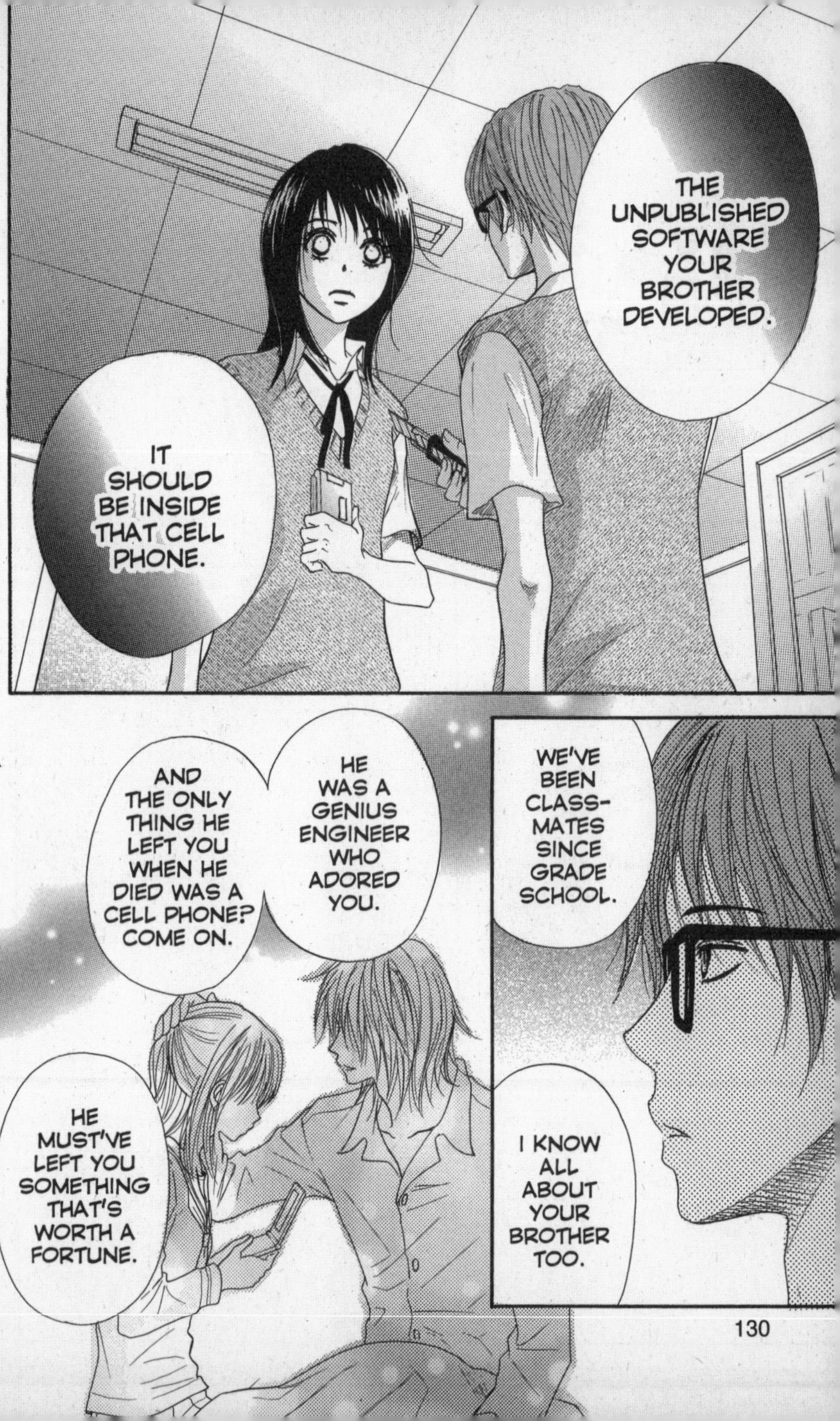
THE UNPUBLISHED SOFTWARE YOUR BROTHER DEVELOPED.
IT SHOULD BE INSIDE THAT CELL PHONE.
WE'VE BEEN CLASS-MATES SINCE GRADE SCHOOL.
I KNOW ALL ABOUT YOUR BROTHER TOO.
HE WAS A GENIUS ENGINEER WHO ADORED YOU.
AND THE ONLY THING HE LEFT YOU WHEN HE DIED WAS A CELL PHONE? COME ON.
HE MUST'VE LEFT YOU SOMETHING THAT'S WORTH A FORTUNE.

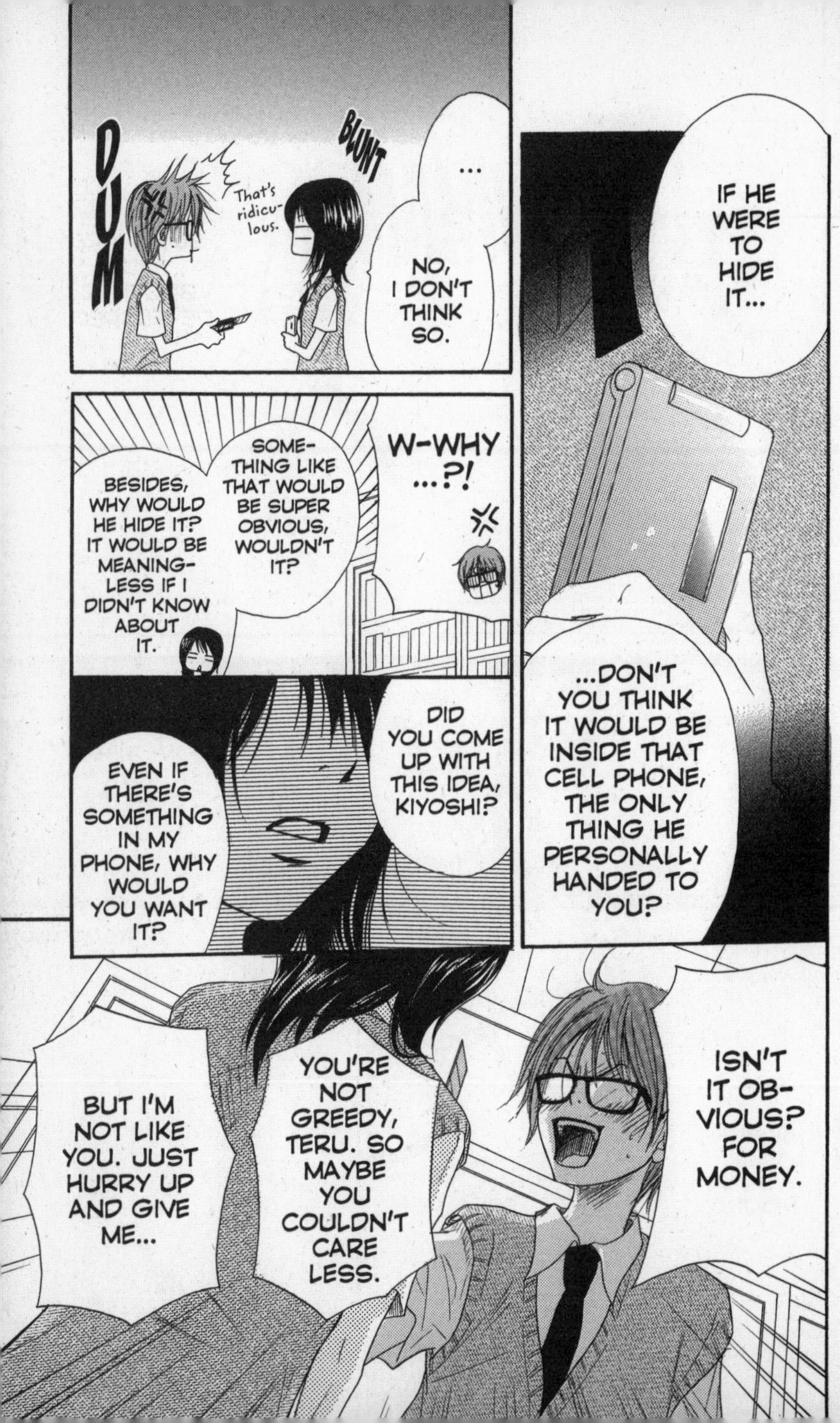
...
NO, I DON'T THINK SO.
BLUNT
That's ridicu-lous.
DUM
W-WHY ...?!
SOME-THING LIKE THAT WOULD BE SUPER OBVIOUS, WOULDN'T IT?
BESIDES, WHY WOULD HE HIDE IT? IT WOULD BE MEANING-LESS IF I DIDN'T KNOW ABOUT IT.
IF HE WERE TO HIDE IT...
...DON'T YOU THINK IT WOULD BE INSIDE THAT CELL PHONE, THE ONLY THING HE PERSONALLY HANDED TO YOU?
DID YOU COME UP WITH THIS IDEA, KIYOSHI?
EVEN IF THERE'S SOMETHING IN MY PHONE, WHY WOULD YOU WANT IT?
ISN'T IT OB-VIOUS? FOR MONEY.
YOU'RE NOT GREEDY, TERU. SO MAYBE YOU COULDN'T CARE LESS.
BUT I'M NOT LIKE YOU. JUST HURRY UP AND GIVE ME...

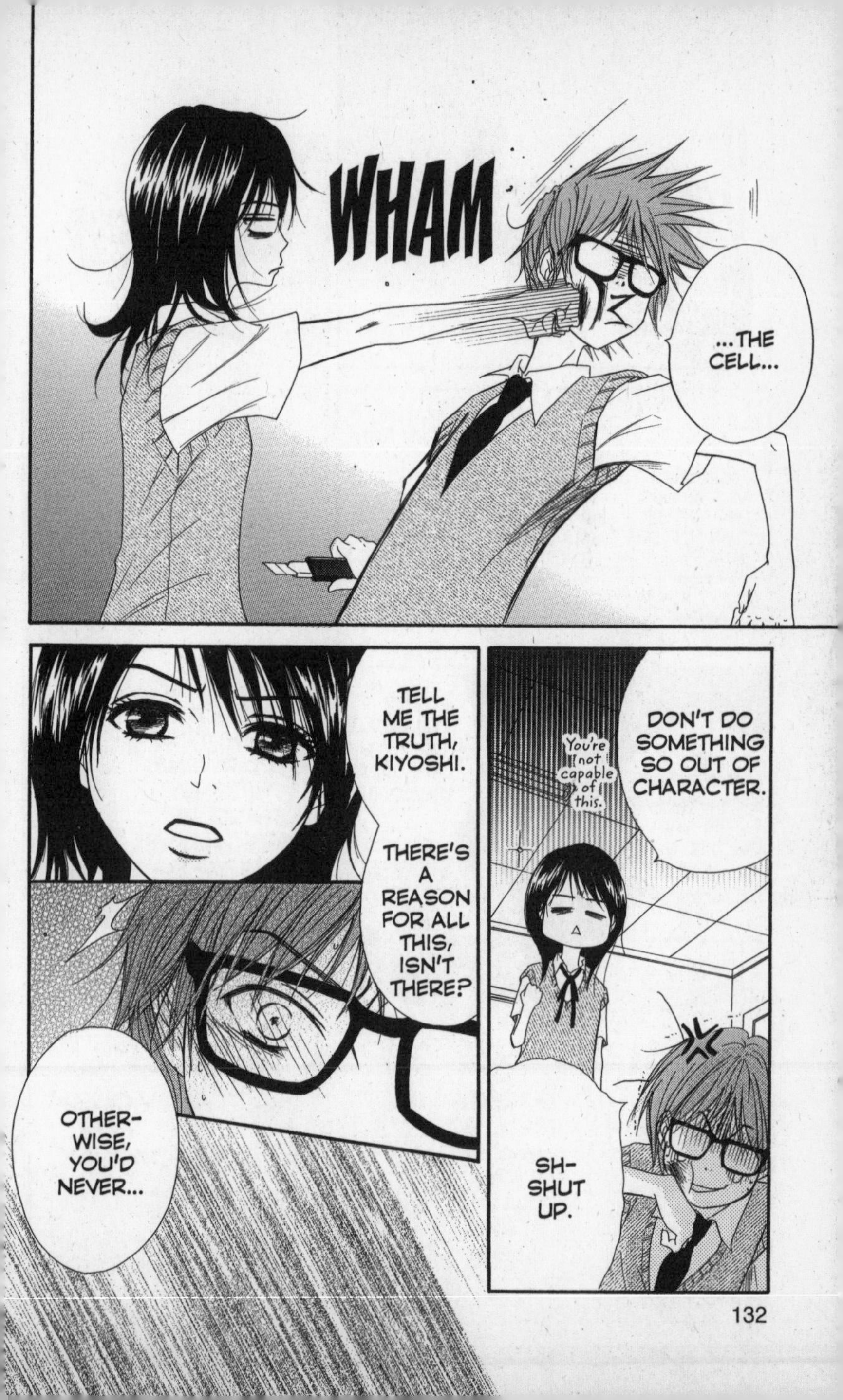
...THE CELL...
WHAM
DON'T DO SOMETHING SO OUT OF CHARACTER.
You're not capable of this.
SH-SHUT UP.
TELL ME THE TRUTH, KIYOSHI.
THERE'S A REASON FOR ALL THIS, ISN'T THERE?
OTHER-WISE, YOU'D NEVER...

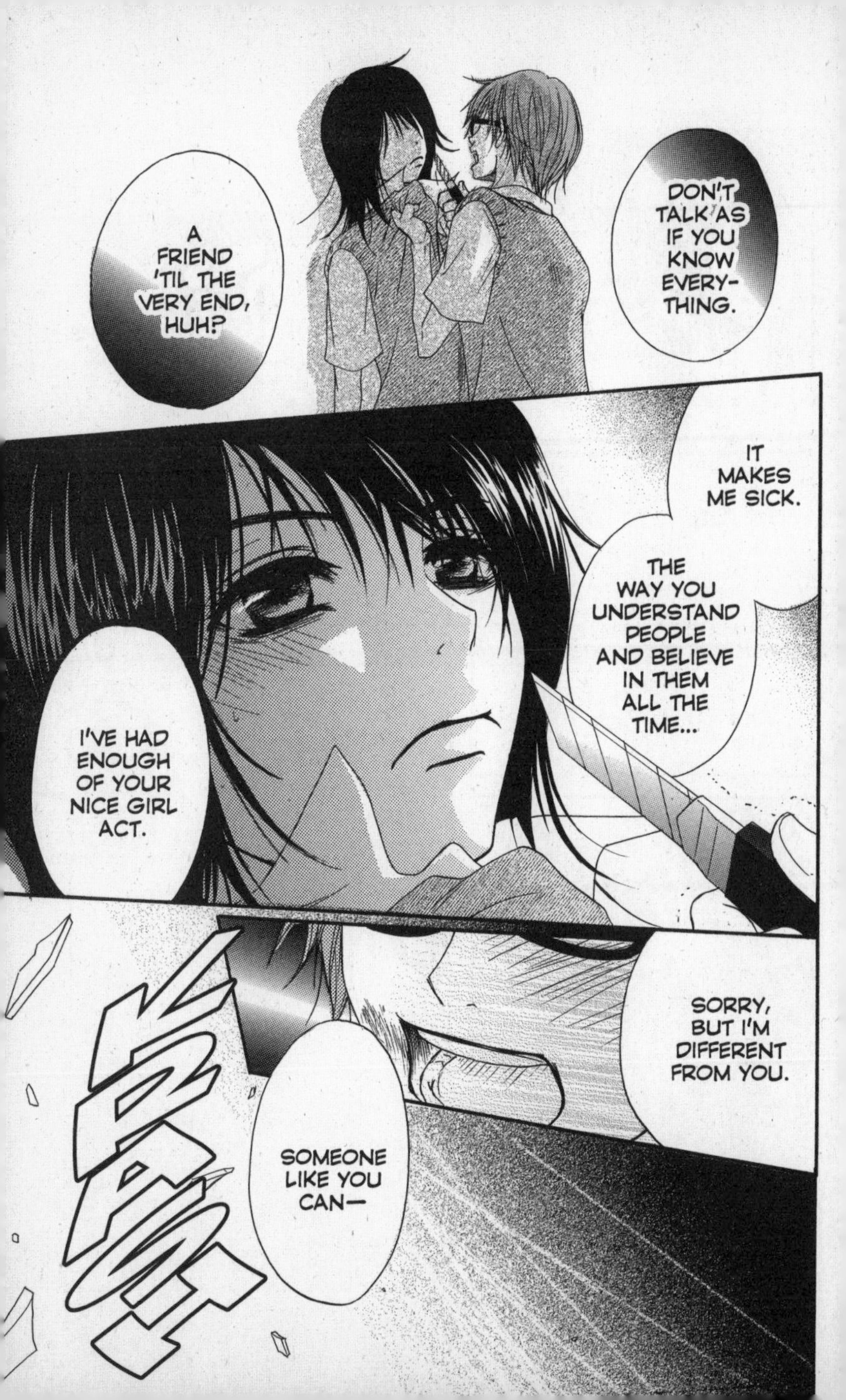
DON'T TALK AS IF YOU KNOW EVERY-THING.
A FRIEND 'TIL THE VERY END, HUH?
IT MAKES ME SICK.
THE WAY YOU UNDERSTAND PEOPLE AND BELIEVE IN THEM ALL THE TIME...
I'VE HAD ENOUGH OF YOUR NICE GIRL ACT.
SORRY, BUT I'M DIFFERENT FROM YOU.
SOMEONE LIKE YOU CAN—

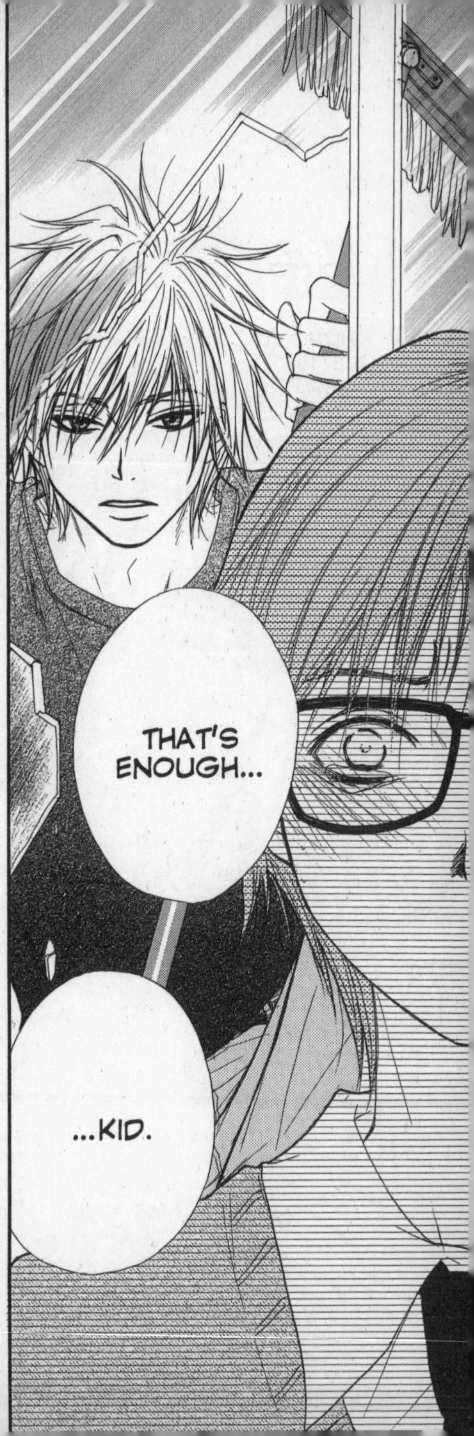
THAT'S ENOUGH...
...KID.

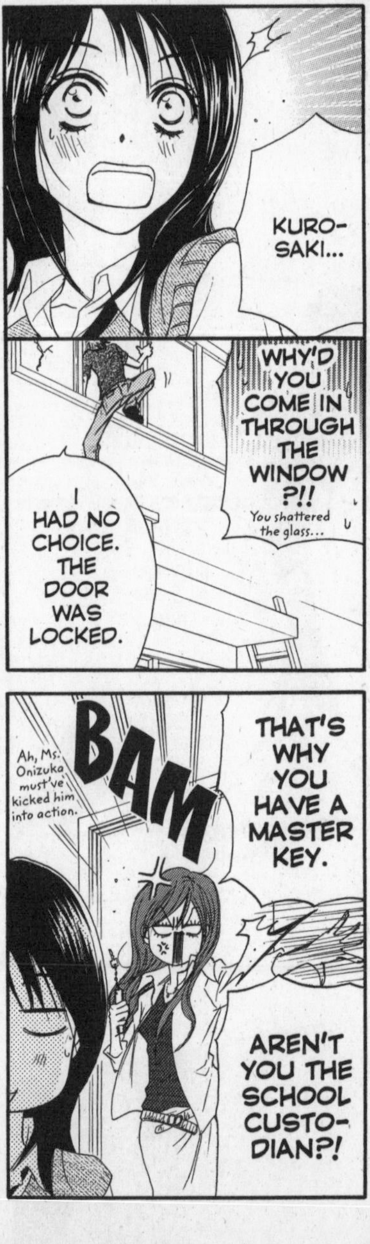
KURO-SAKI...
WHY'D YOU COME IN THROUGH THE WINDOW?!!
You shattered the glass...
I HAD NO CHOICE. THE DOOR WAS LOCKED.
BAM
THAT'S WHY YOU HAVE A MASTER KEY.
AREN'T YOU THE SCHOOL CUSTO-DIAN?!
Ah, Ms. Onizuka must've kicked him into action.

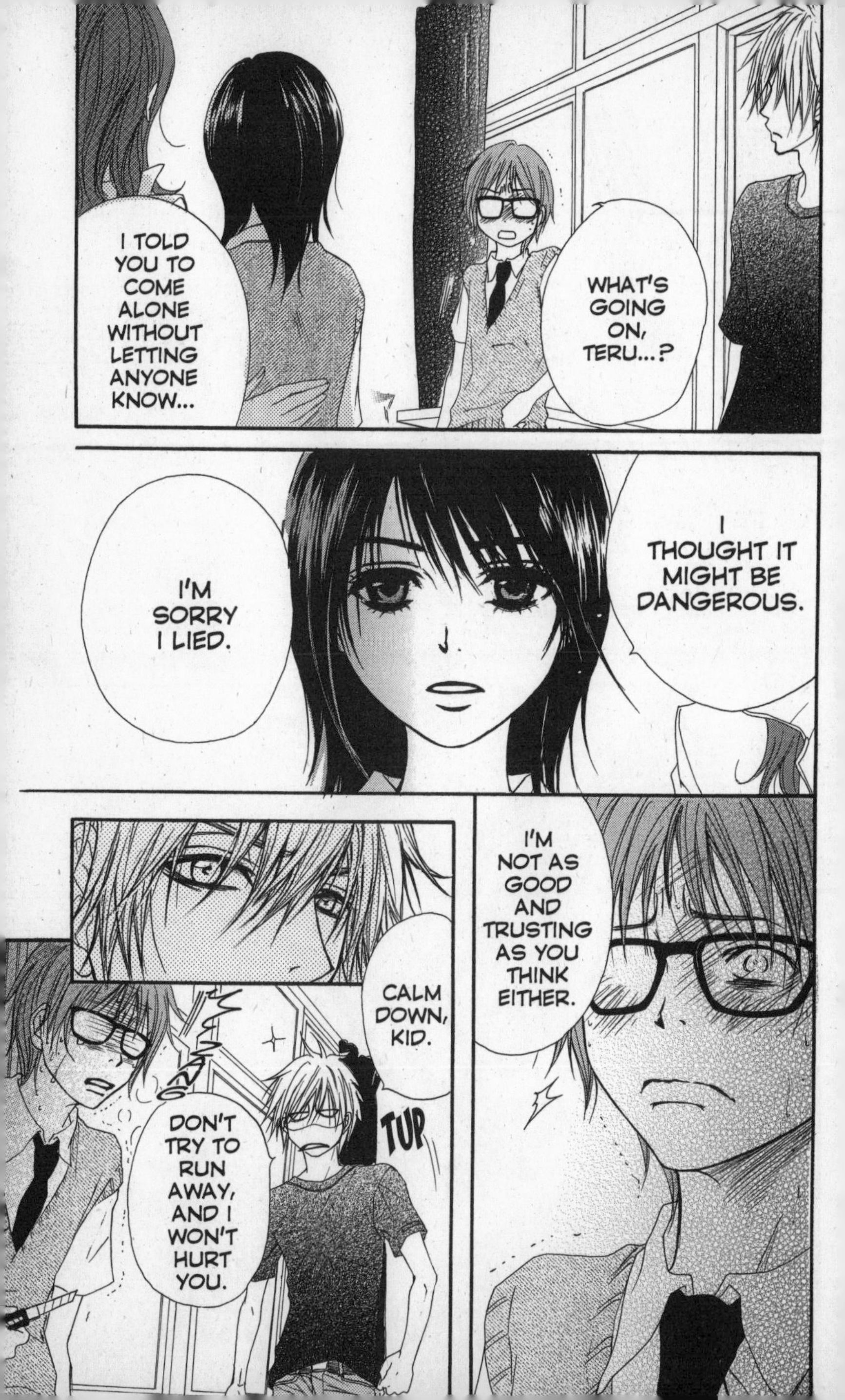
WHAT'S GOING ON, TERU...?
I TOLD YOU TO COME ALONE WITHOUT LETTING ANYONE KNOW...
I THOUGHT IT MIGHT BE DANGEROUS.
I'M SORRY I LIED.
I'M NOT AS GOOD AND TRUSTING AS YOU THINK EITHER.
CALM DOWN, KID.
TUP
DON'T TRY TO RUN AWAY, AND I WON'T HURT YOU.

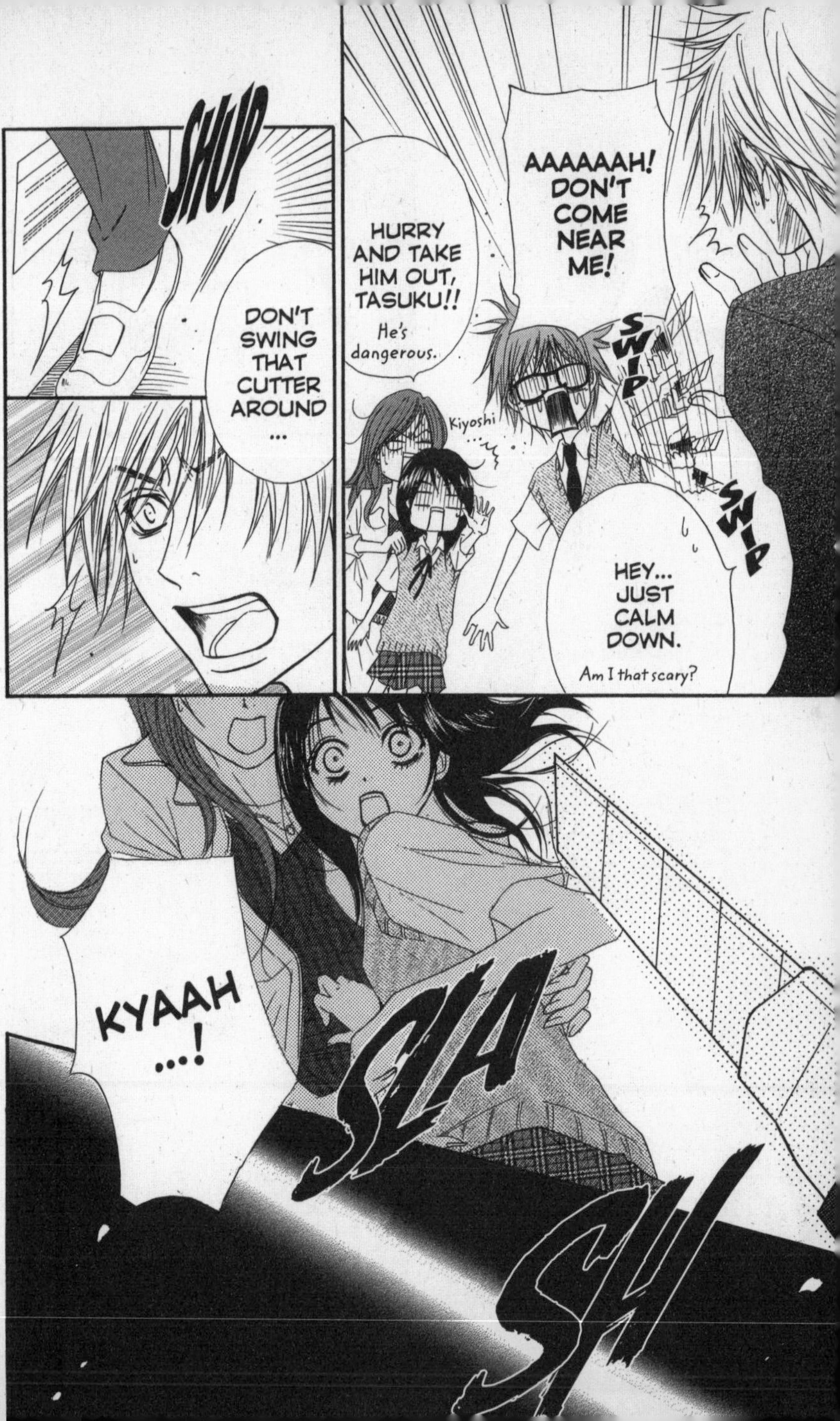
AAAAAAH! DON'T COME NEAR ME!
SWIP
HURRY AND TAKE HIM OUT, TASUKU!!
He's dangerous.
Kiyoshi...
SWIP
HEY... JUST CALM DOWN.
Am I that scary?
SHUP
DON'T SWING THAT CUTTER AROUND...
KYAAH...!

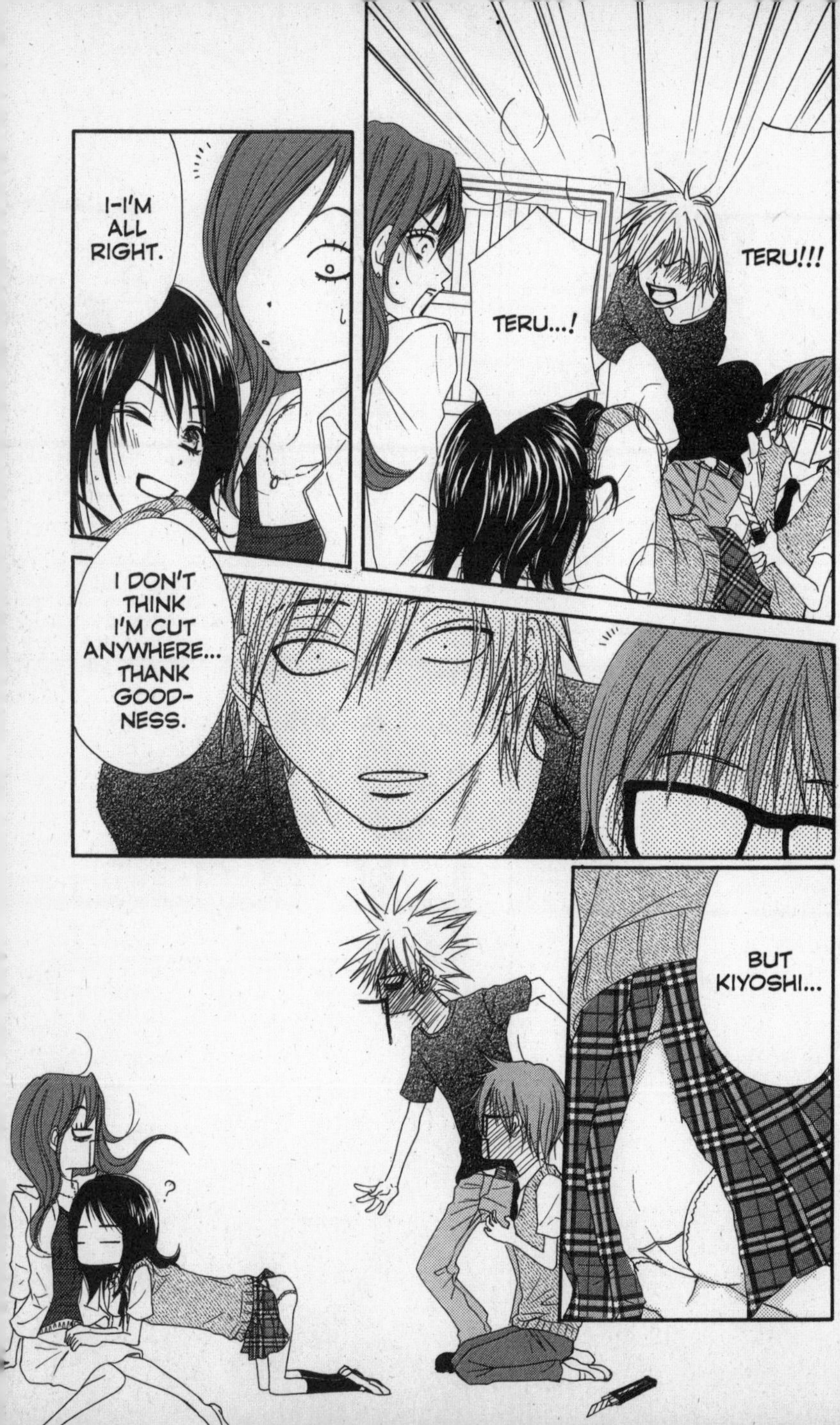
TERU!!!
TERU...!
I-I'M ALL RIGHT.
I DON'T THINK I'M CUT ANYWHERE... THANK GOODNESS.
BUT KIYOSHI...

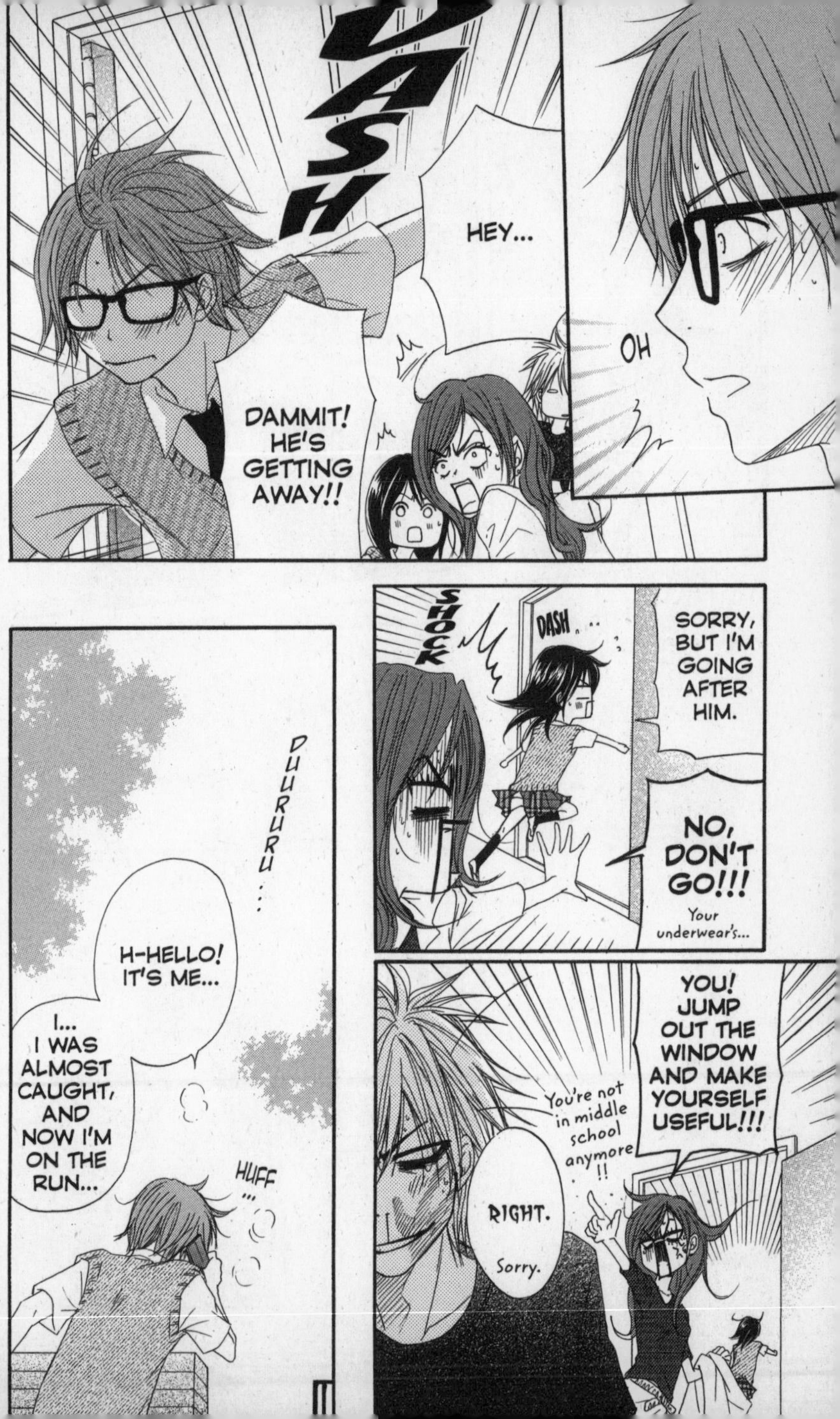
OH
DASH
HEY...
DAMMIT! HE'S GETTING AWAY!!
SHOCK
DASH ...
SORRY, BUT I'M GOING AFTER HIM.
NO, DON'T GO!!!
Your underwear's...
YOU! JUMP OUT THE WINDOW AND MAKE YOURSELF USEFUL!!!
You're not in middle school anymore!!
RIGHT.
Sorry.
DUURURU...
H-HELLO! IT'S ME...
I... I WAS ALMOST CAUGHT, AND NOW I'M ON THE RUN...
HUFF...

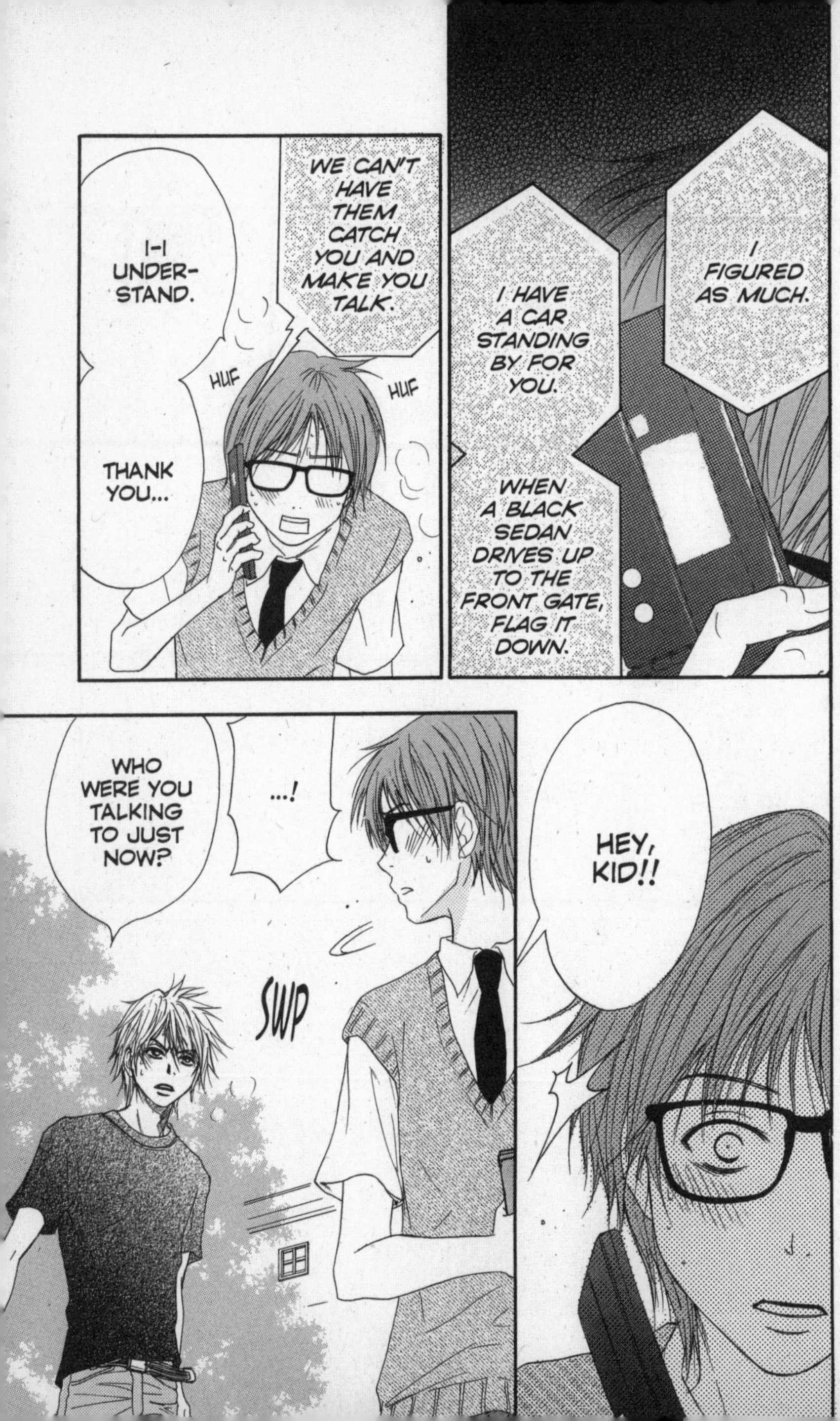
I FIGURED AS MUCH.
I HAVE A CAR STANDING BY FOR YOU.
WHEN A BLACK SEDAN DRIVES UP TO THE FRONT GATE, FLAG IT DOWN.
WE CAN'T HAVE THEM CATCH YOU AND MAKE YOU TALK.
I-I UNDER-STAND.
HUF
HUF
THANK YOU...
HEY, KID!!
...!
WHO WERE YOU TALKING TO JUST NOW?
SWP

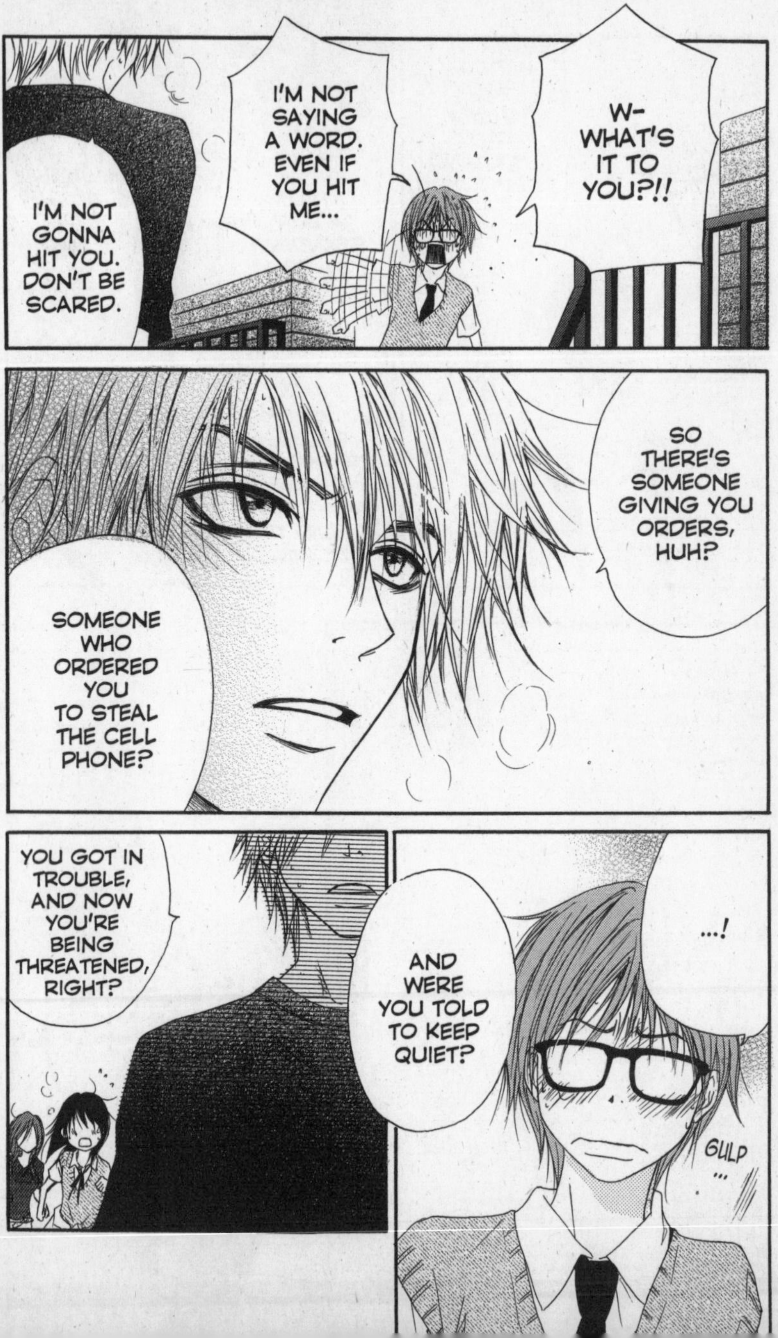
W- WHAT'S IT TO YOU?!!
I'M NOT SAYING A WORD. EVEN IF YOU HIT ME...
I'M NOT GONNA HIT YOU. DON'T BE SCARED.
SO THERE'S SOMEONE GIVING YOU ORDERS, HUH?
SOMEONE WHO ORDERED YOU TO STEAL THE CELL PHONE?
...!
AND WERE YOU TOLD TO KEEP QUIET?
GULP ...
YOU GOT IN TROUBLE, AND NOW YOU'RE BEING THREATENED, RIGHT?

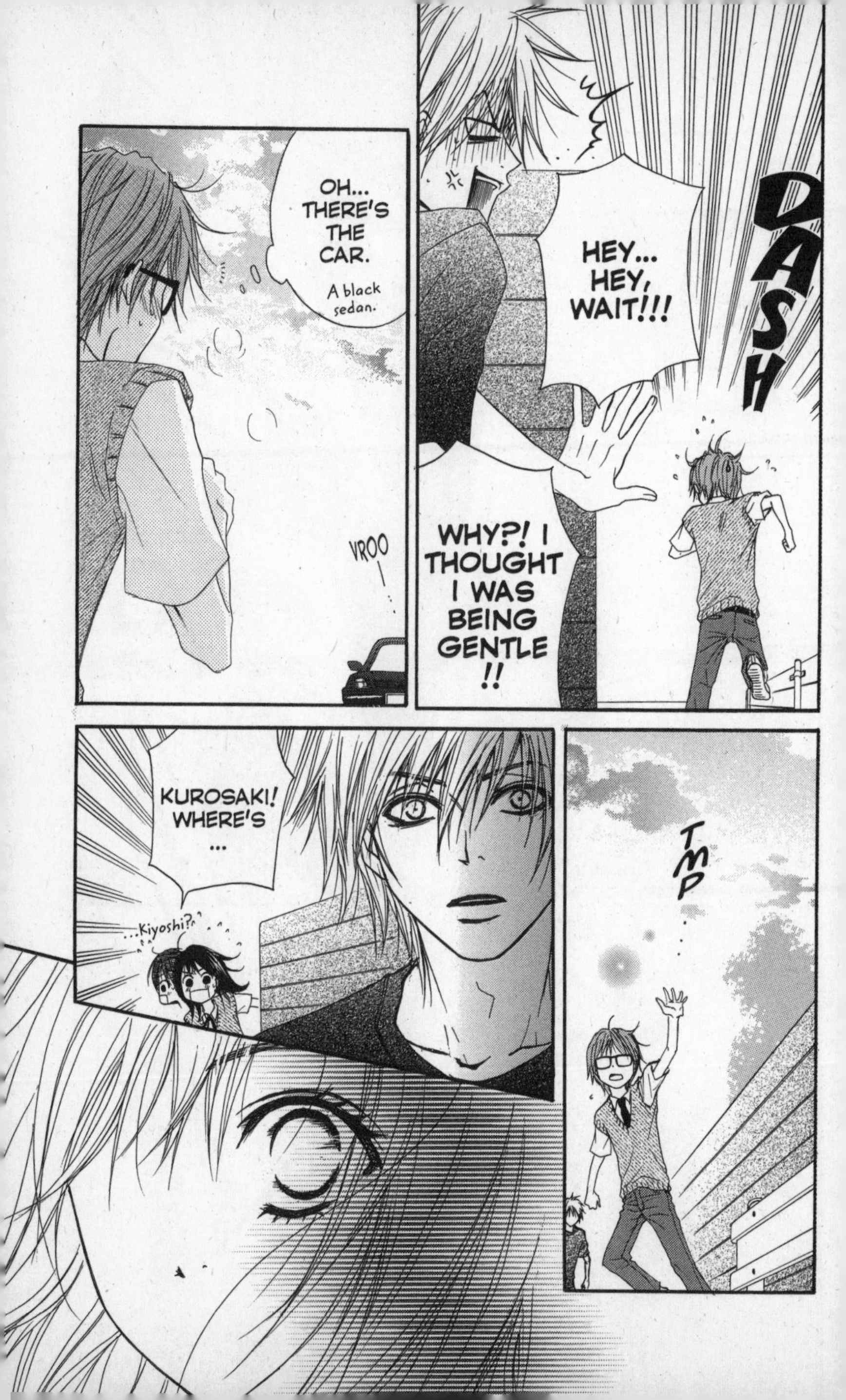
HEY... HEY, WAIT!!!
DASH
WHY?! I THOUGHT I WAS BEING GENTLE!!
OH... THERE'S THE CAR.
A black sedan.
VROO
TMP
KUROSAKI! WHERE'S ...
...Kiyoshi?

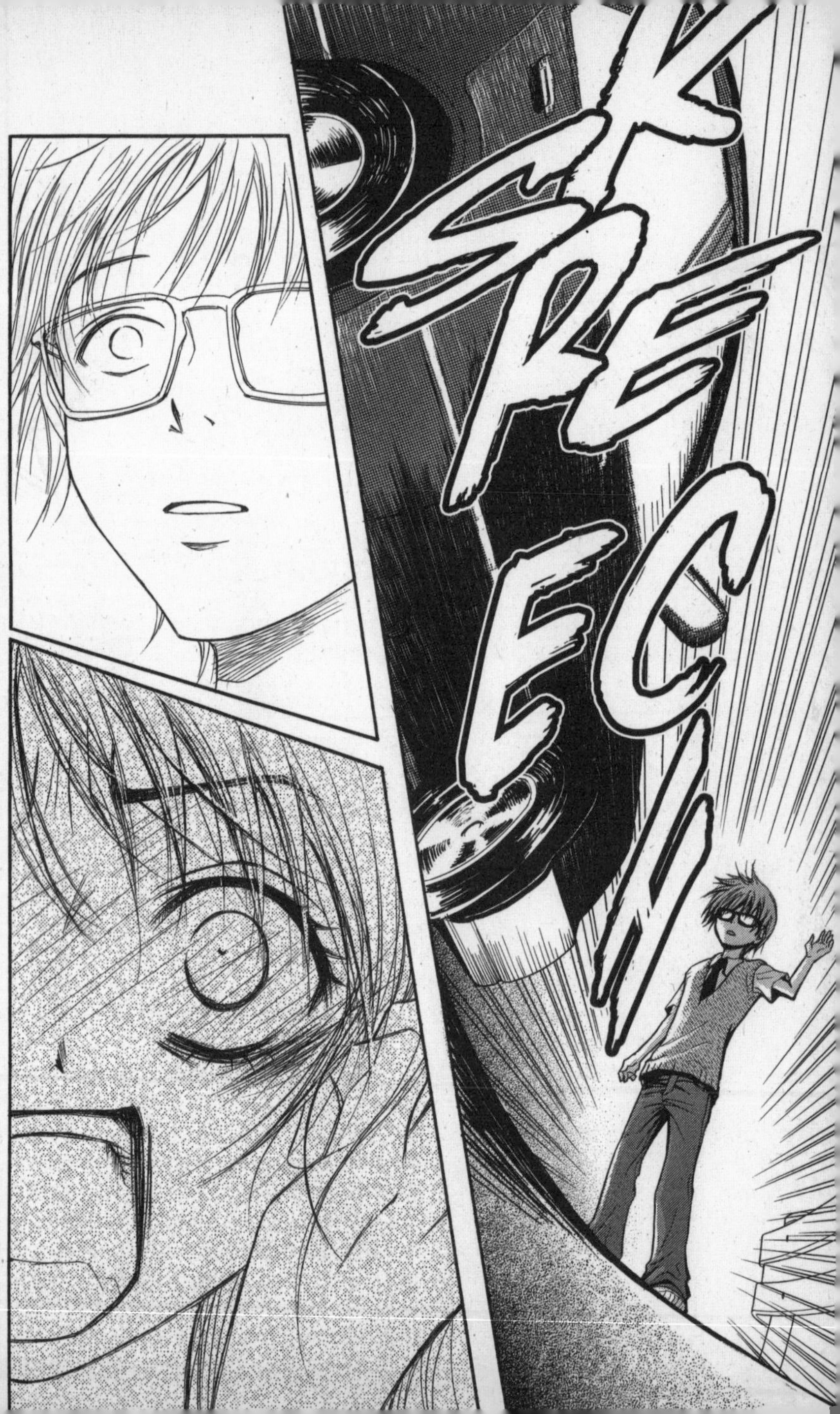
SKREEECH

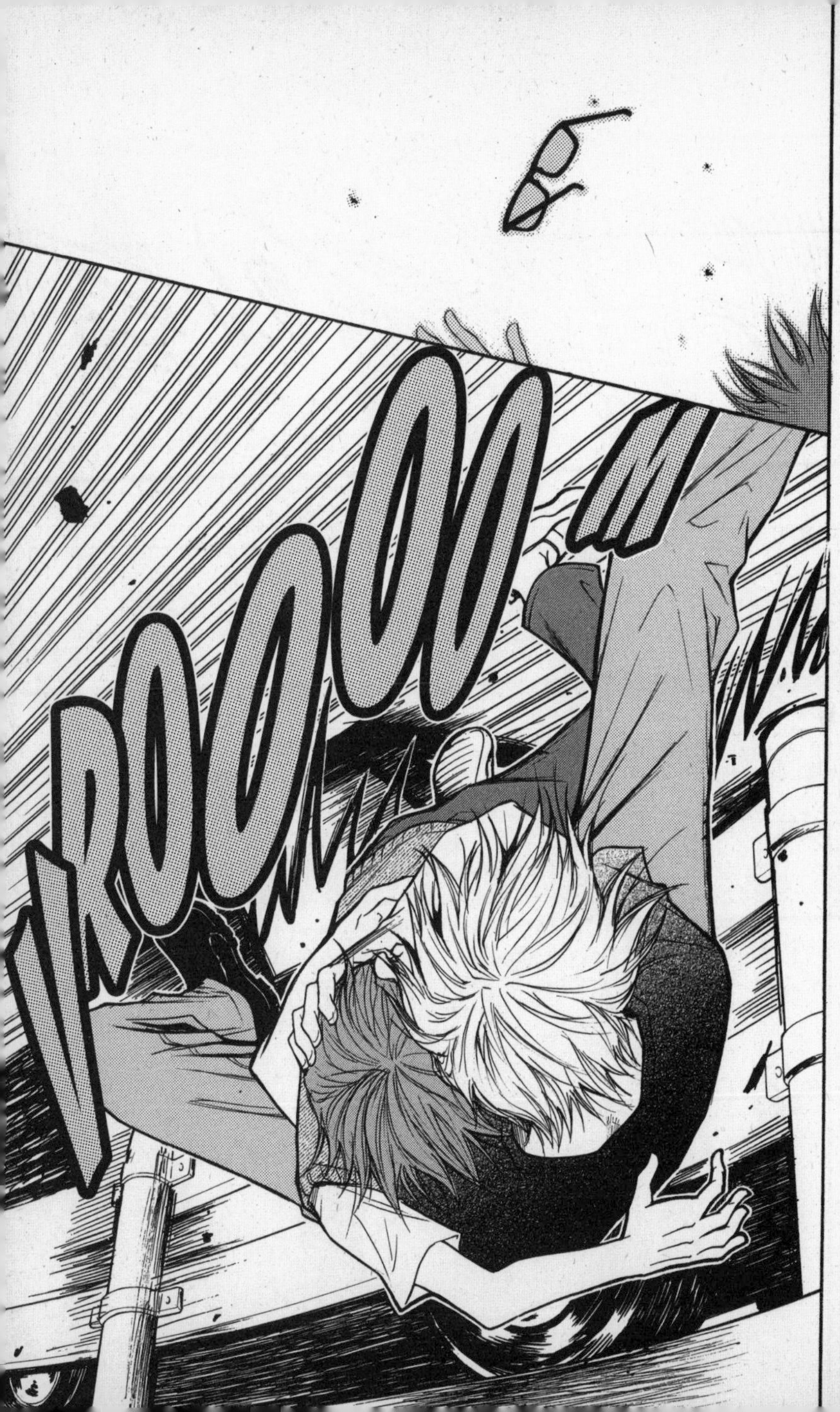
VROOOOOM

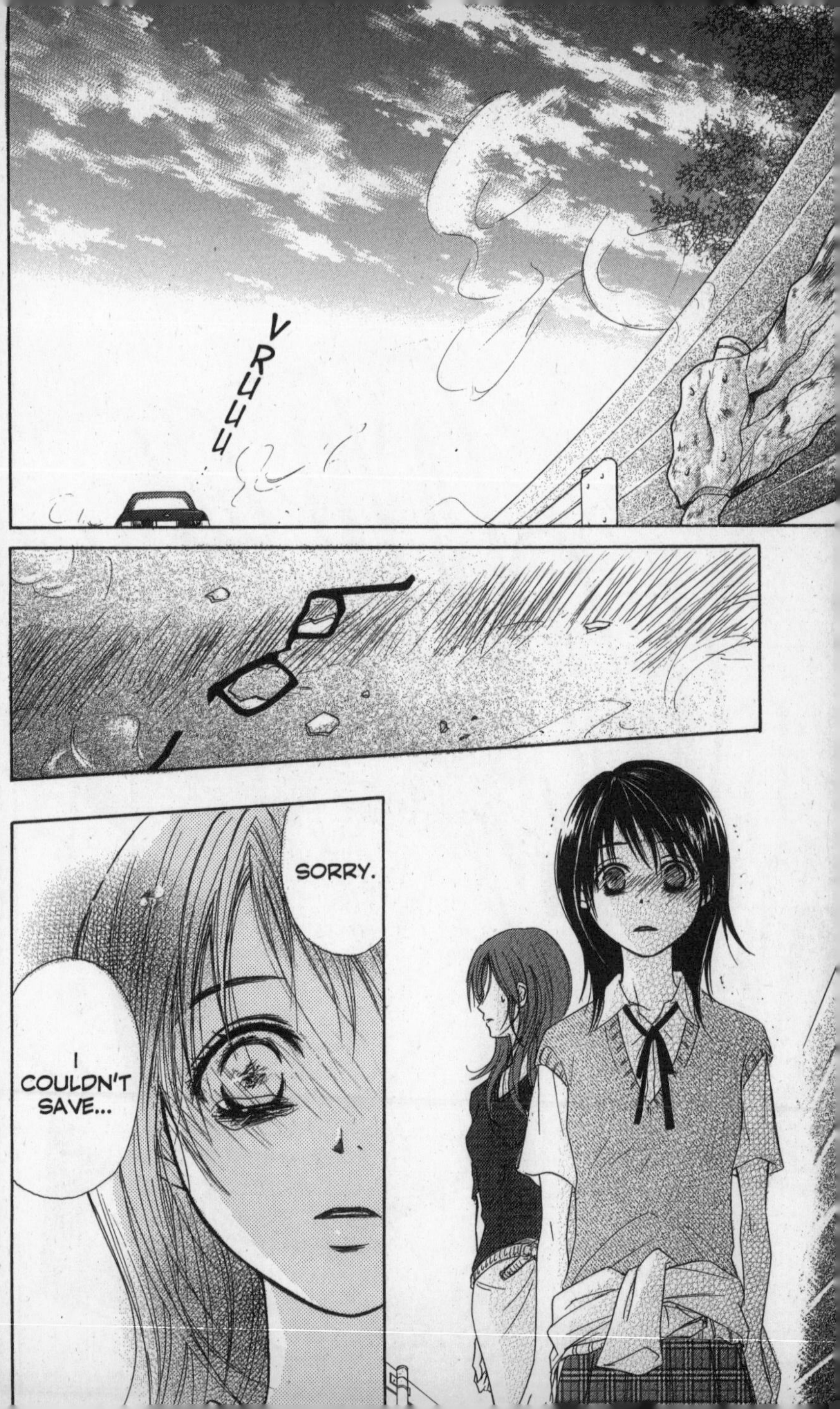
VRUUU
SORRY.
I COULDN'T SAVE...

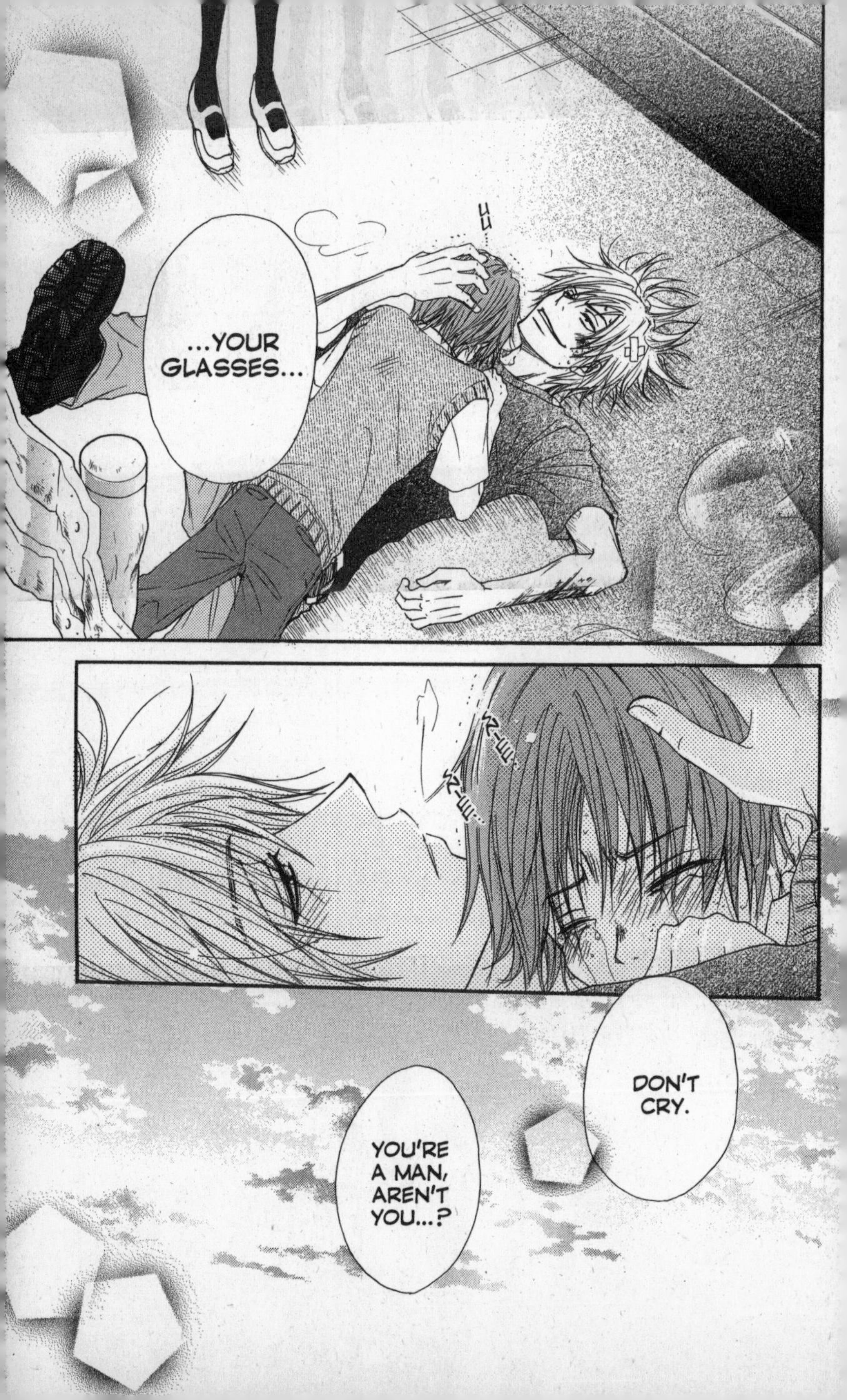
UU...
...YOUR GLASSES...
SN-E...
SN-E...
DON'T CRY.
YOU'RE A MAN, AREN'T YOU...?

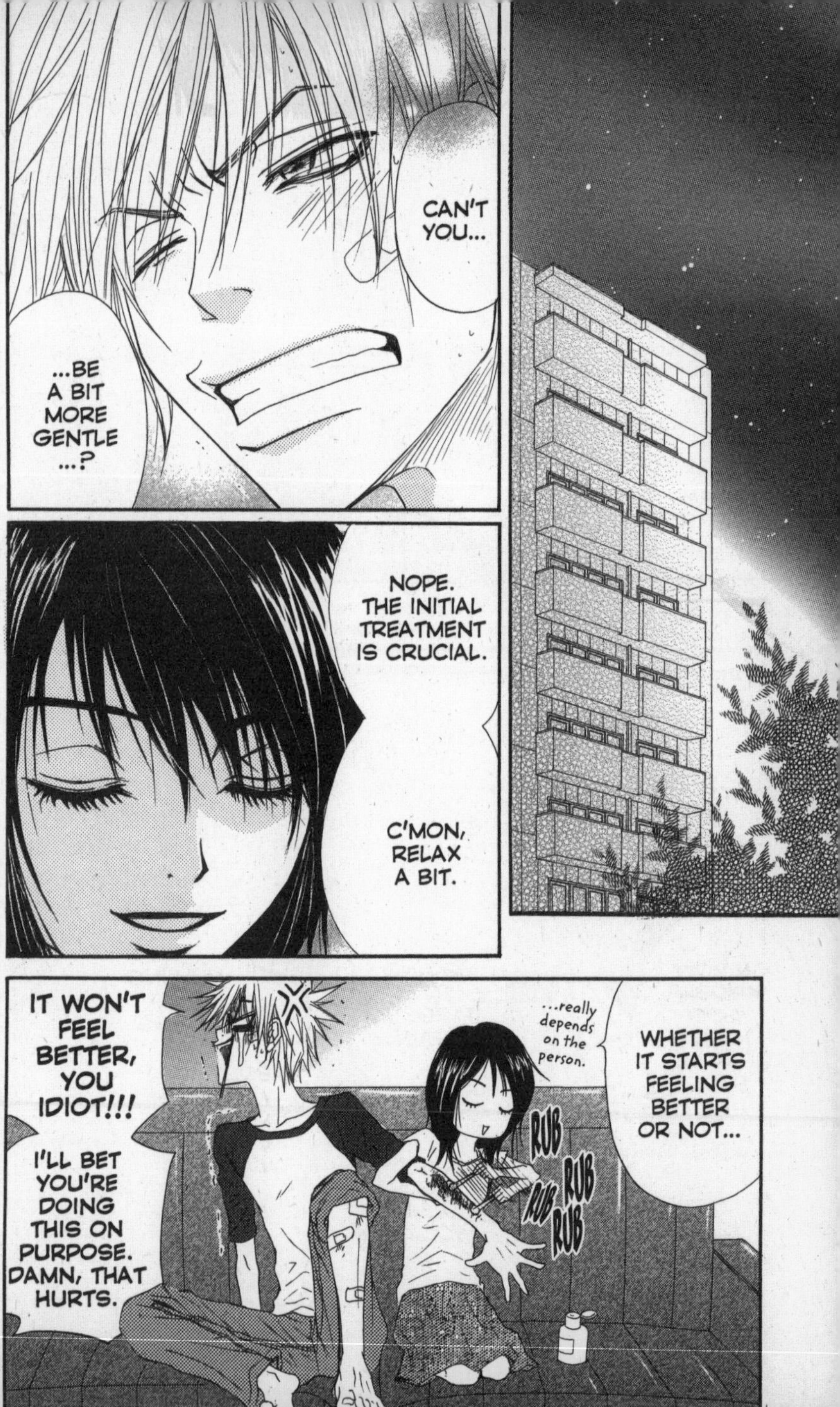
CAN'T YOU...
...BE A BIT MORE GENTLE ...?
NOPE. THE INITIAL TREATMENT IS CRUCIAL.
C'MON, RELAX A BIT.
WHETHER IT STARTS FEELING BETTER OR NOT...
...really depends on the person.
RUB RUB RUB RUB
IT WON'T FEEL BETTER, YOU IDIOT!!!
I'LL BET YOU'RE DOING THIS ON PURPOSE. DAMN, THAT HURTS.

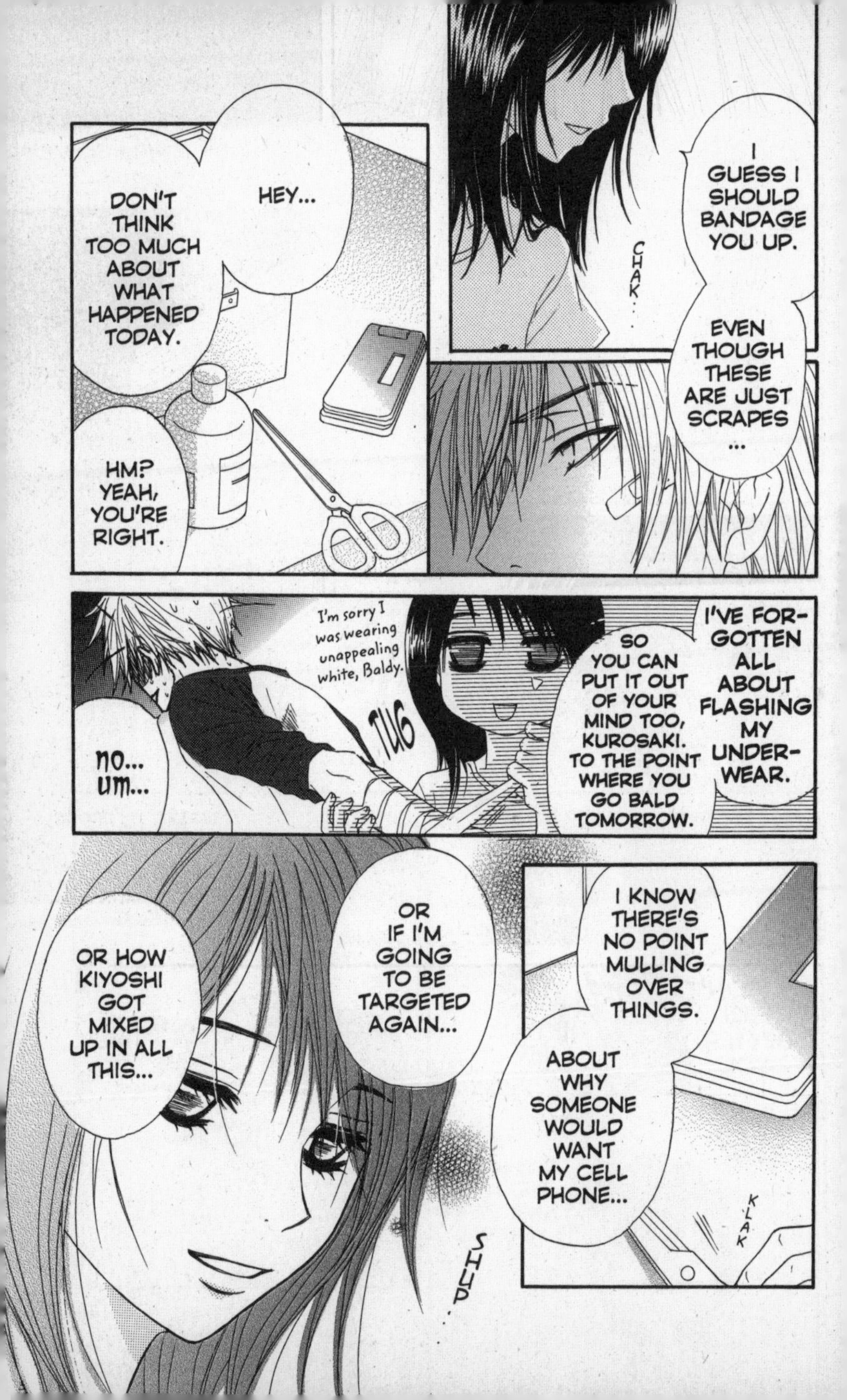
I GUESS I SHOULD BANDAGE YOU UP.
CHAK...
EVEN THOUGH THESE ARE JUST SCRAPES...
HEY...
DON'T THINK TOO MUCH ABOUT WHAT HAPPENED TODAY.
HM? YEAH, YOU'RE RIGHT.
I'VE FORGOTTEN ALL ABOUT FLASHING MY UNDERWEAR.
SO YOU CAN PUT IT OUT OF YOUR MIND TOO, KUROSAKI. TO THE POINT WHERE YOU GO BALD TOMORROW.
I'm sorry I was wearing unappealing white, Baldy.
TUG
no... um...
I KNOW THERE'S NO POINT MULLING OVER THINGS.
ABOUT WHY SOMEONE WOULD WANT MY CELL PHONE...
KLAK
OR IF I'M GOING TO BE TARGETED AGAIN...
OR HOW KIYOSHI GOT MIXED UP IN ALL THIS...
SHUP.

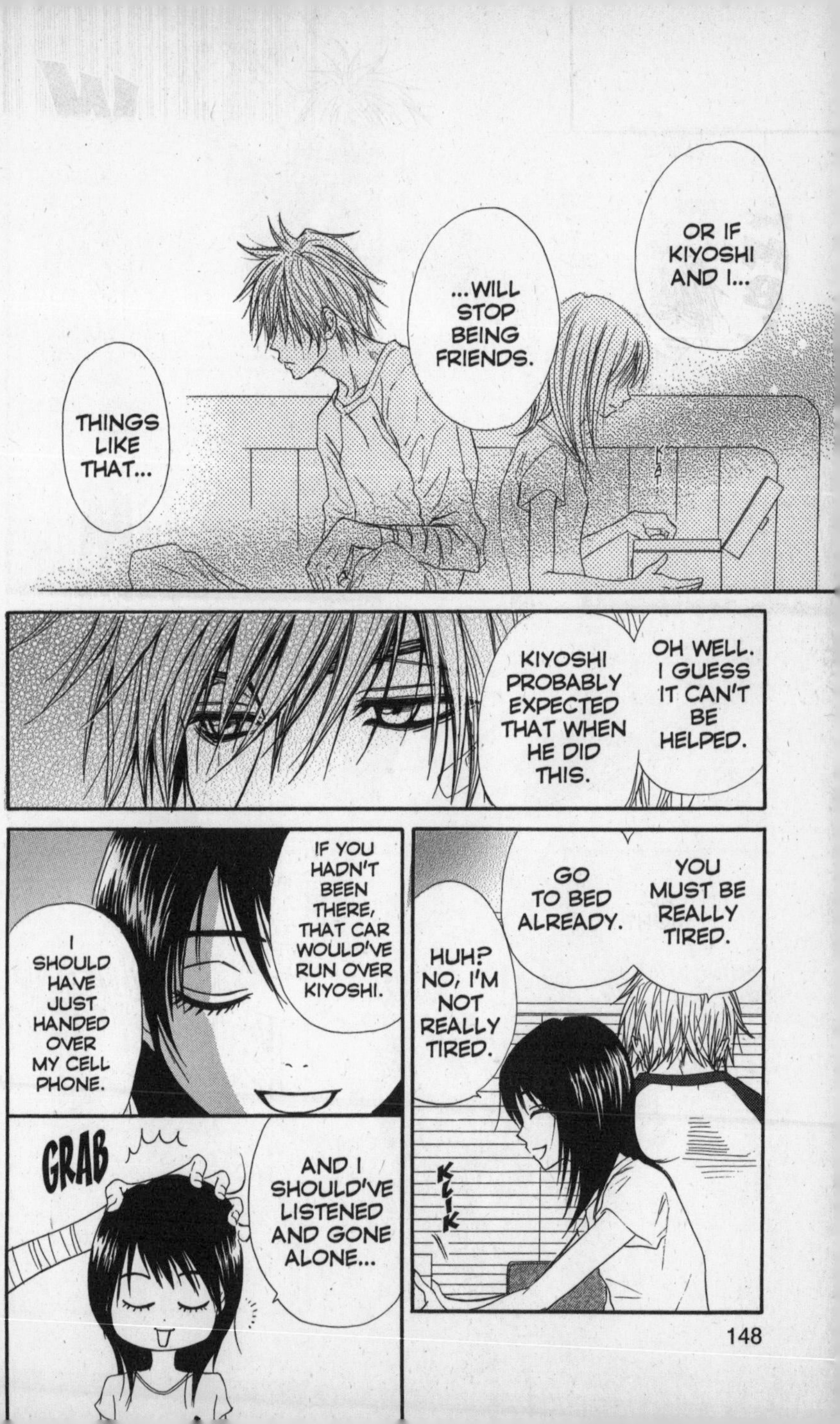
OR IF KIYOSHI AND I...
...WILL STOP BEING FRIENDS.
THINGS LIKE THAT...
OH WELL. I GUESS IT CAN'T BE HELPED.
KIYOSHI PROBABLY EXPECTED THAT WHEN HE DID THIS.
YOU MUST BE REALLY TIRED.
GO TO BED ALREADY.
HUH? NO, I'M NOT REALLY TIRED.
KLIK
IF YOU HADN'T BEEN THERE, THAT CAR WOULD'VE RUN OVER KIYOSHI.
I SHOULD HAVE JUST HANDED OVER MY CELL PHONE.
AND I SHOULD'VE LISTENED AND GONE ALONE...
GRAB

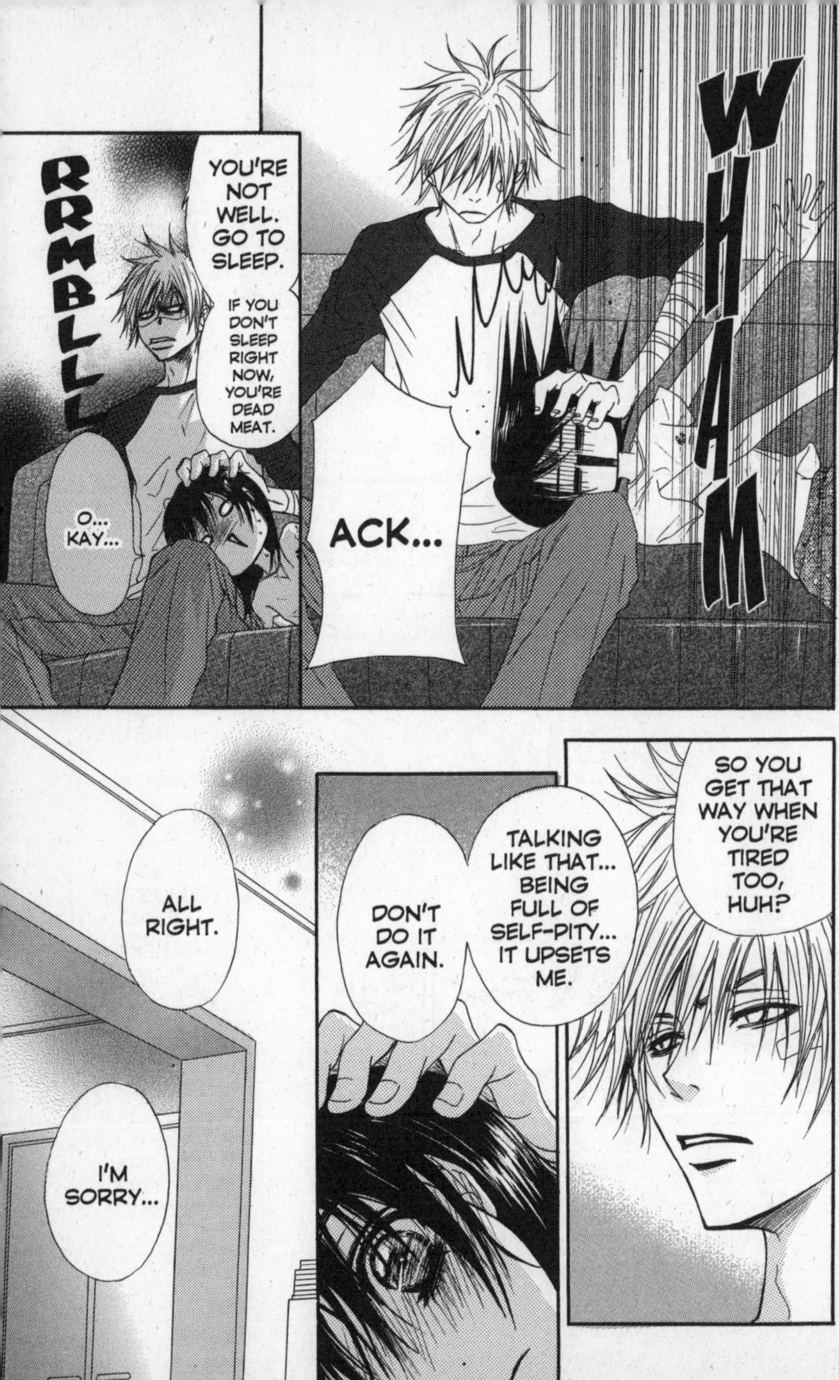
WHAM
ACK...
RRMBLLL
YOU'RE NOT WELL. GO TO SLEEP.
IF YOU DON'T SLEEP RIGHT NOW, YOU'RE DEAD MEAT.
O... KAY...
SO YOU GET THAT WAY WHEN YOU'RE TIRED TOO, HUH?
TALKING LIKE THAT... BEING FULL OF SELF-PITY... IT UPSETS ME.
DON'T DO IT AGAIN.
ALL RIGHT.
I'M SORRY...

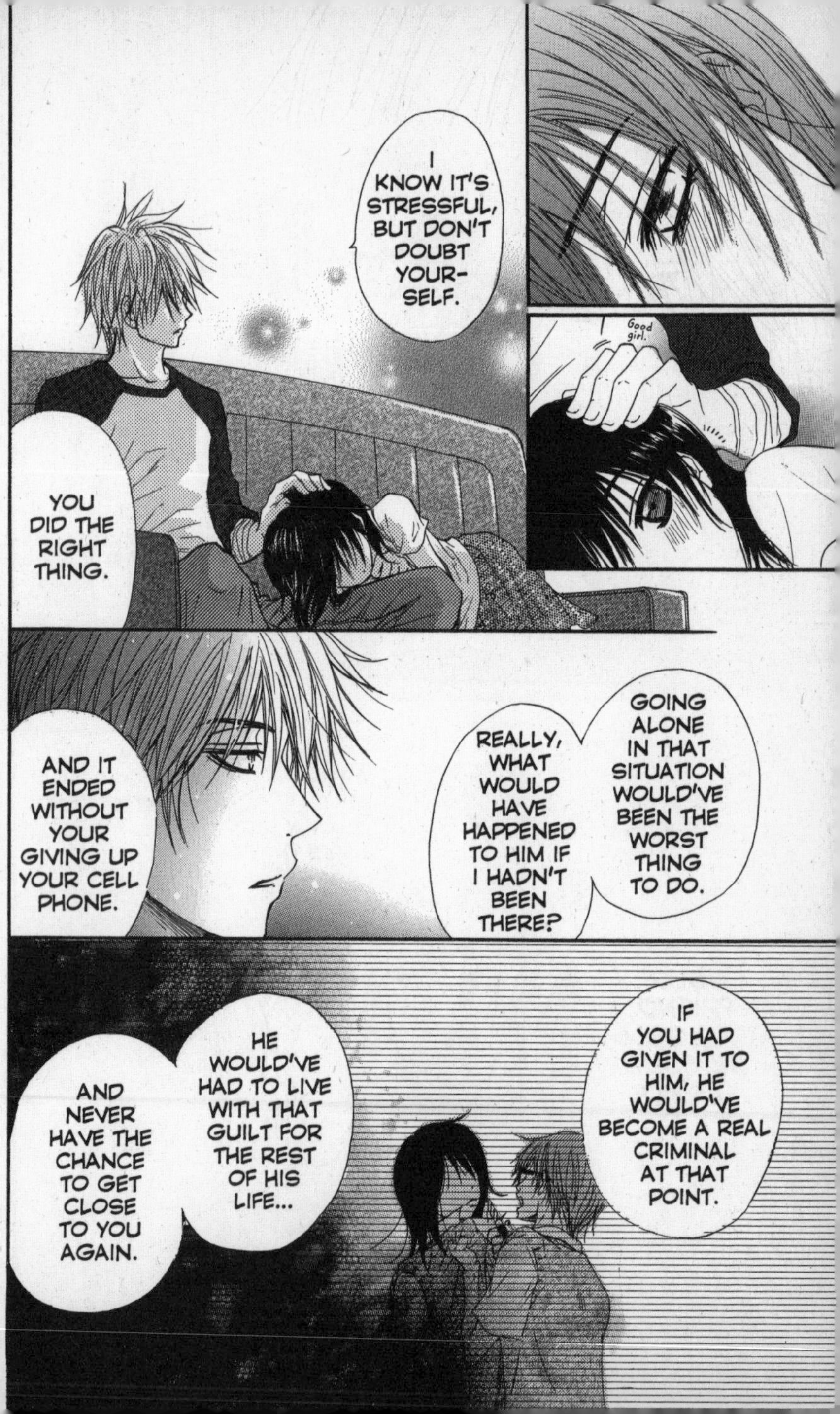
Good girl.
I KNOW IT'S STRESSFUL, BUT DON'T DOUBT YOURSELF.
YOU DID THE RIGHT THING.
GOING ALONE IN THAT SITUATION WOULD'VE BEEN THE WORST THING TO DO.
REALLY, WHAT WOULD HAVE HAPPENED TO HIM IF I HADN'T BEEN THERE?
AND IT ENDED WITHOUT YOUR GIVING UP YOUR CELL PHONE.
IF YOU HAD GIVEN IT TO HIM, HE WOULD'VE BECOME A REAL CRIMINAL AT THAT POINT.
HE WOULD'VE HAD TO LIVE WITH THAT GUILT FOR THE REST OF HIS LIFE...
AND NEVER HAVE THE CHANCE TO GET CLOSE TO YOU AGAIN.

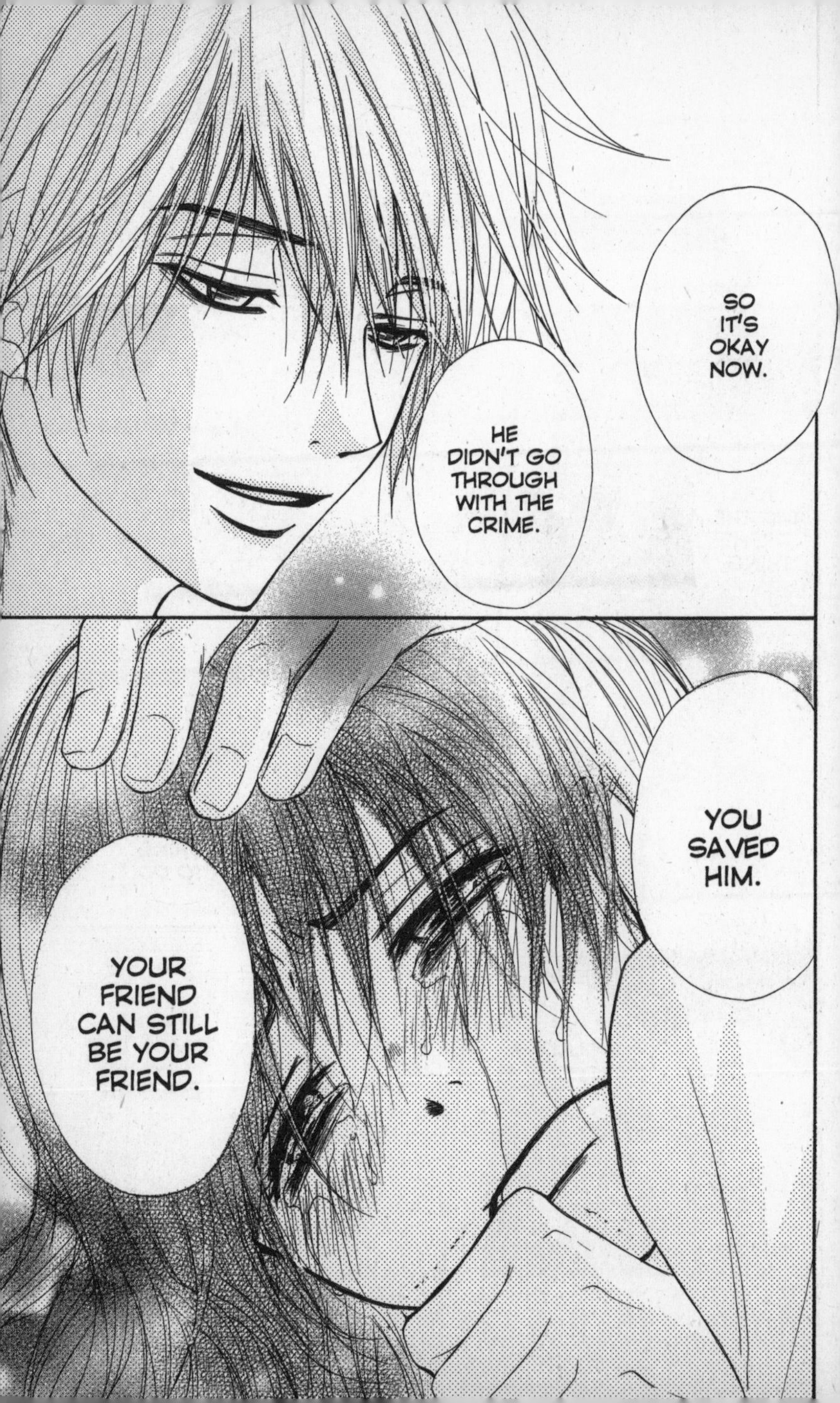
SO IT'S OKAY NOW.
HE DIDN'T GO THROUGH WITH THE CRIME.
YOU SAVED HIM.
YOUR FRIEND CAN STILL BE YOUR FRIEND.

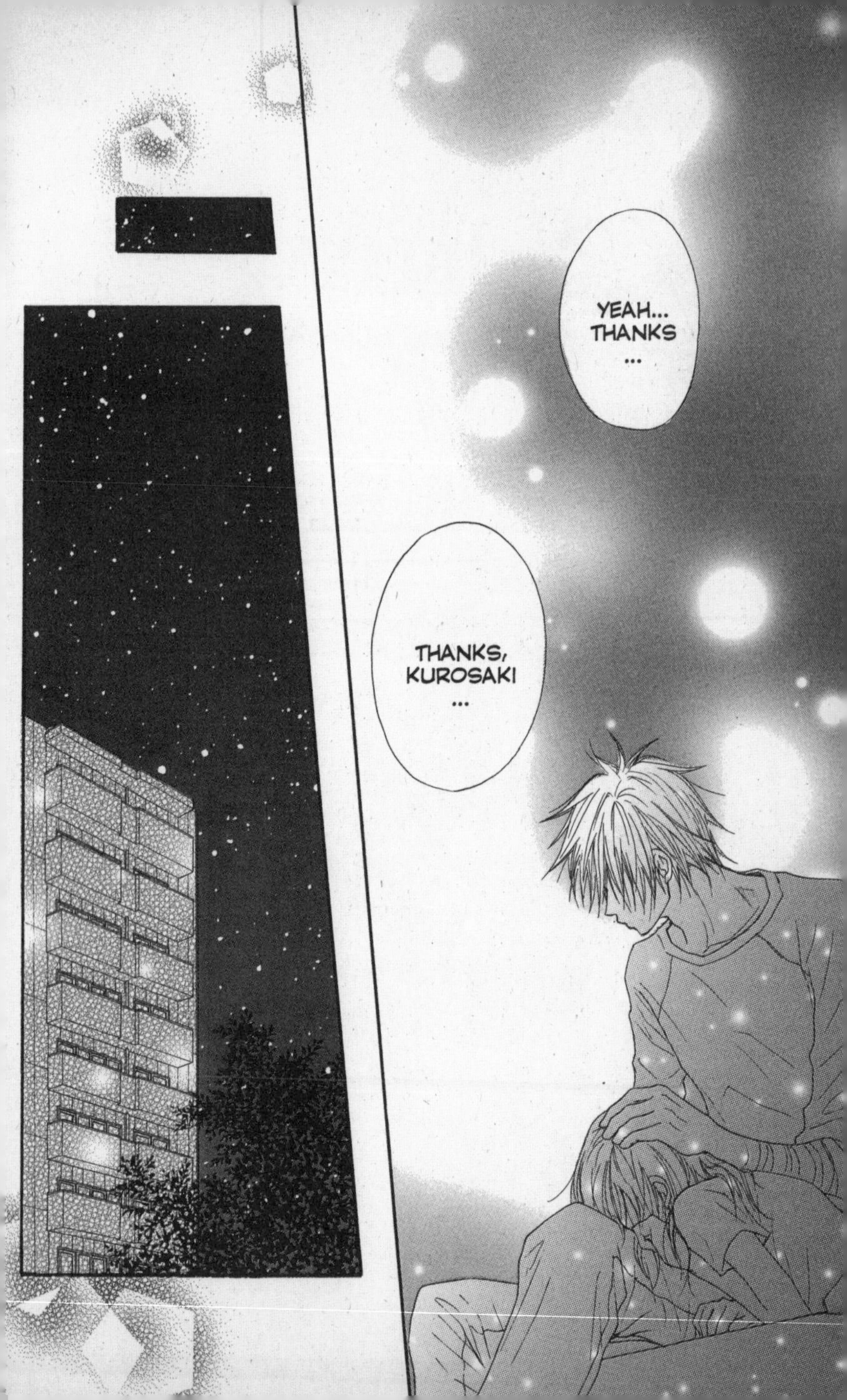
YEAH... THANKS ...
THANKS, KUROSAKI ...

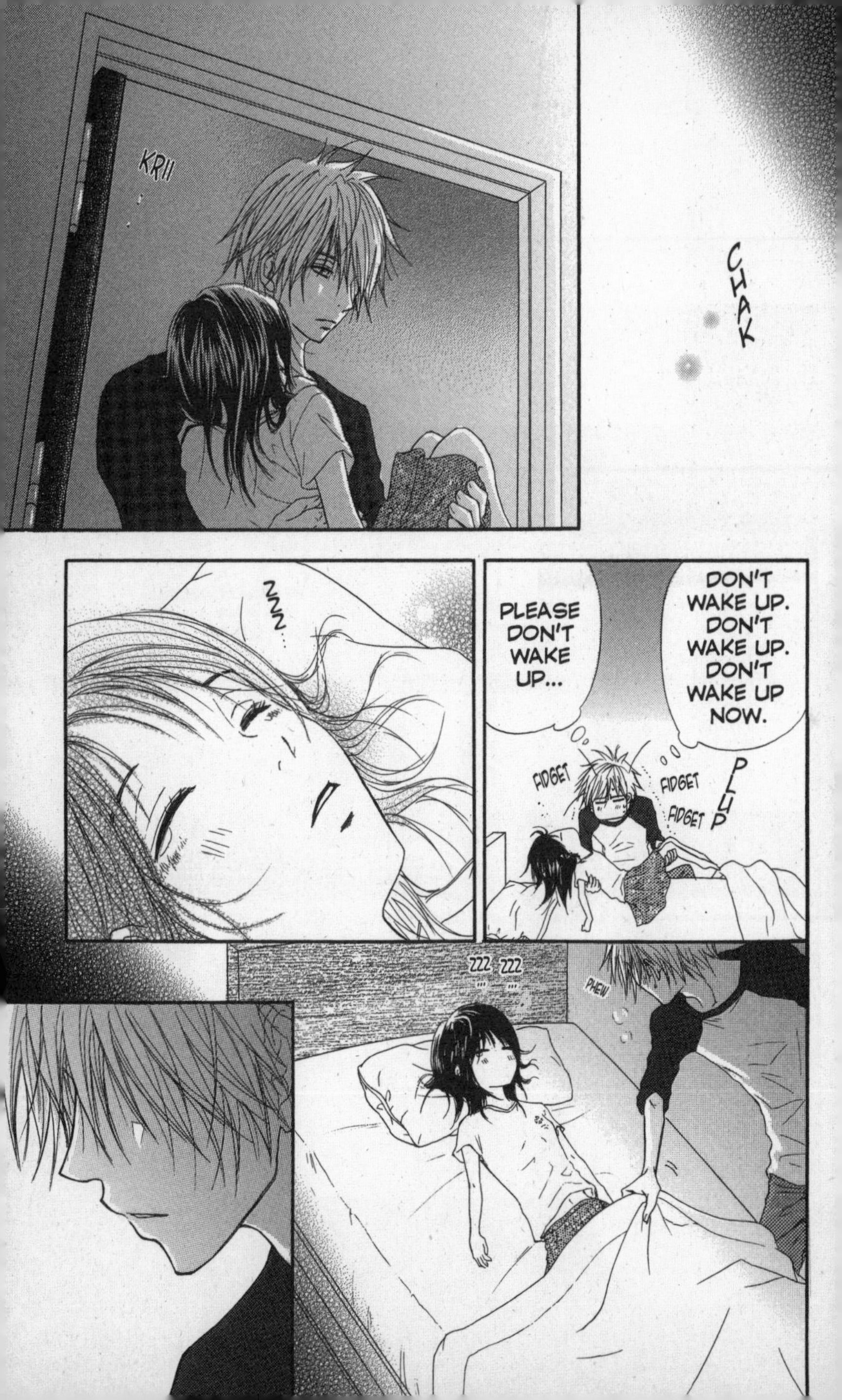
CHAK
KRII
DON'T WAKE UP. DON'T WAKE UP. DON'T WAKE UP NOW.
PLEASE DON'T WAKE UP...
PLUP
FIDGET
FIDGET
FIDGET
ZZZ...
PHEW
ZZZ ZZZ

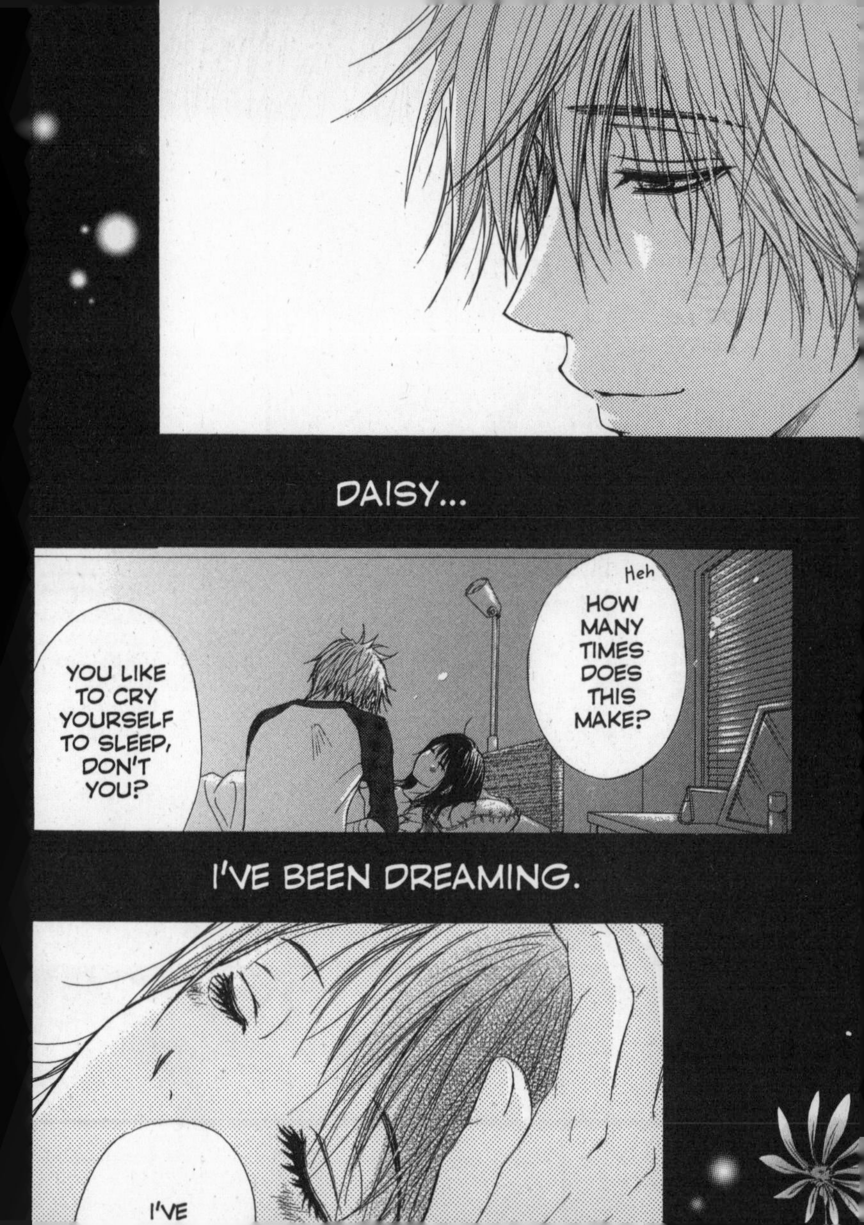
DAISY...
Heh
HOW MANY TIMES DOES THIS MAKE?
YOU LIKE TO CRY YOURSELF TO SLEEP, DON'T YOU?
I'VE BEEN DREAMING.
I'VE

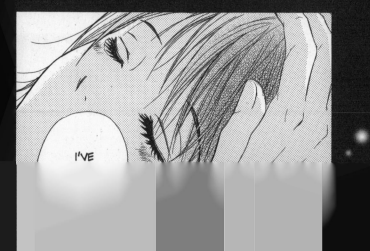

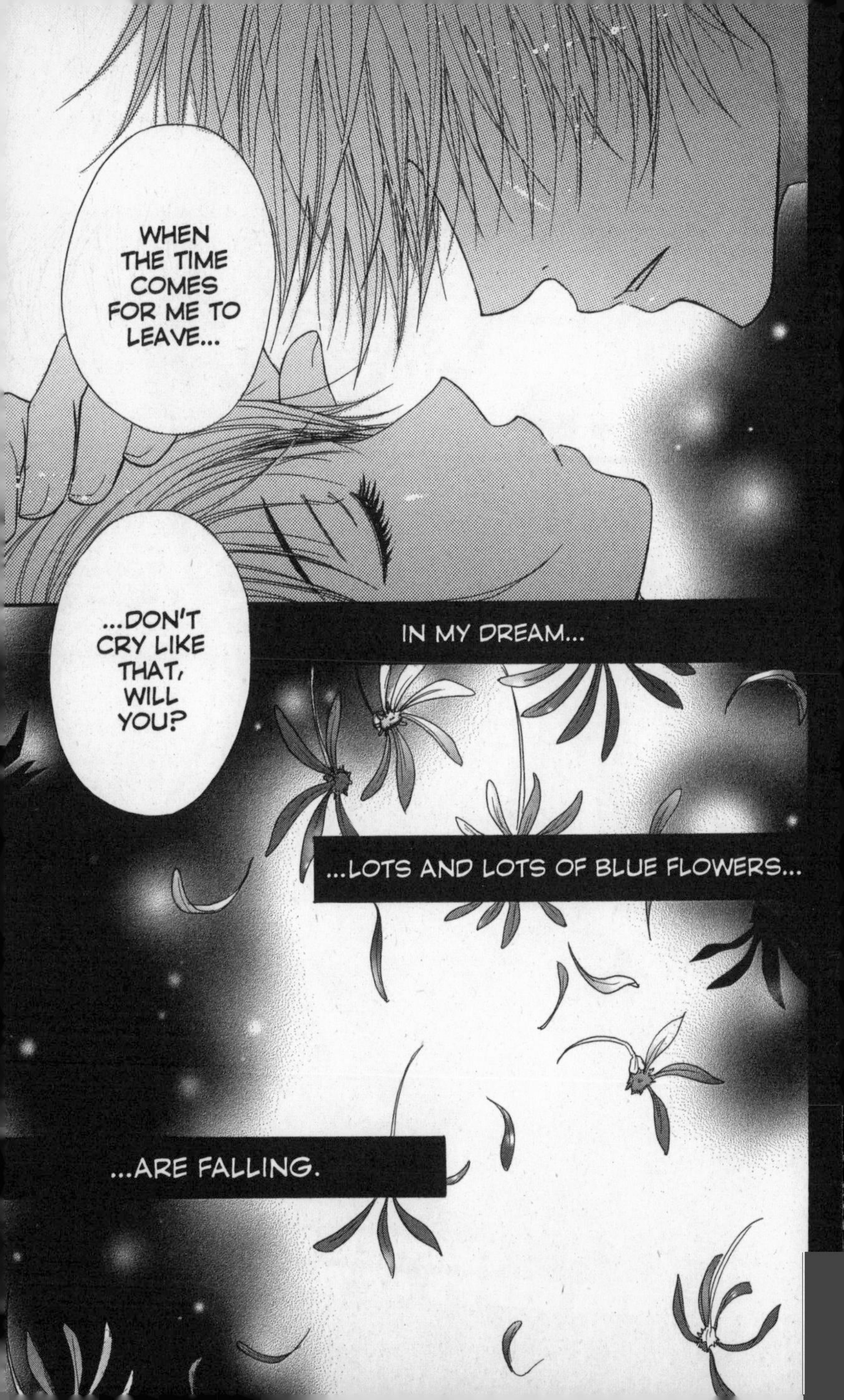
WHEN THE TIME COMES FOR ME TO LEAVE...
...DON'T CRY LIKE THAT, WILL YOU?
IN MY DREAM...
...LOTS AND LOTS OF BLUE FLOWERS...
...ARE FALLING.

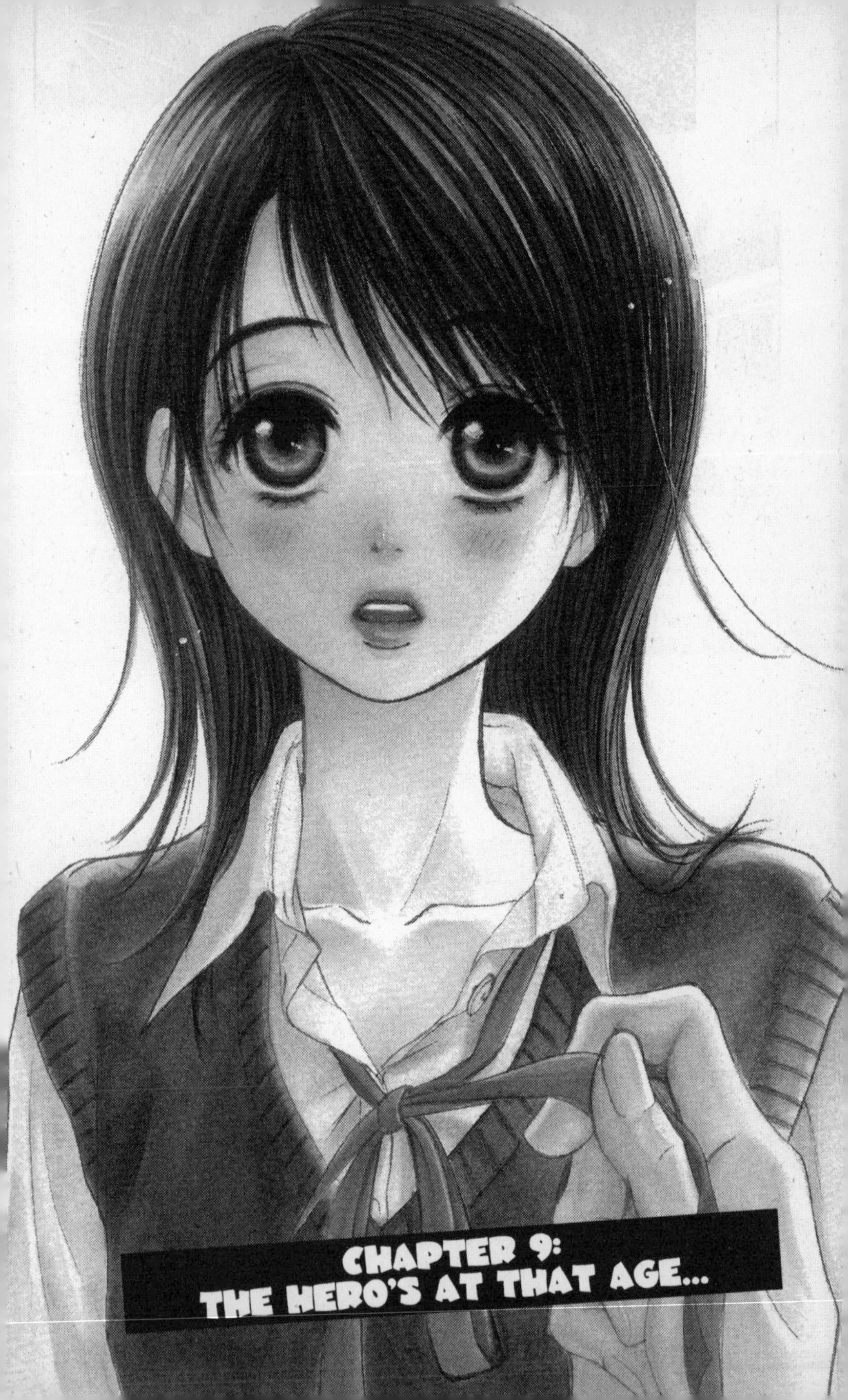
CHAPTER 9:
THE HERO'S AT THAT AGE...

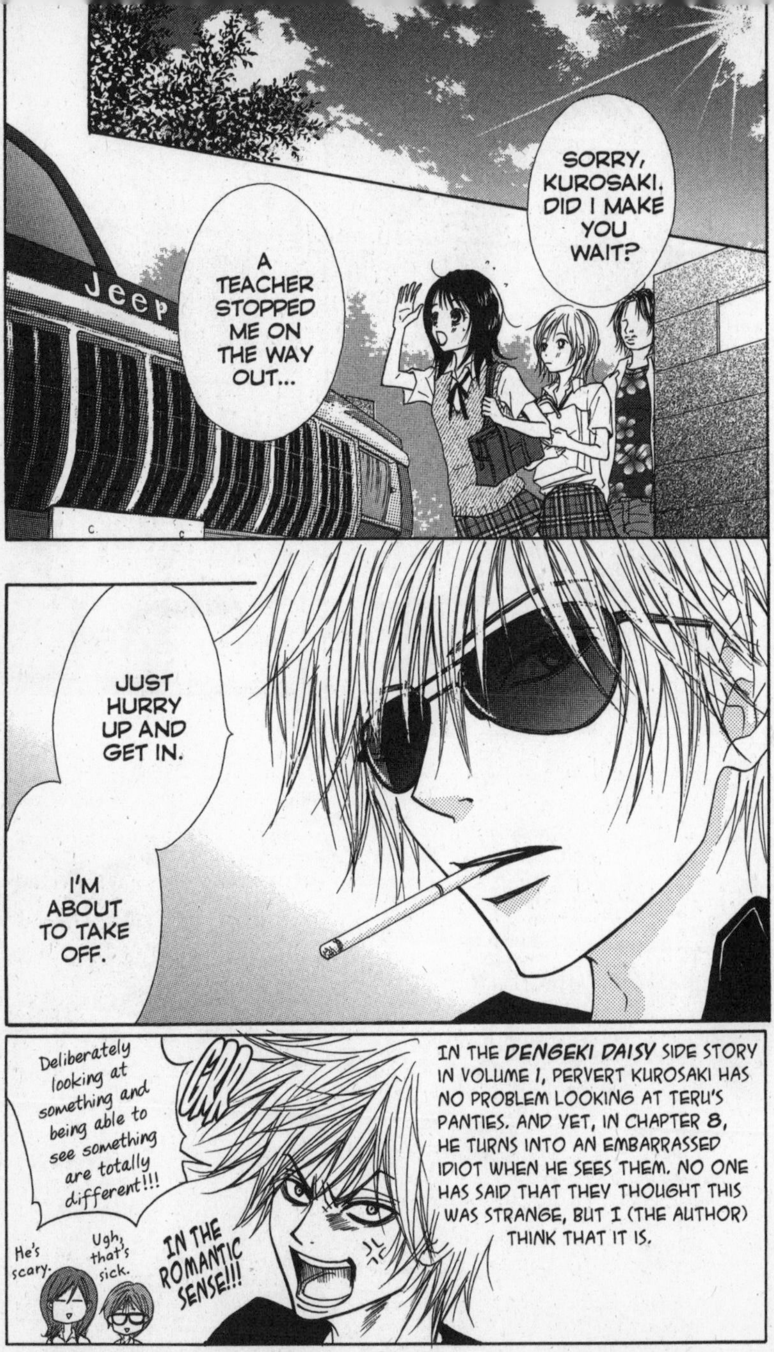
SORRY, KUROSAKI. DID I MAKE YOU WAIT?
A TEACHER STOPPED ME ON THE WAY OUT...
Jeep
JUST HURRY UP AND GET IN.
I'M ABOUT TO TAKE OFF.
IN THE DENGEKI DAISY SIDE STORY IN VOLUME 1, PERVERT KUROSAKI HAS NO PROBLEM LOOKING AT TERU'S PANTIES. AND YET, IN CHAPTER 8, HE TURNS INTO AN EMBARRASSED IDIOT WHEN HE SEES THEM. NO ONE HAS SAID THAT THEY THOUGHT THIS WAS STRANGE, BUT I (THE AUTHOR) THINK THAT IT IS.
Deliberately looking at something and being able to see something are totally different!!!
IN THE ROMANTIC SENSE!!!
Ugh, that's sick.
He's scary.

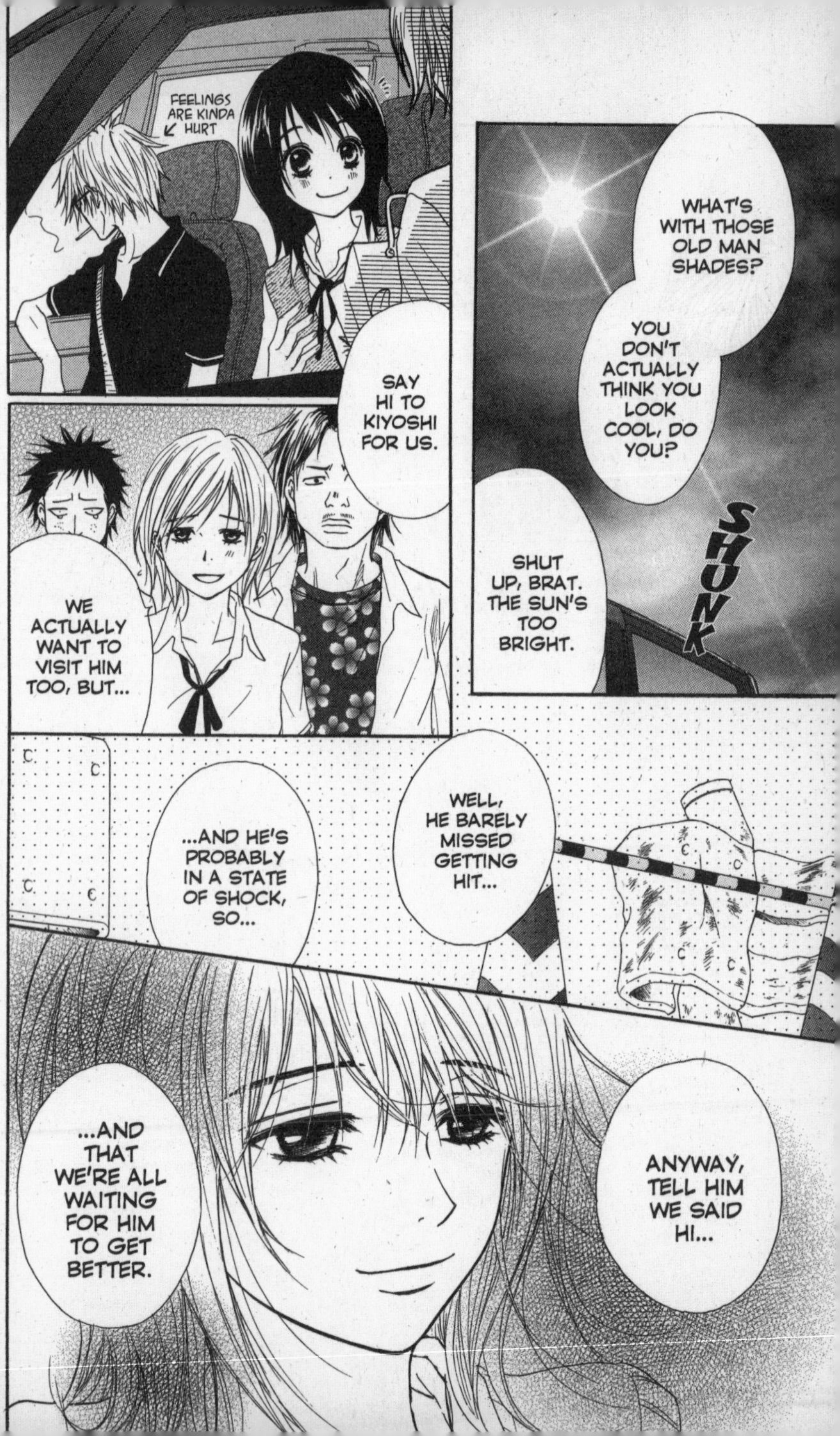
WHAT'S WITH THOSE OLD MAN SHADES?
YOU DON'T ACTUALLY THINK YOU LOOK COOL, DO YOU?
SHUT UP, BRAT. THE SUN'S TOO BRIGHT.
SHUNK
FEELINGS ARE KINDA HURT
SAY HI TO KIYOSHI FOR US.
WE ACTUALLY WANT TO VISIT HIM TOO, BUT...
WELL, HE BARELY MISSED GETTING HIT...
...AND HE'S PROBABLY IN A STATE OF SHOCK, SO...
ANYWAY, TELL HIM WE SAID HI...
...AND THAT WE'RE ALL WAITING FOR HIM TO GET BETTER.

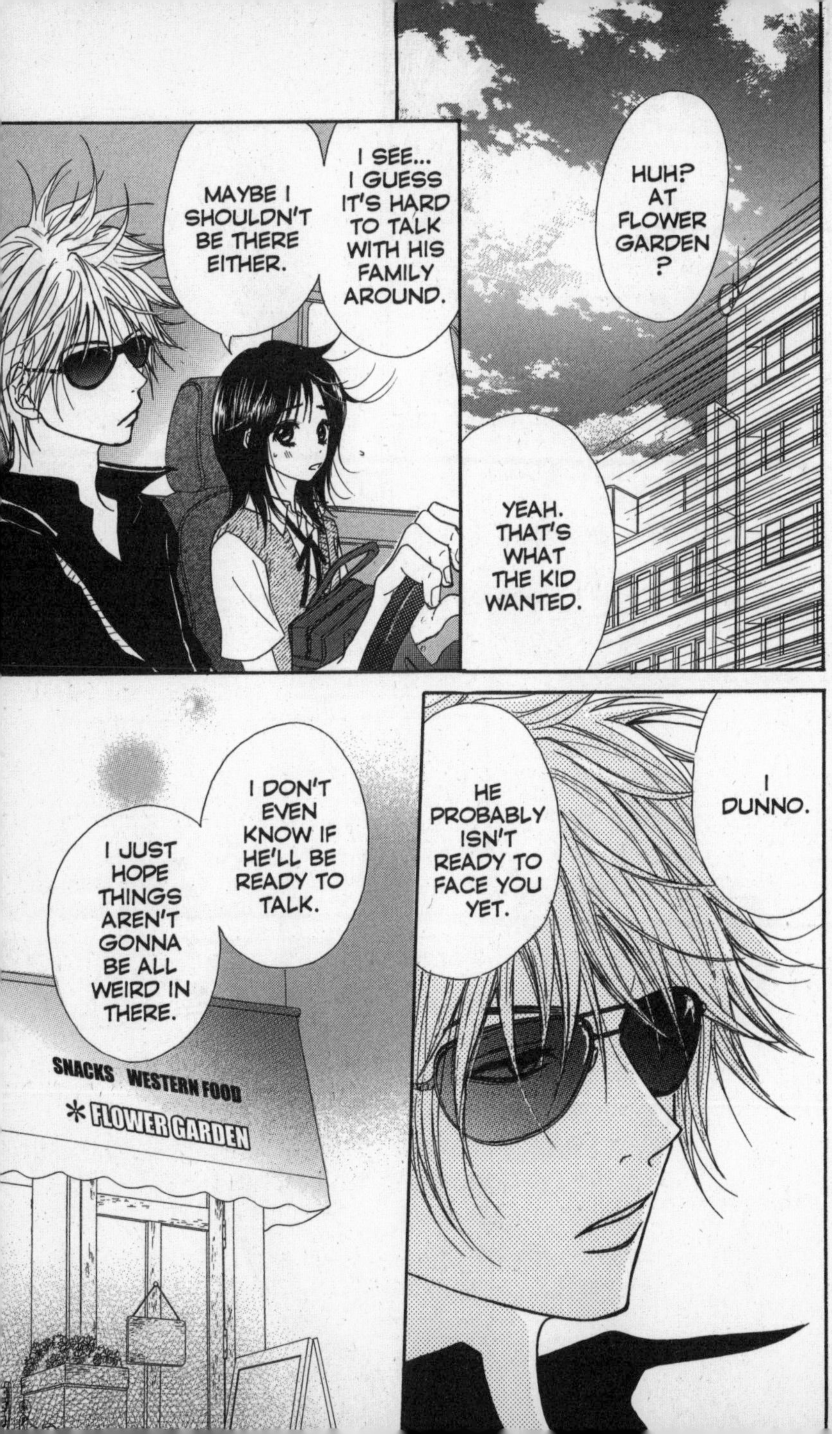
HUH? AT FLOWER GARDEN?
YEAH. THAT'S WHAT THE KID WANTED.
I SEE... I GUESS IT'S HARD TO TALK WITH HIS FAMILY AROUND.
MAYBE I SHOULDN'T BE THERE EITHER.
I DUNNO.
HE PROBABLY ISN'T READY TO FACE YOU YET.
I DON'T EVEN KNOW IF HE'LL BE READY TO TALK.
I JUST HOPE THINGS AREN'T GONNA BE ALL WEIRD IN THERE.
SNACKS WESTERN FOOD
* FLOWER GARDEN

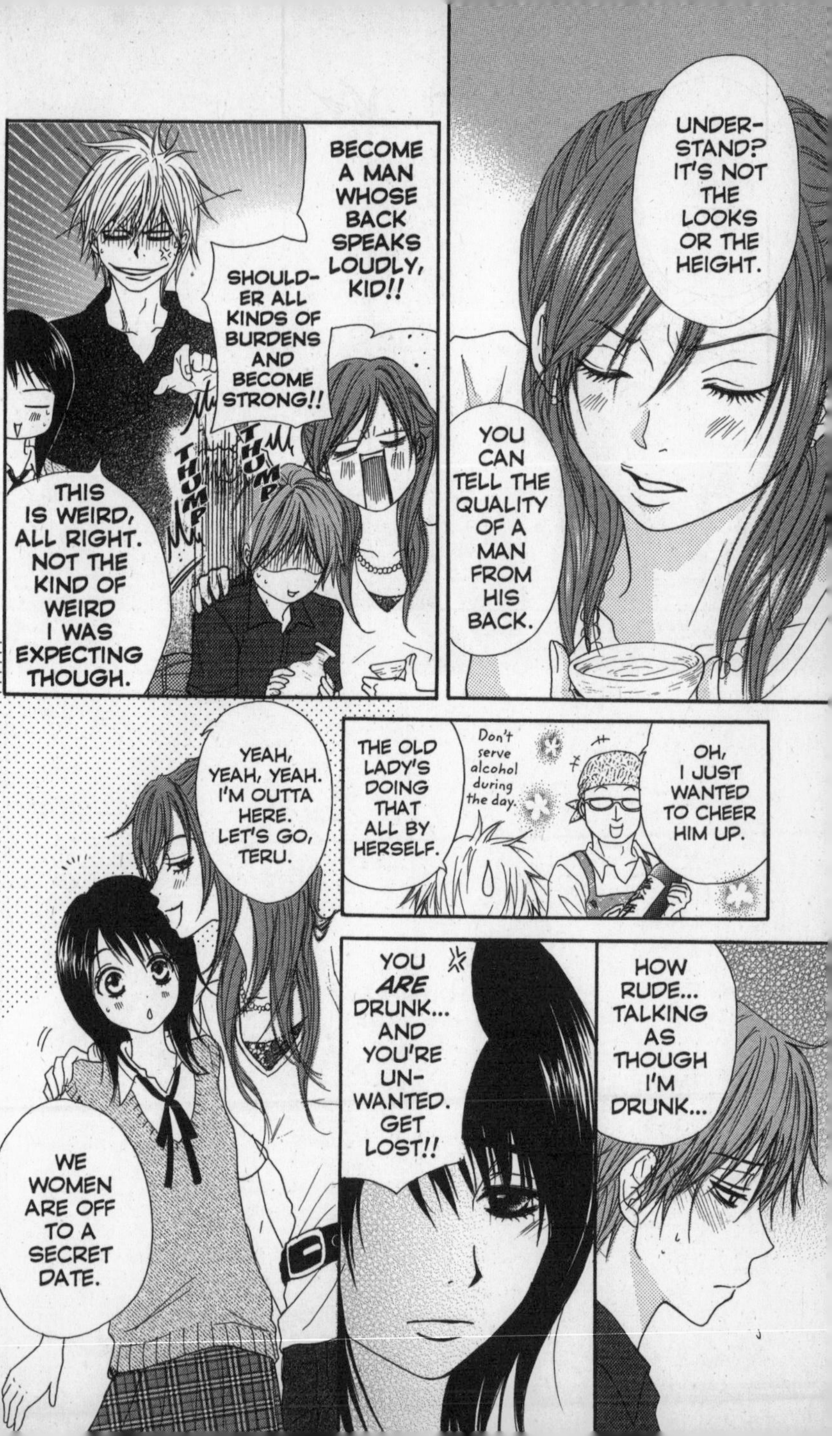
UNDER-STAND? IT'S NOT THE LOOKS OR THE HEIGHT.
YOU CAN TELL THE QUALITY OF A MAN FROM HIS BACK.
BECOME A MAN WHOSE BACK SPEAKS LOUDLY, KID!!
SHOULDER ALL KINDS OF BURDENS AND BECOME STRONG!!
THUMP
THUMP
THIS IS WEIRD, ALL RIGHT. NOT THE KIND OF WEIRD I WAS EXPECTING THOUGH.
OH, I JUST WANTED TO CHEER HIM UP.
Don't serve alcohol during the day.
THE OLD LADY'S DOING THAT ALL BY HERSELF.
HOW RUDE... TALKING AS THOUGH I'M DRUNK...
YOU *ARE* DRUNK... AND YOU'RE UNWANTED. GET LOST!!
YEAH, YEAH, YEAH. I'M OUTTA HERE. LET'S GO, TERU.
WE WOMEN ARE OFF TO A SECRET DATE.

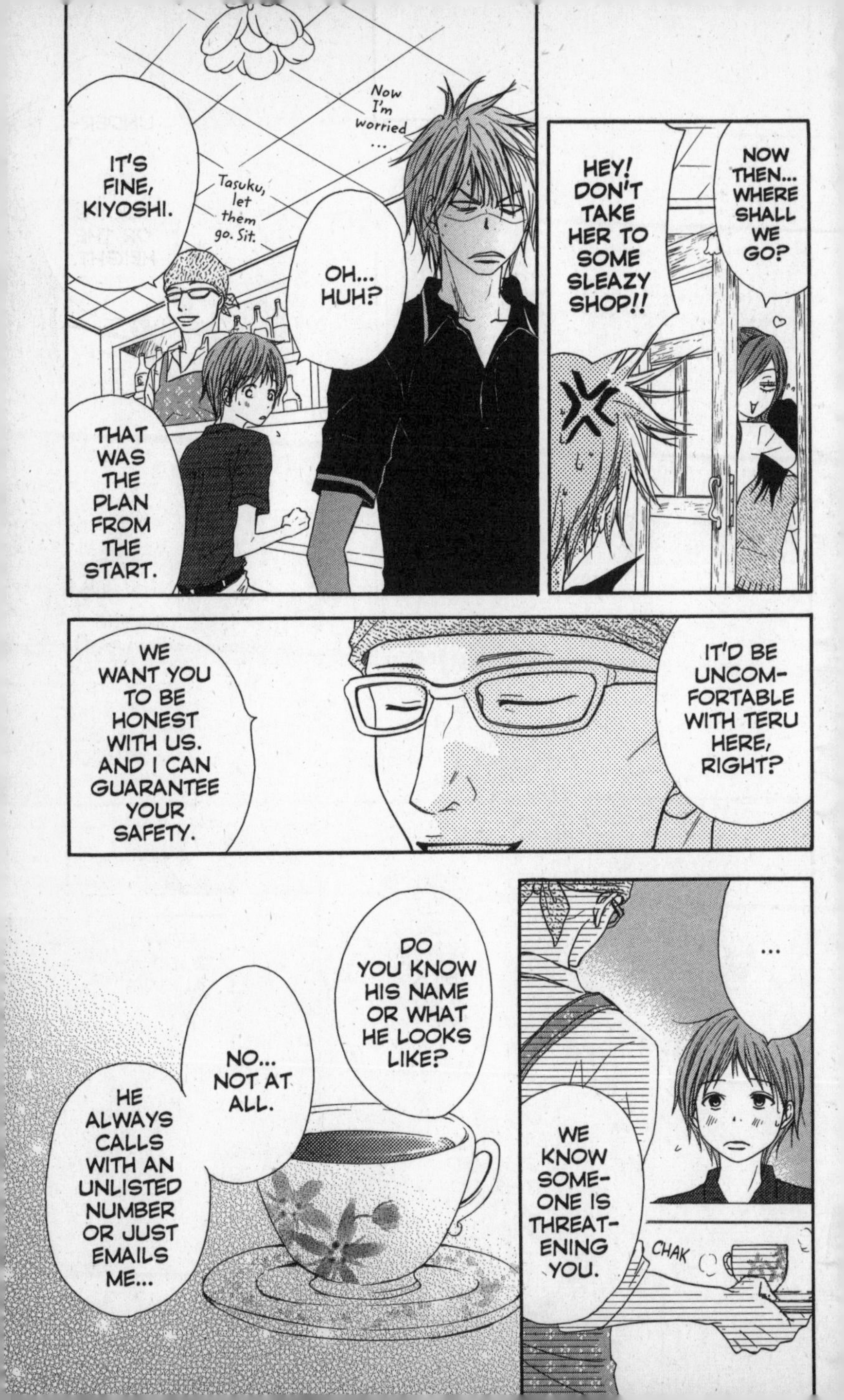
NOW THEN... WHERE SHALL WE GO?
HEY! DON'T TAKE HER TO SOME SLEAZY SHOP!!
Now I'm worried...
OH... HUH?
Tasuku, let them go. Sit.
IT'S FINE, KIYOSHI.
THAT WAS THE PLAN FROM THE START.
IT'D BE UNCOM-FORTABLE WITH TERU HERE, RIGHT?
WE WANT YOU TO BE HONEST WITH US. AND I CAN GUARANTEE YOUR SAFETY.
...
WE KNOW SOME-ONE IS THREAT-ENING YOU.
CHAK
DO YOU KNOW HIS NAME OR WHAT HE LOOKS LIKE?
NO... NOT AT ALL.
HE ALWAYS CALLS WITH AN UNLISTED NUMBER OR JUST EMAILS ME...

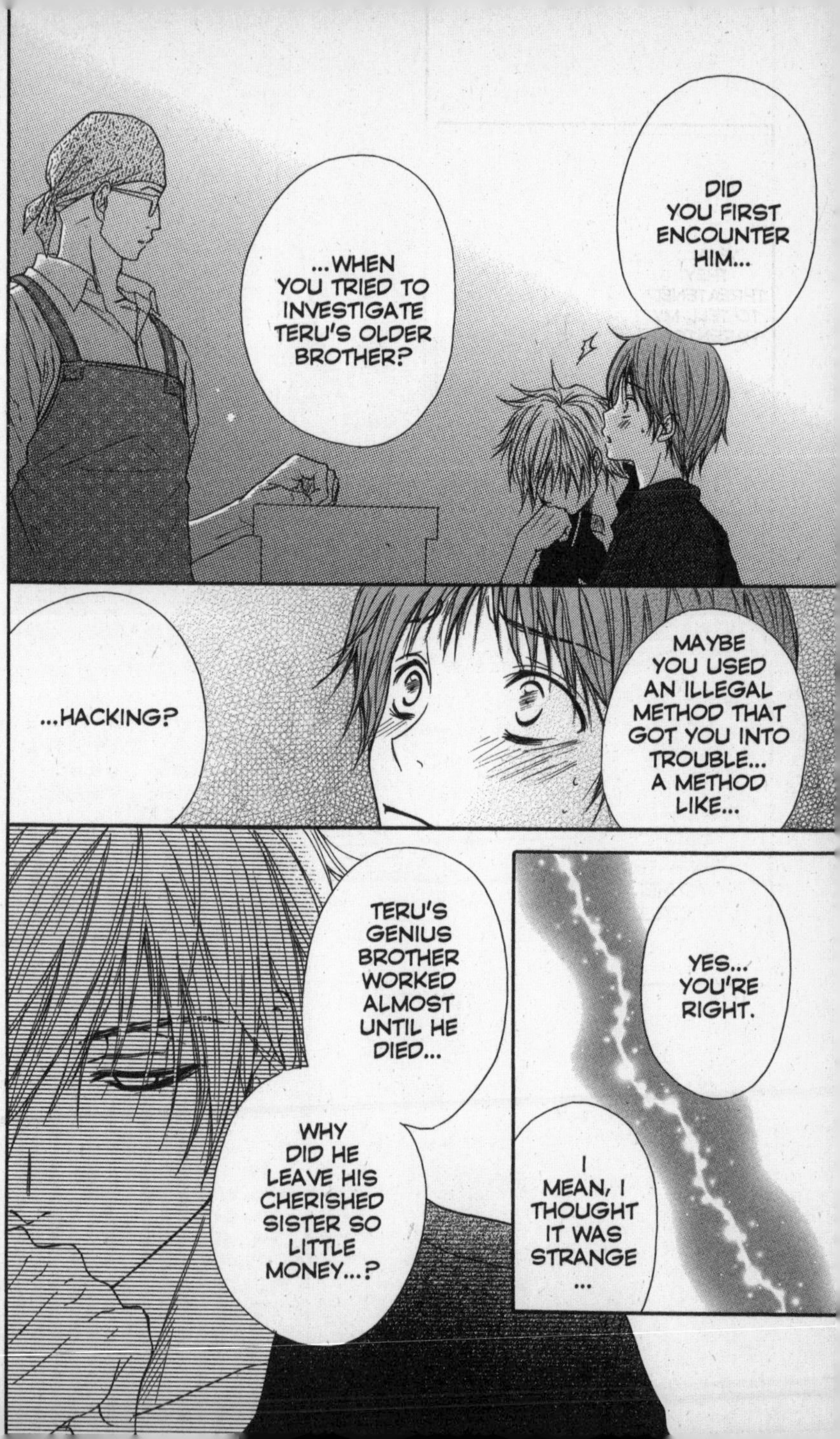
DID YOU FIRST ENCOUNTER HIM...
...WHEN YOU TRIED TO INVESTIGATE TERU'S OLDER BROTHER?
MAYBE YOU USED AN ILLEGAL METHOD THAT GOT YOU INTO TROUBLE... A METHOD LIKE...
...HACKING?
YES... YOU'RE RIGHT.
I MEAN, I THOUGHT IT WAS STRANGE...
TERU'S GENIUS BROTHER WORKED ALMOST UNTIL HE DIED...
WHY DID HE LEAVE HIS CHERISHED SISTER SO LITTLE MONEY...?

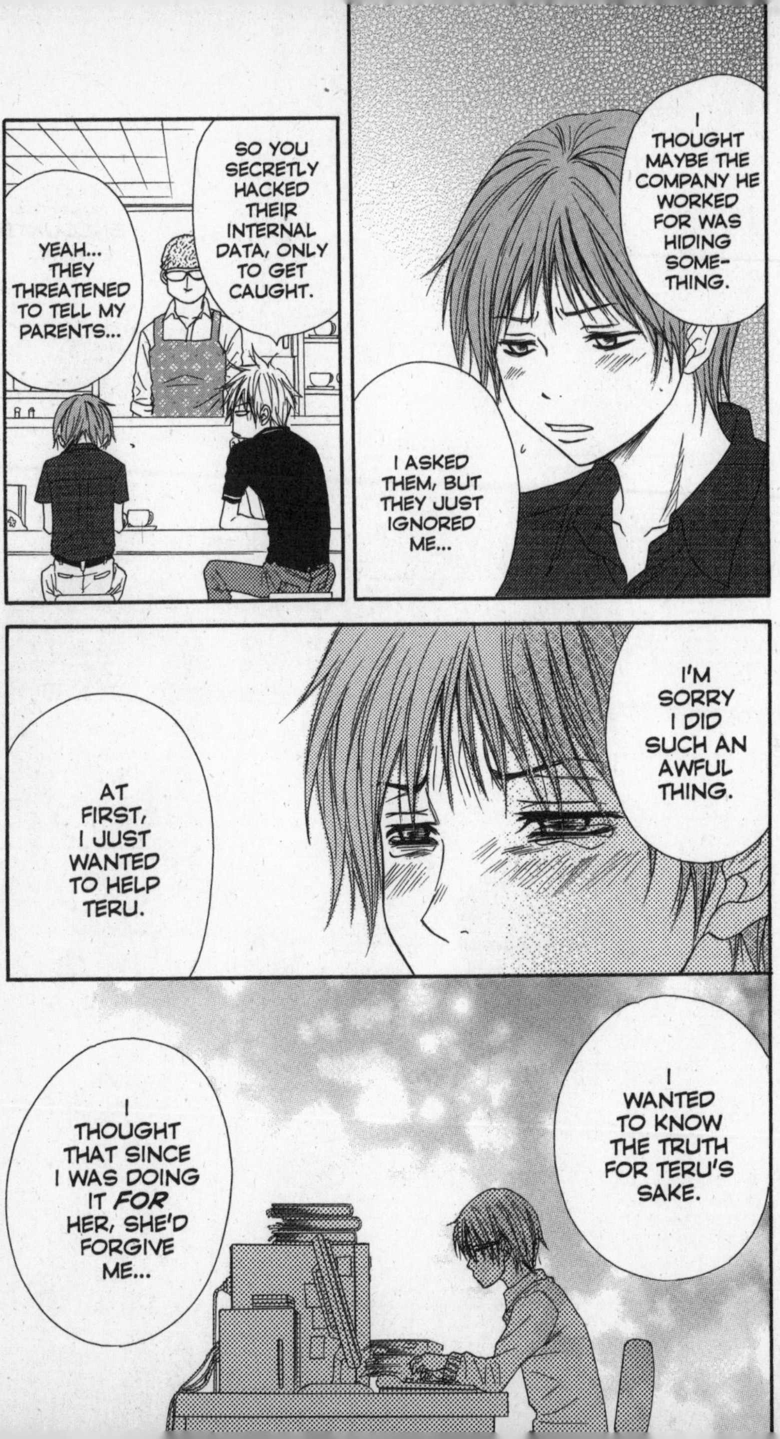
I THOUGHT MAYBE THE COMPANY HE WORKED FOR WAS HIDING SOME-THING.
I ASKED THEM, BUT THEY JUST IGNORED ME...
SO YOU SECRETLY HACKED THEIR INTERNAL DATA, ONLY TO GET CAUGHT.
YEAH... THEY THREATENED TO TELL MY PARENTS...
I'M SORRY I DID SUCH AN AWFUL THING.
AT FIRST, I JUST WANTED TO HELP TERU.
I WANTED TO KNOW THE TRUTH FOR TERU'S SAKE.
I THOUGHT THAT SINCE I WAS DOING IT *FOR* HER, SHE'D FORGIVE ME...

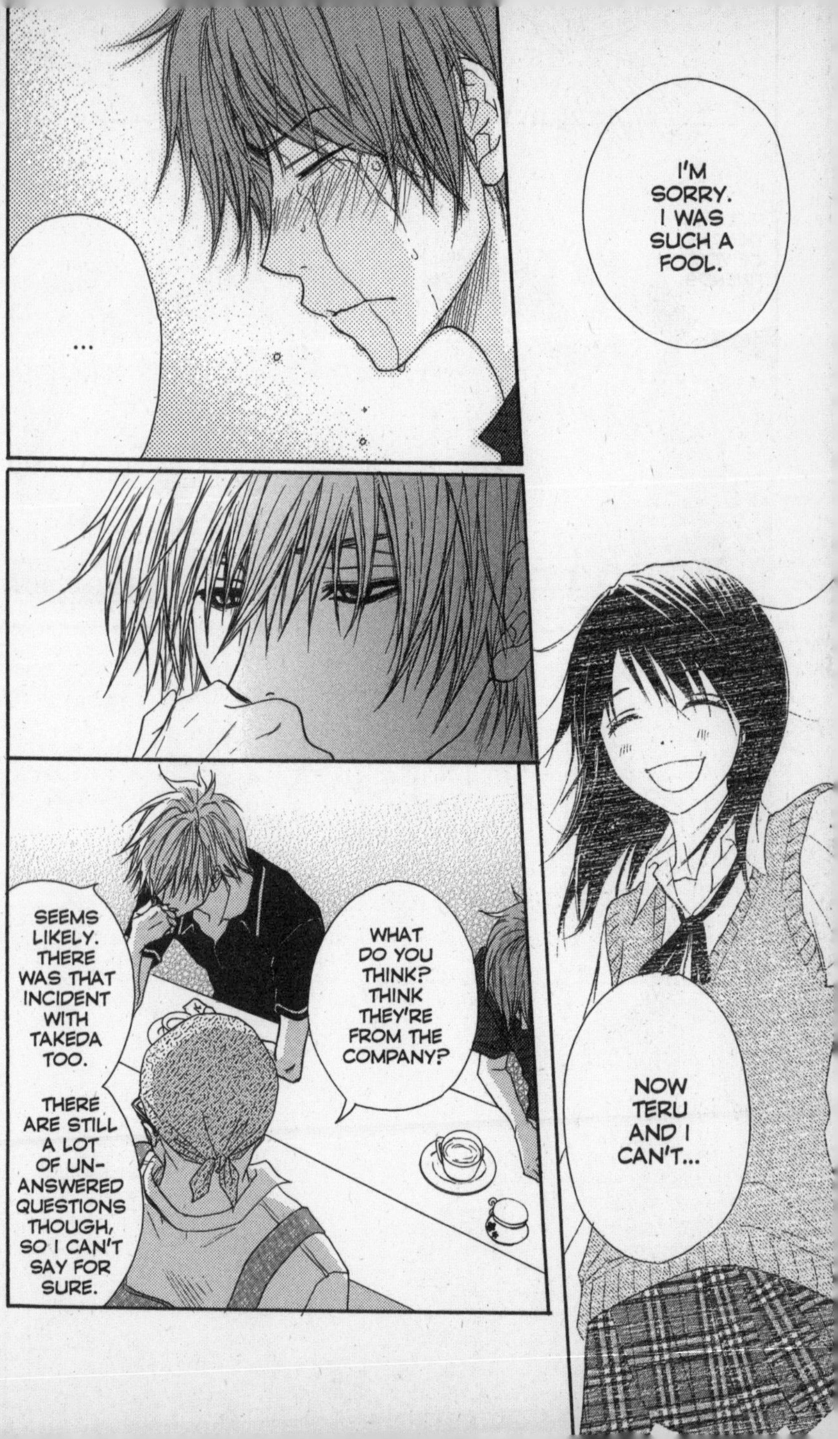
I'M SORRY. I WAS SUCH A FOOL.
NOW TERU AND I CAN'T...
...
WHAT DO YOU THINK? THINK THEY'RE FROM THE COMPANY?
SEEMS LIKELY. THERE WAS THAT INCIDENT WITH TAKEDA TOO.
THERE ARE STILL A LOT OF UN-ANSWERED QUESTIONS THOUGH, SO I CAN'T SAY FOR SURE.

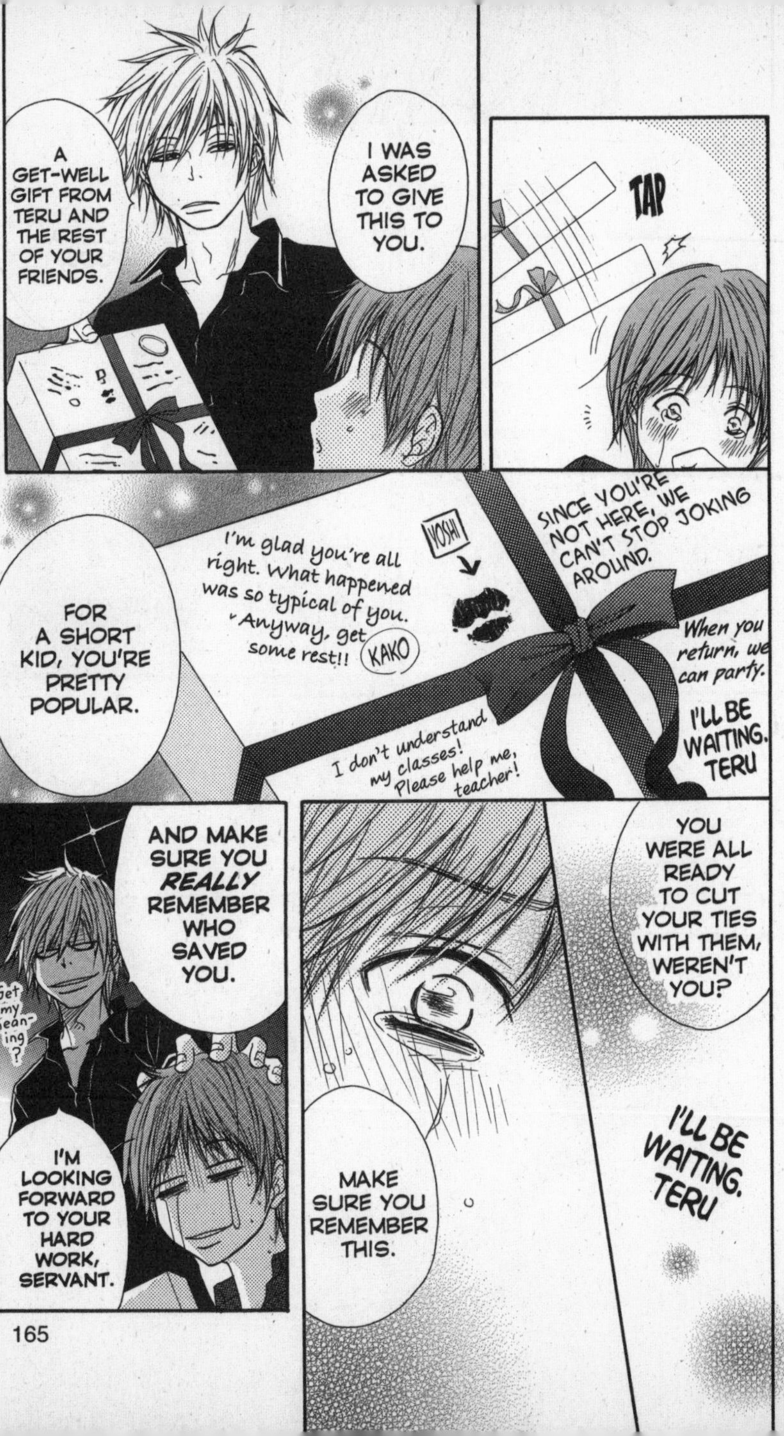
TAP
I WAS ASKED TO GIVE THIS TO YOU.
A GET-WELL GIFT FROM TERU AND THE REST OF YOUR FRIENDS.
SINCE YOU'RE NOT HERE, WE CAN'T STOP JOKING AROUND.
When you return, we can party.
I'LL BE WAITING. TERU
YOSHI
I'm glad you're all right. What happened was so typical of you. Anyway, get some rest!!
KAKO
I don't understand my classes! Please help me, teacher!
FOR A SHORT KID, YOU'RE PRETTY POPULAR.
YOU WERE ALL READY TO CUT YOUR TIES WITH THEM, WEREN'T YOU?
I'LL BE WAITING. TERU
MAKE SURE YOU REMEMBER THIS.
AND MAKE SURE YOU *REALLY* REMEMBER WHO SAVED YOU.
Get my meaning?
I'M LOOKING FORWARD TO YOUR HARD WORK, SERVANT.

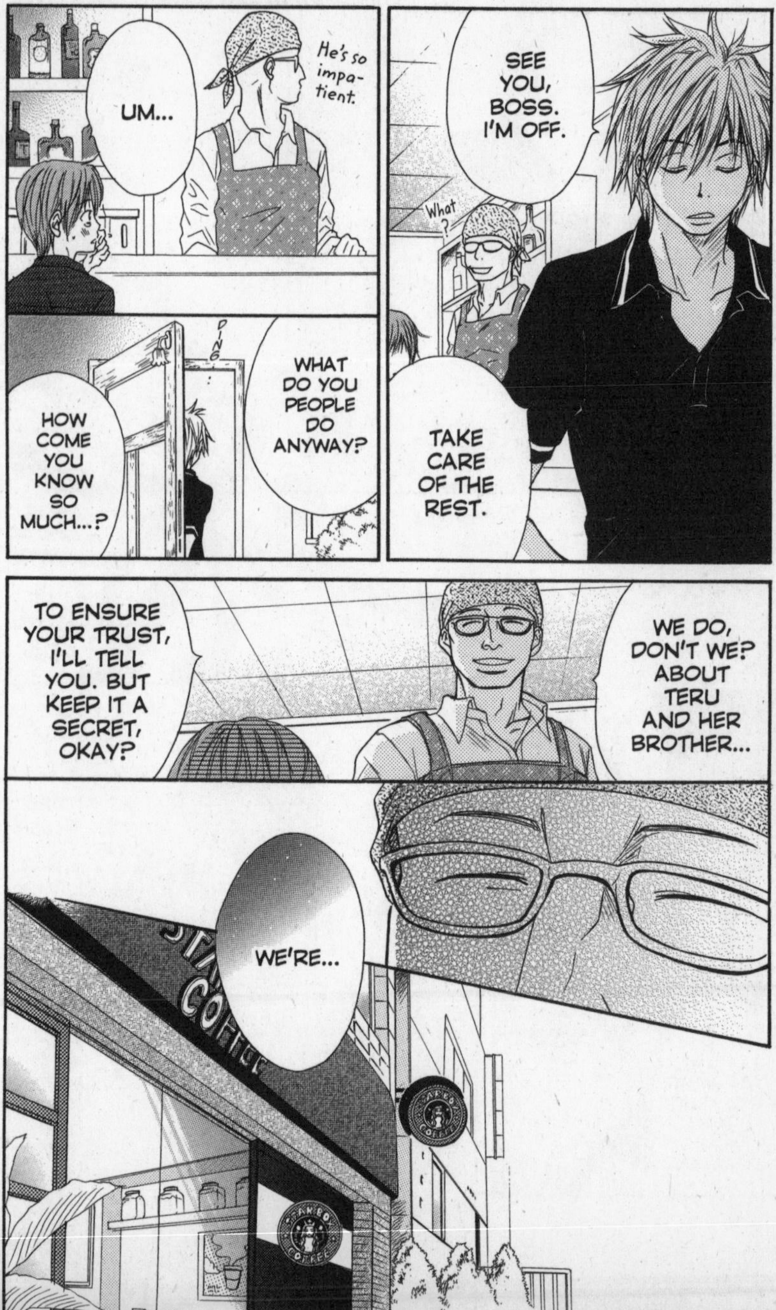
SEE YOU, BOSS. I'M OFF.
What?
TAKE CARE OF THE REST.
He's so impatient.
UM...
WHAT DO YOU PEOPLE DO ANYWAY?
DING...
HOW COME YOU KNOW SO MUCH...?
WE DO, DON'T WE? ABOUT TERU AND HER BROTHER...
TO ENSURE YOUR TRUST, I'LL TELL YOU. BUT KEEP IT A SECRET, OKAY?
WE'RE...

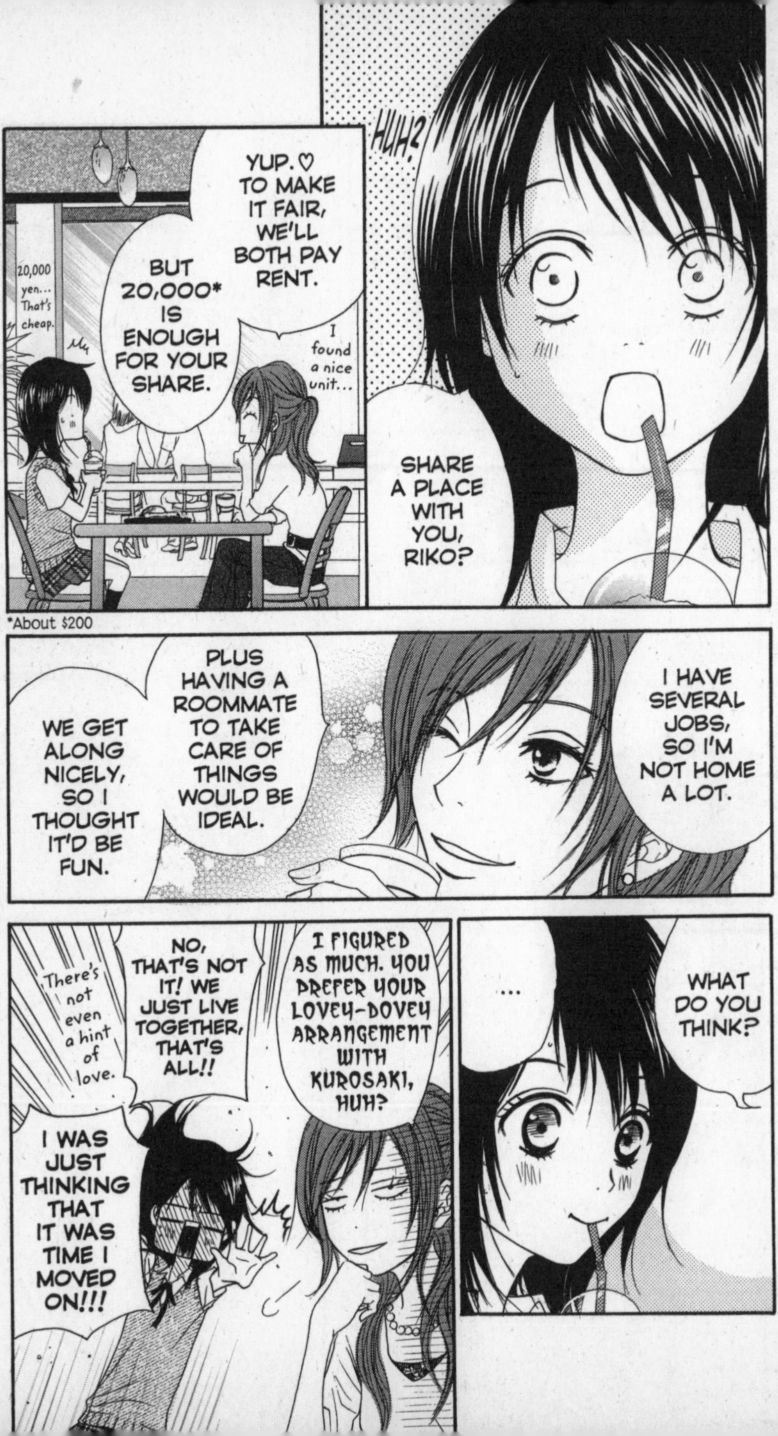
HUH?
SHARE A PLACE WITH YOU, RIKO?
YUP. ♡ TO MAKE IT FAIR, WE'LL BOTH PAY RENT.
I found a nice unit...
BUT 20,000* IS ENOUGH FOR YOUR SHARE.
20,000 yen... That's cheap.
I HAVE SEVERAL JOBS, SO I'M NOT HOME A LOT.
PLUS HAVING A ROOMMATE TO TAKE CARE OF THINGS WOULD BE IDEAL.
WE GET ALONG NICELY, SO I THOUGHT IT'D BE FUN.
WHAT DO YOU THINK?
...
I FIGURED AS MUCH. YOU PREFER YOUR LOVEY-DOVEY ARRANGEMENT WITH KUROSAKI, HUH?
NO, THAT'S NOT IT! WE JUST LIVE TOGETHER, THAT'S ALL!!
There's not even a hint of love.
I WAS JUST THINKING THAT IT WAS TIME I MOVED ON!!!

*About $200

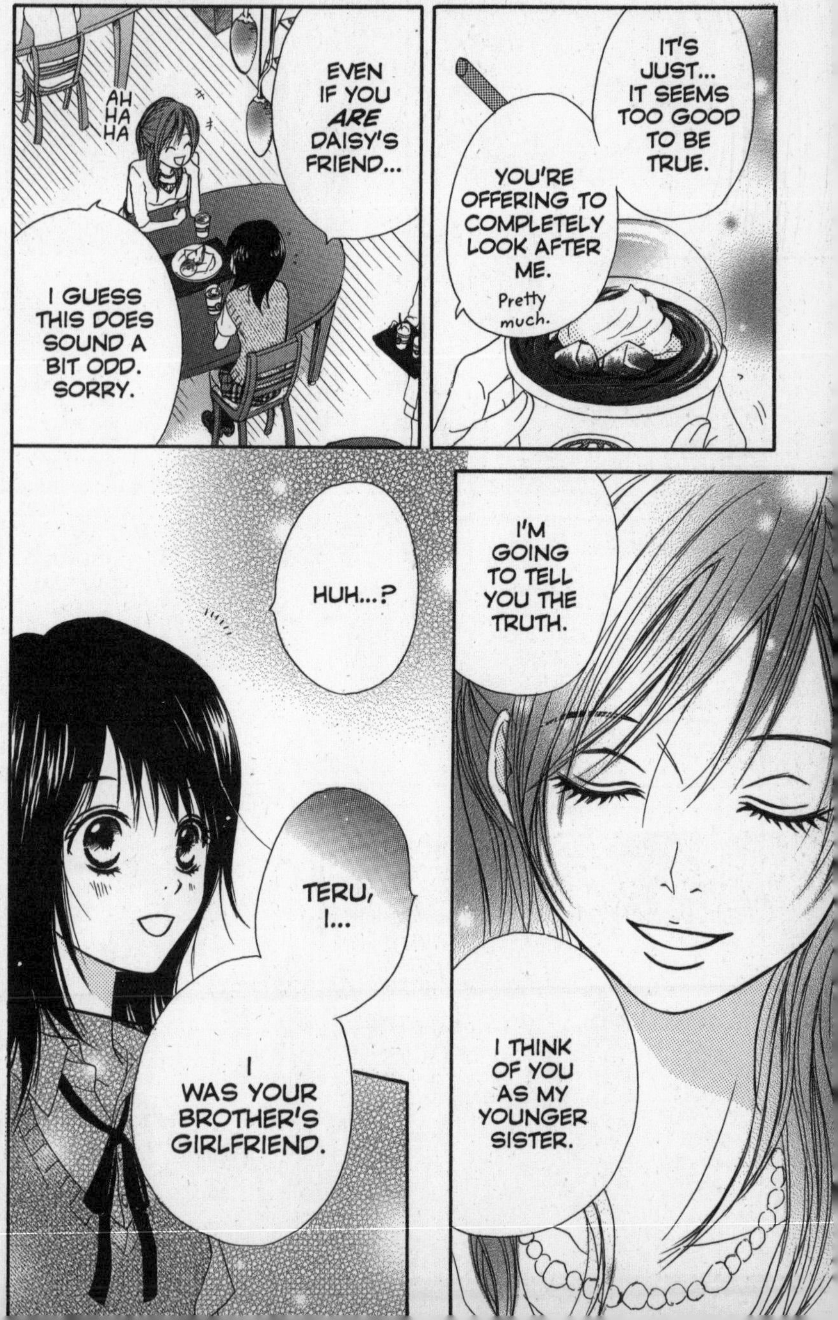
IT'S JUST... IT SEEMS TOO GOOD TO BE TRUE.
YOU'RE OFFERING TO COMPLETELY LOOK AFTER ME.
Pretty much.
EVEN IF YOU *ARE* DAISY'S FRIEND...
AH HA HA
I GUESS THIS DOES SOUND A BIT ODD. SORRY.
I'M GOING TO TELL YOU THE TRUTH.
I THINK OF YOU AS MY YOUNGER SISTER.
HUH...?
TERU, I...
I WAS YOUR BROTHER'S GIRLFRIEND.

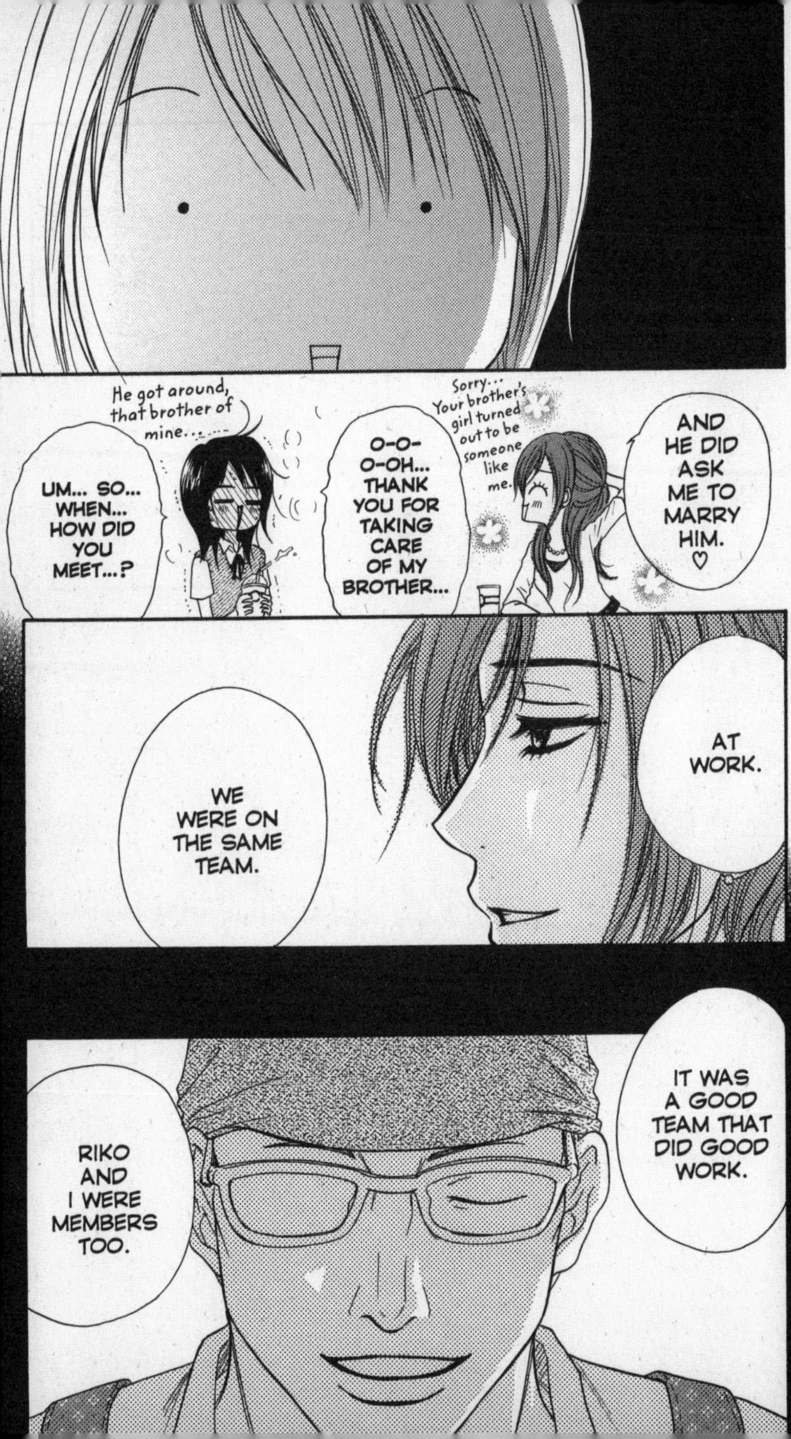
AND HE DID ASK ME TO MARRY HIM. ♡
Sorry... Your brother's girl turned out to be someone like me.
O-O-O-OH... THANK YOU FOR TAKING CARE OF MY BROTHER...
He got around, that brother of mine...
UM... SO... WHEN... HOW DID YOU MEET...?
AT WORK.
WE WERE ON THE SAME TEAM.
IT WAS A GOOD TEAM THAT DID GOOD WORK.
RIKO AND I WERE MEMBERS TOO.

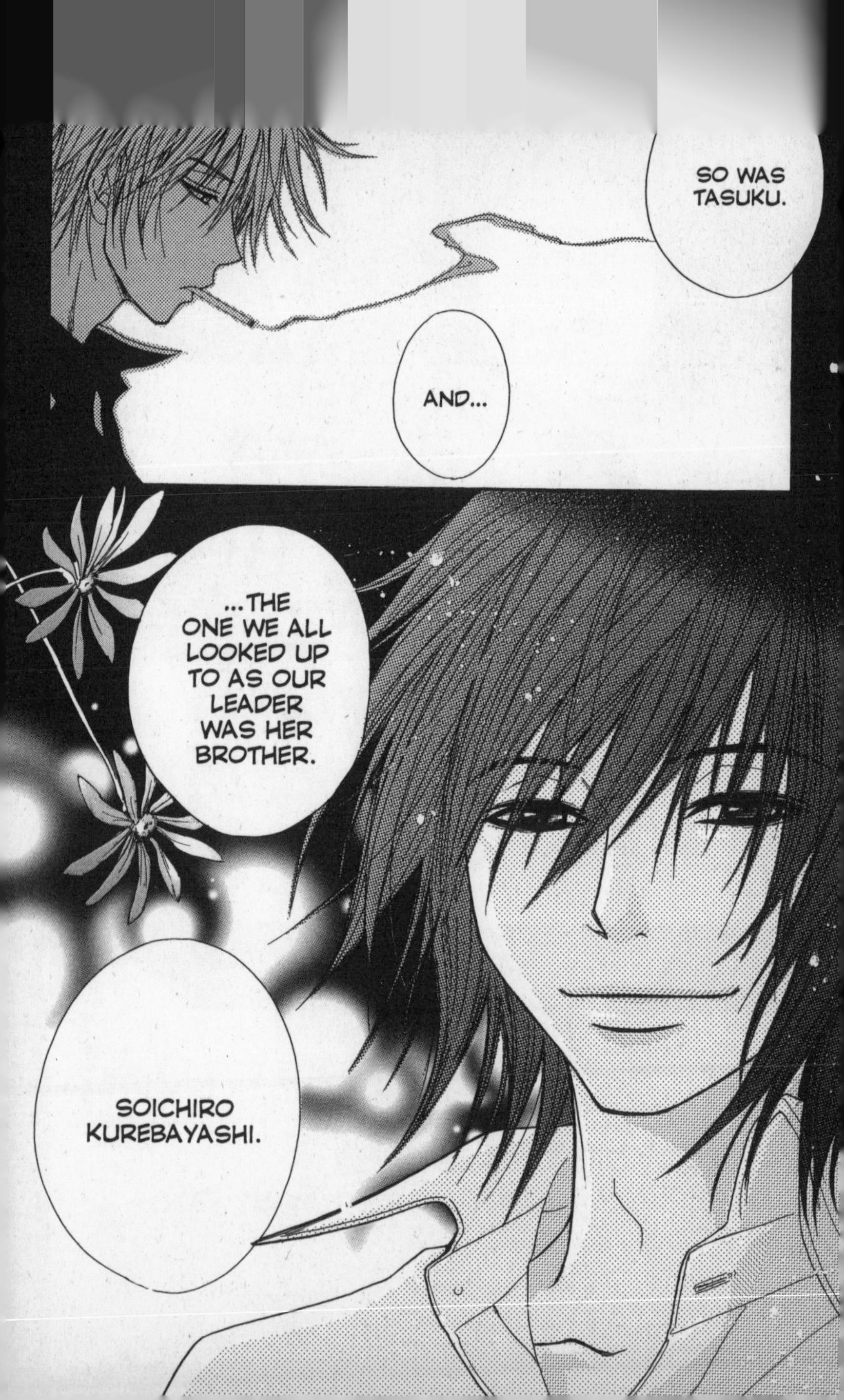
SO WAS TASUKU.
AND...
...THE ONE WE ALL LOOKED UP TO AS OUR LEADER WAS HER BROTHER.
SOICHIRO KUREBAYASHI.

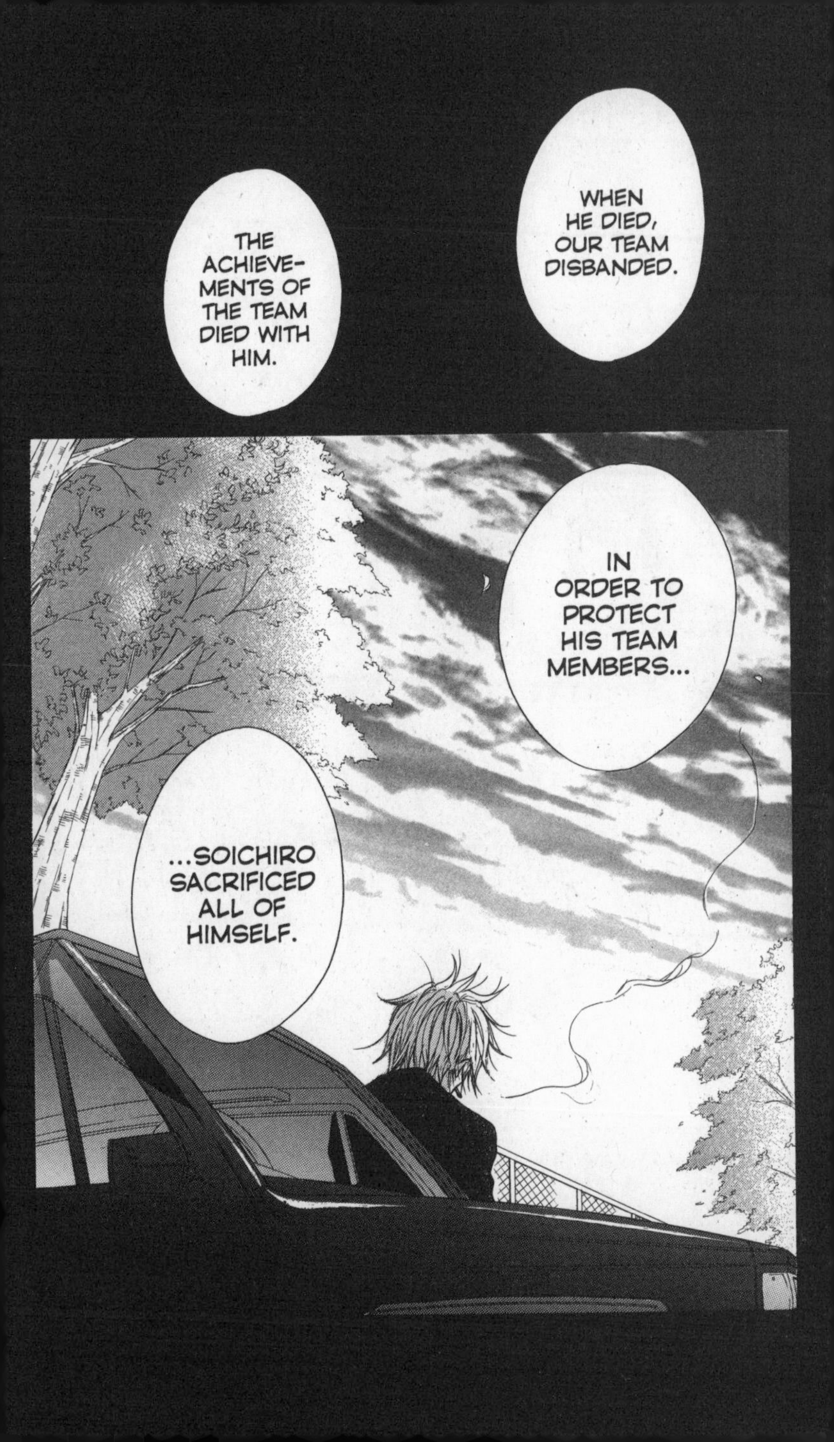
WHEN HE DIED, OUR TEAM DISBANDED.
THE ACHIEVE-MENTS OF THE TEAM DIED WITH HIM.
IN ORDER TO PROTECT HIS TEAM MEMBERS...
...SOICHIRO SACRIFICED ALL OF HIMSELF.

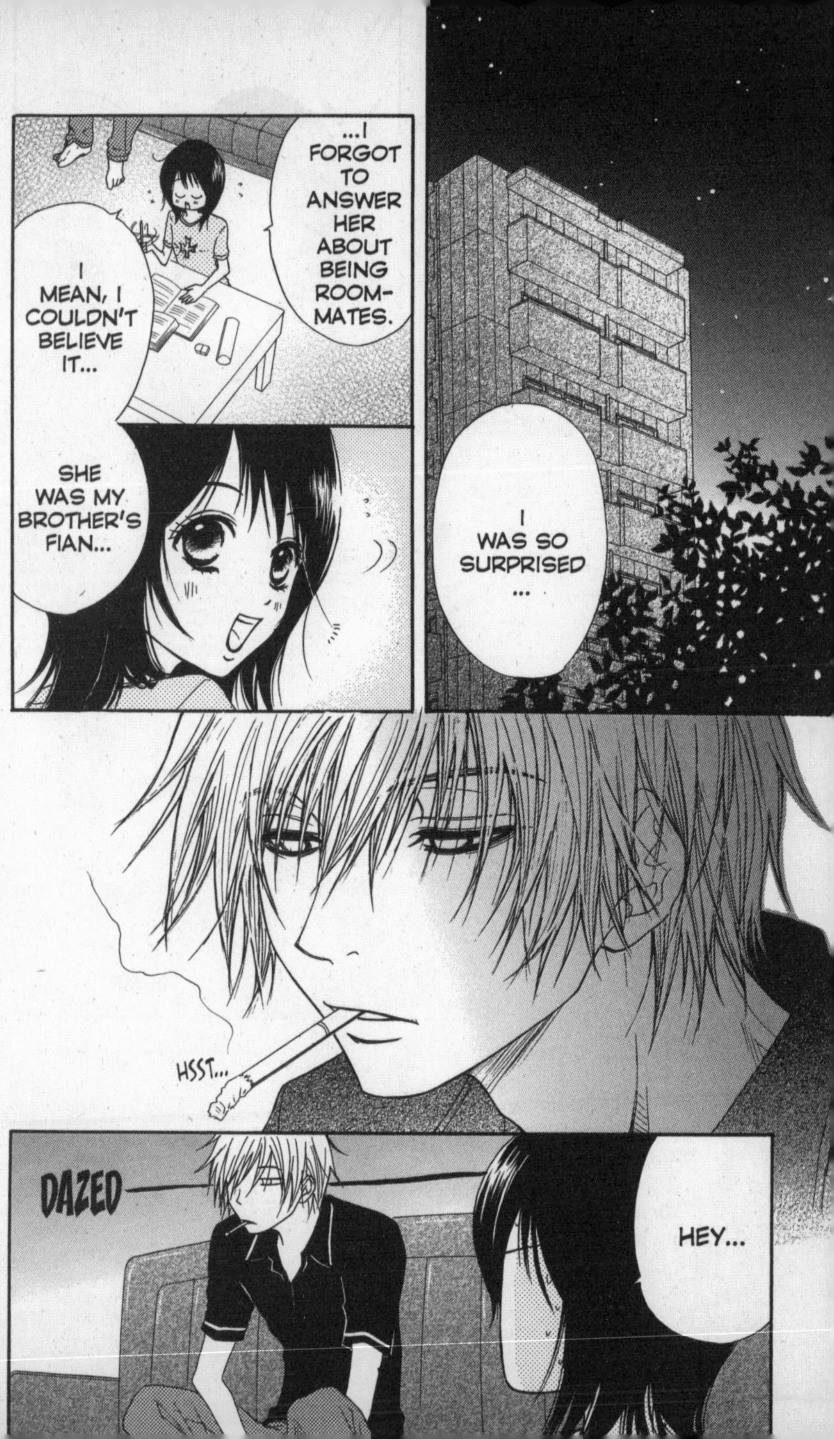
I WAS SO SURPRISED...
...I FORGOT TO ANSWER HER ABOUT BEING ROOM-MATES.
I MEAN, I COULDN'T BELIEVE IT...
SHE WAS MY BROTHER'S FIAN...
HSST...
HEY...
DAZED

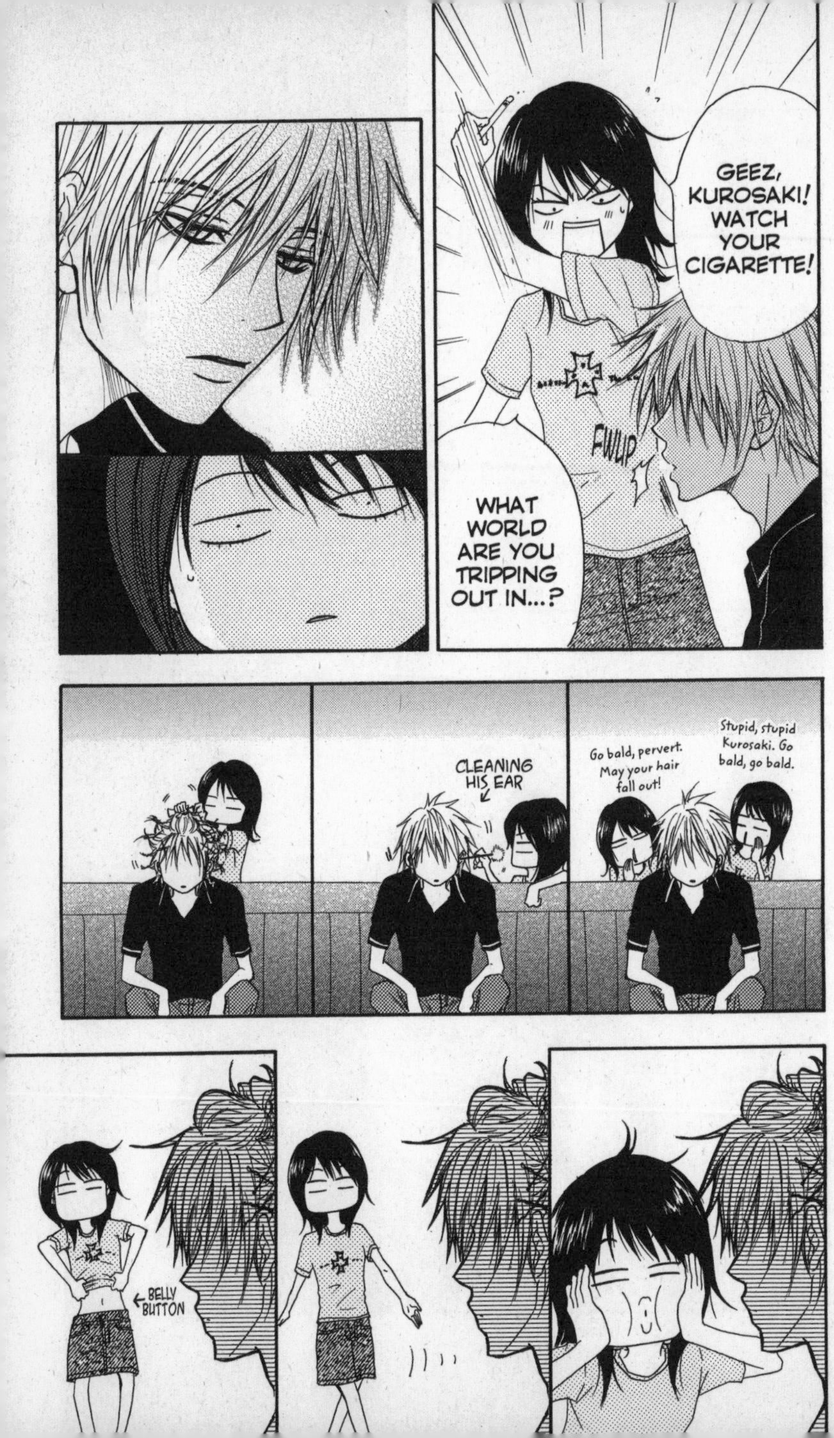
GEEZ, KUROSAKI! WATCH YOUR CIGARETTE!
FWUP
WHAT WORLD ARE YOU TRIPPING OUT IN...?
Stupid, stupid Kurosaki. Go bald, go bald.
Go bald, pervert. May your hair fall out!
CLEANING HIS EAR
BELLY BUTTON

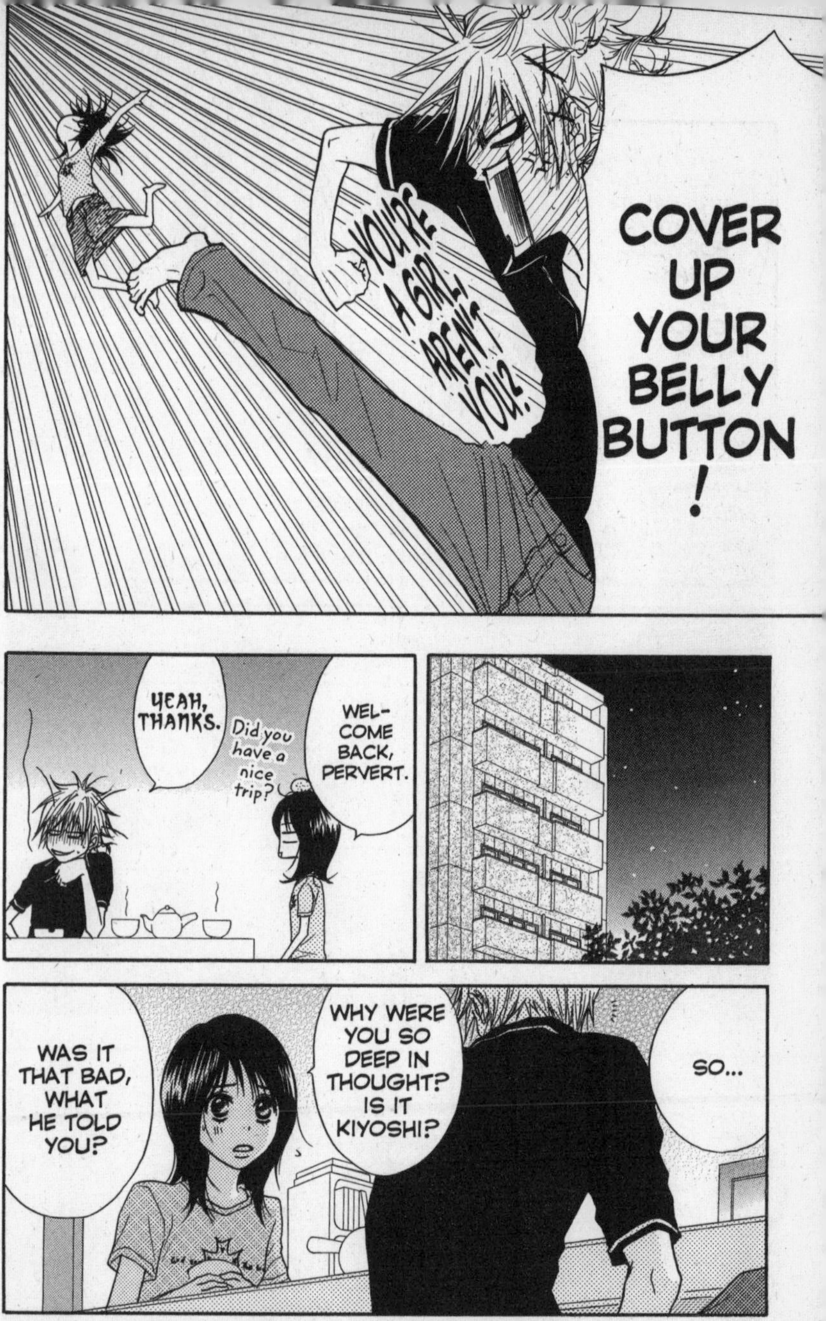
COVER UP YOUR BELLY BUTTON!
YOU'RE A GIRL, AREN'T YOU?!
WEL-COME BACK, PERVERT.
Did you have a nice trip?
YEAH, THANKS.
SO...
WHY WERE YOU SO DEEP IN THOUGHT? IS IT KIYOSHI?
WAS IT THAT BAD, WHAT HE TOLD YOU?

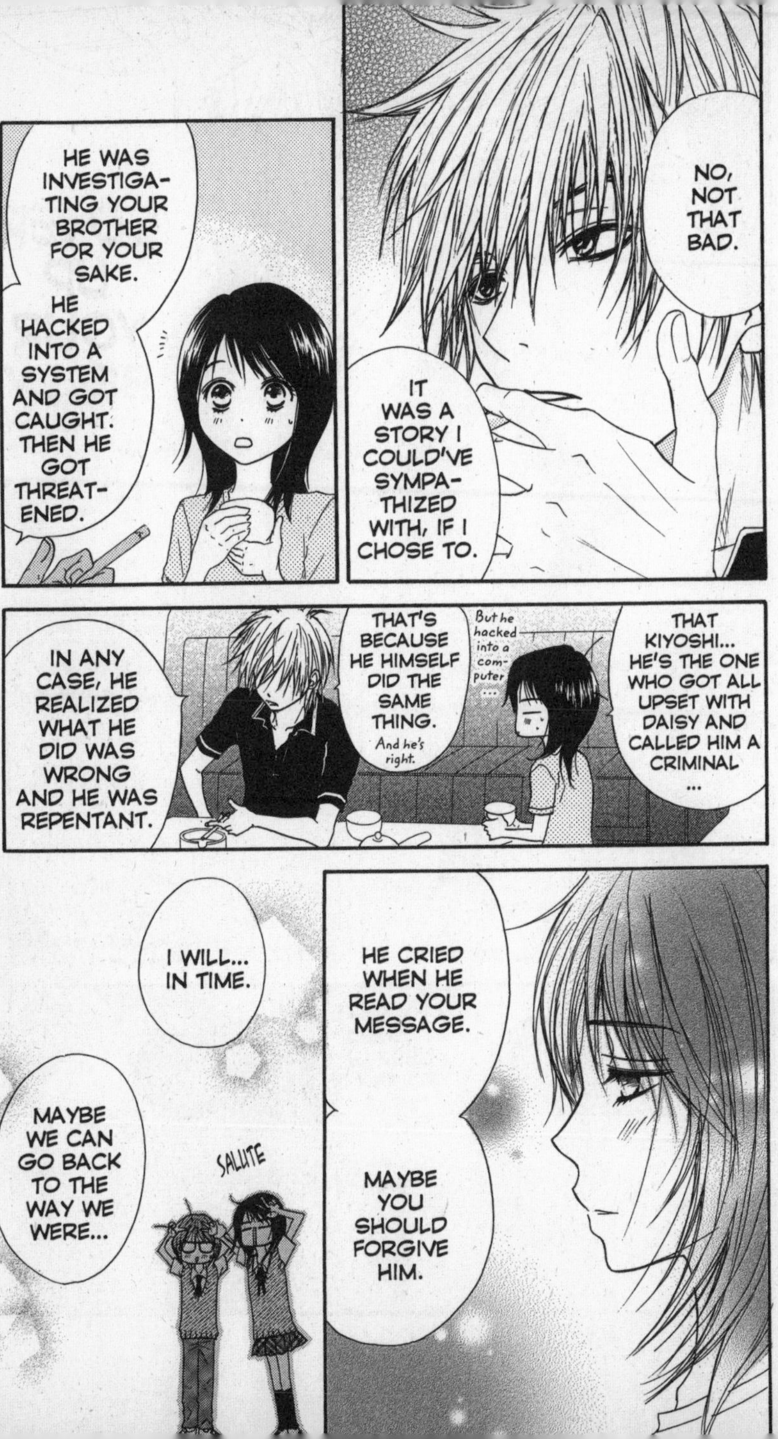
NO, NOT THAT BAD.
IT WAS A STORY I COULD'VE SYMPATHIZED WITH, IF I CHOSE TO.
HE WAS INVESTIGATING YOUR BROTHER FOR YOUR SAKE.
HE HACKED INTO A SYSTEM AND GOT CAUGHT. THEN HE GOT THREATENED.
THAT KIYOSHI... HE'S THE ONE WHO GOT ALL UPSET WITH DAISY AND CALLED HIM A CRIMINAL...
But he hacked into a computer...
THAT'S BECAUSE HE HIMSELF DID THE SAME THING.
And he's right.
IN ANY CASE, HE REALIZED WHAT HE DID WAS WRONG AND HE WAS REPENTANT.
HE CRIED WHEN HE READ YOUR MESSAGE.
MAYBE YOU SHOULD FORGIVE HIM.
I WILL... IN TIME.
MAYBE WE CAN GO BACK TO THE WAY WE WERE...
SALUTE

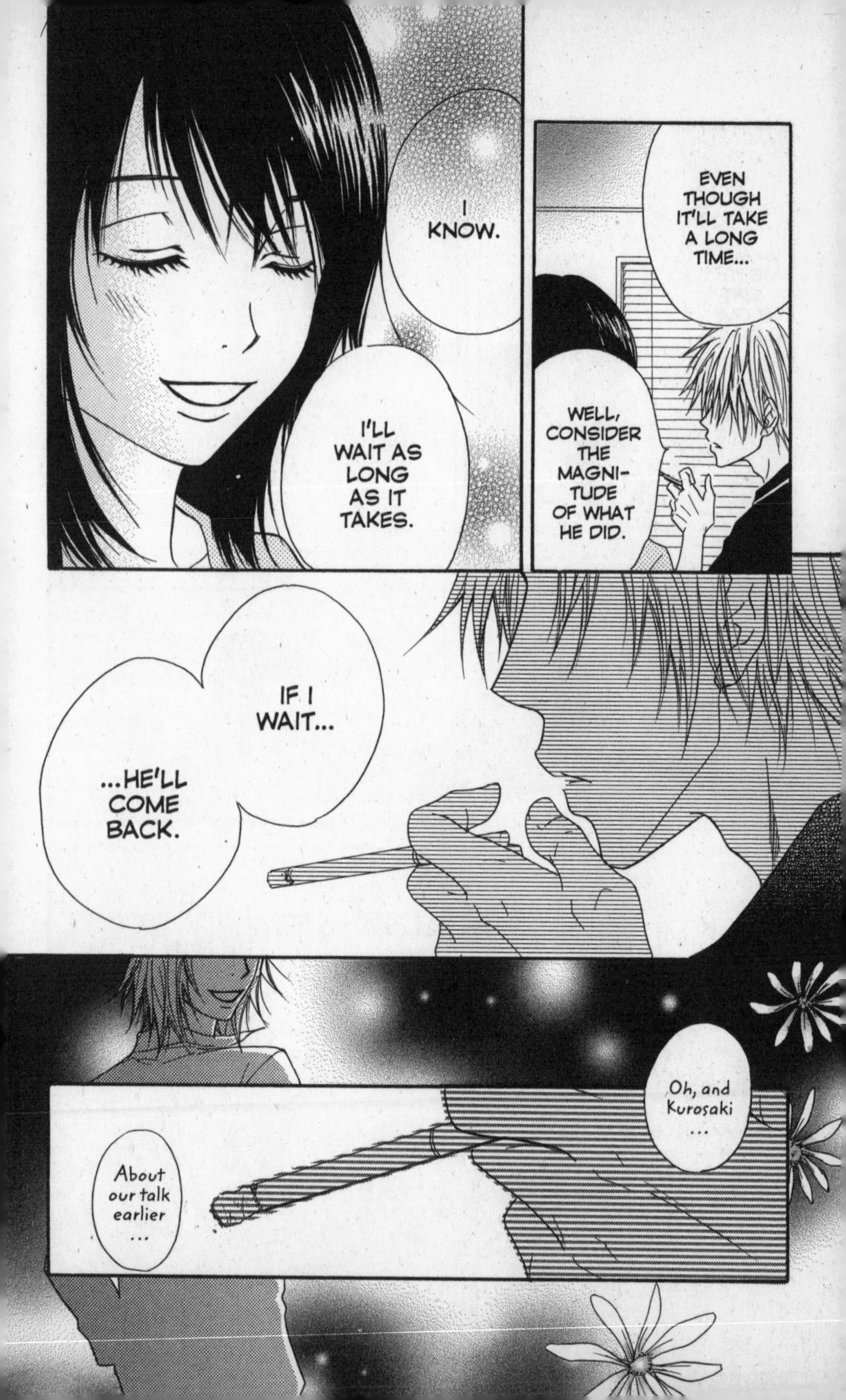
EVEN THOUGH IT'LL TAKE A LONG TIME...
WELL, CONSIDER THE MAGNITUDE OF WHAT HE DID.
I KNOW.
I'LL WAIT AS LONG AS IT TAKES.
IF I WAIT...
...HE'LL COME BACK.
Oh, and Kurosaki...
About our talk earlier...

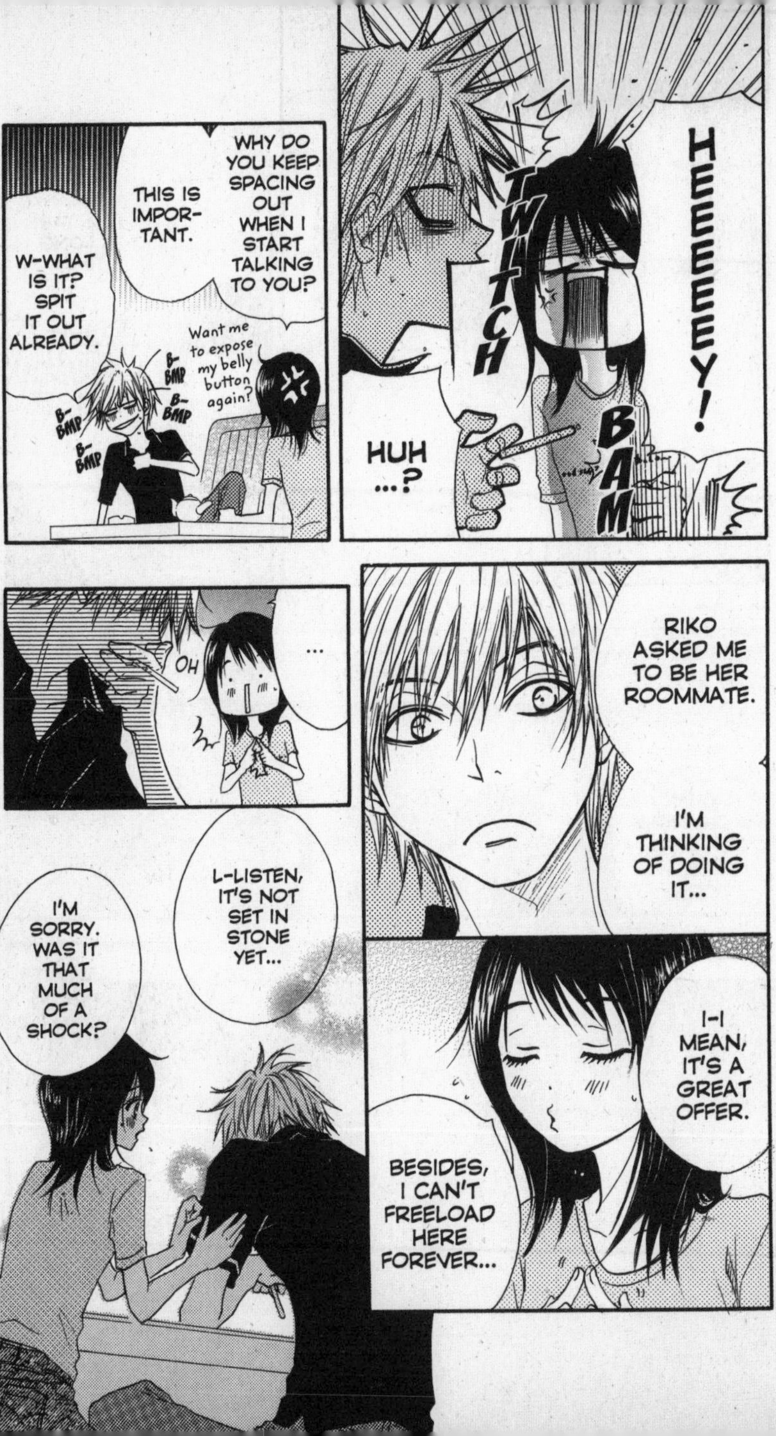
HEEEEEEY!
TWITCH
BAM
HUH ...?
WHY DO YOU KEEP SPACING OUT WHEN I START TALKING TO YOU?
THIS IS IMPOR-TANT.
W-WHAT IS IT? SPIT IT OUT ALREADY.
Want me to expose my belly button again?
B-BMP
B-BMP
B-BMP
B-BMP
RIKO ASKED ME TO BE HER ROOMMATE.
I'M THINKING OF DOING IT...
OH
...
I-I MEAN, IT'S A GREAT OFFER.
BESIDES, I CAN'T FREELOAD HERE FOREVER...
L-LISTEN, IT'S NOT SET IN STONE YET...
I'M SORRY. WAS IT THAT MUCH OF A SHOCK?

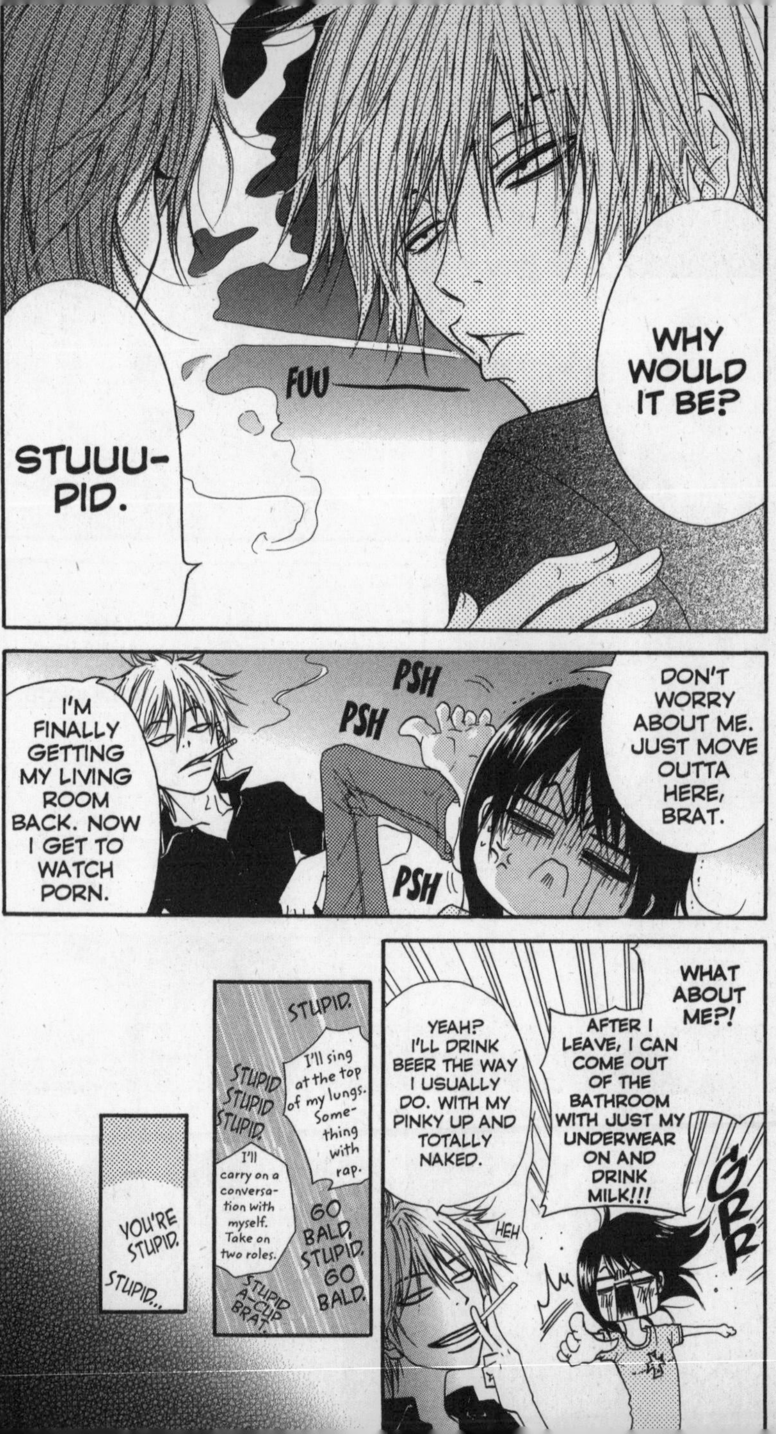
WHY WOULD IT BE?
FUU
STUUU-PID.
DON'T WORRY ABOUT ME. JUST MOVE OUTTA HERE, BRAT.
PSH
PSH
PSH
I'M FINALLY GETTING MY LIVING ROOM BACK. NOW I GET TO WATCH PORN.
WHAT ABOUT ME?!
AFTER I LEAVE, I CAN COME OUT OF THE BATHROOM WITH JUST MY UNDERWEAR ON AND DRINK MILK!!!
GRR
YEAH? I'LL DRINK BEER THE WAY I USUALLY DO. WITH MY PINKY UP AND TOTALLY NAKED.
HEH
STUPID.
I'll sing at the top of my lungs. Something with rap.
STUPID STUPID STUPID.
I'll carry on a conversation with myself. Take on two roles.
GO BALD, STUPID, GO BALD.
STUPID A-CUP BRAT.
YOU'RE STUPID.
STUPID...

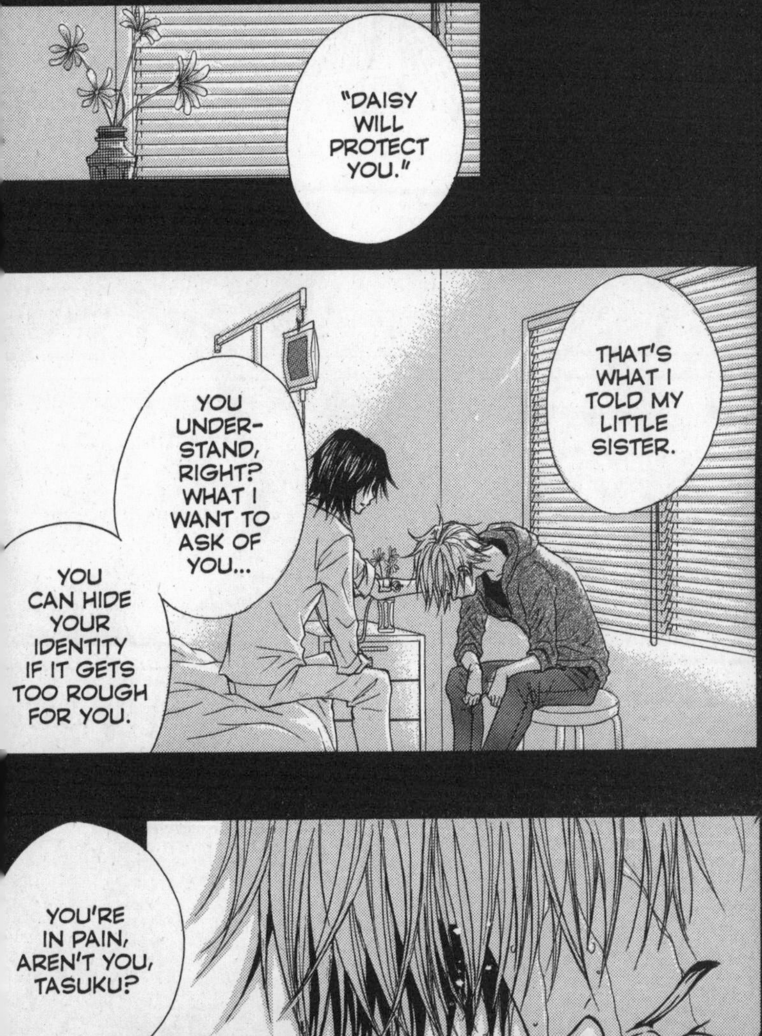
"DAISY WILL PROTECT YOU."
THAT'S WHAT I TOLD MY LITTLE SISTER.
YOU UNDER-STAND, RIGHT? WHAT I WANT TO ASK OF YOU...
YOU CAN HIDE YOUR IDENTITY IF IT GETS TOO ROUGH FOR YOU.
YOU'RE IN PAIN, AREN'T YOU, TASUKU?

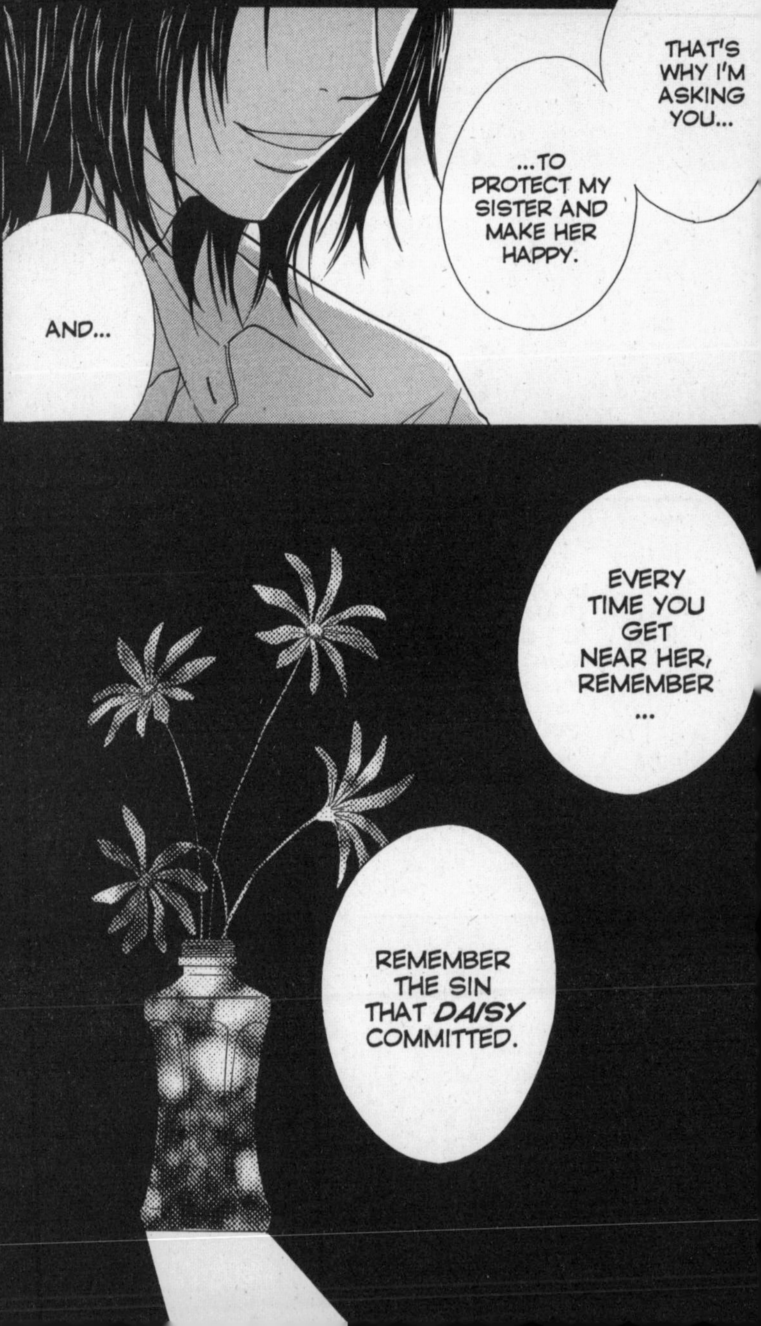
THAT'S WHY I'M ASKING YOU...
...TO PROTECT MY SISTER AND MAKE HER HAPPY.
AND...
EVERY TIME YOU GET NEAR HER, REMEMBER ...
REMEMBER THE SIN THAT *DAISY* COMMITTED.

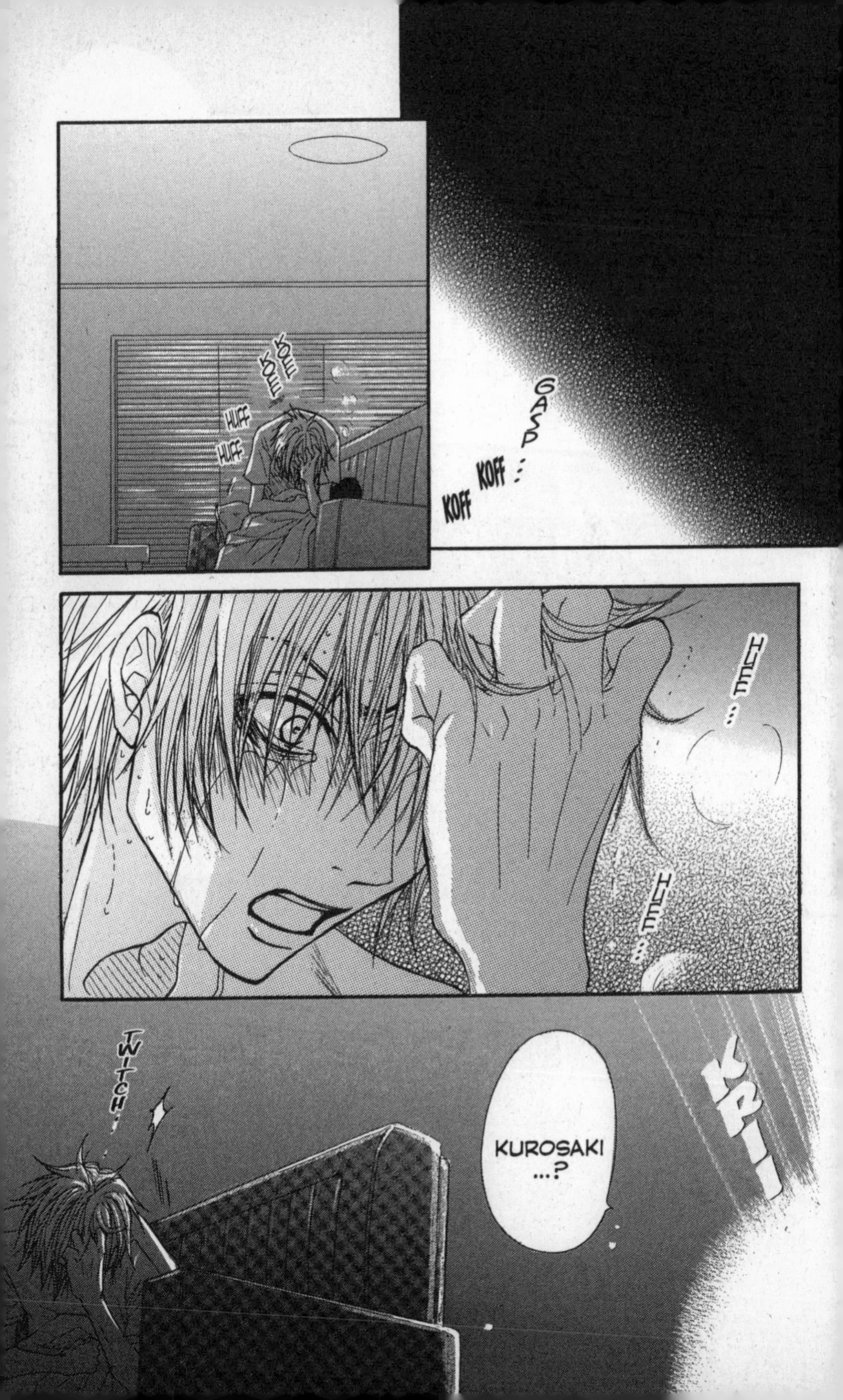
GASP...
KOFF
KOFF
KOFF
KOFF
HUFF
HUFF
HUFF...
HUFF...
KRII
KUROSAKI
...?
TWITCH...

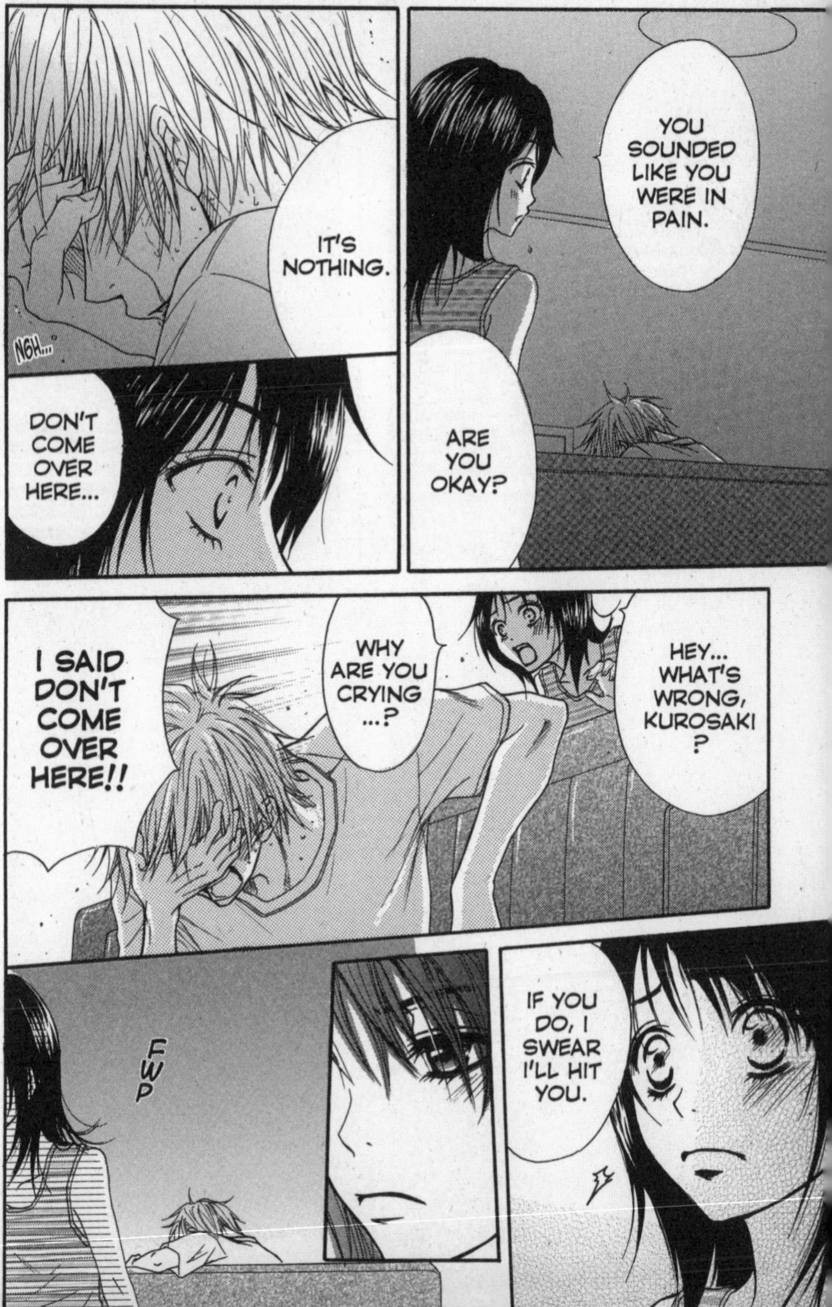
YOU SOUNDED LIKE YOU WERE IN PAIN.
ARE YOU OKAY?
IT'S NOTHING.
NGH...
DON'T COME OVER HERE...
HEY... WHAT'S WRONG, KUROSAKI?
WHY ARE YOU CRYING ...?
I SAID DON'T COME OVER HERE!!
IF YOU DO, I SWEAR I'LL HIT YOU.
FWP

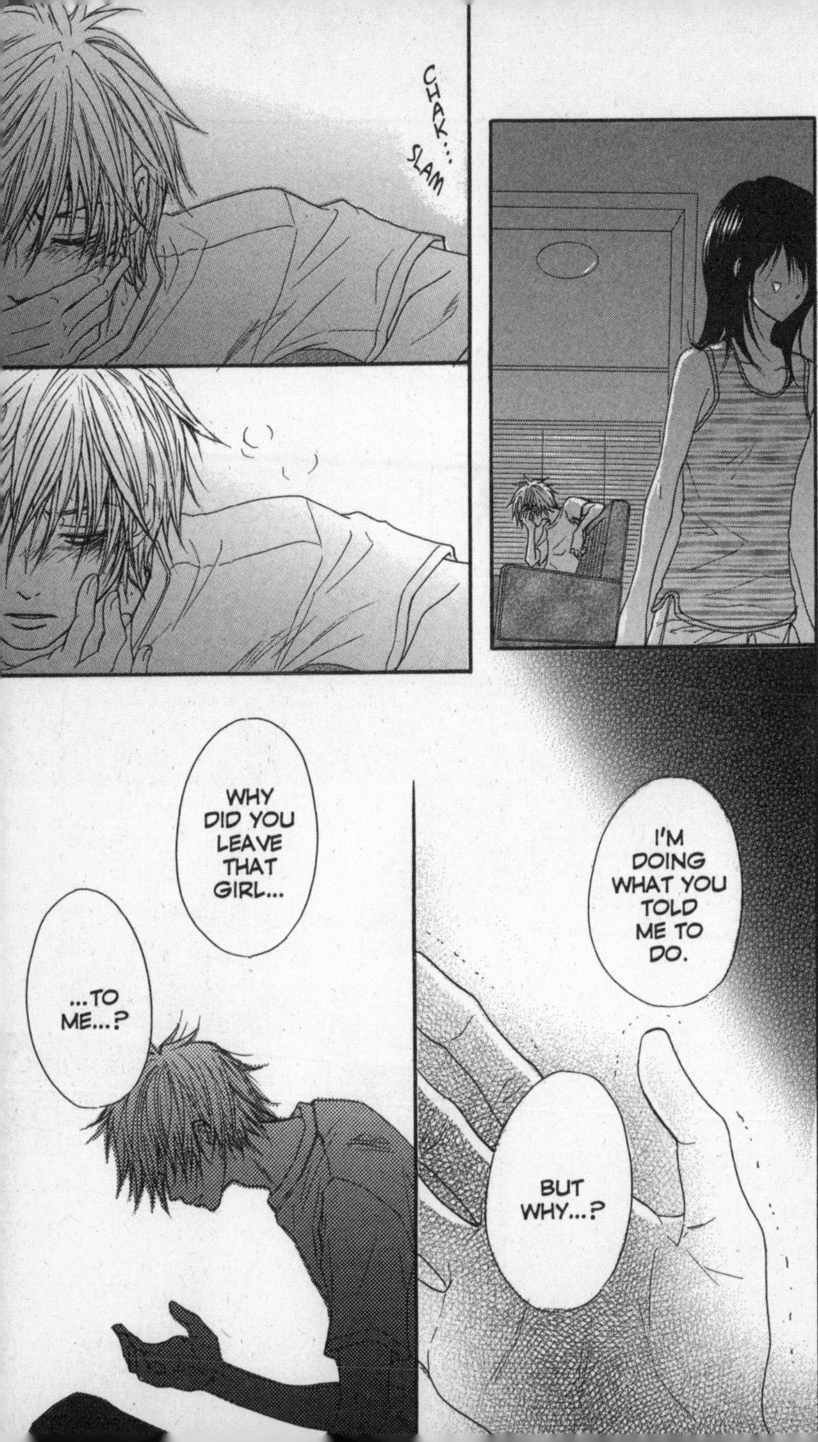
CHAK...
SLAM
I'M DOING WHAT YOU TOLD ME TO DO.
BUT WHY...?
WHY DID YOU LEAVE THAT GIRL...
...TO ME...?

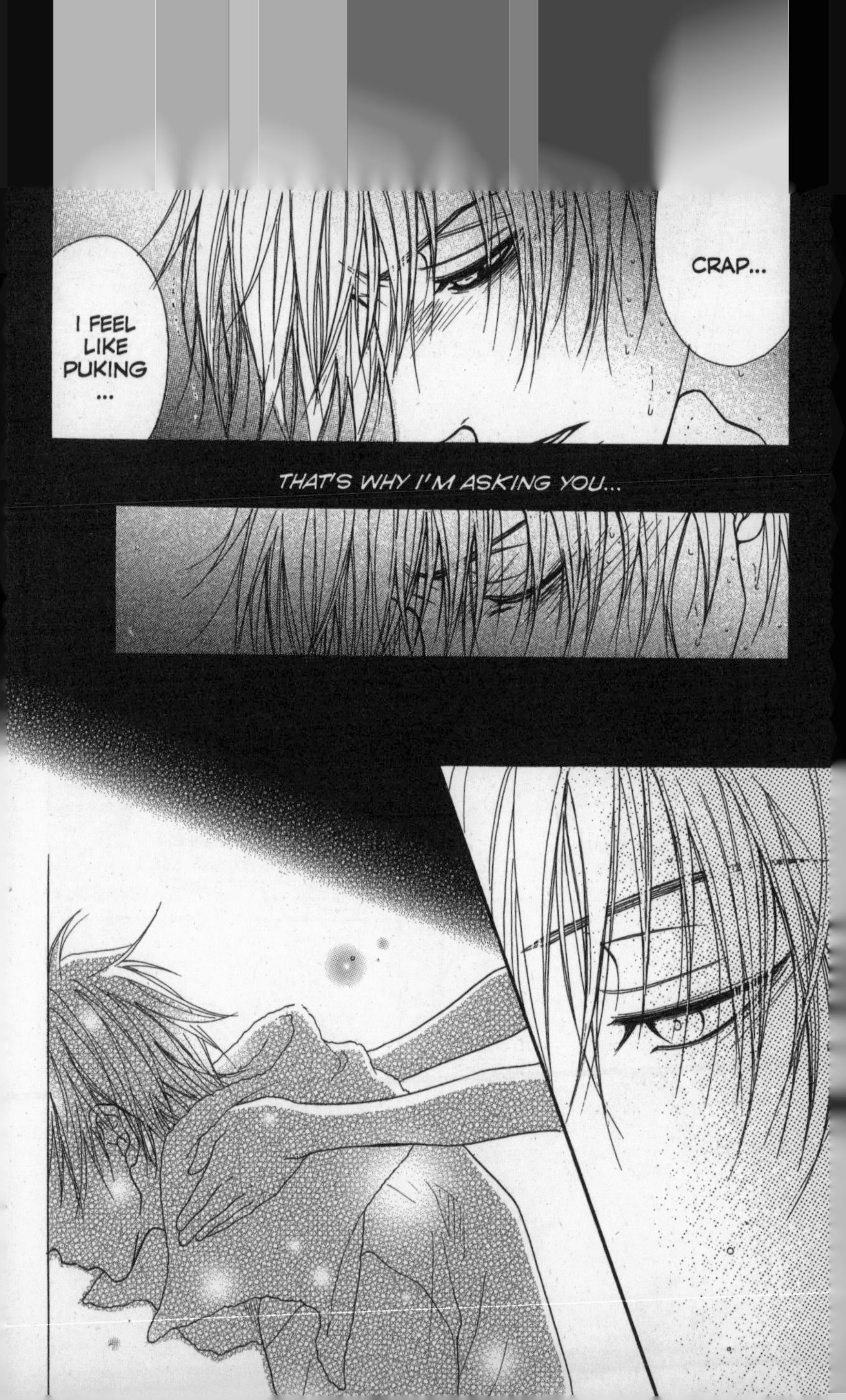
CRAP...
I FEEL LIKE PUKING ...
THAT'S WHY I'M ASKING YOU...

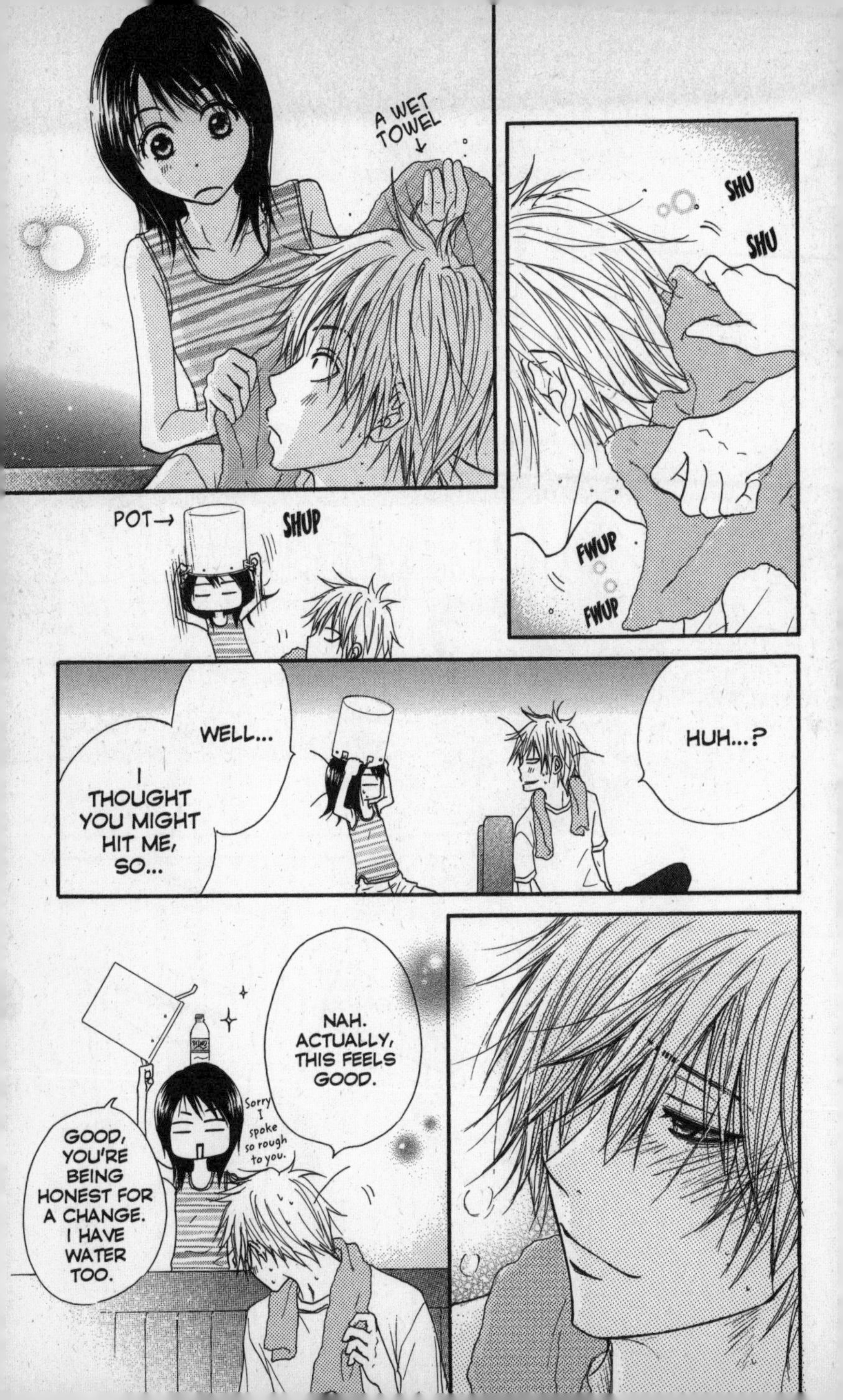
SHU
SHU
FWUP
FWUP
A WET TOWEL ↓
POT→
SHUP
HUH...?
WELL...
I THOUGHT YOU MIGHT HIT ME, SO...
NAH. ACTUALLY, THIS FEELS GOOD.
Sorry I spoke so rough to you.
GOOD, YOU'RE BEING HONEST FOR A CHANGE. I HAVE WATER TOO.

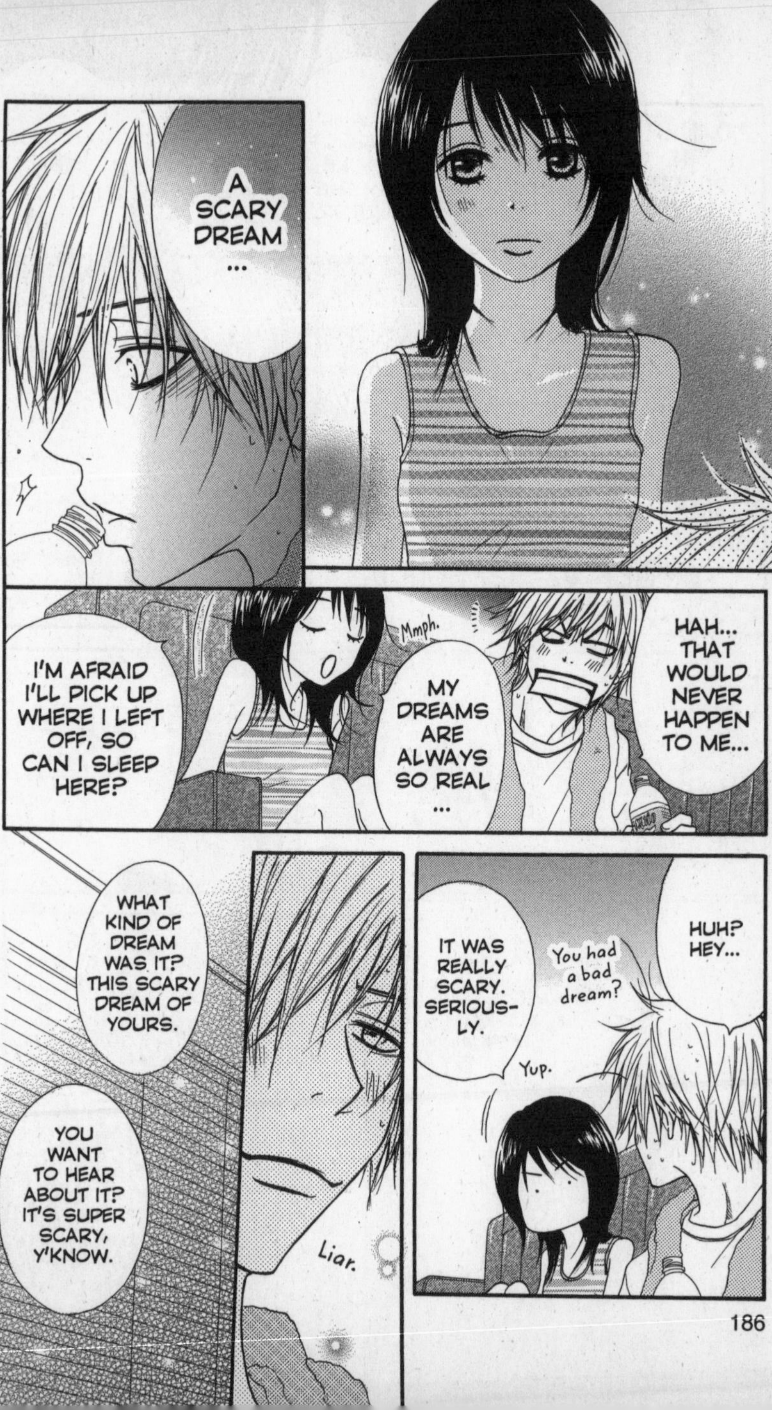
A SCARY DREAM ...
HAH... THAT WOULD NEVER HAPPEN TO ME...
Mmph.
MY DREAMS ARE ALWAYS SO REAL ...
I'M AFRAID I'LL PICK UP WHERE I LEFT OFF, SO CAN I SLEEP HERE?
HUH? HEY...
You had a bad dream?
IT WAS REALLY SCARY. SERIOUS-LY.
Yup.
WHAT KIND OF DREAM WAS IT? THIS SCARY DREAM OF YOURS.
YOU WANT TO HEAR ABOUT IT? IT'S SUPER SCARY, Y'KNOW.
Liar.

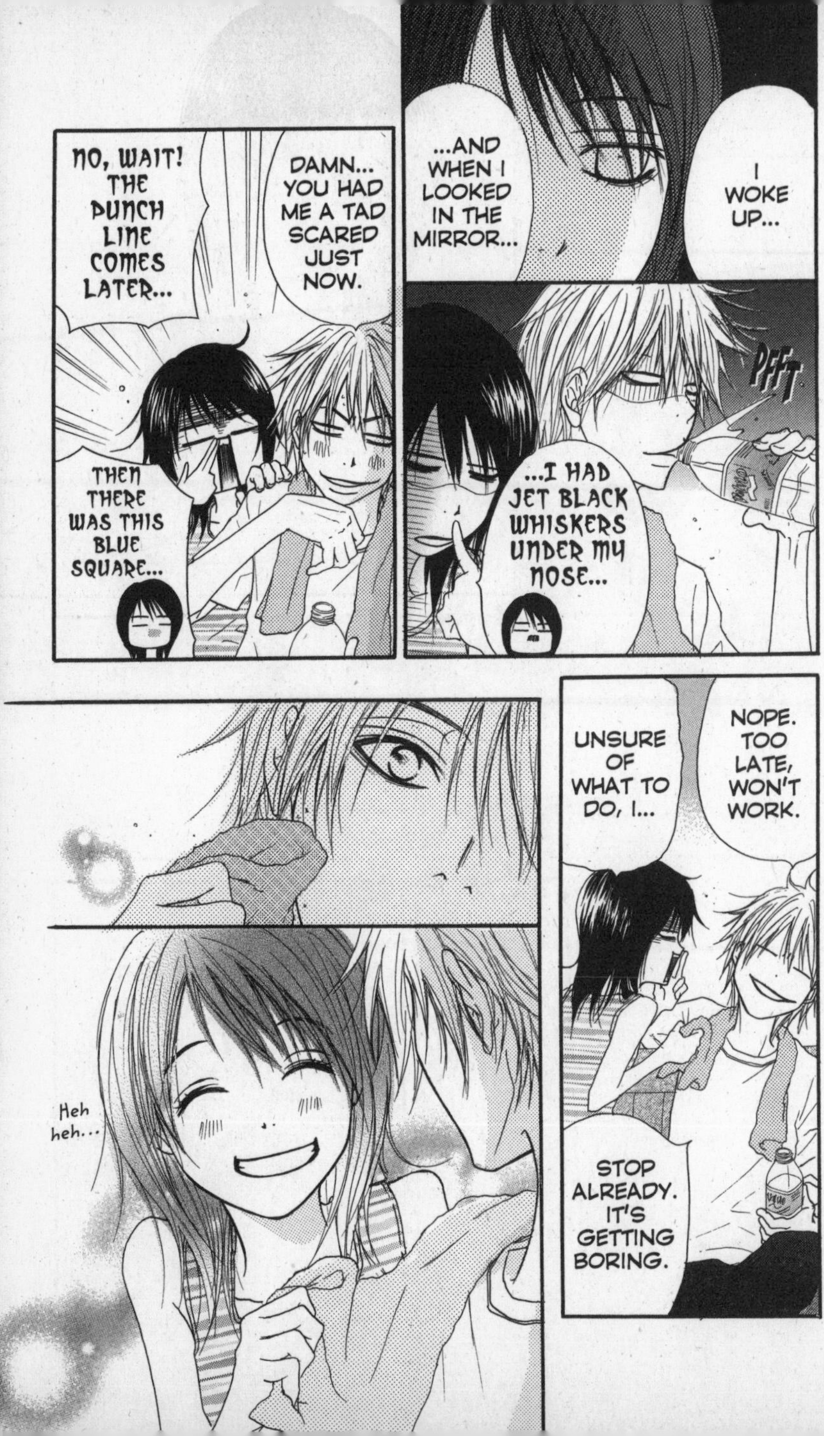
I WOKE UP...
...AND WHEN I LOOKED IN THE MIRROR...
...I HAD JET BLACK WHISKERS UNDER MY NOSE...
PFFT
DAMN... YOU HAD ME A TAD SCARED JUST NOW.
NO, WAIT! THE PUNCH LINE COMES LATER...
THEN THERE WAS THIS BLUE SQUARE...
NOPE. TOO LATE, WON'T WORK.
UNSURE OF WHAT TO DO, I...
STOP ALREADY. IT'S GETTING BORING.
Heh heh...

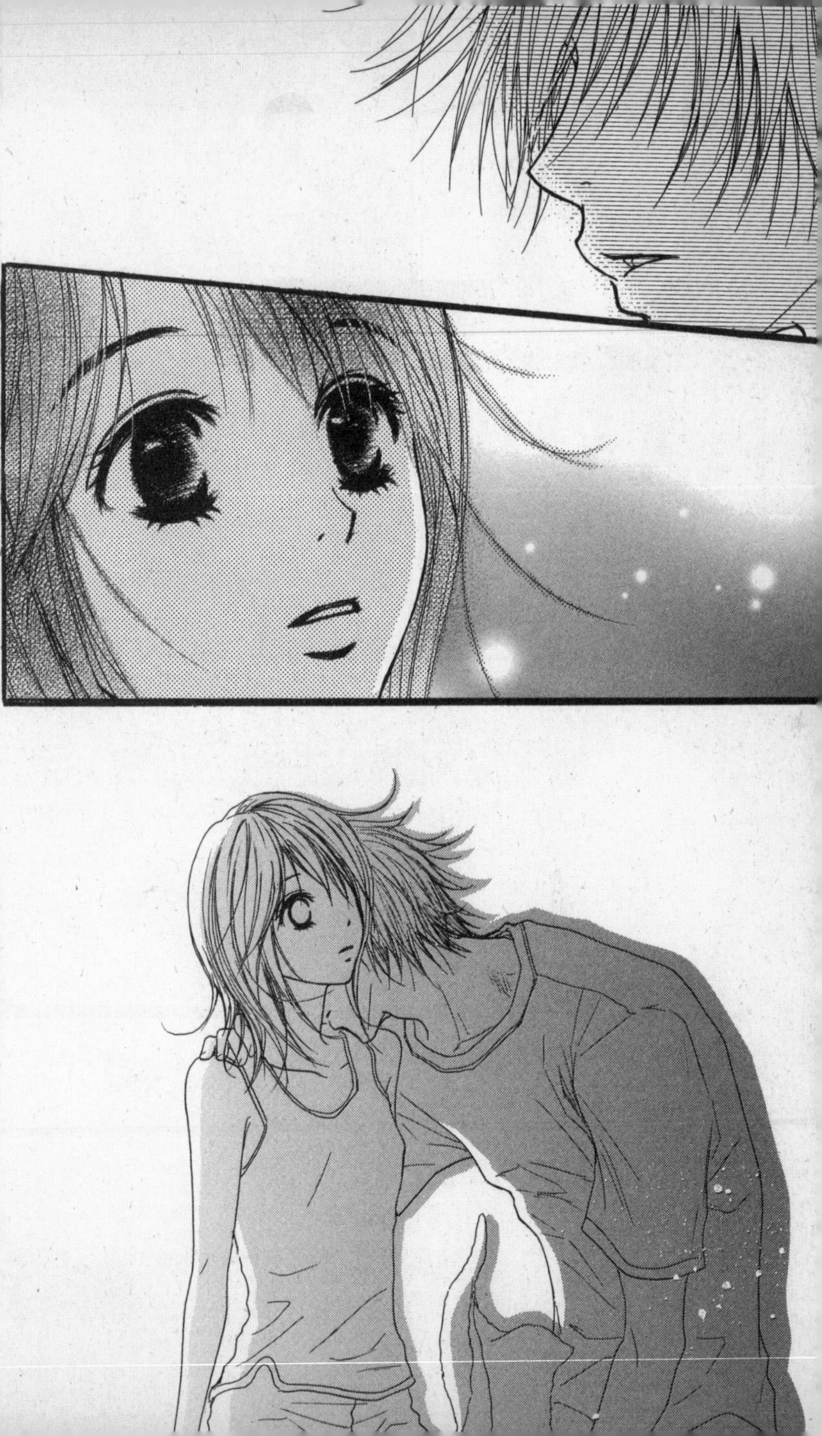

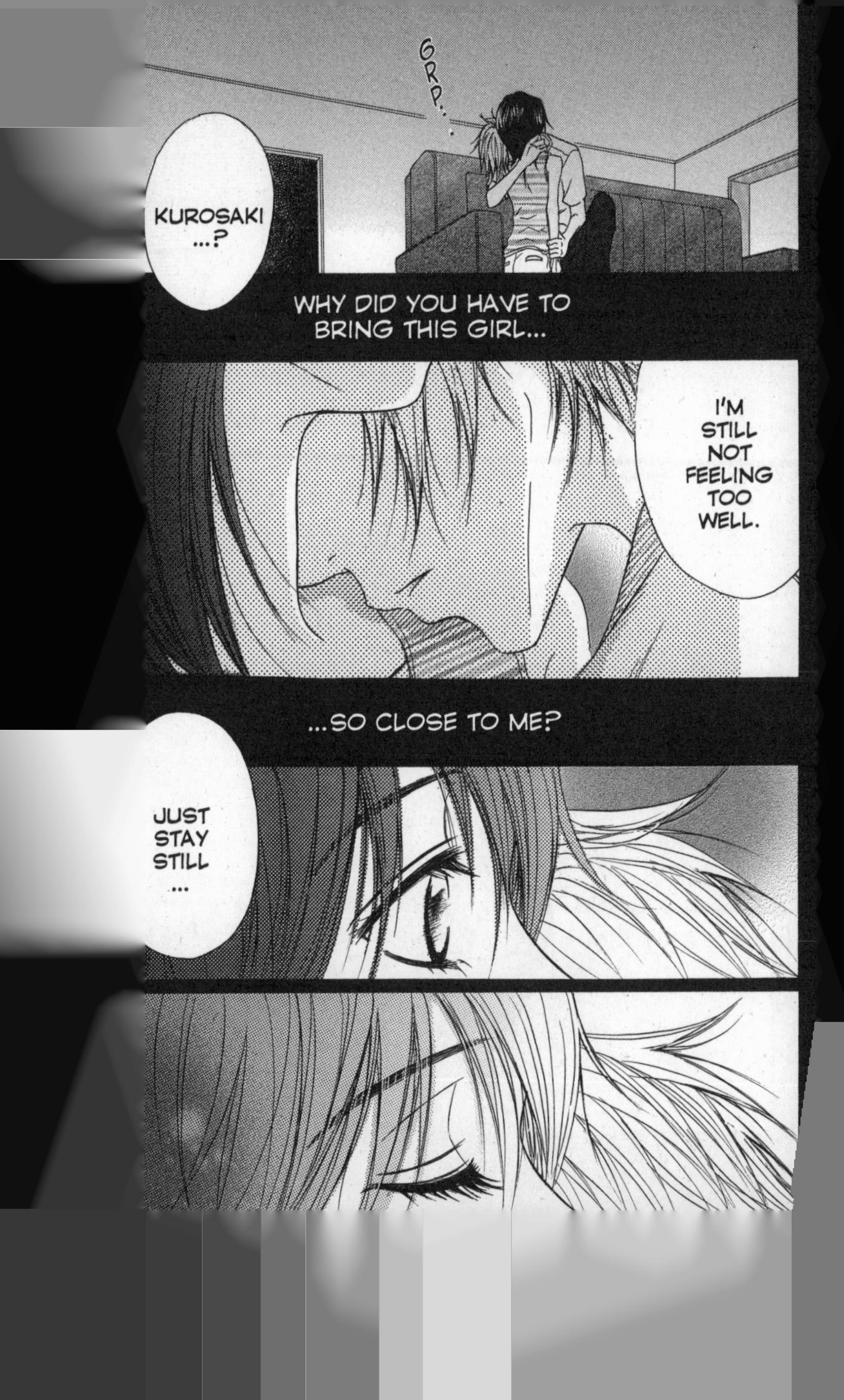
GRP...
KUROSAKI ...?
WHY DID YOU HAVE TO BRING THIS GIRL...
I'M STILL NOT FEELING TOO WELL.
...SO CLOSE TO ME?
JUST STAY STILL ...

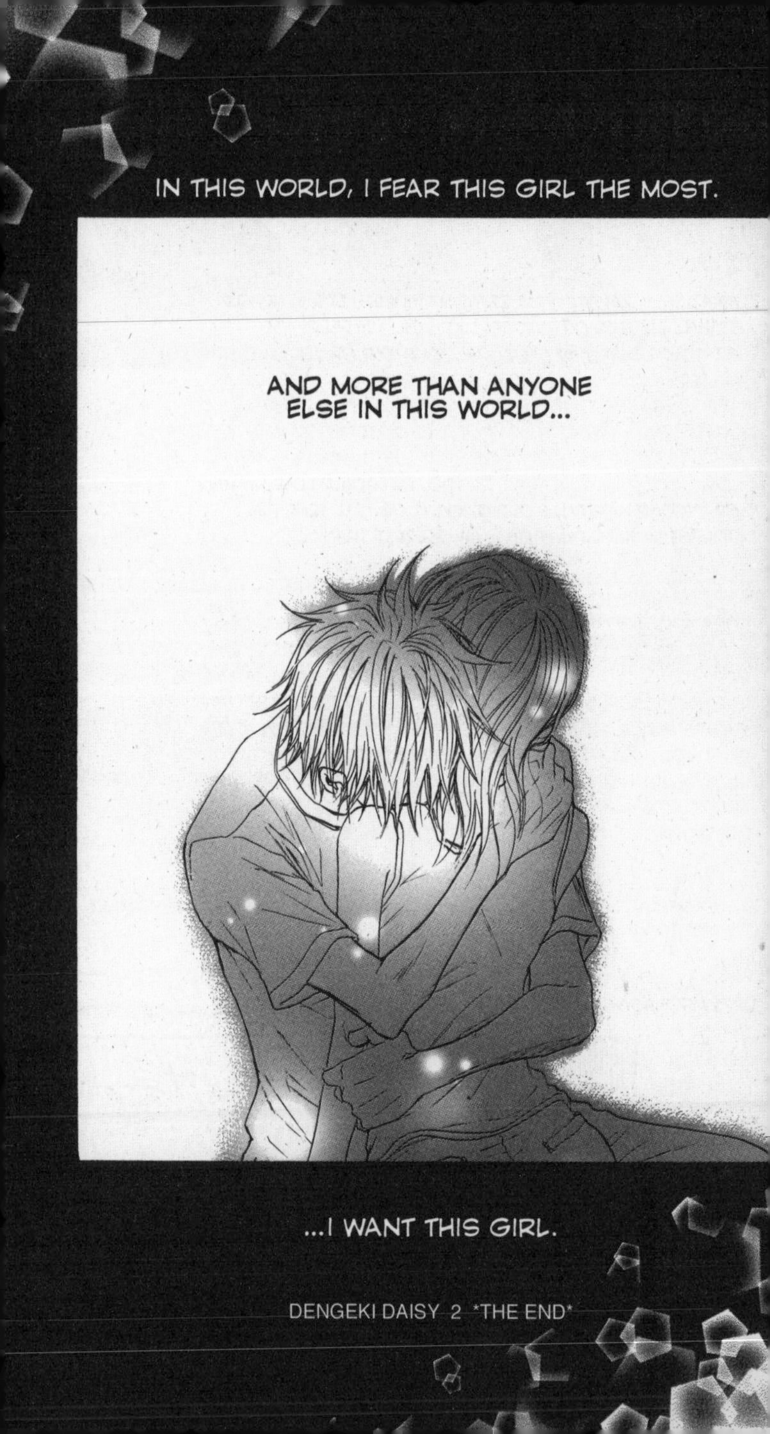
IN THIS WORLD, I FEAR THIS GIRL THE MOST.
AND MORE THAN ANYONE ELSE IN THIS WORLD...
...I WANT THIS GIRL.
DENGEKI DAISY 2 *THE END*

THIS IS THE END OF VOLUME 2 OF ***DENGEKI DAISY.***
THANK YOU FOR READING IT UNTIL THE END!

AMAZINGLY, ***DAISY*** IS STILL BEING SERIALIZED. (IT'S A MIRACLE.) IT'S ALL BECAUSE OF READERS LIKE YOU. I'M FILLED WITH GRATITUDE EACH AND EVERY DAY. TO THOSE OF YOU WHO SEND LETTERS AND EMAILS... THOSE MESSAGES REALLY ENERGIZE ME. THANK YOU FROM THE BOTTOM OF MY HEART. NO, REALLY. MESSAGES LIKE "KEEP IT UP, KYOUSUKE MOTOMI" OR "DO YOUR BEST, TERU" OR "KUROSAKI, GO BALD" OR "ABSOLUTELY DO NOT LOSE YOUR HAIR, KUROSAKI" OR "NO, HE SHOULD LOSE HIS HAIR" OR "BLOND HAIR FALLS OUT QUICKLY" OR "I'LL SEND HIM HAIR-GROWTH MEDICATION"... MY DEEPEST THANKS.

FOR THOSE WHO'D LIKE TO FIND OUT SOONER ABOUT KUROSAKI'S HAIR-LOSS SITUATION, PLEASE READ THE MONTHLY MAGAZINE ***BETSUCOMI***. I'VE SAID IT OFTEN, BUT IT'S A FUN MAGAZINE. ONCE IN A LOOOONG WHILE, I'M ASKED TO DO A COLOR COVER PAGE. AND THERE'S ALSO A FAN PAGE FEATURING CONTENT FROM READERS. EACH MONTH'S FAN PAGE IS GREAT, WITH LOTS ABOUT BALDY. IT'S EVEN MORE FUN THAN THE MANGA ITSELF (OH, FAN PAGE TOPICS AREN'T CONFINED TO BALDING. OTHER COMMENTS AND ILLUSTRATIONS WILL BE PUBLISHED TOO, SO PLEASE DON'T WORRY!!)

(Kurosaki)
ANYWAY, PLEASE CONTINUE TO SUPPORT THE SAGA OF TERU AND THE PERVERT. (I WANT TO REITERATE THAT THEY'RE NOT DATING.)

LET'S MEET AGAIN IN VOLUME 3!!!

最富 キョウスケ
KYOUSUKE MOTOMI

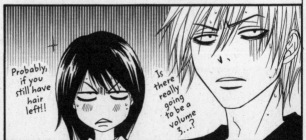

Is there really going to be a volume 3...?
Probably, if you still have hair left!!

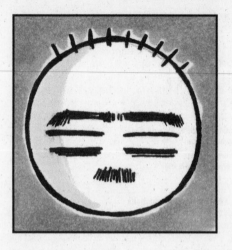

Lately, my facial hair has been growing very quickly. Even my eyebrows. (But not the hair on my head.)

-Kyousuke Motomi

Born on August 1, Kyousuke Motomi debuted in *Deluxe Betsucomi* with *Hetakuso Kyupiddo* (No-Good Cupid) in 2002. She is the creator of *Otokomae! Biizu Kurabu* (Handsome! Beads Club), and her latest work, *Dengeki Daisy*, is currently being serialized in *Betsucomi*. Motomi enjoys sleeping, tea ceremonies and reading Haruki Murakami.

DENGEKI DAISY
VOL. 2
Shojo Beat Edition

STORY AND ART BY
KYOUSUKE MOTOMI

© 2007 Kyousuke MOTOMI/Shogakukan
All rights reserved.
Original Japanese edition "DENGEKI DAISY"
published by SHOGAKUKAN Inc.

Translation & Adaptation/JN Productions
Touch-up Art & Lettering/Rina Mapa
Design/Yukiko Whitley
Editor/Amy Yu

Printed in Canada

Published by VIZ Media, LLC
P.O. Box 77010
San Francisco, CA 94107

10 9 8 7 6 5 4 3
First printing, October 2010
Third printing, January 2011

www.viz.com   www.shojobeat.com

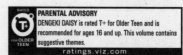

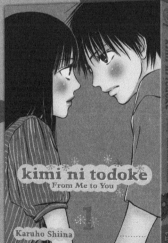

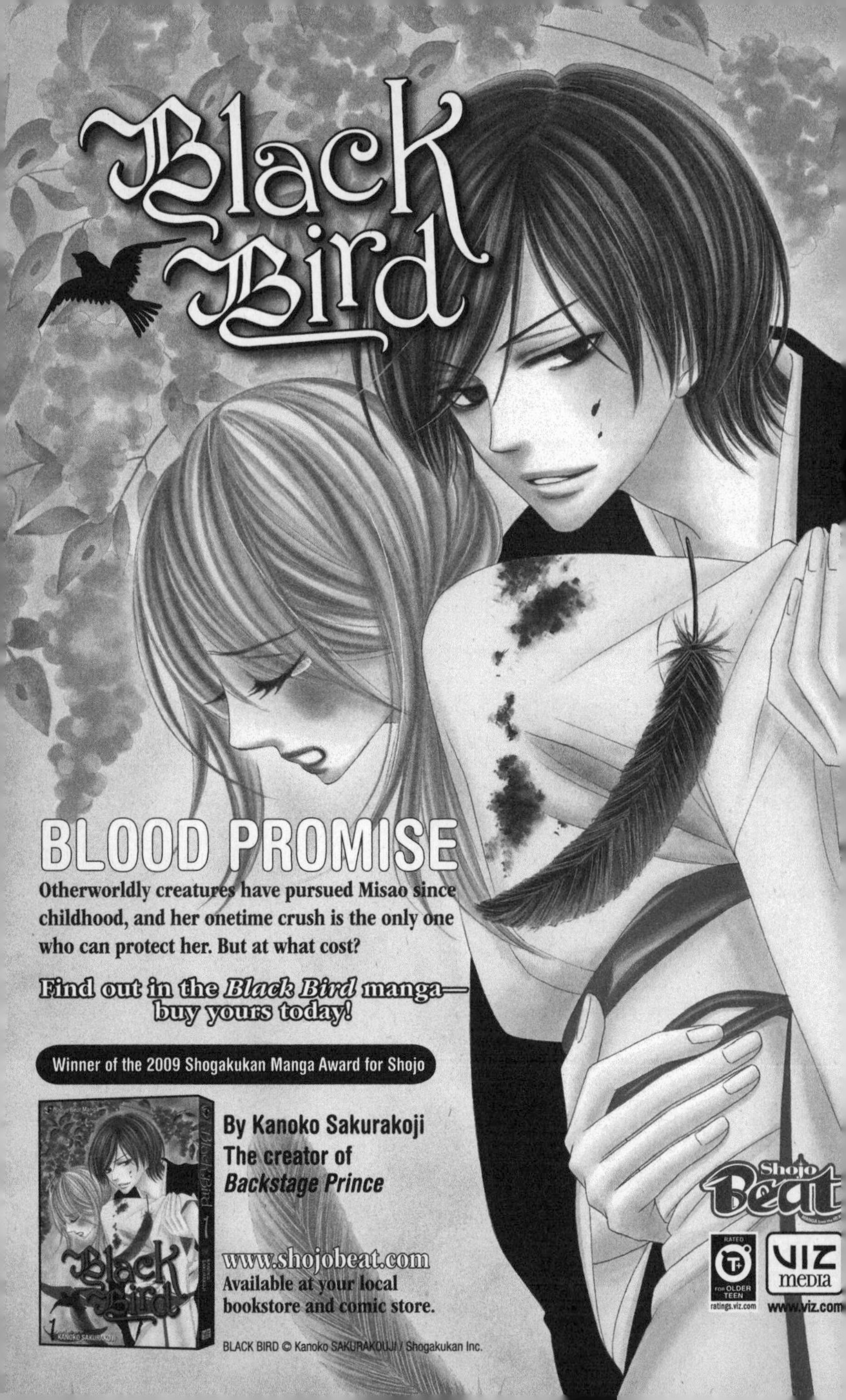
Black Bird
BLOOD PROMISE
Otherworldly creatures have pursued Misao since childhood, and her onetime crush is the only one who can protect her. But at what cost?
Find out in the Black Bird manga— buy yours today!
Winner of the 2009 Shogakukan Manga Award for Shojo
By Kanoko Sakurakoji
The creator of Backstage Prince
www.shojobeat.com
Available at your local bookstore and comic store.
BLACK BIRD © Kanoko SAKURAKOUJI / Shogakukan Inc.
Shojo Beat
RATED T+ FOR OLDER TEEN
ratings.viz.com
VIZ media
www.viz.com

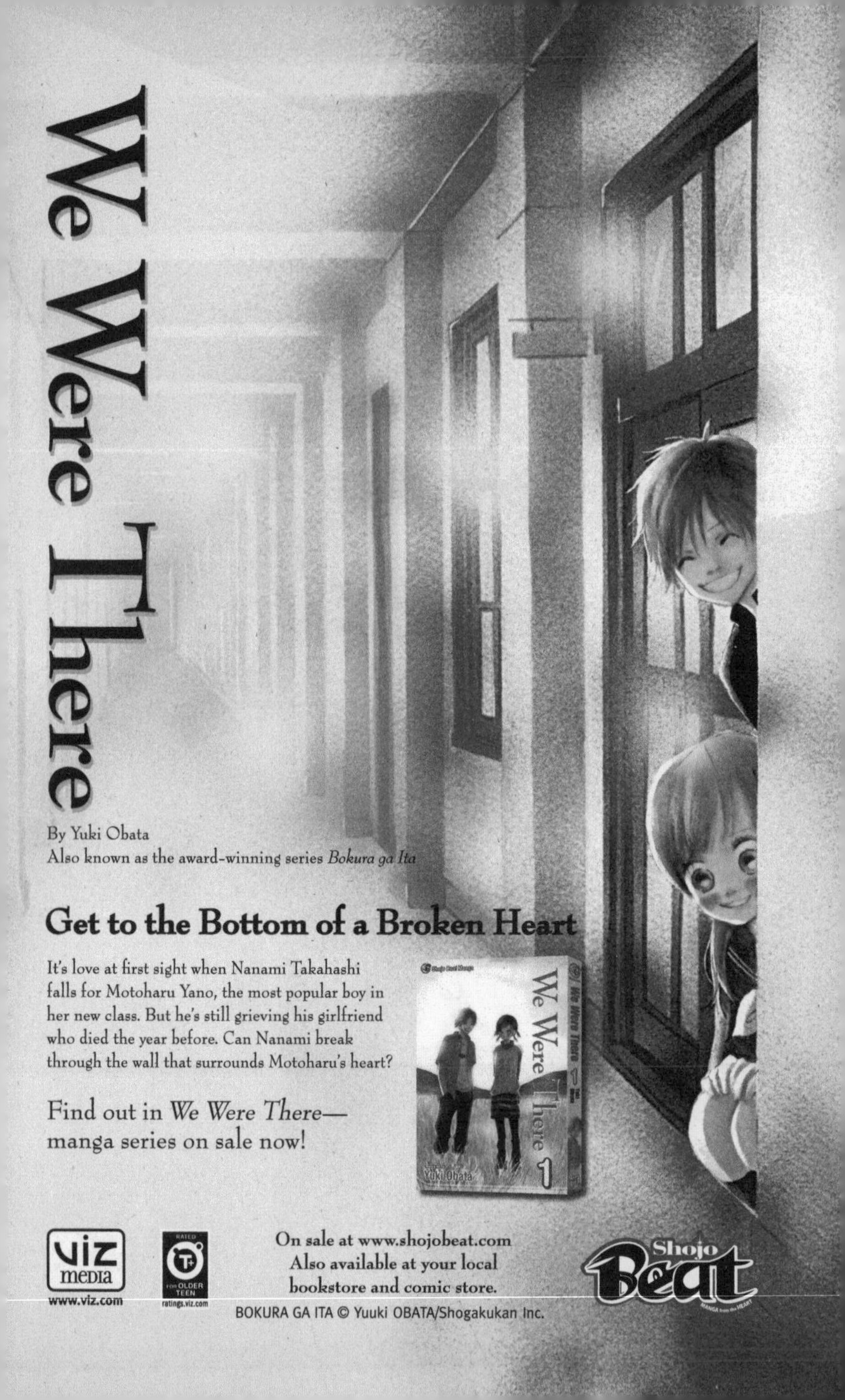
We Were There
By Yuki Obata
Also known as the award-winning series *Bokura ga Ita*
Get to the Bottom of a Broken Heart
It's love at first sight when Nanami Takahashi falls for Motoharu Yano, the most popular boy in her new class. But he's still grieving his girlfriend who died the year before. Can Nanami break through the wall that surrounds Motoharu's heart?
Find out in *We Were There*—
manga series on sale now!
Shojo Beat Manga
We Were There
Yuki Obata
1
viz media
www.viz.com
RATED T+ FOR OLDER TEEN
ratings.viz.com
On sale at www.shojobeat.com
Also available at your local
bookstore and comic store.
Shojo Beat
BOKURA GA ITA © Yuuki OBATA/Shogakukan Inc.